Research in Classrooms

*The Study of Teachers, Teaching,
and Instruction*

Other titles of related interest

DUNKIN   The International Encyclopedia of Teaching and Teacher Education

REYNOLDS   Knowledge Base for the Beginning Teacher

ANDERSON, RYAN   The IEA Classroom Environment Study
& SHAPIRO

Pergamon Journals of related interest

Teaching & Teacher Education

International Journal of Educational Research

Research in Classrooms

The Study of Teachers, Teaching and Instruction

LORIN W. ANDERSON
University of South Carolina, USA

and

ROBERT B. BURNS
Far West Laboratory for Educational Research and Development, USA

PERGAMON PRESS
Member of Maxwell Macmillan Pergamon Publishing Corporation
OXFORD · NEW YORK · BEIJING · FRANKFURT
SÃO PAULO · SYDNEY · TOKYO · TORONTO

U.K.	Pergamon Press plc, Headington Hill Hall, Oxford OX3 0BW, England
U.S.A.	Pergamon Press Inc., Maxwell House, Fairview Park, Elmsford, New York 10523, U.S.A.
PEOPLE'S REPUBLIC OF CHINA	Pergamon Press, Room 4037, Qianmen Hotel, Beijing, People's Republic of China
FEDERAL REPUBLIC OF GERMANY	Pergamon Press GmbH, Hammerweg 6, D-6242 Kronberg, Federal Republic of Germany
BRAZIL	Pergamon Editora Ltda, Rua Eça de Queiros, 346, CEP 04011, Paraiso, São Paulo, Brazil
AUSTRALIA	Pergamon Press Australia Pty Ltd., P.O. Box 544, Potts Point, N.S.W. 2011, Australia
JAPAN	Pergamon Press, 5th Floor, Matsuoka Central Building, 1-7-1 Nishishinjuku, Shinjuku-ku, Tokyo 160, Japan
CANADA	Pergamon Press Canada Ltd., Suite No. 271, 253 College Street, Toronto, Ontario, Canada M5T 1R5

Copyright © 1989 L. W. Anderson & R. B. Burns

First edition 1989

Library of Congress Cataloging-in-Publication Data
Anderson, Lorin W.
Research in classrooms: the study of teachers, teaching, and instruction/Lorin W. Anderson and Robert B. Burns.
p.   cm.
Bibliography: p.
1. Education—Research.   I. Burns, Robert B. (Robert Bounds).
1951–   .   II. Title.
LB1028. A475 1989   370′ 7′8—dc20   89–16156

British Library Cataloguing in Publication Data
Anderson, Lorin W.
Research in classrooms: the study of teachers, teaching and instruction.
1. Schools. teaching. Research
I. Title   II. Burns, Robert B.
371.1′02′072

ISBN 0-08-034060-1 Hard cover
ISBN 0-08-034059-8 Flexi cover

Printed in Great Britain by BPCC Wheatons Ltd, Exeter

Contents

Foreword

MANY who have reviewed research on teaching and learning over the decades have apparently felt obliged to criticize the efforts of those who could only have been either pioneers or early consolidators in the field. The reviews have usually concluded with discussions of implications for practice and for research. There has been a negative correlation between the lengths of those two discussions because lack of guidance for practice tended to be blamed on flaws in the research. The research was said to be either methodologically unsound, epistemologically misguided, or both. It was positivistic and quantitative when it should have been hermeneutic and qualitative, cried some. It did not use observations of classroom events by independent observers when it should have, or it used such observation when it should have relied on the phenomenological perceptions of the participants, shouted others. The debates have shown signs of abating recently with some polarization rather loosely depicted as between the "quantifiers" and the "qualitatives." Between the two has been a large group unpersuaded by either camp, seeing value in both and wanting to get on with the exploration with all the tools and ideas at their disposal.

Unfortunately, this unpersuaded group has had great trouble identifying the tools, obtaining their specifications, realizing their strengths and limitations, and learning how to use them. This is because the present volume has not existed until now, some decades after the need for it came to exist.

This book is not yet another substantive review of the findings of classroom research. It makes no attempt to portray the current state of knowledge of such topics as teacher praise, student initiations, teacher interactive decision making, student deviance, homework, student engagement, and the like. This is more a book about classroom research for those who want to know how to think about and conduct such research. It is not for those who want to learn how to teach by digesting the products of research, and it does not justify its existence in the deficiencies of the past. Indeed, it sees strengths and shortcomings in many different approaches.

This book is the only one to date which takes up epistemological issues concerning classroom research and pursues them in relation to design and methodological matters with depth and balance. It deals with all of the perennial issues that have divided scholars in the field and contributes more to achieving points of reconciliation than has been available to date. A good example of the balance contained in it is to be seen in the three main sections or "units" into which it is organized: "Conceptualizing Classroom Research;" "Designing Classroom Research;" and "Illustrative Classroom Research." The connectedness of these three is such that it is possible to pursue conceptual issues raised in the first through to discussion of implications for research design and methodology in the second and on to examples of applications in the third. This gives the book tremendous potential for students to capitalize on the experience and accumulated wisdom of decades of scholars so as to emerge from it with high level understanding and knowledge of the field.

I know of no other writing in the area of paradigms for research on classrooms that penetrates so deeply and intelligibly into the philosophical fundamentals involved. The coverage of insights provided by scholars of the status of Kuhn makes this section of the book challenging as well as enlightening, and certainly should equip students well to engage in discussion and debate over contending views. Kant and hypocrisy contained in the so-called quantitative/qualitative debate are exposed and dealt with objectively, while the deeper and more genuine issues are presented faithfully.

Although it need not have been, the book is also very useful for the historical material it contains. In other words, it has avoided the common mistake of assuming that nothing of value was achieved in the early decades of this research enterprise. Instead, it provides a good record of developments over time and contains many fully described examples of earlier achievements. Moreover, the book is not wholly American like so many others written by American authors in this field. The contributions of scholars in Europe, the UK, Australia, Canada and New Zealand are represented.

One of the most helpful features of the book is the distinction among research on teachers, research on teaching, and research on instruction. I found it a useful way of organizing the research and of highlighting important issues.

I think the authors are to be congratulated heartily for this excellent book. It will become the standard text and reference in the field for those seeking guidance on such questions as "What is classroom research about?," "What are the different approaches of this type of research?," "What methods and techniques are most suitable?," "What directions should this research take in the future?"

M J Dunkin

Sydney, Australia
April 1989

Preface

OUR purpose in writing this book was to help students of education develop sufficient knowledge and understanding of classroom research to be able to conceptualize, plan, and conduct sound, defensible studies of classrooms and to properly interpret the results of those studies. In order to accomplish this purpose, we have chosen to rely heavily on studies of classrooms that have been conducted over the past half-century or more. Our belief is that students are more likely to develop an understanding of classroom research by reading about how the research *has been* conducted, than by reading about how it *should be* conducted. At the same time, however, we must admit to sprinkling a few "shoulds" throughout the book.

Given our approach, it would have been impossible to include all of the studies of classroom research that have been conducted over the years. We have chosen to include those studies that we believe best illustrate the major concepts and principles of classroom research. In other words, the set of studies we have chosen to highlight are intended to be instructive, not exhaustive.

As all authors do, we bring to this book a particular point of view. Stated simply, we believe that the primary purpose of classroom research is to help educators improve the conditions of learning and the quality of learning of increasingly large numbers of students. As a consequence, we believe that four conditions must be met if defensible, meaningful, and useful classroom research is to be designed and conducted.

First, classroom research must be guided by an explicit conceptual framework which includes clearly and precisely defined concepts and a set of hypothesized relationships among the concepts. As we shall see in later chapters, this framework guides not only the planning and conduct of the study, but the interpretation of the results as well. At present, we believe that the statement made some 35 years ago by Barr and his colleagues still applies:

> . . . research too often proceeds without explicit theoretical framework, in intellectual disarray, too often to the testing of myriads of arbitrary, unrationalized hypotheses. The studies too often interact little with each other, do not fall into place within any scheme, and hence add little to the understanding of the teaching process (Barr et al., 1953, p. 651).

Second, a clear statement of purpose for which the study is being conducted is needed. Some studies are intended to provide complete, accurate descriptions of classrooms—the participants, the events that occur within them, and/or the consequences of the participants being in the classrooms and engaging in the various events over some period of time. What is the typical class size in public schools and how does class size change across grade levels? This question is about the description of participants (students). How frequently do teachers work with individual students in their classrooms (as opposed to groups of students)? This question is about the description of a classroom event (teachers working with individual students).

Other studies are planned so that the relationships among participants, events, and consequences can be examined. Do teachers talk more in classrooms than do students? This question is about the relationship between participants (teachers, students) and events (talking). Do teachers who ask more questions requiring students to think about the answer or express and defend their opinion produce students who have higher levels of achievement? This question is about the relationship between events (teacher questioning) and consequences (student achievement).

Still other studies are planned so that cause-effect relationships among participants, events, and consequences can be established. In raising the previous question about the relationship between teacher questioning and student achievement, the researcher may be seeking to establish a causal relationship. If so, this fact has great implications for the type of study that is planned and conducted.

Knowing the purpose for which a study is conducted is important if the study is to be properly planned and the results are to be properly interpreted. Since cause-effect relationships are relationships or associations by definition, we will emphasize two general purposes of classroom research in this volume: descriptive and associational.

Third, defensible and reasonable plans for conducting the research are needed. These plans would include procedures for carrying out the study, means of obtaining the needed evidence, and methods for analyzing and otherwise examining the evidence once collected. For these plans to be defensible, they must be consistent with both the purpose of the study and the conceptual framework which guides it.

Fourth, knowledgeable and wise people who are able to interpret the results of the studies and examine implications of those results for thinking about classrooms and doing something about classrooms are needed. Contrary to some people's opinions, evidence does not speak for itself. The translation of evidence into thought and action requires people who understand both the research *and* the classroom.

This book is organized around these four conditions of sound, defensible classroom research. In the first three chapters, the emphasis is on conceptual frameworks and research plans. In Chapters 4 through 7, the methodological details that must be attended to in order to design and conduct classroom research of high quality are described. In Chapters 8 through 10 we examine a variety of studies of teachers, teaching, and instruction that have been conducted over the past 60 years. The intent of this examination is that students of classroom research should learn from those who have designed and conducted such research in the past. Finally, in Chapter 11 our emphasis shifts to an understanding and application of our current knowledge of research on teachers, teaching, and instruction.

As we reflect on our work on this volume, we are very grateful to many people. Our thinking has been greatly stimulated by the work and writings of many of the pioneers of classroom research: A. S. Barr, A. A. Bellack, N. A. Flanders, N. L. Gage, P. V. Gump, D. M. Medley, D. G. Ryans, and B. O. Smith chief among them. We have benefitted tremendously from our associations over time with a number of contemporary classroom researchers: Rebecca Barr, David Berliner, Jere Brophy, Robert Dreeben, Walter Doyle, Carolyn Evertson, Charles Fisher, Thomas Good, Judith Green, Greta Morine-Dershimer, Barak Rosenshine, and Susan Stodolsky.

Three colleagues deserve our special thanks. Neville Postlethwaite suggested to several people at Pergamon Press that we write the book. Throughout the entire process he has been a source of strength and inspiration. Bruce Biddle reviewed the initial outline for the book, and provided us with encouragement to proceed when we needed it most. Michael Dunkin has "stuck with us" through it all. His comments, suggestions, and insights have provided us with a vast storehouse of "food for thought."

We are extremely grateful to Barbara Barrett of Pergamon Press. Despite several missed deadlines, she remained patient, confident, and supportive. We also are grateful to Michèle Norton of Pergamon who successfully "shepherded" this project from initial draft to publication. We would like to thank our secretaries, Cathy Schachner and Ann Wallgren, for keeping our professional lives in order. We also wish to thank Mabel Henderson for her excellent work in drawing figures and preparing camera-ready copies.

Finally, we are indebted to Jo Anne Anderson, who put up with our long distance telephone conversations, meetings at the house, and long hours at the word processor. Now that the book has been completed, we are pleased that she has chosen to remain married to one of us and a good friend of the other.

LWA
Columbia, SC

March, 1989

RBB
San Francisco, CA

Unit I—Introduction
Conceptualizing Classroom Research

THE THREE chapters in this unit are intended to provide the reader with the "big picture." While specific research techniques and the application of these techniques to particular research questions are the emphases of Units II and III, respectively, the chapters in this first unit deal with the larger issues surrounding the design and conduct of classroom research. Basic concepts will be defined and discussed, and essential differences between and among the concepts will be made.

In the first chapter, distinctions are drawn among three concepts: teachers, teaching, and instruction. Each of these concepts is associated with a long, distinguished research tradition (as we shall see in the third unit). At the same time, however, failure to differentiate among these concepts has led, we believe, to some of the apparently conflicting results of classroom research studies. Chapter 1 ends with a discussion of the role of the researcher's values in the design, conduct, and interpretation of classroom research.

In the second chapter our attention shifts to various ways in which classrooms and the events and objects in those classrooms have been conceptualized. Paradigms and research programs, theories, and models are central to these conceptualizations. Each of these "conceptual systems" is described in some detail in the chapter. Since models of classrooms are more common than theories, a large portion of the chapter is spent discussing the nature and function of these models. Furthermore, since many of these models assume but do not explicate student learning, a brief postscript entitled "What about student learning?" concludes the chapter.

The focus of the third chapter is on research methodology. Four studies are summarized as examples of the variety of methodologies currently used to study classrooms. Several key distinctions are made in this chapter; distinctions between knowing and knowledge, and confirmatory and interpretive inquiry chief among them. Classroom research is seen as disciplined inquiry, and the importance of this conception of research is described.

1

Some readers may view the chapters in this unit as too "philosophical." Others may suggest that some of our distinctions are "semantic." We would disagree on both counts. We believe that all research rests on philosophical underpinnings. Thus, it behooves classroom researchers to understand the variety of philosophical orientations that currently underlie much of classroom research and to confront their own philosophical predispositions. We further believe that the language system currently used to describe and discuss classroom research lacks the necessary precision to move us forward in our understanding of classrooms. Our distinctions among concepts are intended to provide some of this needed precision.

1

Teachers, Teaching, and Instruction

THIS is a book about research on teachers, teaching, and instruction. To the uninitiated, the title of both the book and this chapter may seem somewhat redundant. After all, in most countries throughout the world, teachers teach or provide instruction to students in classrooms. Consistent with this view, teachers are those who teach, while instruction and teaching are synonymous. We wish it could be so simple and straightforward.

Consider the following realities, however. Four definitions of the word "teacher" appear in the *Dictionary of Education* (Good, 1973). A teacher is:

> (1) a person employed in an official capacity for the purposes of guiding and directing the learning experiences of pupils or students in an educational institution, whether public or private; (2) a person who because of rich or unusual experience or education or both in a given field is able to contribute to the growth and development of other persons who come in contact with him; (3) a person who has completed a professional curriculum in a teacher education institution and whose training has been recognized by the award of an appropriate teaching certificate; and (4) a person who instructs others (p. 586).

Thus, there are people who are teachers because of their status (i.e., they are certified as teachers), *not* because of their behavior or the impact of that behavior on others (definition 3). There are those who are teachers solely because of their behavior, with no apparent status at all (definition 4). Finally, there are those who are teachers because of their status *and* their behavior or skill. Furthermore, this status may be formally granted (definition 1) or informally earned (definition 2).

To complicate matters further, teachers are expected to fulfill a variety of roles.

> It is customary to think of the teacher as: a. a director of learning, b. as a friend or counselor of pupils, c. as a member of a group of professional workers, and d. as a citizen participating in various community activities—local, state, national, and international (Barr, 1952, p. 1446).

Only one of these roles, the first one, is typically associated with teaching or instruction (although to confuse matters even more Amidon and Hunter (1967) include counseling as a teaching activity).

As in the case of the term "teacher," there are several definitions of "teaching" (Smith, 1987). Historically, teaching has been defined as the imparting of knowledge or skill. This apparently simple definition has given rise to several questions, each leading to a definition with a somewhat different emphasis.

For example, when a person is clearly intending to impart knowledge, but does not do so, is that person teaching? Some definitions of teaching emphasize the *intentional* nature of the act.

When a person acts in a way that is consistent with practices generally known (through research) or suspected (by professional educators) to lead to the acquisition of knowledge, but none of the students in that particular classroom learn the knowledge or acquire the skill, is that person teaching? Some definitions emphasize the *scientific* nature of teaching (Smith, 1987). Soar, Medley, and Coker (1983), for example, argue in favor of this "best practice" definition of teaching.

Finally, when a person actually does impart knowledge or skill to another or others, is that person teaching? Although few would respond negatively to this question, such a *success* (Smith, 1987) or *effectiveness* definition of teaching often leads to circularity. Such a definition, for example, prohibits the differentiation of one who is simply teaching from one who is teaching well.

Like the terms "teacher" and "teaching," the term "instruction" also has several definitions. At the most general level, instruction is synonymous with teaching (Good, 1973). That is, saying that teachers teach or that teachers instruct is saying the same thing. Other, more precise, definitions of instruction do exist, however.

Some educators have suggested that instruction is a subset or one component of the act of teaching. Stiles (1960), for example, defines the relationship between instruction and teaching in this manner:

> If we regard teaching as a purposeful activity of man, then this activity has identifiable aspects of purpose or plan, of means or operations, and of results or effects. The term curriculum may be used to emphasize the first aspect of the activity, the term instruction to emphasize the second, and the term evaluation to emphasize the third (p. 710).

A similar relationship between instruction and teaching can be found in Good (1973).

Other educators define teaching as a subset of instruction. Weil and Murphy (1982), for example, define instruction as a

> broad term that may encompass most of the activities taking place in the classroom and the school as well as many activities taking place in the home. [It includes] duration, source, group size, nature of the instructional activities, and specific teacher or student behaviors (p. 890).

Similarly, Barr and Dreeben's (1983) definition of instruction includes "patterns of interaction, aspects of class organization, curriculum content, and the intellectual and social demands made by the nature of the schoolwork itself " (p. 69).

As should be evident to the reader, then, multiple definitions of teachers, teaching, and instruction currently exist. It should be equally clear that these multiple definitions of these related terms make it very difficult to understand much of what we read and hear as we seek to improve the quality of school learning of students in classrooms throughout the world.

Defining Teachers, Teaching, and Instruction

As we shall see throughout this volume, the precise definition of key educational concepts is a necessary precondition for planning and carrying out sound research studies. Furthermore, studies that focus on either teachers, teaching, or instruction have their unique advantages and disadvantages. In this section, we shall offer our definitions of these terms and speculate on the primary advantages and disadvantages of studies of teachers, teaching, and instruction, respectively.

Teachers

We limit our view of teachers to Good's (1973) first definition. That is, our study of teachers is limited to those persons who are employed in schools in an official capacity for the expressed purpose of "guiding and directing the learning experiences" of children. Once we have limited our study to this group of people, our job is not over; rather, it has just begun. One fundamental question remains, namely, "What characteristics or qualities of teachers should we study?"

The answer to this question depends on the purpose for which the question is asked (Ryan and Phillips, 1982). If the purpose is to describe the characteristics and qualities of the current teaching force, then certain characteristics or qualities are likely to be included. Sex of teachers, race or ethnicity of teachers, years of teaching experience, level of education, and type or level of certification are characteristics and qualities frequently used to describe teachers. Opinions and attitudes on a variety of issues are often solicited for the purpose of describing the teachers in the current teaching force.

If, on the other hand, the purpose of asking about teacher characteristics and qualities is to identify those characteristics or qualities that set excellent or effective teachers apart from other teachers, a different set of characteristics and qualities may be necessary. This latter purpose, which is consistent with the overall purpose of this book as described in the preface, has been the focus of studies for almost a century (see Kratz, 1896, for one the earliest studies). Over time, in our attempts to identify those characteristics and qualities, we have asked different people (e.g., students, "experts," the teachers themselves), asked different questions (e.g., asked them to recall qualities of excellent teachers that made them excellent, asked them to rate teachers on various scales), and focused on different types of characteristics and qualities (e.g., personality traits, attitudes and beliefs, subject matter and pedagogical knowledge).

The study of teachers has several advantages. First, most of the characteristics and qualities that have been identified in past research studies possess a reasonable amount of "face validity" or credibility. Who can argue, for example, that teachers should know the subject matter they are expected to teach, exercise good judgment, or be enthusiastic or honest? Second, and by definition, characteristics such as personality traits and subject matter knowledge tend to be relatively stable over time. They are not likely to change dramatically from week to week, or month to month. As a consequence, reliable estimates of them can be obtained fairly easily. Third, once such characteristics and qualities are identified, they can be used to select individuals who are likely to be or become good teachers. Furthermore, knowledge of these characteristics and qualities may be useful in helping teachers become better teachers. Thus, the study of teachers has practical as well as theoretical value.

At the same time, however, the study of teachers has several disadvantages. First, there traditionally has been a great deal of disagreement on the characteristics and qualities possessed by excellent or effective teachers (Medley, 1972). In one of the earliest studies conducted in this area, only one teacher characteristic was mentioned by the majority of the students surveyed (Kratz, 1896). Many of the characteristics and qualities were mentioned by fewer than ten percent of the students. Furthermore, supervisors, students, and the teachers themselves have tended to disagree on the characteristics of good teachers (Charters and Waples, 1929).

Second, the characteristics and qualities identified typically are too global or vague to be useful in selecting or attempting to improve teachers. Medley (1972) has made this point succinctly.

> When asked to describe a good teacher, [the typical student] produces a mixture of trivia, banality, and common sense that adds nothing to what is already generally believed. Not only are such descriptions devoid of new content, they tend also to be couched in terms too vague to be useful to a teacher who needs specific information rather than pious generalities (p. 432).

Third, and perhaps most damaging, there is very little evidence that characteristics and qualities of teachers identified in prior research are linked in any way with the excellence or effectiveness of teachers. While honesty may be an important trait for teachers to possess as employees of the school district or pillars of the community, honesty may not differentiate those teachers who are likely to be more successful in their classrooms and with their students from those teachers who are likely to be less successful. Getzels and Jackson's (1963) conclusion made a quarter of a century ago still holds today.

> Very little is known for certain . . . about the relation between teacher personality and teaching effectiveness. The regrettable fact is that many of the studies so far have not produced significant results. Many others have produced only pedestrian findings (p. 574).

Teaching

Our definition of teaching is an amalgam of definitions offered by Gage (1963a), Amidon and Hunter (1967), Klauer (1985), and Robertson (1987). Gage (1963a) defines teaching as "any form of interpersonal influence aimed at changing the ways in which other persons can or will behave" (p. 96), while Amidon and Hunter (1967) define teaching as "an interactive process, primarily involving classroom talk, which takes place between teacher and pupils and occurs during certain definable activities" (p. 1). Klauer (1985) defines teaching as an "interpersonal activity directed toward learning by one or more persons" (p. 5). Finally, Robertson (1987) suggests that teaching "denotes action undertaken with the intention of bringing about learning in another" (p. 15). Several common critical attributes of the concept "teaching" emerge from these definitions.

First, teaching is an activity or process; in Robertson's (1987) terms, teaching is action. You can see teaching take place; you need not (and, some would argue, should not) infer it from learning. In this regard, "teaching may be effective or not as far as student learning is concerned. Thus, circularity in definition is avoided" (Klauer, 1985, p. 5).

Jackson (1986) also argues for teaching as an activity or process:

> When we say "Look, there's a person teaching," what we mean is "There's a person trying to teach." The "trying to" is understood. Its omission is simply a kind of verbal shorthand (p. 81).

Second, teaching is an *interpersonal* activity or process. Interpersonal means that teaching involves interactions between a teacher and one or more students (Klauer, 1985). Most of these interactions are verbal (Amidon and Hunter, 1967). Furthermore, these interactions are bi-directional (that is, teachers talk to and influence students and students talk to and influence teachers) (Klauer, 1985).

Third, teaching is *intentional*. There is some purpose or set of purposes for which teaching occurs. Klauer (1985) suggests that teaching is "directed toward learning," while Gage (1963a) asserts that teaching is "aimed at changing the ways in which other persons can or will behave." Thus, while the use of the term "teaching" does not imply that learning has taken place, it does imply that learning is intended.

In this regard, two corrolaries of the third critical attribute should be noted. The act of teaching seems to require what Jackson (1986) refers to as the "presumption of ignorance." That is, before teaching begins, students do not know or can not do what they are to be taught. If they already know or can do what they are being taught, they can not learn it. Furthermore, as Robertson (1987) contends, teaching can be judged to be successful "at least to the extent that [the student] *tries to learn*" what is being taught. That is, in lay terms, if students pay attention, concentrate, or put forth effort when a teacher is teaching, that teaching can be said to be successful.

When these three defining attributes are combined, a single definition of teaching can be formulated. Teaching is an interpersonal, interactive activity, typically involving verbal communication, which is undertaken for the purpose of helping one or more students learn or change the ways in which they can or will behave.

Like the study of teachers, the study of teaching has several advantages. First, the study of teaching moves us one step closer to understanding and improving learning. As Bloom (1972) asserts:

> It is the *teaching*, not the *teacher*, that is the key to the learning of students. That is, it is not what teachers are *like* but what they *do* in interacting with their students that determines what students learn and how they feel about the learning and about themselves (p. 339).

Second, while characteristics and qualities of teachers are relatively stable, teaching is malleable and alterable (Bloom, 1981). Thus, while changing the basic characteristics or qualities of teachers may be quite difficult, changing teachers' approaches, strategies, practices, or behaviors relative to teaching may be somewhat easier.

Third, many of the methodological problems involved in the study of teachers (e.g., the use of recall measures and rating scales) are ameliorated in the study of teaching. Teaching is both observable and *observed*. And, as we shall see in Chapter 5, the value of observation as a research tool has been generally accepted. As the Committee on the Criteria of Teacher Effectiveness suggested:

> Sitting in classrooms and letting the sights and sounds interact with apperceptive processes may give some workers the concepts and hypotheses with which to order the phenomena fruitfully (Barr et al., 1952, p. 261).

The study of teaching also has disadvantages. First, while teaching is indeed malleable, it may perhaps be too unstable for scientific study. The ways in which teachers interact with their students differ from day to day, and from week to week (Anderson, Ryan, and Shapiro, 1989). Second, the same behaviors may have quite different results in different settings and situations (e.g., different age or ability students, different subject matters, different learning goals or objectives) (Barr et al., 1952, p. 253). Stated somewhat differently, the influence of teaching on learning tends to be context-specific.

Third, there tend to be problems with many of the observation systems themselves. Nuthall and Snook (1973) have argued that the current emphasis on observational studies has produced a proliferation of observational systems and frequency counts of the minutiae of teacher and student behaviors in their daily situations (pp. 71–72).

Similarly, since different observation systems emphasize quite different events or behaviors, the results of any given study may depend in part on the system used to collect the data. Adams (1972), for example, examined some 100 observational systems and identified more than 200 distinct categories or types of teacher behavior. Only two behaviors—"teacher directs" and "teacher questions"—were included on more than one-third of these systems.

Fourth, and related to the previous point, any single observation system is likely to focus on or emphasize only a small portion of all of the activities and interactions occurring in most classrooms. For example, in their reanalysis of the classic Flanders' (1965) study, Barr and Dreeben (1977) point out that only about 17 percent of all interactions can be classified as either "direct" or "indirect" (the two types of interactions Flanders was studying). In Barr and Dreeben's words:

> Flanders, however, attributes mean differences in achievement only to the 17% of interactive events, while ignoring the other 83%. Moreover, while in indirect classrooms, there is about 5–6% more indirect teaching compared to direct classrooms, there is close to 9% more *lecturing*. Accordingly, an equally plausible interpretation of the achievement findings—in fact, a slightly more plausible one—is that the superior achievement in the indirect classrooms is attributable to lecturing, a rather direct form of instruction (p. 107).

Instruction

As has been mentioned, instruction can be defined either as a subset of teaching (that is, one of several teaching acts) or as inclusive of teaching (that is, teaching is one aspect or component of instruction). We prefer the latter definition. We believe that most teacher behaviors, student behaviors, and teacher-student interactions occur within the larger context of instruction. Stated simply, instruction "contextualizes" teaching. Knowing something about instruction helps us gain a more complete understanding of teaching.

This view of instruction is similar to that of several educators, most notably Gump (1967), Weil and Murphy (1982), Barr and Dreeben (1983), and Stodolsky (1988). Gump includes five components of instruction: concern (e.g., academic, social and recreational), teacher leadership pattern, group quality (defined in terms of the group configuration in the classroom), pupil activity (that is, the behavioral and/or academic demands of the activity), and action sequencing (that is, pacing).

In their definition of instruction (or, more appropriately, "instruction processes"), Weil and Murphy include "duration, source, group size, nature of the instructional activities, and specific teacher or student behaviors"

(p. 890). Barr and Dreeben (1983) suggest that instruction consists of "patterns of interaction, aspects of class organization, curriculum content, and the intellectual and social demands made by the nature of the schoolwork itself" (p. 69). Finally,. Stodolsky (1988) uses 11 dimensions to conceptualize instruction: instructional format, teacher leadership role, cognitive level, task options, options when done, expected student interaction, feedback, pacing, student location, student behavior, and student involvement.

Much like our definition of teaching, our definition of instruction is an amalgam of these definitions. Specifically, we would emphasize six defining features of instruction. These defining features and their relationship with the perspectives offered by Gump, Weil and Murphy, Barr and Dreeben, and Stodolsky are displayed in Table 1.1.

The first component of instruction is its aim or purpose. Like teaching, instruction is intended to promote learning on the part of students. However, the aim or purpose of instruction is far more global and broad-based than that of teaching. Instruction is addressed toward the

TABLE 1.1
Six Primary Components of Classroom Instruction

Our Label	Gump	Weil/Murphy	Barr/Dreeben	Stodolsky
Subject Matter	Concern		Curriculum Content	Subject Matter
Task Demands	Pupil Activity	Instructional Activities	Intellectual & Social Demands	Cognitive Level
Instructional Format	Teacher Leadership Pattern	Source of Instruction		Instructional Format
Grouping Arrangement	Group Quality	Group Size	Class Organization	Expected Student Interaction
Time/Pacing/ Coverage	Action Sequencing	Duration	Content* Coverage/ Pacing	Pacing
Classroom Behaviors and Interactions	Teacher and Student Behaviors	Teacher and Student Behaviors	Patterns of Interaction	Student Behavior and Student Involvement

Note. Those entries marked with an asterisk (*) are *not* part of the definition of instruction provided by Barr and Dreeben or Stodolsky. Nonetheless, they can be inferred as major components of instruction from the studies conducted by these researchers.

learning of some organized body of knowledge. Gump refers to this component as the instructional "concern," Barr and Dreeben discuss "curriculum content," while Stodolsky uses the more traditional term, "subject matter."

The second component of instruction is the demands placed on the students by the subject matter, teacher, or students themselves. What tasks are students expected to perform and complete while in the classroom? These tasks may be intellectual or social (Barr and Dreeben, 1983; Erickson, 1982). They may be easier or more difficult (Stodolsky, 1988). Nonetheless, within the context of the subject matter being taught, demands are placed on students so they will learn the subject matter within the confines of the classroom as organized by the teacher.

The third component of instruction is the instructional format. Instruction is characterized as "standing or characteristic ways of conducting interaction" (Dunkin and Biddle, 1974, p. 181), "patterns of teacher behavior that are recurrent, applicable to various subject matters, characteristic of more than one teacher, and relevant to learning" (Gage, 1969, p. 1446), and "global descriptions of the overall action pattern in the classroom" (Stodolsky, 1988). These "characteristic ways," "recurrent patterns" or "action patterns" are referred to as instructional formats. Instructional formats determine the teachers leadership pattern (e.g., talking, supervising) (Gump, 1967) and identify the source of instruction (e.g., teacher, discussion group, television) (Weil and Murphy, 1982). Instructional formats are similar to what Corey and Monroe (1941) refer to as patterns of instruction and Gage (1969) terms teaching methods.

The fourth component of instruction is the grouping arrangement in place in the classroom. Instruction can be addressed to the whole class, subgroups, or individual students. If groups are formed within classrooms, then different task demands may be placed on members of the various groups and the teacher's leadership role or pattern may shift from group to group during the lesson. Each of the authors listed in Table 1.1 refers to grouping arrangement in their discussion of instruction, although the emphasis is somewhat different. Barr and Dreeben (1983) refer to it simply as "class organization." In contrast, Gump uses the label "group quality," Weil and Murphy discuss "group size," while Stodolsky emphasizes the relationship of students within groups, or the "expected student interaction."

The fifth component of instruction is the length of time during which instruction takes place. Stated simply, instruction takes time; teaching, in contrast, may be instantaneous. As mentioned earlier, the aims and purposes of instruction are long-term. Similarly, instructional formats are defined in terms of teachers' roles, characteristic ways of behaving, or patterns of behavior. Students need time to learn; teachers need time to provide instruction to those students so they can and will learn. Barr and Dreeben (1983) make this point explicit:

Instruction entails 1. a teacher's attempt to adapt 2. available materials to 3. the characteristics of groups over 4. *some period of time* (pp. 106–107) (emphasis ours).

As used by the various authors cited in Table 1.1, however, instructional time is a multi-faceted component. Some, like Weil and Murphy, appear to focus exclusively on the obvious temporal aspect of time, using the term "duration" as one of their primary components of instruction. Barr and Dreeben (1983), on the other hand, tend to emphasize the amount and type of content that gets covered during that time. "Content coverage," then, becomes an important element in Barr and Dreeben's model of instruction. Gump (1967) and Stodolsky (1988), while fully recognizing the temporal aspect of instruction, are primarily concerned with identifying the person or persons responsible for determining how fast the content is actually presented or delivered during the available time. Is it the teacher, the student or students, or some mechanical devise (such as a television set or movie projector)? Thus, three facets of this component of instruction have been identified: the time during which instruction takes place (instructional time), the amount of content covered during that time (content coverage), and the pacing of the instruction (particularly, who or what is responsible for pacing it).

As might be expected, the sixth and final component of instruction is, in fact, teaching (that is, the behavior of teachers and students, either individually or collectively). While in classrooms, teachers act alone (e.g., they lecture, they grade papers at their desks, and they watch over their students), students act alone (e.g., they work at their seats or desks, they daydream, and they punch their classmates), and teachers and students interact (e.g., they ask questions of one another, they engage in conversations, they respond to each other using methods of "non-verbal communication" such as hand-raising, frowns, and scowls).

Like research on teachers and teaching, there are advantages and disadvantages in the study of instruction. Three primary advantages are quite evident. First, as mentioned earlier, instruction contextualizes teaching. It does so in two ways. Instruction has as its major dimensions the subject matter being taught, the intellectual and social demands placed on students, the instructional format or formats in place, the grouping arrangements or classroom organization, and the time available for covering the subject matter (including the portions of that subject matter covered and the pace at which it is covered). Armed with such knowledge, researchers are more likely to observe and interpret teaching as it takes place in the classroom. In other words, teaching is quite likely to be "read" more accurately (Jackson, 1986) when the components of instruction are known and considered.

Second, instruction provides a level of stability similar to that of teachers, but far greater than that of teaching. Studies of instruction search for reasonably stable patterns of teacher behaviors and teacher-student interactions over some specified time period. These patterns are likely to be quite distinct from the typical means of summarizing teacher behaviors, namely, cumulative frequency counts over time. In addition, the study of instruction requires that long-term, longitudinal investigations are conducted. The value of such studies has long been recognized. Flanders and Simon (1969) ended their review of teacher effectiveness by asserting, rather bluntly, that "consistent, long-range research programs are still few in number, and single-shot correlation studies much too frequent" (p. 1434).

Third, and as will be discussed in greater detail in Chapter 11, several of the components of instruction are associated with student achievement. The nature of grouping arrangements, for example, is a very promising instructional variable. Accelerated instruction provided to homogeneous groups of high ability students (Kulik and Kulik, 1987) and cooperative learning arrangements for groups of heterogeneous students (Slavin, 1987; Johnson and Johnson, 1989) appear to be quite effective in terms of facilitating student learning. Similarly, instructional time (Fisher and Berliner, 1985) and content coverage (Barr, 1987) have substantial empirical support for their importance in learning.

There are at least two disadvantages of current studies of instruction, however. First, instruction is a complex phenomenon. Unfortunately, most studies of instruction have focused on only one or two of the major components, often confounding them. Studies of teaching methods are a good example of such confounding. If, for example, the effectiveness of the lecture method is compared with small group discussions, both instructional format (lecture vs. discussion) and grouping arrangement (whole class vs. small group) are included under the general rubric "teaching methods." Some confounding is likely to occur because the six components are not completely independent. Other types of confounding, however, can be avoided. The point is that few studies of instruction have included most or all of the components, have examined the complex set of interrelationships among them, or have investigated the impact of the components, individually and collectively, on student achievement.

Second, in studies of instruction, differences among teachers or teaching are traditionally treated as error. In studies of teaching methods, for example, teachers are likely to differ in their understanding and use of the methods being compared. Some teachers understand the discussion method better than, say, the lecture method; some teachers are better able to lead discussions, while others are more dynamic lecturers. When the achievement of students learning under the discussion method is compared with that of students learning under the lecture method using traditional statistical techniques such as *t*-tests or analyses of variance, these differences among teachers within each of the teaching methods become part of the within group or error variance. This within group variance is compared with the average achievement difference between students in the two methods, the between group variance. The larger the between group variance relative to the within group variance, the more likely it is that differences in student achievement can be attributed to differences in teaching methods. Conversely, the greater the differences in teachers or teaching within any study of instruction, the *less likely* it is that differences in instruction will be reliably identified.

Researchers and Research: The Issue of Human Values

Thus far we have defined teachers, teaching, and instruction and have discussed several strengths and weaknesses associated with research on each. In this final section, we address an issue that often is given short-shrift in research textbooks. Many researchers are unable or unwilling to confront their values or the role values play in educational research, in general, or classroom research, in particular.

We believe that values play a major role in classroom research. Our values determine whether a particular type of research topic or problem is worthwhile. If we deem research on teacher effectiveness to be worthwhile, our values determine what we mean by effectiveness. In this regard, we would agree with Rabinowitz and Travers (1953) that:

> the effective teacher does not exist pure and serene, available for scientific scrutiny, but is instead a fiction of the minds of men. No teacher is more effective than another, except as someone so decides and designates (p. 586).

A variety of criteria of effectiveness currently exist, ranging from ratings of effectiveness made by students, supervisors, or independent observers to gains in student achievement. Since each of these criteria has strengths and weaknesses associated with them, the choice of an effectiveness criterion will likely depend in large part on the values of the person or persons doing the choosing.

Dunkin and Biddle (1974) have suggested that researchers have Commitments, that is, motivations to conduct research that support their value orientations concerning how best to improve education. These Commitments impact on the planning and conduct of our research in a number of ways. For example, some researchers

> have clung to weak research instruments or orientations, despite confusing and contradictory evidence and in defiance of severe criticism, apparently because they could not abandon their Commitments (p. 51).

Similarly, debates over the relative merits of experimental, quantitative research and naturalistic, qualitative research are based, not on the inherent value of the research *per se*, but on the inherent values of the researcher. Thus, our values influence the plans we make and use to conduct research.

Finally, our values influence our interpretation of the results of our research studies. When confronted with evidence, we have basically three choices. We can accept the evidence as is, we can ignore it, or we can modify it to "fit" with our belief system or value orientation. Unfortunately, at times, ignoring or modifying evidence seems to be the easy way out. As Dunkin and Biddle (1974) have pointed out, some researchers

> have simply ignored evidence accumulated by others that contradicts their Commitments or, worse, become advocates for a particular program of teacher training or curricular innovation in violation of their own published results (p. 51).

In combination, then, our values influence our decisions as to the topics and problems that are worthy of study, the plans we design and carry out to study these topics and problems, and our interpretation of the results. Bussis, Chittenden, and Amarel (1976) summarize our position on this matter:

> Decision-making is invariably a subjective, human activity involving value judgments . . . placed on whatever evidence is available. . . . Depending on the extent to which parties to a decision agree that the available evidence has been impartially gathered and represents "important" information, people may or may not agree on the meaning of the evidence. Even when there is virtual consensus of the "facts of the matter," such facts do not automatically lead to decisions regarding future action. People render decisions; information does not (p. 19).

Given the role of values in research, we ask but two things of those intending to engage in research in classrooms. First, be aware of your values and their impact on the decisions you make concerning research. Second, research by its very nature requires that you make your values explicit. Explicit values are needed if others are to critically examine your research studies and accurately replicate them. Many of our values were stated in the Preface.

2

Conceptualizing Classrooms

One of the first things a classroom researcher learns is that classrooms are difficult to study. Since the primary purpose of instruction and teaching is learning, a major goal of classroom research is to connect instruction and teaching with the learning of students. Although this may seem easy enough, it must be remembered that classrooms are settings in which (1) teachers and groups of students engage in activities with frequent verbal exchanges and academic work, (2) the intended result of these activities—student learning—occurs gradually over time and is largely unobservable, and (3) decisions made during instructional planning and teaching are also unobservable. Not only do these phenomena occur frequently and are often unobservable, they occur together in a complex chain of interrelated events whose sequence in time is important to their understanding. As if this were not enough, these phenemona are on vastly different time scales: teacher decision-making occurs virtually instantaneously, teacher-student interactions occur over seconds and minutes of classroom time, and student learning occurs over days and months, but with flashes of insight and understanding on the part of students.

There are, of course, other sources of classroom complexities. The point here is not to chronicle them, but simply to illustrate them. To understand classrooms, then, classroom researchers must come to grips with the way in which they conceptualize classroom phenemona. A major point of this chapter is that theory is the only way that classroom researchers will be able to sort out and understand the complex relationships which exist among teachers, teaching, instruction, and learning.

In this chapter, we examine the nature of various types of conceptual frameworks and present examples of how researchers have conceptualized classroom phenomena. As we will see, the level of theorizing about classrooms is at a relatively low level. There are at least three types of conceptual systems for describing classrooms and research in classrooms: paradigms or research programs, theories, and models. Unfortunately, classroom researchers have not been particularly careful in their definitions and use of these concepts. This has caused considerable confusion about the meaning of these terms and probably contributed to the low level of classroom theory.

16

Paradigms and Research Programs

Thomas Kuhn (1962, 1970) has outlined a theory of scientific progress that has the paradigm as its core concept. Kuhn's influential book concerns characteristics of normal and revolutionary science and the nature and course of scientific revolutions. Much of his discussion is tangential to our purposes and will not be presented here. But because the concept of scientific paradigm has been used frequently in discussions of research on teaching, we will consider some of the issues surrounding the concept here.

According to Kuhn, a paradigm is a shared commitment and belief within a scientific community as to the nature of the legitimate problems, theories, and methods of their discipline. Paradigms, often recounted as outstanding past achievements in a discipline's textbooks, are a major means by which students are prepared for membership in the scientific community. Paradigms not only provide model problems and solutions for future work in the discipline, but determine how scientists make sense of the world. "Men whose research is based on shared paradigms are committed to the same rules and standards for scientific practice. That commitment and the apparent consensus it produces are prerequisites for normal science, i.e., for the genesis and continuation of a particular research tradition." (Kuhn, 1970, p. 11).

Kuhn characterized the early stages of a science as pre-paradigmatic: "The pre-paradigmatic period, in particular, is regularly marked by frequent and deep debates over legitimate methods, problems, and standards of solution, though these serve rather to define schools than to produce agreement" (Kuhn, 1970, p. 48). According to Kuhn, it was only after a given paradigm emerged by solving a particularly acute problem or set of problems, ending interschool debate and freeing scientists to do more focused and directed work, that a science would begin to mature. Kuhn called this period of paradigmatic work "normal science" and characterized it as "puzzle-solving;" cumulative work on relatively minor problems dictated by the paradigm and accepted by the scientific community holding the paradigm as worthy of study.

As research becomes more focused and precise during normal science, Kuhn argued that significant anomolies appear. Although many anomolies are subsumed by the paradigm as puzzles and solved or set aside, some are capable of producing a crisis and plunging the scientific community into a period of extraordinary science where a new paradigm replaces the old one: "The transition from a paradigm in crisis to a new one from which a new tradition of normal science can emerge is far from a cumulative process, one achieved by the articulation or extension of the old paradigm. Rather it is reconstruction of the field from new fundamentals, a reconstruction that changes some of the field's most elementary theoretical generalizations as well as many of its paradigm methods and applications" (Kuhn, 1970, pp. 84–85).

Kuhn also argued that competing paradigms are incommensurate, that each paradigm will satisfy its own criteria but will fall short of criteria dictated by its competitor: ". . . the early development stages of most sciences have been characterized by continual competition between a number of distinct views of nature, each partially derived from, and all roughly compatible with, the dictates of scientific observation and method. What differentiated these various schools was not one or another failure of method—they were all 'scientific'—but what we shall come to call their incommensurable ways of seeing the world and of practicing science in it" (Kuhn, 1970, p. 4). Problems are different, standards of science are different, and most importantly, each paradigm has its own world view with which to interpret phenomena. "Practicing in different worlds, the two groups of scientists see different things when they look from the same point in the same direction" (Kuhn, 1970, p. 150). It is because paradigms establish standards for viewing and studying the world that a shift in paradigms is revolutionary, as when Einsteinian physics, which could explain more phenomena, replaced Newtonian physics. When a new paradigm is adopted, the scientific community has a new view of the world and new standards as to what constitutes legitimate science in their discipline.

Kuhn's book has generated an enormous amount of debate and criticism (see, for example, Gutting, 1980; Suppe, 1974). Much of the criticism has been directed at his inconsistent use of the term paradigm and also to how he characterized the social structure of the scientific communities that supposedly share paradigms.

In a postscript to a 1970 second edition of his work, Kuhn acknowledged the imprecision in the concept of paradigm but suggested there were really only two different uses of paradigm in the original work, not dozens as had been suggested. The first use was sociological and renamed "disciplinary matrix" by Kuhn. A disciplinary matrix has (1) a set of symbolic generalizations (mathematical laws like force = mass × acceleration), (2) shared commitments to models, including metaphors and analogies, and (3) shared values about theory and science in general. A fourth component to the disciplinary matrix was exemplars, the second use of the term paradigm. Exemplars are the solutions to past problems students are exposed to during their advanced training. They are the past achievement of the paradigm and serve as models of how to approach similar unsolved problems of the paradigm.

Kuhn also outlined in his postscript what he meant by the structure of scientific communities. The question is whether paradigms are shared by whole disciplines, like physics or astronomy, or whether a discipline is to be divided into groups of scholars, each studying his or her own substantive area within the discipline and each with his or her own paradigm and scientific revolutions. Kuhn specified three readily identified levels of the (natural) scientific community: the community of all natural scientists, the professional groups identified by a discipline (e.g., biologists, chemists, physicists, astronomers), and major sub-groups within disciplines (theoretical physicists, radio astronomers, organic chemists). To identify the next lower level of the scientific community, however, requires one to analyse communication networks among scientists (for example, exchange of draft manuscripts, attendance at special conferences, correspondence). Kuhn speculated that communities at this level number about 100 scientists, sometimes less. He also characterized this level as the level of the paradigm: "Communities of this sort are the units that this book has presented as the producers and validators of scientific knowledge. Paradigms are something shared by the members of such groups" (Kuhn, 1970, p. 178).

In his postscript, then, Kuhn suggests that paradigms are shared by relatively small groups of scientists. There could be many such paradigms within a discipline. Kuhn also revised his ideas about the transition from pre-paradigmatic to post-paradigmatic science. He suggested that it was not the acquisition of a first paradigm that characterized paradigmatic science since "members of all scientific communities, including the schools of the 'pre-paradigm' period, share the sorts of elements which I have collectively labeled 'a paradigm' " (p. 179). Rather, it was the nature of the paradigm itself. A mature paradigm characterizes a developed science, one that "identifies challenging puzzles, supplies clues to their solution, and guarantees that the truly clever practitioner will succeed" (p. 179). Kuhn does not, however, define what an immature paradigm looks like or how it functions for the competing schools prior to some "notable scientific achievement" that reduces the number of competing schools to one and pushes the mature paradigm to the top.

Paradigms in Classroom Research

Kuhn's book and concept of paradigm have been widely used and cited in the social sciences. In classroom research, several notable papers have used paradigms as a way of characterizing different areas of research within the field. Doyle (1978), for example, outlined three teacher effectiveness paradigms: process-product, mediating process, and classroom ecology. The process-product paradigm is characterized by relating quantitative measures of teacher behavior (process) to student achievement measures (product). The mediating process paradigm adds a third class of variables to the process-product paradigm, placing student information-processing constructs (mediating process) between instructional conditions and student learning. A third paradigm—classroom ecology—is less well characterized structurally. Doyle draws upon two literatures, classroom ethnography and ecological psychology, and outlines two stages of research to characterize this paradigm: ". . . identifying environmental demands and speculating about the mediational strategies necessary to meet these demands successfully" (Doyle, 1978, p. 176).

In a second, more recent paper on paradigms for classroom research, Doyle (1987) only refers to the first two paradigms by name and greatly expands the domain boundaries of the third. He suggests that the latter two, mediating process and "descriptive studies" of classrooms, are only "emerging paradigms" because "differences in types of questions and interpretive frameworks militate against the development of a coherent perspective or a common research program" (Doyle, 1987, p. 119). Doyle's description fits well with Kuhn's postscript suggestion that it is not the presence of a paradigm but its nature that characterizes a "paradigmatic" science.

If we take Kuhn's concept of paradigm seriously, we need to ask questions about the level of scientific community we are discussing when we talk about paradigms for classroom research. For example, are process-product, mediating process, and classroom ecology competing *schools* (each with paradigmatic elements) for the *field* of research on teaching, with one ultimate winner guiding puzzle-solving science in the field, or are there competing schools within the field of say, classroom ecology, schools attempting to push their paradigm to the top of the field of classroom ecology with some notable achievement? Given Doyle's classroom ecology paradigm, the community of scientists characterized by this label is composed of at least two schools—ecological psychologists and classroom ethnographers. Should they be viewed as competing schools for a field of classroom ecology or the field of classroom research?

We also need to ask questions about how many mature paradigms are possible in a field? Can multiple paradigms exist in a field? Is it necessary to have winning and losing paradigms in the social and behavioral sciences as there have been in Kuhn's view of the natural sciences? Are there multiple questions that a field needs to answer, necessitating multiple paradigms? We ask these questions because they seem to go to the heart of how we conceptualize the field of classroom research.

Among those educators concerned with classroom research, N. L. Gage has written the most on paradigms. His chapter on "Paradigms for Research on Teaching" in the first *Handbook of Research on Teaching* was written without his knowing the work of Kuhn (see Gage, 1985). In his chapter, Gage defined paradigms as:

> . . . models, patterns, or schemata. Paradigms are not theories; rather, they are ways of thinking or patterns for research that, when carried out, can lead to the development of theory . . . . When one has chosen a paradigm for his research, he has made crucial decisions concerning the kinds of variables and relationships between variables that he will investigate . . . . A second characteristic of paradigms is that they often represent variables and their relationships in some graphic or outline form" (Gage, 1963a, p. 95).

Gage went on to define three paradigms for research on teaching: criterion-of-effectiveness, teaching process, and machine paradigms. The criterion-of-effectiveness paradigm first identifies a criterion of teacher effectiveness and then finds correlates of this criterion by determining the correlation between the two. A shift away from teacher effectiveness criteria to other criteria gives rise to Gage's second paradigm—the teaching process paradigm. These other criteria are the perceptual and cognitive processes of teachers and students and the behavior of each (see Gage, 1963a, pp. 127–129). Gage's final paradigm involves drawing parallels between the functions of components of teaching machines and teaching and teacher characteristics.

More recently, Gage (1985) has defined paradigms in a manner more similar to that of Kuhn. He characterizes a paradigm as:

> an integrated cluster of *substantive* concepts, variables and problems attached with corresponding *methodological* approaches and tools . . .. A paradigm gathers unto itself a community of investigators. By sharing information within itself, this community gives itself intellectual and social support. It tends not to communicate with investigators who follow different paradigms. Citation of others' work is frequent within a paradigm but much less frequent, perhaps nonexistent, across paradigms. Hence the followers of a paradigm tend to have their own journals, scientific societies, and meetings, because the paradigm has won their allegiance to an integrated set of concepts, variables, problems, and methods (p. 42).

He outlines seven paradigms for research on teaching: process-product, the extended process-product, behaviour modification, interactive educational technology, instructional design, intact teaching styles, and ethnographic-sociolinguistic. The extended process-product paradigm, by the way, incorporates key concepts from both the classroom ecology and mediating process paradigms mentioned by Doyle (1978). As shown in Figure 2.1, "pupils cue resources and interpretations" and "pupils mediating responses" are concepts associated with the classroom ecology and mediating process paradigms, respectively, which have been added by Gage to intervene between "process" and "product."

Over the years, Gage has been perhaps the staunchest defender of the process-product paradigm. One example is his expansion of the paradigm to include Doyle's additional variables. He has also "liberalized" the process-product paradigm to include all ways of describing or measuring process variables, including ethnographic and case study methodologies (see Gage, 1985; Gage and Needels, 1989). Thus, the paradigm is being adapted in response to new ideas about how research on teaching should proceed. The

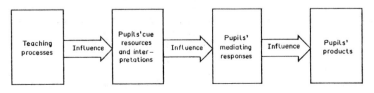

FIG 2.1   The extended process-product paradigm (from Gage, 1985).

question is whether the paradigm can continue to exist as a viable paradigm and not as a historical relic or whether, as Doyle (1987) suggests, it will share the limelite with a new emerging paradigm.

Before leaving paradigms, a final example helps round out the discussion and introduces a somewhat different view of scientific progress. Shulman (1986) prefers the "research program" concept of Lakatos (1978) to Kuhn's concept of "paradigm." A research program is a series of successive theories linked by a set of shared, temporarily irrefutable assumptions or theoretical "hard core." A research program also has a "positive heuristic" which defines problems and outlines hypotheses to be tested. A "protective belt" of auxillary hypotheses, generated by the theoretical hard core, shields the hard core from direct empirical falsification. A research program attempts to improve the fit between the theoretical hard core and the phenemonon being explained by modifying auxillary hypotheses through empirical tests. Only when changes in auxillary hypotheses can no longer fit the hard core to the phenemonon is the hard core modified or dropped altogether. Thus, research programs develop and change as empirical studies are carried out and a better fit is attempted between the theoretical hard core and the phenomena being explained. This is quite different from the traditional Popperian (1959) view that a single counter example to a hypothesis is sufficient to falsify and abandon a hypothesis.

Research programs progress theoretically as long as its theories continue to make new predictions; research programs progress empirically as long as the predictions receive empirical support. Because research programs do not necessarily progress on both levels simultaneously, scientists can sometimes disregard negative empirical evidence as long as the program is progressing theoretically. However, research programs "degenerate" when the theories can only yield *post hoc* explanation. If one research program explains more than another, it can supercede the rival. However, it is difficult to determine when a research program has completely degenerated or when one program has achieved a decisive advantage over another.

Shulman suggests that Kuhn's characterization of the social sciences as being in a state of "preparadigmatic retardation" was incorrect and that the existence of multiple schools of thought could and does characterize a mature social science, not a developmentally retarded one. Simultaneous research paradigms—programs—can and do exist side by side in a mature science. Because of the complexity of classroom phenomena and the inability of a given research program to encompass classroom phenomena in their entirety, Shulman advocates multiple research programs and the blending of features across programs. To this end, he offers the "synoptic map" for research on teaching shown in Figure 2.2.

The map outlines the research perspectives, relationships, contexts, and events of teaching for research on teaching. A given research program can be characterized by a particular unit or set of units from the map, but no

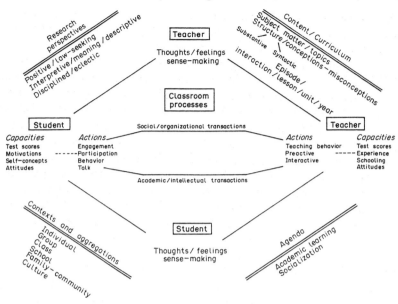

FIG 2.2   Synoptic map of classroom research (from Shulman, 1986)

research program could cover all the units that are represented. Shulman's chapter develops a beautifully crafted argument about paradigms and research programs, part of which he states as follows:

> The argument of this chapter is that each of the extant research programs grows out of a particular perspective, a bias of either convention or discipline, necessarily illuminating some part of the field of teaching while ignoring the rest. The danger for any field of social science or educational research lies in its potential corruption (or worse, trivialization) by a single paradigmatic view. In this manner, the social sciences and education can be seen as quite different from Kuhn's conception of a mature paradigmatic discipline in the natural sciences, which is ostensibly characterized by a single dominant paradigm whose principles define "normal science" for that field of study (p. 4).

Theory and Classroom Research

For knowledge to be useful, it must be organized. Isolated facts serve little purpose. Mouly (1963), for example, argues that only when facts are integrated into some conceptual scheme do we obtain understanding of a phenomena.

Most scientists would agree that theory is useful because it brings order to empirical facts and events in the world. Theory outlines the kinds of facts that are important in understanding phenomena and specifies the relationships among the facts necessary to produce that understanding. Theory provides a shorthand version of the world, sometimes allowing us to anticipate and make predictions about what to expect. Scientists, in other words, invent theories to facilitate understanding. George Kelly (1955), a personality theorist, does not even restrict theorizing to scientists, believing all people, not just scientists, theorize and predict as a way of controlling the course of events in their lives. His concept of "man-as-scientist" undergirds his personal construct theory.

While there is no denying that all people theorize, as Kelly suggests, it is also true that the products of theorizing are different for scientists than for lay people. For one thing, scientific theories are written down and shared with other scientists for evaluation. For another, scientific theories are typically more complex than everyday observation, with formal and logical connections between the concepts stated as propositions of the theory. Furthermore, there is some degree of consensus in the scientific community about what constitutes "good theory." There are formal procedures for submitting theories, or more precisely, hypotheses derived from the theories, to verification.

While scientists generally agree on the broad view of theory presented above, they are less consistent in the language used to describe the process of theorizing and they disagree on approaches for generating theory. We will discuss some of these issues in the next chapter. Here we will present a brief description of the function of theory, different types of theory, and criteria for selecting among competing theories. We begin with an often-quoted definition of theory given by Kerlinger, an educational psychologist.

According to Kerlinger (1973), "A theory is a set of interrelated constructs (concepts), definitions, and propositions that present a systematic view of phenomena by specifying relations among variables, with the purpose of explaining and predicting the phenomena" (p. 9). Kerlinger's definition suggests a number of different elements and purposes of theory (see Hage, 1972, for a more systematic presentation of theory).

Theories are made up of concepts and propositions. Concepts can be "primitive terms," undefined except by illustration or intuition, and derived terms, terms defined by using the primitive terms or other derived concepts. Theoretical concepts refer to events that cannot be directly observed, and are typically called constructs by scientists, since they are constructed by a scientist's thinking. Propositions are statements that connect two or more concepts, and are unfortunately called by many names that are often intended to convey subtle meanings: axioms, postulates, premises, assumptions, theorems, or hypotheses are some of the names. We will not go into those subtle meanings here, leaving that task for the philosophers of science (see, for example, Kaplan, 1964). Suffice it to say that axioms or postulates are propositions that state general assumptions from which other theoretical statements can be derived, most notably hypotheses. Hypotheses are simply unconfirmed statements.

What is important about theories is that they specify relations among concepts, and in the process, *attempt to explain why a particular relationship holds.* The concepts and propositions are interrelated and provide a systematic description of the phenomena. It is from this systematic description that explanation and prediction eminate.

We can expand our presentation of theory slightly by considering another definition of theory, this time from a personality theorist. Rychlak (1968, p. 42) defines theory as follows: "A theory may be thought of as a series of two or more constructions (abstractions), which have been hypothesized, assumed, or even factually demonstrated to bear a certain relationship, one with the other." Rychlak describes four functions of theory: describing phenomena with concepts and propositions, delimiting the boundary conditions of the phenomena to be described, generating hypotheses and ideas from the propositions, and integrating the concepts and propositions into a consistent whole. Before we turn our attention to these four functions of theory, however, it will be helpful to have a theory to illustrate each of these functions. To do this, we will use Bloom's (1976) theory of school learning.

Suppose you were interested in developing a theory of classroom learning, a task many educational psychologists have attempted in the past. How would you go about developing the theory? What concepts would you use to explain learning? What propositions would you use to relate the concepts? How much of school learning would you attempt to understand? What language system would you use to convey your concepts and propositions? What predictions would your theory make about classroom learning?

Bloom was interested in how groups of students could learn as well as an individual student who receives excellent tutoring. Deviations from this quality of learning were perceived as errors, and Bloom wanted to identify and define those variables that were associated with these errors. "Our theory is an attempt to determine a small number of variables which will account for much of the variation in school learning" (Bloom, 1976, p. 10). Once these variables were identified, school conditions could be altered to reduce the errors. Three sets of variables were identified:

"a. The extent to which the student has already learned the basic prerequisites to the learning to be accomplished,
b. The extent to which the student is (or can be) motivated to engage in the learning process,
c. The extent to which the instruction to be given is appropriate to the learner" (pp. 10–11).

These three sets of variables are labeled cognitive entry behaviors affective entry characteristics, and quality of instruction, respectively. Bloom hypothesizes that variations in each of these three sets of variables determine the nature of learning outcomes. When the two sets of student characteristics and the quality of instruction are favorable, then there will be little variation in measures of learning outcomes and learning will be uniformly high. When these variables are less favorable, there will be variation in learning outcomes, the extent of which will be determined by the amount of variation in the student characteristics and the extent to which the quality of instruction is less than optimal.

In his book presenting his theory, Bloom defines each of his concepts, demonstrates how each of the three concepts is related to student learning, and amasses existing evidence as to the validity of each of these three relationships. Most importantly, Bloom makes clear what he means by "favorable" and "less favorable." Quality of instruction, for example, is defined in terms of cues, participation, reinforcement, and the use of feedback/correction procedures. Bloom also justifies his theory in terms of its usefulness, showing how the three sets of variables can be altered to produce better learning, which for Bloom rests on two values: that higher levels of learning are better than lower levels of learning and that less variation in student learning is better than more variation.

We can use this brief outline of Bloom's theory to illustrate the different functions of theory. The first function of theory is to *describe phenomena*. A theorist organizes concepts and propositions into a language system that attempts to characterize the nature of the phenomena. According to Rychlak, a fully described phenomena is one that explains the conditions under which the phenomena varies. This usually means that the theorist's language system becomes more abstract and further removed from the layman's description of the phenomena. However, such a language system can still be understood and checked by other scientists sharing a similar background to the theorist.

Bloom's theory defines a set of three concepts and relates these concepts to the phenomena of student learning, itself a concept. Cognitive entry behaviors, affective entry characteristics, and quality of instruction are first operationalized and then the research literature is reviewed to estimate the strength of relationship between each of the three concepts and student learning. The relationship between cognitive entry behaviors and student learning was estimated by Bloom to be + .70, or about 50 percent of the variation in student achievement (square the correlation coefficient and multiply by 100 to obtain the percentage of shared variation). The correlation between affective entry behaviors and student achievement was estimated to be + .50, or about 25 percent of the variability in student learning. Finally, quality of instruction was estimated to account for about 25 percent of the variation in student achievement. Bloom then estimated the joint relationship of the three sets of variables and student achievement as shown in Figure 2.3.

Ninety percent of the variation in student learning was estimated to be a direct function of the three sets of variables. Such propositions, specifying

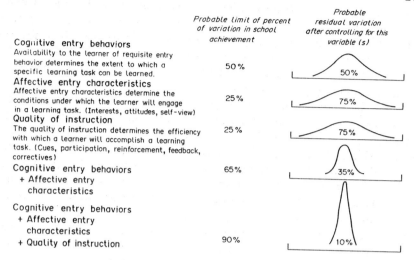

FIG 2.3 Estimated effect of selected variables on variation in school achievement (from Bloom, 1976). Reproduced with permission from Bloom, B. S., *Human Characteristics and School Learning* (1976) © McGraw-Hill.

relationships among the theory's concepts, offer one explanation of student learning by accounting for a large percentage of the variation in student achievement. If Bloom's marshalling of evidence and his reasoning are convincing to you, then his theory is quite powerful.

A second function of theory is to *delimit the boundary conditions and scope of the phenomena* the theory purports to describe and explain. A theories' concepts and propositions do not explain all phenomena, but rather focus on a single phenomenon or perhaps some small set of phenomena. Bloom's theory, for example, is about school conditions affected student learning, not personality development nor teacher stress nor other significant problems educators face. Perhaps physics will develop its grand, unifying theory uniting the four known forces—gravitational, electromagnetic, strong, and weak—but it is doubtful that a comparable theory will ever exist in the social sciences. Middle-range or substantive theory (see Denzin, 1970, pp. 68 ff), focusing on particular problem areas or topics, is more realistic. Such theories are of medium scope, focusing on particular topics such as a theory of school learning or theory of personality development or a theory of teacher stress.

A third function of theory, in Rychlak's view, is to *generate new ideas or hypotheses* about the phenomenon with the goal of producing new knowledge and understanding. Theories must continue to generate new ideas or else they stagnate and wither from lack of use. A theory that stimulates new ideas to study and hypotheses to test is useful heuristically. This includes the use of metaphors and analogies to suggest new ideas about phenomena. Bloom, for example, used the relatively error-free tutor-learner situation to argue for analogous learning with larger groups of students. Rychlak (1968) offers an interesting quote by Robert Oppenheimer on the use of analogy in science:

> Whether or not we talk of discovery or of invention, analogy is inevitable in human thought, because we come to new things in science with what equipment we have, which is how we have learned to think, and above all how we have learned to think about the relatedness of things. We cannot, coming into something new, deal with it except on the basis of the familiar and the old-fashioned (p. 55).

To help generate ideas, theorists often use models of the phenomenon being explained. Although most models are more formalized than analogies or metaphors, as we will see in the next section, they serve essentially the same function. Models can provide a graphic representation of salient aspects of the theory, assisting the theorist's thinking about the phenomena under consideration. Bloom's model of school learning, presented in Figure 2.4, is a shorthand version of the theory, outlining the major concepts and their interrelationships. Such models can also stimulate others to think in similar ways, perhaps expanding a particular concept, or adding new concepts and relationships to the model. Thus, both theories and models serve a generative function.

The fourth and final function of theory is *integration*. Theories bring together concepts and propositions into a theoretical system, a consistent perspective or view of the phenomenon. As more and more concepts are added to a theoretical system, it is necessary to organize the concepts. Theory integrates because it uses abstract concepts and propositions capable of unifying less abstract concepts and propositions. Integration requires that theories be parsimonious, using only what concepts and propositions are necessary to describe and explain its phenomenon. The goal is to explain as much of the phenomenon with as few concepts and propositions as possible. Thus, simpler theories are preferred to more complex ones, and theories with fewer assumptions and concepts are valued over those with more assumptions and concepts.

Bloom's theory is powerful because it purports to explain most of the

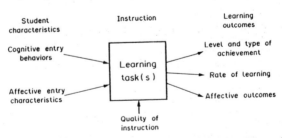

FIG 2.4   Major variables in a theory of school learning (from Bloom, 1976). Reproduced with permission from Bloom,, B. S., *Human Characteristics and School Learning* (1976) © McGraw-Hill.

variation in school learning with only three sets of variables. In this sense, Bloom's theory is fulfilling the integration function of theory. What must be kept in mind, however, is the scope of the theory and its ability to generate testable hypotheses. Some broad theories may appear to explain more with fewer assumptions or propositions, but in fact have difficulty generating hypotheses to be submitted to test.

In summary, then, theory serves multiple functions. Theory attempts to describe and explain some delimited phenomena in a parsimonious way. It also attempts to generate testable hypotheses for study, as well as stimulate new ways of thinking about the phenomena.

When multiple theories exist, researchers need some criteria and standards to use in choosing among them. A set of criteria for use in evaluating theories of instruction was developed in the mid-1960s by the Commission on Instructional Theory of the Association for Supervision and Curriculum Development (Gordon, Fattu, Hughes, Lund, Smith, and Travers, 1968). The purpose of the Commission was to "provide guidelines for supervisors and teachers as they look critically at proposed statements of instructional theory" (p. v). The members of the Commission decided to write criteria applicable to scientific theory in general, rather than specifically to instructional theory. As a consequence, the document is an excellent statement of criteria for assessing theory in general and summarizing the "good" qualities in theory, but is not particularly good for evaluating

TABLE 2.1
Criteria for a Theory of Instruction

Descriptive Function of Theory
1. A statement of an instructional theory should include a set of postulates and definition of terms involved in the postulates.
2. An instructional theory must not only explain past events but also must be capable of predicting future events.

Delineating Function of Theory
3. The statement of an instructional theory or sub-theory should make explicit the boundaries of its concern and the limitations under which it is proposed.

Generative Function of Theory
4. An instructional theory must be capable of generating hypotheses.
5. An instructional theory must contain generalizations which go beyond the data.
6. An instructional theory must be verifiable.
7. An instructional theory must be stated in such a way that it is possible to collect data to disprove it.

Integrative Function of Theory
8. A theoretical construction must have internal consistency—a logical set of inter-relationships.
9. An instructional theory should be congruent with empirical data.

Note. Adapted from Gordon et al. (1968).

instructional theory. In Table 2.1 we present nine of the ten criteria included in that document which we have organized according to Rychlak's four functions of theory. Since the criteria displayed in Table 2.1 should be familiar from our previous discussion we shall not elaborate on them here.[1]

Models and Classroom Research

In the previous section, we suggested similarities between theories and models. This is to be expected since modeling in classroom research is a major source of theorizing. In this section we begin by defining models and present several examples of models used in classroom research.

According to Snow (1973), we can ". . . consider models well-developed descriptive analogies used to help visualize, often in a simplified or imitative way, phenomena that cannot be easily or directly observed. Each model is thus a projection of a possible system of relationships among phenomena, realized in verbal, material, or symbolic terms" (p. 81). Snow distinguishes two kinds of models. The first kind are replica models, usually material or pictorial representations made with a change in spatial or temporal scale. Symbolic models are the second kind, which tend to be intangible, using abstract verbal, graphic, or symbolic representation to stand for conceptual systems.

Simon and Newell (1956) distinguish theories and models in the following ways. First, models are useful rather than true. That is, models serve as a heuristic device rather than provide detailed description of a phenomenon. Second, models are less sensitive to empirical evidence in that disconfirming evidence are more damaging to a theory than to a model. However, this is less true today in at least the case of structural regression techniques (see Pedhazur, 1982). Structural regression modeling techniques such as LISREL (the acronym for "*l*inear *s*tructural *rel*ations") are designed specifically to test conceptual models. Third, models are more likely to make false claims than are theories.

To use Snow's terminology, virtually all models in classroom research are symbolic models. They are not meant to be miniature replicas of classrooms or events that occur within them; rather, models function to simplify the complexities of classrooms and to identify salient features of classroom phenomena. In so doing, they help researchers think about the relationships among these features.

There are no shortages of models in classroom research. During the preparation of this book we have encountered about thirty graphically-presented models that have as their primary emphasis teachers, teaching, instruction, and/or school learning. Interestingly, most of these models were developed after 1960. In analyzing these various models, we have identified

---

[1]The tenth criterion included in the document is more a general statement than a criterion.

four general uses for models and modeling. Models and modeling are used to:

1. summarize and organize the results of a set of studies,
2. provide a conceptual framework for analyzing classroom phenomena,
3. direct or guide a specific research study, and
4. formally test hypothesized causal relationships.

Each of these purposes are discussed below, with examples given to illustrate each.

Summarizing Research Findings

Of all the models that exist, the Dunkin and Biddle (1974) model is arguably the best known. The model was developed primarily to organize their excellent review of literature and to consider the "research in an economical and thoughtful manner" (p. 31). The model includes broad classes of variables and outlines the hypothesized relationships among them. (See Figure 2.5.)

The model is not an explanation for student learning or for teacher-student interaction. It is constructed with general terms that provide little in the way of explanation. It is a model *for* research on teaching which identifies classes of variables to study. Other models whose primary purpose is to organize

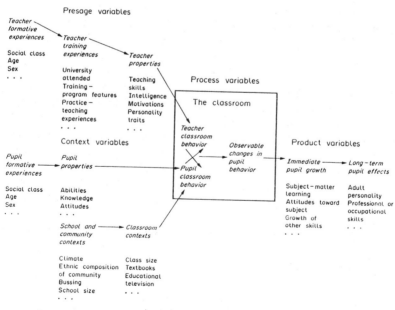

FIG 2.5 A model of the study of classroom teaching (from Dunkin and Biddle, 1974).

research findings have been developed by Bennett (1978), Centra and Potter (1980), and Walberg (1984).

Providing a Conceptual Framework

A second use of models in classroom research is for conceptual analysis. The models are generated in an attempt to help the researcher analyze the phenomenon being studied in a meaningful and organized way. While these models may be derived from previous research, typically they are generated from the researcher's own observations and reflections about the phenomenon itself. Excellent examples of such models can be found in Smith and Geoffrey (1968). Both Geoffrey, the classroom teacher, and Smith, the outside observer, maintained daily field notes of their observations of Geoffrey's class. They met frequently to discuss their observations and began to construct the "jigsaw puzzle" of what teaching was really like. The pieces of this puzzle were in the form of models.

In their report of the study, Smith and Geoffrey actually describe their process of model building as follows:

> As we have tried to abstract from our observations our operational definitions, in effect, we have named phenomena. Then we have tried to define theoretically the new term we have coined or borrowed. As we wrote down our conceptual definitions we found that they usually contained some terms already in our growing glossary and some new terms. Ultimately we found our way back to our "undefined" primitive list. . . . As a further step, we tried to find in our data the antecedents and consequences of the conception. This led us into forming hypotheses with concepts already in our theory, as well as creating new concepts. . . . As we sketched out our propositions we found we were drawing diagrams (pp. 16–17).

Their diagrams, or models, then, are actually hypothesized relationships based on their observations in Geoffrey's classroom. According to Smith and Geoffrey, these hypotheses "need verification through quantitative research in the laboratory and the field" (p. 19). Although some would disagree whether their hypotheses would, in fact, need verification, few can argue that the richness of description ethnographic description provides ample opportunity for hypothesis generation.

As one example, consider the model illustrated in Figure 2.6. This model outlines Smith and Geoffrey's conception of "ringmastership," an analogy to the fact that operating and reacting to the multiple and simultaneous events in a classroom is like emceeing the simultaneous acts of a three-ring circus. They hypothesize that a teacher's ability as a ringmaster directly affects the effectiveness and efficiency of the classroom that, in turn, affects student learning. This is a reasonable hypothesis, although it is less clear how ringmastership influences pupil esteem and they do not explain the model. Presumably student needs are better met by a teacher equipped to handle the simultaneity of classroom events. Enhanced peer and superior esteem, which they also do not explain, likely refers to the rewarding effects a good

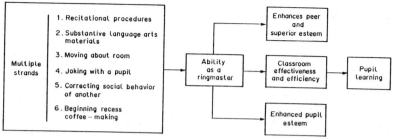

FIG 2.6   Clarification of "ringmaster phenomenon" (from Smith and
Geoffrey, 1968).

ringmaster derives from recognition by other teachers and the principal. In any case, our point is not to discuss the model so much as it is to show how their conceptual analysis was carried out.

Another example of a model designed for conceptual analysis is one developed by the authors of this book. Much of the research in teaching and instruction neglects, in our view, the instructional environment. Teaching methods research, for example, treats different methods or models of teaching as qualitatively different when, in fact, they vary along certain dimensions. The purpose of our conceptual analysis of lessons, therefore, was to outline what some of the dimensions might be.

The starting point of our conceptual analysis was a view of classrooms as behavior settings (Barker, 1968). Generally, a behavior setting "involves time, place, and thing elements coordinated to behavior phenomena; this coordination is expressed in the label used: *behavior setting*" (Gump, 1968, p. 236). A behavior setting is a place where certain kinds of purposeful behavior are supposed to occur. Because classrooms are places where a teacher attempts to influence the learning of a group of students, they have a different physical arrangement and props than say banks, for example, and people behave differently in classrooms than in banks. The concept of behavior setting was developed by Barker as a way of distinguishing, in our example, classrooms from banks, or more generally, to characterize "human behavior and its environment in situ" (Barker, 1986, p. 1).

Borrowing from the work of Gump (1967), Berliner (1983), and Stodolsky (1983), we related the structural features of lessons to the kinds of tasks both teachers and students were required to perform in their roles as teacher and student (see Burns and Anderson, 1987). Our model, shown in Figure 2.7, characterizes lessons as sequences of lesson segments, each segment defined in terms of purpose, activity format, and topic or assignment. A particular segment configuration suggested roles for both the teacher and students, the roles determining tasks to be accomplished and the type of behavioral interaction likely to occur.

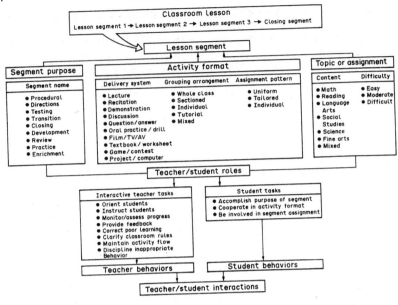

FIG 2.7   The activity structure of lesson segments (from Burns and Anderson, 1987).

Guiding Classroom Research

Nuthall and Snook (1973) argue that most research on teaching has been guided not by the desire to discover and accumulate empirical knowledge about teaching but by "debate and controversy over certain highly provocative pedagogical concepts and claims about how teaching ought to be viewed" (p. 48). They "discard the popular notion of a model as a formal symbolic representation of variable relationships and entertain, instead, a conception of 'model' as a more general and influential point of view with certain significant functions in guiding and structuring research" (p. 48).

Models have been used to guide several research studies since the publication of Nuthall and Snook's argument. The model presented in Figure 2.8, for example, helped to guide the Beginning Teacher Evaluation Study (BTES) (Fisher et al., 1980). The model outlines a specific sequence of teaching functions considered to be critical for student learning. The model separates instructional planning, where the teacher diagnoses and prescribes, from actual teaching, where the teacher presents material or tasks to students, monitors students' responses, and provides feedback to the students. Each of these teaching functions can be accomplished using different teacher behaviors.

Another example of a model used to guide research comes from the Instructional Dimensions Study (Cooley and Leinhardt, 1980). The study

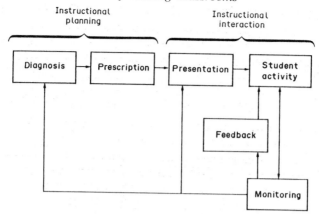

FIG 2.8   Teaching functions in the academic learning time model of classroom instruction (from Fisher et al., 1980).

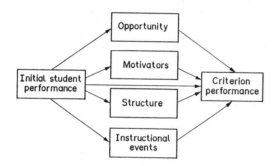

FIG 2.9   Model of classroom processes (from Cooley and Leinhardt, 1980).

was part of a Congressionally-mandated evaluation of compensatory education with a specific focus on the effectiveness of individualized instruction with low-income students. Cooley and Leinhardt argued that such an evaluation ought to consider individualized and regular instruction as differing along certain dimensions, hence, the name of the study. The model used to guide the selection and organization of variables, taken from Cooley and Lohnes (1976) is presented in Figure 2.9. This model was used to "identify the domains of relevant variables that should be 'kept in mind' when considering the variables that might be included in exploratory studies of particular phenomenon" (Cooley and Leinhardt, 1980, footnote 2, p. 8).

Four classes of variables, in addition to initial student levels of performance, are hypothesized to "explain the variation in student perform-ance that occurs among classrooms after an extended period of instruction in those classrooms" (p. 8). Opportunity refers to a student's opportunity

TABLE 2.2
Variables and Measures Associated with the Concept "Structure"

Variable	Measure	Source
Placement &	Curr. ref. placement test	C
Pretest	Place. proc.—standard test	T
	Place. proc.—curr. test	T
	Place. proc.—teacher test	T
	Place. proc.—obs. wk. sample	T
	Curriculum pretests	C
Mastery	Curriculum posttests	C
	Curric. meth. assess. mastery	T
	Teach. assess.—curr. test	T
	Teach. assess.—teacher test	T
	Teach. assess.—in-class assign	T
	Teach. assess.—compl. wk. unit	T
	Teach. assess.—observe work	T
	Teach. assess.—conf. w/pupil	T
Matching	# days since last test ($-$)	T
Practices	Range days since last test ($-$)	T
	% correct last test	T
	Frequency of testing	T
	Tests for assessing mastery	T
	Tests for diagnosis	T
	Tests for prescription	T
Grouping &	% unique assignments	T
Assignments	To whom assign. made	T
	% time—entire class ($-$)	T
	% time—subgr. 11+ ($-$)	T
	% time—subgr. 2–4	T
	% time—1 to 1	T
	# students in group ($-$)	T
	Frequency of regrouping	T
Meeting	Diff.—curr.—addn. practice	C
Individual	Diff.—curr.—repeat incomplete	C
Needs	Teacher alt.—repeat material	T
	Teacher alt.—1 to 1 remedial	T
	Teacher alt.—curr. sugg. remed.	T
	Teacher alt.—cont on, back later	T
	Readability level	C
Sequence	Clarity of sequence	T
	Teacher follows sequence	T
	Sequence varies w/in classroom	T
	Teach. create supple. to imp. seq.	T
	Ea. seg. instr. prereq. to next	C
	Diff. alt. based on stud. pref.	C
	Self-pacing	T
	Rules/guide for pacing	C
	Amount of review	C

Note. T = teacher, V = videotape, C = curriculum analysis

Source: Cooley and Leinhardt, 1980.

to learn what is measured in the criterion performance. Motivators refer to curricular and interpersonal behavior related to student engagement. Instructional events are complex, consisting of a variety of more specific variables related to classroom interaction. Structure is also complex, referring to the level of organization in the curriculum, the curricular objectives, and the match of student to curriculum. Each of these constructs identified more specific variables for investigation. For example, the variables used to define the construct of "structure" are given in Table 2.2.

Testing Causal Relationships

A fourth and final purpose of models is to test the causal relationships between constructs specified in a model. As mentioned earlier, structural regression modeling techniques specifically test hypothesized causal relationships among variables or constructs (see Pedhazur, 1982). Such regression techniques require the researcher to specify the model to be tested in advance of data analysis. The more sophisticated approaches, like LISREL (see Hayduk, 1987; Jöreskog and Sorbom, 1986) or partial least squares (see Wold, 1982; also see Anderson et al., 1989), explicitly separate the structural model, which specifies the relations among the constructs being considered in the causal analysis, from the measurement model, which links the measures of the constructs to the constructs themselves. In effect, the structural equation model specifies the researchers' theory of the phenomena to be tested.

Examples of structural regression are still relatively rare in research on teaching. One of the first uses of such techniques in research on teaching was from Phase II of the Beginning Teacher Evaluation Study conducted by Educational Testing Service (McDonald and Elias, 1975/76). This large scale correlational study was designed to develop hypotheses about the relationships between teacher behavior and student achievement and to develop measurement procedures for future phases of the study (Phase III was conducted at the Far West Laboratory). The model in Figure 2.10 guided the development of instrumentation and was formally tested using path analytic techniques. Even though data were collected in forty-one second-grade and fifty-four fifth-grade classrooms, the complexity of the model and the large number of variables required that portions of the model be tested separately. Still, the McDonald and Elias study represents one of few attempts to test causal models in a large-scale process-product paradigm.

Another example from instructional research is the study reported by Schneider and Treiber (1984). Schneider and Treiber were interested in developing a "better" model of achievement. To do so, they argued, required (1) that achievement be measured longitudinally with multiple measurements over time, (2) that instruction be conceptualized more

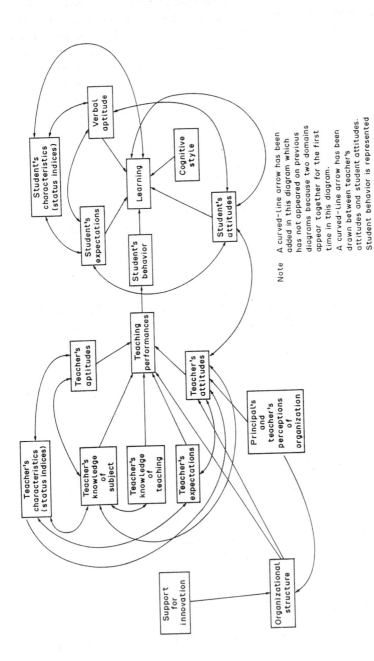

Note A curved-line arrow has been
      added in this diagram which
      has not appeared on previous
      diagrams because two domains
      appear together for the first
      time in this diagram.
      A curved-line arrow has been
      drawn between teacher's
      attitudes and student attitudes.
      Student behavior is represented
      for the first time in this diagram.

FIG 2.10 A structural model of the domains of variables influencing teaching
performances and children's learning from McDonald and Elias (1975–76).
Reproduced by permission of Educational Testing Service

realistically by selecting appropriately compatible variables, and (3) that comparative models across different types of students and or classrooms be made. They proposed, therefore, that the model depicted in Figure 2.11 be tested empirically for two different types of classrooms: those with steep achievement on aptitude slopes and those with shallow achievement on aptitude slopes. Their reasoning was that the differential slopes were indicators of fundamentally different instructional processes occurring in the classrooms which should directly affect how achievement should be "modeled." Specifically, student achievement in classrooms having a steep slope meant that aptitude played an important role in learning. In classrooms with shallow slopes, however, student aptitude was less important, presumably reflecting a compensatory approach focusing on the lower aptitude students in the classroom.

Their model displays both the structural and measurement components. The structural model specifies the hypothesized causal relations between the constructs of the model; they are indicated by the arrows between circles in the model. The measurement model specifies how each construct is to be measured as well as how measurement error between measures is to be modeled, if at all. Measures of the constructs are indicated in the model by squares. Examination of the model in Figure 2.11 indicates that aptitude is measured by six measures and instruction by two. Both aptitude and instruction are hypothesized to affect achievement measured at four sequential points in time. The purpose of the study was to test this model

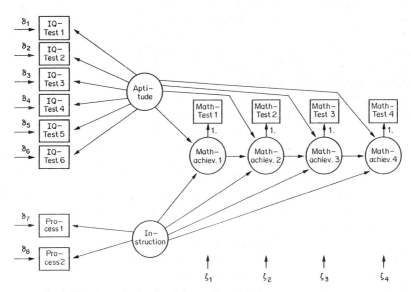

Fig 2.11   Theoretically plausible causal model explicating achievement in mathematics (from Schneider and Treiber, 1984)

of achievement and estimate the strength of relationships hypothesized in the model. As they summarized their theoretical framework, it consisted of the following components:

"● an *explanatory* component that introduces three different hypothetical constructs— "Achievement," "Aptitude," and "Instruction"—as analytic units for describing and explaining achievement processes;
● a *structural* component that specifies the causal links between these three constructs as indicated in Figure 1 [our Figure 2.11];
● a *longitudinal* component that describes the statistical properties of a multiwave achievement data set in a simplex growth model (see above); and
● a *measurement* component that defines the relationship among these three un-measured constructs and their observed indicators" (p. 199).

Discussion

We have covered a great deal of territory in this chapter, having examined paradigms, theories and models as ways of conceptualizing classrooms. We began with paradigms because the concept of paradigm has generated a good deal of interest (and misuse) in the social sciences in general and classroom research in particular. The concept is useful for thinking about the sociology of knowledge and how members of the scientific community actually exchange and share ideas. As classroom researchers we have particular disciplinary roots, philosophical commitments, and method-ological strengths that lead us to acceptance or endorsement of particular paradigms. In turn, these paradigms organize and shape our view of classrooms and classroom phenomena. They guide our thinking about questions we might ask and suggest where we might look for answers. Paradigms also can provide language systems for describing classroom phenomena. In so doing, they affect the kinds of theory that researchers generate about these phenomena.

Theory serves a number of useful functions. It allows us to describe and explain phenomena, to delimit the boundaries of the phenomena, to generate new ideas, and to integrate our concepts and propositions into a consistent and parsimonious system. Theory simplifies our world by using abstract concepts and propositions that provide a mental scaffolding for interpreting phenomena. Without some type of theory, it is virtually impossible to integrate empirical evidence and make sense of our experi-ences. Finally, theory enables us to make predictions about the phenomena that allow us to test and refine our understanding of them.

Unfortunately there has been a definite lack of theory about classrooms.[2]

[2]Many of these points about theory were also made by Nuthall (1968) over 20 years ago. At the conclusion of a review of the research on teaching conducted to that time Nuthall wrote: "It must be obvious to the critical reader that what is missing from many of the reported studies is the sense of direction and controlled orderliness, which can only be provided by adequate theory" (p. 143).

This lack of theory has allowed researchers to move considerable distances from their evidence and, in some cases, make claims that are not supported by the evidence at all. The lack of theory, we believe, provides a breeding ground for "blind empiricism" and permits one to form a Commitment, that faith in a given approach or method of teaching as mentioned in Chapter 1, to guide the interpretation of evidence.

Unlike the paucity of theory, there is an abundance of models of classrooms. Interesting, the majority of these models offer about the same characterization of classroom phenomena. All seem to offer some combination of concepts based on time (duration), behavior (frequency) or things (presence or absence). Somewhat surprisingly, psychological constructs are not as common in these characterizations as one might think. When they do exist, they exist in the form of rather common constructs such as student aptitude and learning, teacher self-efficacy, and the like.

Much has been written about the complexity of classrooms. Doyle (1977), for example, describes classrooms in terms of their multidimensionality, simultaneity, and unpredictability. Similarly, Shulman (1986) has argued that no single research program could include all of the classroom phenomena. The models described in this chapter also attest to this complexity. Classrooms do have physical, social, and instructional features operating simultaneously. While the activity structure of classrooms is fairly predictable, the particular teacher and student behaviors are not. There is an undercurrent of unpredictability that operates in classrooms, forcing teachers to move classroom events along while at the same time behaving reactively as the activities unfold and behaviors are exhibited.

As researchers we must agree with such a characterization of classrooms. We must note, however, that for the participants, those teachers and students who live and work together in those classrooms, such is not the case. To the participants, teachers and students alike, classrooms appear to be rather affectless and routinized settings that are not at all complex. One of the ironies of classroom research is the great difficulty we have as researchers attempting to describe and understand a phenomenon that appears to us so complex, but to the participants so mundane. This irony leads us to a postscript to this chapter.

A Postscript: What About Student Learning?

Perhaps because student learning is always the "thing" to be predicted, learning is often tacked on to models of classrooms as an afterthought. Perhaps this neglect stems from the inability of learning theory to generate classroom theory—theory pertaining to instruction and teaching. Whatever the reason for the neglect, we believe that more attention needs to be given to the nature of school learning.

The fact of the matter is that school learning is typically gradual and cumulative over time.. Although we recognize periodic discontinuous leaps of insight and cognitive restructuring, we are in agreement with Rumelhart and Norman (1978) who state: "we are impressed with the fact that real learning takes place over periods of years, not hours" (p. 39). While this view of learning makes classroom research more difficult, we can not ignore the fact that student learning (often in the guise of achievement tests) is the phenomenon that classroom researchers are the most interested in understanding, explaining, and, ultimately, improving.

Many contemporary views of student learning begin with the premise that the student is active, not only accumulating knowledge gradually during learning, but also interpreting that knowledge and reorganizing existing knowledge structure in new ways (see, for example, Rumelhart and Norman, 1978). These views recognize the interplay between the ways in which students organize their existing knowledge and the changes in that organization that are necessary to accommodate new information and experiences.

The active role of the student is facilitated or inhibited by his or her abilities. Abilities can be defined as acquired, overlearned strategies for perceiving, organizing, and manipulating information (Messick, 1984; Snow, Federico, and Montague, 1980). Abilities work from the top down, transfering to new learning situations over the short term to influence learning. In contrast, knowledge that is "to-be-acquired" works from the bottom up, being assimilated into existing knowledge structures to become the material students can draw upon based on their abilities for future learning over the long term.

To understand school learning and the impact of student abilities on that learning, classroom researchers must begin to model the relationships among student abilities, classroom conditions, and student learning. Bennett, Desforges, Cockburn, and Wilkinson (1984) provide a rare example of this type of modeling. Their model is based on the conceptualization of learning developed by Rumelhart and Norman (1978) who distinguished among three modes of learning: the gradual accumulation of information, the fine tuning of knowledge already possessed, and the restructuring of existing knowledge. These three modes are referred to as "learning accretion," "tuning," and "restructuring," respectively. Before we examine Bennett et al.'s model, let us briefly explore each mode.

Accretion is the most common type of learning. It is the "normal kind of fact learning, daily accumulation of information in which most of us engage" (p. 38). Such learning occurs through proper exposure to the information and concepts to be acquired, and a person's knowledge base is thought to simply increment with the addition of the new information. Learning by tuning is different. Tuning involves actual change in the categories people use to assimilate and interpret new information. Such tuning presumably is occurring continuously, as our categories for interpreting experience are undergoing minor modifications to better reflect that experience. Tuning would, for example, account for more effective performance with practice or a richer understanding of a concept. Restructuring refers to the learning involved when an entirely new knowledge structure is created for interpreting new information and creating a new organization of existing knowledge. Restructuring, according to Rumelhart and Norman, takes place after a critical mass of information has been accumulated first and a need for restructuring is felt to handle the unstructured information. Restructuring allows for new interpretations of experience and new accessibility to knowledge for interpretation and acquisition of new knowledge. It is a qualitative change in knowledge organization.

Quite interestingly, the distinction between accretion and restructuring corresponds to Jackson's (1986) distinction between the mimetic and transformative traditions in teaching. He labels the first tradition "mimetic" because "it gives a central place to the transmission of factual and procedural knowledge from one person to another, through an essentially *imitative* process" (p. 117). In contrast, "the adjective 'transformative' describes what this tradition deems successful teaching to be capable of accomplishing: a transformation of one kind or another in the person being taught—a qualitative change often of dramatic proportion, a metamorphosis, so to speak" (p. 120).

Bennett and his colleagues were able to develop a schematic representation which corresponded to Rumelhart and Norman's three modes of

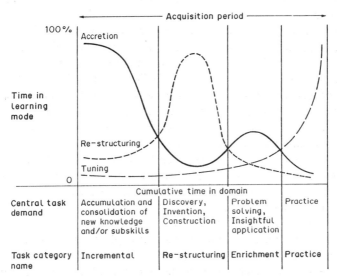

FIG 2.12   Task categories in relation to growth of knowledge (from Bennett et al., 1984)

learning (and by analogy Jackson's two traditions of teaching). This representation is shown as Figure 2.12. In the initial stage of learning, the emphasis is on accretion (as it quite likely should be).

As learning progresses over time, however, the emphasis shifts toward restructuring (which constitutes the second stage of Bennett et al.'s model). During the third stage of teaching and learning (termed "enrichment"), accretion, restructuring, and enrichment are all touched upon in a fairly minimal sense. Finally, in the fourth stage, "practice," the emphasis once again shifts. This time the shift is toward tuning (and away from accretion and restructuring).

Our analysis of the Bennett et al. model is not to suggest that it is correct. Rather, the point here is that paradigms, theories, and models of classrooms should include the learner as a focal point in learning. Paradigms, theories, and models that can neither predict nor explain student learning over the long term are of lesser value to classroom researchers.

3

Studying Classrooms

In the previous chapter, we discussed issues related to conceptualizing classrooms. In this chapter, we take up issues related to the methodology of classroom research. What questions will be asked? What procedures will be used to study classroom phenomena? What language system will convey knowledge gained to others? Underlying these questions are assumptions about the purpose of research, assumptions about the proper focus for study, and assumptions about the type of evidence necessary to answer questions legitimately. In this chapter we attempt to uncover these assumptions and examine what influence they have on researchers studying classrooms.

What is Methodology?

What do we mean by methodology? What distinguishes research methodology from other forms of discourse? Is methodology different from speculation, opinion, or experience? Is there a difference, for example, between a principal observing in a teacher's classroom for 30 minutes and developing an opinion about the teacher's ability to teach, and a researcher making narrative accounts of the teacher's classroom for 30 minutes and rating the extent to which the classroom was stimulating, task-oriented, orderly, and so on? There is a difference, and the difference has to do with existing conventions in the scientific community about what constitutes legitimate methodology. We will develop this theme throughout this chapter.

Methodology refers to how evidence is gathered and meaning derived from it. According to Rychlak (1968), a method is the means or manner of determining whether a theoretical construct or proposition is true or false. Each of the scientific disciplines has developed criteria and conventions about what constitutes legitimate tests of theory and what lines of development researchers are to follow as they move from data to knowledge claims. Methodology has as much to do with reasoning as it does with data. There are rules for testing knowledge, and it is this set of rules that define methodology in a discipline.

Thus, methodology is different from the specific research techniques used in any given study. While specific techniques are associated with particular methodologies, they are not the same. We follow a distinction used by Willems and Raush (1969) and separate the broader concept of methodology from specific research techniques and measurement instruments such as interviews, tests, narrative records, and the like. Methodology, to Willems and Raush, is concerned with two basic questions that are more general than issues of research technique:

> 1. "How do I obtain interpretable data? or How do I obtain data for which the ambiguity of evaluation is reduced to the lowest possible degree?"
> 2. "Given a purpose or set of purposes, a question or set of questions, what kinds of investigative exercises, operations, and strategies should I embark upon to fulfill the purposes and answer the questions?" (p. 3).

These two questions are about research design, that is, how to ask questions and test whether the answers are compelling. Questions about research design, whether one should conduct a laboratory experiment or a field-based case study, for example, are more general than issues of research techniques. By comparison, we might illustrate comparable questions for research techniques by asking, for example, "Does this standardized achievement test yield scores that reflect the content that was taught? or "Given that I want to find out why the teacher organized the lesson in a particular format, will this post-lesson interview provide me with the answer? or "Will having students identify the relevant and irrelevant information in a mathematical story problem yield information about the student's ability to solve problems in mathematics?" These questions, while certainly being influenced by the particular methodological stance of the researcher, are issues of research techniques. The terms methodology, methods, and techniques are often used interchangeably by researchers.

So this chapter is about methodology. The fact that we have separated theory and method between Chapter Two and Chapter Three is only logistical. The close interplay between theory and method, between how classroom phenomena are conceptualized and what methods are used to gather evidence about classrooms, is what *paradigmatic* research is all about. Fields of study—like the field of research on teaching—are characterized by both the objects or events they describe and the way they generate knowledge about those objects or events (Rychlak, 1977). As Shulman (1981) has stated, "Selecting the method most appropriate for a particular disciplined inquiry is one of the most important, and difficult, responsibilities of a researcher. The choice requires an act of judgment, grounded both in knowledge of methodology and the substantive area of investigation" (p. 11).

Examining the close interplay between theory and method is not an easy task in education. For one reason, a particularly acrimonious and divisive schism has arisen during the 1980s between "quantitative" and "qualitative" methodologies. Quantitative methodology has come to be characterized by the techniques of random assignment, treatment contrasts, experimental control, objective tests, statistical analyses, and so on. In contrast, qualitative methodology has been primarily associated with case studies, ethnographic description, interviews and long-term observation, and the discovery of meaning in social phenomena. Advocates of both approaches often seem more intent on playing partisan politics than understanding the value inherent in each methodology. This makes reasonable discussion of the merits of each approach considerably more difficult.

A second reason, perhaps part of the cause of the first, is the nature of education itself. Because education is a professional field and not an academic discipline like sociology, anthropology, or psychology, it borrows and adapts techniques from these social and behavioral sciences. The case study methodology that has become popular in education in recent years, for example, has been borrowed from field methods in sociology and anthropology. Experimental and correlational methodology was borrowed from psychology. Even some research design and statistical principles were borrowed from agricultural research. While such eclecticism gives education a broad range of tools with which to work, it also interferes with developing consensus about the proper approach to conducting educational research in general and classroom research in particular.

A final difficulty in examining the relationship between theory and method is the fact that the nature of paradigms as encompassing both theory and method is not always recognized or is easily glossed over in discussions of paradigms. Some have identified a paradigm by the particular subject matter examined. As we will see in this chapter, others have identified paradigms by their methodology. This is especially true in the case of quantitative and qualitative "paradigms." How helpful such a distinction will be in the long run is unclear. Rychlak (1977) has suggested that Kuhnian paradigmatic revolutions occurred not because of new methodology but because of new theory:

> But when we are speaking of a Kuhnian revolution we are referring to dramatic shifts in the theoretical viewpoints of scientists. Indeed since the turn of the seventeenth century and the rise of modern science, though there have been a number of quite startling paradigm shifts in scientific theory, *there has never been a paradigmatic shift in the theory of knowledge defining scientific method* (p. 186).

In this chapter, we take a middle-of-the-road position with respect to methodology. We see value in both quantitative and qualitative methods, although we will avoid these labels in favor of the more descriptive ones of confirmatory and interpretive inquiry. The issues that separate these two approaches to inquiry are more significant than whether one uses *numbers or words* to study and describe phenomena. The job of science, as Cronbach (1957, p. 671) so succinctly stated, is to "ask questions of Nature." We see ample room for different approaches to asking questions in education.

Indeed, it may be critical that we seek multiple methods in education, as Shulman (1981) argues:

> We must avoid becoming educational researchers slavishly committed to some particular method. The image of the little boy who has just received a hammer for a birthday present and suddenly finds that the entire world looks to him like a variety of nails, is too painfully familiar to be tolerated. We must first understand our problem, and decide what questions we are asking, then select the mode of *disciplined inquiry* most appropriate to those questions. If the proper methods are highly quantitative and objective, fine. If they are more subjective or qualitative, we can use them responsibly as well (p. 12).

In summary, then, methodology refers to the rules or principles used in a discipline to test theoretical propositions about phenomena. Methodology is the way we discover or create knowledge. It is how we test whether our hunches about phenomena are sound so that we can claim to "know" something. Two fundamental modes of inquiry in the social and behavioral sciences are confirmatory and interpretive. Before we present these two approaches to inquiry, however, we need to preface our comments with a brief analysis of what it means to have knowledge. After all, we have just argued that knowledge is what methodology is all about. Much of our discussion draws directly from the excellent text of Krathwohl (1985).

Knowing and Knowledge

One of the functions of science is to describe patterns in and discover relationships among phenomena in the world around us. When a pattern or relationship has been identified and an explanation for it offered, we believe we have gained some knowledge of the phenomenon we are studying. But what does it mean to know something? How do we come to know what we know? How does science allow us to discover patterns and regularities in the world?

There are many ways of knowing and there are different sources of knowledge. *Personal experience* is the most common way we come to know the world. It has long been recognized that beginning teachers, for example, by virtue of their extensive educational experiences as students, have a rich repertoire of models to emulate in their own teaching. Novice teachers have personal knowledge of what classrooms are supposed to be like and how teachers are supposed to behave.

But there are many occasions where personal experience does not provide a basis for knowing something. When one does not have personal experiences to use, *authorities* are often consulted as a source of knowledge. A teacher, facing a large group of students with special language, learning, or emotional needs for the first time, is likely to consult a resource specialist in the district for teaching advice.

Tradition is a third source of knowledge. "We do it this way because it has always been done this way at our school" is sometimes heard by new teachers at a school. Traditional knowledge possesses legitimacy because it has "passed the test of time" and presumably has worked for others in the past. But tradition is not infallible, as history continually reminds us. Student memorization of passages and class recitals of the passages were "traditional" teaching techniques around the turn of the century.

Intuition is still another source of knowledge. Some things are so obviously true that they are accepted without question or taken as self-evident. The logic of deductive reasoning is sometimes based on self-evident premises. A simple syllogism, for example, has a major premise based on a self-evident or known fact, a minor premise to which the major premise applies, and a conclusion: "All humans are fallible; all teachers are humans; therefore, all teachers are fallible" is a deductively reasoned conclusion that logically is self-evident.

All these sources of knowing, from personal experience to intuition, require us to make a decision, a judgment as to whether we will believe the something to be true. We must accept or reject something as known by making a personal decision based on our experience, an authority, tradition, or our intuition. Knowing, then, is a personal judgment. And, of course, we are sometimes wrong in our judgments.

If knowing is a personal experience, what is knowledge? Krathwohl (1985) makes the case that knowledge is merely a collection of individual judgments of the same conclusion. Knowledge, according to Krathwohl, is a consensus of individual judgments. He points out that consensual knowing is rather disturbing in the case for which there is no way of gathering evidence other than by the personal testimony of humans. Religious cults, for example, often have their own consensus about their beliefs even though others in the community may not hold to their truths. For most knowledge, however, confirmation beyond belief is required. We typically want evidence that we can interpret or someone we trust can interpret. This is where science comes in.

Krathwohl points out that scientific knowledge is also consensual knowing, but with three important differences from other sources of knowledge. First, consensus is formed around evidence. The basis for the knowledge claim is something tangible that can be examined, discussed, and critiqued publically. Speculation has its place in science, but eventually evidence must be submitted to test the knowledge claims.

Second, evidence is presented to and screened by the scientific community, a community that has developed norms to prevent unwarranted and arbitrary consensus from developing. Merton has outlined four such norms (see Merton, 1982; originally published in 1942): universalism, "communism", disinterestedness, and organized skepticism. *Universalism* means that knowledge claims are to be judged by "preestablished impersonal criteria" and not on the personal or social attributes of the one making the claim. *Communism* means that the products of scientific discovery are part of the scientific community to be shared by all. The demand for *disinterestedness* in science refers to the press on scientists for integrity through rigorous public scrutiny by members of the scientific community. Finally, *organized skepticism*, interrelated with the other three norms, refers to the close and careful scrutiny of new knowledge claims. The four norms define an ethos of science designed to ensure knowledge claims are carefully considered and certified.

Third, the evidence must meet certain criteria, criteria used to judge the acceptability of the evidence presented. Since evidence is generated by particular research methodologies, criteria to evaluate evidence are indirectly criteria to judge the acceptability of research methodologies. As we will see shortly, there is much debate in education over what constitutes legitimate methodology.

Sandra Scarr (1985) also argues that science is constructed knowledge. Science "is an agreed-upon set of procedures, not constructs or theories. At any one time there are prevailing views with favored constructs to explain and make consistent the facts as we construe them. But it is the procedures for gathering observations (sensory data) that are the rules of the scientific enterprise" (p. 500).

Scientific knowledge, then, is consensual knowing developed from public examination of evidence by a community of scholars following certain rules. The evidence, the criteria used to judge the evidence, and the norms of the formal scientific community that guide the evaluation of knowledge claims are what distinguishes scientific knowledge from know- ledge produced through personal observation, or knowledge based on tradition, authority, or intuition.

Disciplined Inquiry in Education

The debate over appropriate methodology is critical to social and behavioral science. Scientists and scholars who share similar views about methods find it much easier to discuss the results of their investigations than scientists who pursue different methods or who have different criteria for acceptability of evidence. If methodology is similar, then a common ground exists for researchers to discuss the results of particular studies. When methodologies are different, that common ground is absent and it is more difficult for scientists to communicate about the results of their studies. Kuhn (1970) characterized different paradigms as being incommensurate, partly because proponents of different paradigms "practice their trades in different worlds" and "see different things when they look from the same point in the same direction" (p. 150).

To concretize our discussion of different methodologies, it will be helpful to detour momentarily and consider four contrasting classroom studies. The four studies represent quite different approaches to conducting classroom research. While certainly not representing the entire range of possible classroom studies, they are diverse enough to help ground the reader in some of the ways that researchers have approached classroom research.

The Worthen (1968) Study

Worthen was interested in the effects on student achievement, retention, and transfer of discovery methods of instruction relative to expository methods of instruction. At the time this quasi-experiment was carried out, there was considerable interest in discovery methods of teaching and studies comparing competing methods of instruction were common.

Over 400 students in 16 classes of fifth- and sixth-grade students were divided into two groups, one group receiving expository teaching and one group receiving discovery teaching in arithmetic. Eight teachers taught one class of each group in an attempt to control for teacher effects other than method of instruction. Each group received the same amount of instructional time, teacher verbalization, and curricular materials. No homework was assigned during the six weeks of instruction. An attempt was made to equalize the two groups on background concepts by teaching both groups a two-month unit covering necessary prerequisites. Instruction occurred daily for 40 minutes. Both cognitive and affective pretests and posttests were administered, and the posttests included achievement, transfer, and 5-week and 11-week retention measures. Two measures of teacher behavior were taken to ensure that the teachers were, in fact, behaving in ways dictated by discovery and expository methods. Finally, to ensure each class received adequate coverage of curriculum, a criterion was established that a minimum of 85% of each class meet a minimum standard on each concept before the teacher was allowed to move to the next concept. Items were built into the curriculum materials to provide evidence on this criterion.

Teacher training occurred for 2 to 6 hours a week for 20 weeks, 13 prior to the study and 7 during the study. Instruction in each method was determined by the teacher following the structure inherent in the curricular materials. Briefly, in expository teaching, verbalization and presentation of the concept to be learned is made first and then the student works examples of the concept. Discovery teaching, on the other hand, delays verbalization and presentation of the concept until an ordered series of examples, designed to elicit the concept, are presented to the student. The curricular materials provided this sequence of presentation for teachers.

In addition to the sequence of curricular materials, there were specific teacher behaviors independent of the curriculum that were considered part of the difference between expository and discovery teaching. Teachers received training in five specific areas of teacher behavior for each type of method. For example, teachers were trained, for expository teaching, to answer questions by "reiterating and explaining the rule and relating it to

TABLE 3.1

Means and Standard Deviations (SD) for Selected Posttest Measures from the Worthen Study

Measure	Treatment	Mean	SD	Direction of Result[1]
Achievement	Discovery (D)	52.5	17.1	E > D
	Expository (E)	54.0	18.0	
5-Week Retention	Discovery	48.9	20.9	D > E
	Expository	46.7	21.3	
11-Week Retention	Discovery	48.9	20.7	D > E
	Expository	46.1	23.2	
Transfer	Discovery	34.9	19.5	D > E
	Expository	31.5	18.3	

[1]The statistical analyses were based on adjusted posttest scores using analysis of covariance procedures. All differences were significant at the 0.05 level.

the question . . . [and] then [giving] examples which will further clarify the way the rule is used in the solution of that type of problem" (p. 5). For discovery teaching, they changed their question answering style: "The teacher answers questions by referring to the model or the computational sequence which the student has used. If a student is still confused, the teacher takes him back to the model and goes through it carefully. The teacher may make use of sequenced examples as a clue, but no verbal hint of the rule is given" (p. 5). Ratings of teacher behavior and audiotapes of classroom discourse during the study revealed that the teachers could and did, in fact, teach in very different ways.

Although not a true experiment (no random assignment of subjects to groups), this study is exemplary in its attempt to control for extraneous variables. In fact, one of the justifications of the study offered by the author was that it was carried out in real schools and classrooms and not in the laboratory under artificial conditions. He felt that results of such a study, using representative curricular materials and learning tasks, would generalize better to classroom practice. The major results are presented in Table 3.1. Worthen found that expository methods were superior on immediate achievement, but that discovery methods were superior on retention and transfer measures.

The Hughes (1959) Study

The purpose of this study was to develop a description of teaching in elementary schools. It was also desired to develop a useable model of "good teaching." This study, funded through a Cooperative Research Grant from the United States Office of Education, attempted to develop a "functional" perspective on teaching, where teaching functions are defined as "patterns of teacher acts" (p. 10).

A sample of 41 elementary teachers (K-6) were observed. Twenty-five of these teachers had been nominated as good teachers by a county office of education. Ten teachers at another school nominated by district personnel were considered representative of other teachers at the school but not necessarily "good" teachers. Six other teachers from a pilot study were also included in most analyses, four of which had been nominated as good teachers by district personnel.

Specimen records focusing on the teacher for 30 minutes were used to describe teaching. Specimen records are detailed, sequential written narra-

TABLE 3.2

Teacher Functions from the Hughes Study

1. Controlling Functions (Teacher serves as director of learning activities)
   Structure
   Regulate
   Standard Set
   Judge
2. Imposition of the Teacher (Teacher projects self into the situation)
   Regulate Self
   Moralize
   Teacher Estimate of Need
   Informal Appraisal
   Inform
3. Facilitating Functions (Teacher assists the movement of the activity)
   Clarify Procedure
   Checking
   Demonstrate
4. Functions That Develop Content (Teacher responds to students: academic)
   Resource
   Stimulate
   Clarify
   Evaluate
5. Functions of Personal Response (Teacher responds to students: personal)
   Meets Request
   Clarify Personal
   Interprets
   Acknowledge Teacher Mistake
6. Functions of Positive Affectivity (Teacher responds positively)
   Support
   Does For Personal
   Solicitous
   Encourage
7. Functions of Negative Affectivity (Teacher responds negatively)
   Admonish
   Reprimand
   Verbal Futuristic
   Negative Response Personal
   Accusative
   Threat
   Ignore

Source: Adapted from Hughes (1959).

tives of teacher behavior. Teachers were asked to teach three lessons: a reading lesson, a developmental lesson in arithmetic or social studies, and a work or activity period. Teachers were free to choose the order and time of observation. Each teacher was observed on three separate days within a two-month period (the six pilot teachers were observed four times). Two observers completed specimen records, and different observer pairs were used for each observation. Immediately following the observation, observers filled in their notes and produced a single final record. Final records averaged about 10 pages in length. This procedure produced a data set of 129 specimen records (35 teachers × 3 observations + 6 teachers × 4 observations) on over a thousand typewritten pages.

To analyse the voluminous data, the teaching "function" was selected as the unit of analysis. Each function performed was counted as an act on the part of the teacher. Rules were established for identifying a function and how the process of unitizing the specimen records should proceed. Thirty-one functions, in seven broad categories, were identified and used for coding the records (see Table 3.2). These teaching functions had been derived from reading the specimen records and had not been determined prior to the study. Coding was completed in pairs, with a third person serving to work through disagreements. Some 25,000 acts (functions) were coded; objectivity checks revealed relatively consistent coding for both within and between category coding.

Table 3.3 presents the basic descriptive results. Analysis of the percent of acts falling in the seven function categories revealed considerable variability among teachers, with the majority of acts categorized as "controlling" (a finding, by the way, of virtually every observational study ever done!). A variety of additional comparisons revealed few findings, including an analysis comparing nominated good teachers with the representative teachers, both of whom demonstrated similar ranges of performance. Based

TABLE 3.3

Percent of Teacher Acts Classified into Each of Seven Functions and the Range of Percentages Associated with a "Good" Teacher

	Actual Observation		Theoretical "Good" Teacher
Teaching Function	Mean	Range	Range
Controlling	47	38–68	20–40
Imposition	3	1–7	1–3
Facilitating	7	3–13	5–15
Content Development	16	8–26	20–40
Personal Response	5	2–11	8–20
Positive Affectivity	12	7–21	10–20
Negative Affectivity	10	3–20	3–10

Source: Adapted from Hughes (1959), from p. 223 and Table DII, Appendix D.

on a logical review of the literature on teaching, Hughes then defined a theoretical "good teacher" in terms of these seven functions, including percentages of time that should be spent in each function (see Table 3.3), and illustrated the theoretical model with six observed records from her study that fit the percentage recommendations. Hughes suggested that a definition of good teaching required a reduction in the number of controlling functions performed, an increase in the use of the functions that develop content, an increase in functions of personal response, and minimum use of functions of negative affectivity.

The Jackson (1968) Book

Phillip Jackson (1968) wrote one of the most influential books on research on teaching, and yet there is very little research reported in the book. The purpose of Jackson's book was to "arouse the reader's interest and possibly to awaken his concern over aspects of school life that seem to be receiving less attention than they deserve" (p. vii). The book presents a mixture of reports on research studies, interview data, personal observation of classrooms, and speculation about the experience of school from both the teacher and student perspective. The purpose of describing classrooms using these different approaches, according to Jackson, is that classroom life is too complicated to be viewed from any single approach. "As we try to grasp the meaning of what school is like for students and teachers," Jackson writes, "we must not hesitate to use all the ways of knowing at our disposal" (p. vii).

Jackson's opening chapter is a classic description of the repetitive, routinized, and compulsory nature of elementary classrooms. Jackson organizes his description around three characteristics of classrooms: crowds, praise, and power. These three characteristics combine to "form a hidden curriculum that each student (and teacher) must master if he is to make his way satisfactorily through the school" (pp. 33–34). Jackson raises the possibility that psychological withdrawal or detachment is a generic adaptive strategy open to all students for dealing with the hidden curriculum and the demands of classroom life.

Having characterized classrooms in a less than flattering way, Jackson asks how students feel about classroom life. He presents in some detail the results of four survey studies examining elementary students' liking of school. The general conclusion he draws is that elementary students are "relatively content;" about 80 percent of students say they like as opposed to dislike school. However, based on further review of student attitude studies, he concludes that "most students do not feel too strongly about their classroom experience one way or the other" (p. 60).

Jackson next examines how teachers attempt to maintain student attention. He outlines two different sets of strategies for doing so. One set has to do with maintaining appropriate working conditions and the prevention of disruptions. Jackson describes the rules common to most classrooms and argues that these rules share a common goal, the prevention of disruption. Jackson's second set of strategies for maintaining student attention involves three areas: (1) bring the curriculum closer to the needs and interests of the students, (2) group students to better fit the established curriculum, and (3) enliven classroom lessons with humor, novelty, or appeal to human interest. Thus, Jackson suggests, the teaching problem is not just to maintain an orderly classroom with attending students, but to foster more enduring involvement on the part of students.

Finally, Jackson examines the teacher perspective on classroom life. Fifty teachers nominated as "outstanding" by their administrators were interviewed. Three sets of questions were asked: about how they knew they were doing a good job, about their use of authority and their feelings of having their own work evaluated, and about the personal satisfactions arising from teaching. Four themes emerged from the interview material: immediacy, informality, autonomy, and individuality.

Immediacy refers to the spontaneous quality of classroom life. One aspect of immediacy was the apparent value of student expressions of enthusiasm and interest during teaching as indicators of good teaching, more so than test results. *Informality* refers to the lessening of teachers' use of their authority in the classroom from what it had been in the past. *Autonomy* was expressed through a desire to be "free from inspection" and "on their own" in the classroom. The teachers did not express a desire for total independence; rather, a desire to be able to exercise their creativity, spontaneity, and professional judgment within certain limits. *Individuality* refers to the teacher's concern for the well-being of individual students, demonstrated by the delight teachers derive from seeing the progress of individual students.

Jackson concludes his analysis by discussing the appropriateness of current sources of knowledge about teaching. He argues that the learning theorist and the human engineer do not deal with the reality of classroom events well and that new approaches, "close to the phenomena of the teacher's world," are required. He calls for more attempts to understand teaching before undertaking efforts to change it and suggests that more classroom observation be completed. Furthermore, the use of participant observation techniques may provide useful methodology for observation.

The Cusick (1973) Study

The purpose of the Cusick study was to "describe the way a number of students behave in high school and to explain the way their behavior affects themselves, the teachers, administrators, and the entire school organization" (p. v). The study attempted to understand the student perspective of high school and how those perspectives were used to interpret the social reality of the school environment.

Cusick used the set of research techniques known as participant observation. The participant observer becomes available to and participates in the activities of those being studied. Extensive, long-term observation and participation allows the researcher to come to an understanding of the perspectives of those being studied. Working hypotheses are continually formulated and tested as an understanding emerges. Eventually, the researcher reaches a point where the description and explanation are adequate to answer the basic questions of the study.

There are a number of different participant observation roles a researcher can take with respect to the group being studied. Denzin (1970) outlines four roles: the "complete participant," where a researcher attempts to become a group member and his or her role as a researcher is unknown to those being observed; the "participant as observer," where the researcher joins a group and makes his or her intentions of studying the group known to its members; the "observer as participant," where the researcher makes only brief contact with the group and there is no attempt to establish an enduring relationship with the group; and the "complete observer," where the researcher is completely removed from interaction with members of the group and observations are recorded mechanically, as with videotape, or in the laboratory.

Cusick used the second role, that of participant as observer, to understand student life in the high school he studied. Cusick became a high school student for six months, going to classes every day, attending student meetings, interviewing students informally and formally, examining school records, and generally participating in the social events of the school. At the end of each day, he would write down what occurred during the day, which eventually resulted in some 550 pages in addition to all the records collected from the school itself. The notes were classified, coded in a variety of ways, and considered for emerging perspectives. These per- spectives were then verified by asking group members about the perspective or its applicability to an event or situation.

According to Cusick, his acceptance by students took some time but was not difficult. He was initially introduced to three senior boys who agreed to guide him around the school. These students belonged to a sub-group of eight athletes and they became his opening into the world of the high school student. In time, Cusick came to know several other sub-groups at the school, including a power clique of girls and a music-drama group. Some isolates, students with few or no friends at schools, were also studied. Experiences with about sixty seniors allowed Cusick to develop certain insights into how students view the school environment. In an attempt to see if the student perspective was reasonable given the environment they inhabited, Cusick related the student perspective to characteristics of the

school environment itself. To illustrate the type of conclusion Cusick draws
from his analysis, it is worthwhile to quote from his conclusion extensively:

> I would suggest that the students continue their out-of-school group affiliations in
> school simply because those affiliations can and do provide so much of what the
> organization denies. Whereas the school denies students freedom, masses and fails to
> differentiate them, keeps them powerless and in a state of spectatorship, provides little
> human interaction, and gives them primarily future-oriented and symbolic rewards, the
> groups themselves are rigidly segregated with little cross-communication, give students a
> degree of independence and power over their activity, and give them the immediate
> pleasure of participating in human interaction. This is not particularly revealing until
> the second part is added; that is, that the school, with its emphasis on teacher-initiated
> action, its routine, batch processing, and reliance on maintenance procedures, provides
> an enormous amount of time when students are actually required to do little other than
> be in attendance and minimally compliant. It is this that provides them with the time to
> carry on their group activity, and their group activity seems to consume over half the
> school day (p. 214).

The Worthen, Hughes, Jackson, and Cusick studies represent four very
different approaches to the study of classrooms. Worthen was interested in
establishing which of two methods of teaching was the "best" method for
teaching. He selected a sample of teachers, manipulated the independent
variable, and observed its effects. A major concern was to control as many
of the variables as possible outside of teaching method. Cusick, on the other
hand, studied only one school, and only a handful of the students in the
school (about 60 of 1,100 or so). He did not manipulate variables but rather
attempted to live and understand the perspective of the students in the
school. He did not attempt to control the context of the study but to
understand its effect on the thoughts and behavior of the students making
up the school environment. Hughes collected an enormous amount of
written data about teacher behavior that was subsequently quantified. Her
attempt to define good teaching by distinguishing between teachers nominated as good teachers and other teachers was not successful, primarily
because of the variability of teaching behavior observed. And Jackson
engaged in general discussions of what life in classrooms was all about
based on his reading of the literature, his own research and classroom
observation, and informed opinion.

The four studies represent different views of methodology—how to
answer questions and test whether the answers are sound. For the most
part, the debate over methodology in the social sciences has followed
epistomological lines, dividing along the two great philosophical traditions
emanating from the 17th and 18th centuries, British empiricism with its
emphasis on realist doctrines and German rationalism with its emphasis on
idealism (see Rychlak, 1977, for an extended discussion). These two systems
have come to form the foundation for two major modes of inquiry, which
we will call confirmatory and interpretive inquiry (see Biddle and Anderson,
1986; Erickson, 1986; Soltis, 1984). Within each system, a number of
methodological disciplines or schools have emerged.

Both systems are forms of "disciplined inquiry." Shulman (1981) distinguishes disciplined inquiry from opinion 'by the ways observations are collected, evidence is marshalled, arguments are drawn, and opportunities are afforded for replication, verification, and refutation" (p. 5). The term *disciplined inquiry* comes from Cronbach and Suppes (1969), who characterize it as follows:

> Disciplined inquiry has a quality that distinguishes it from other sources of opinion and belief. The disciplined inquiry is conducted and reported in such a way that the argument can be painstakingly examined. The report does not depend for its appeal on the eloquence of the writer or on any surface plausibility. The argument is not justified by anecdotes or casually assembled fragments of evidence. Scholars in each field have developed traditional questions that serve as touchstones to separate sound argument from incomplete or questionable argument. Among other things, the mathematician asks about axioms, the historian about the authenticity of documents, the experimental scientist about verifiability of observations. Whatever the character of a study, if it is disciplined the investigator has anticipated the traditional questions that are pertinent. He institutes controls at each step of information collection and reasoning to avoid sources of error to which these questions refer. If the errors cannot be eliminated, he takes them into account by discussing the margin of error in his conclusions. Thus the report of a disciplined inquiry has a texture that displays the raw materials entering the argument and the logical processes by which they are compressed and rearranged to make the conclusion credible (pp. 15–16).

In what follows, we will sketch broad outlines of confirmatory and interpretive inquiry as well as some of the schools or disciplines that have emerged within each system. Confirmatory inquiry has been the primary mode of inquiry in the social and behavioral sciences. Periodically, various schools of thought have developed in reaction to confirmatory inquiry, primarily in response to lack of attention given to the meaning of actions and events humans construe from their world. Meaning, in the view of these schools, is what makes us distinctly human. They argue that the social world of the social scientist is different from the physical world of the natural scientist. In other words, the various schools of interpretive inquiry have been concerned about the focus and subject matter of confirmatory inquiry, and, as a result, have offered methodologies that attempt to answer questions about that subject matter neglected in confirmatory inquiry.

Confirmatory Inquiry

The British empiricist tradition is based in the philosophies of Thomas Hobbes (1588–1679), John Locke (1632–1704), George Berkeley (1685–1753), David Hume (1711–1776), John Stuart Mill (1806–1873), and Alexander Bain (1818–1903), among others. A major feature of their thinking was that knowledge was gradually acquired through sensory experience. According to Locke, for example, the mind at birth was a "tabula rasa," a blank slate upon which experiences were gradually impressed. The real world existed outside the individual, with mental activity occurring because of and after the sensory input. He distinguished two sides to knowledge—sensations and perceptions—the former being physical and the latter being mental products of reflection. A basic unit of mind was the simple idea, first recorded by the mind from external sensation and then combined through association into more complex ideas with time. The mind could not invent new ideas and provided little structuring of existing ideas, and in this sense, the mind was quite passive in Locke's view.

The British philosophers provided the foundation for the emergence of American behaviorism in the early part of this century. John Watson (1878–1958) published his famous paper in *Psychological Review* in 1913. This paper started the behaviorism movement in America, and bolstered by concurrent developments in operationalism and logical positivism during the 1920s and 30s, helped to shape the nature of psychological and educational research to the present day.

Watson argued that the current American functional psychology derived in part from German structural psychology and its emphasis on the experimental study of consciousness through introspection, was a mistake. The content was inappropriate and the methods were not objective. He proposed to replace consciousness with behavior as the proper content of psychology, and replace introspection with the objective measurement of behavior as the proper methodology. Since behavior was controlled by stimuli, not mental events, psychologists should focus on events controlling behavior external to the individual. In short, Watson proposed a new system for psychology.

Behaviorism, attempting to make psychology a true science on par with the natural sciences, readily accepted the operationalism of the physicist Percy Bridgman (1927) and the philosophy of science espoused during the 1920s and 30s by the group of philosophers and mathematicians meeting in Vienna to develop a perspective uniting all of science under empirical methodology. By using the language of operationalism, which stated that scientific concepts were to be defined by the procedures or "operations" used to measure them, the "Vienna Circle" attempted to provide a common language system to bring together the various scientific disciplines. Polkinghorne (1983) summarizes the basic doctrine of the logical positivists as follows:

1. Knowledge (*episteme*), as opposed to opinion, is contained only in statements that are descriptions of direct observation or in statements that are deductively linked to those descriptions of direct observations. (Inductively generated statements of probability are recognized as approximations that have not attained the certainty of deductively valid statements; they are acceptable as the best obtainable knowledge thus far.)

2. The goal of science is a network of knowledge statements linked together by the necessity of deductive logic generated from a few axiom statements and grounded ultimately in observation statements.

3. The only kinds of statements free from metaphysical overtones and personal bias—that is, the only kinds of statements assuring certainty—are those grounded in observation and belonging to the axiomatic system. All sciences are to limit their assertions to these kinds of statements, including the sciences of human phenomena.

Unless statements about "values," "reasons," "meaning," and so on can be reduced to the kinds of statements just mentioned, they are beyond the possibility of inclusion in true knowledge—that is, in *science* or (*episteme*) (pp. 90–91). Reproduced with permission from Polkinghorne, D., Methodology for The Human Sciences (1983). State University of New York Press.

The logical positivists were not successful in their attempt to unify scientific statements and we will leave it to the reader to explore why. Polkinghorne (1983) provides a very readable history. But the legacy of the logical positivists is not hard to find in educational research. The dominant system of inquiry in education has been controlled, quantitative, operational, objective, empirical, and replicable research. It posits a realist's point of view, that, in the extreme, takes the position that reality exists independently of the perceiver and that the task of the scientist is to discover the facts of the external world. Emphasis is placed on the explanation of causes of facts in this external world through controlled observation and measurement and the description of such regularities in terms of general laws. Operationism helps ensure objectivity and avoid the intrusion of subjective, and presumably unverifiable, personal accounts. Hypotheses are derived deductively from theory and confirmed or disconfirmed based on the statistical analysis of empirical evidence. Studies are repeated by different researchers with new subjects and settings in an attempt to generalize findings across researchers and contexts.

We have used Biddle and Anderson's (1986) label of "confirmatory" to name this mode of inquiry because of the emphasis on testing hypotheses generated from theory prior to data collection. It is not hard to identify educational researchers operating within the confirmational mode of inquiry. Mouly (1963), for example, states that the purpose of science is to "establish functional relationships among phenomena with a view to predicting and, if possible, to controlling their occurrence" (p. 31). Kerlinger (1973) defines scientific research as "systematic, controlled, empirical, and critical investigation of hypothetical propositions about presumed relations among natural phenomena" (p. 11).

Two major disciplines of confirmational inquiry were discussed in a well-known American Psychological Association Presidential Address given by Lee Cronbach (1957). Cronbach argued that scientific psychology was divided between experimental psychology, with an emphasis on experimental design and the identification of group differences, and correlational psychology, with an interest on naturalistic studies of covariation between variables. These two disciplines, experimental and correlational, developed along relatively independent lines and both have had a major impact on education.

Experimental Psychology

An experiment is a deliberate test of a hunch or hypothesis. People experiment every day as they test their predictions about the world around them against their experience. In science, the experimenter's predictions are also tested, but typically under more controlled conditions. The scientific community requires more stringent criteria of control than what most people require in their everyday lives. In fact, control is the cornerstone of experimental psychology.

Experimental researchers attempt to rule out all causes or explanations of the phenomenon under investigation except the one they are interested in establishing. Such alternative or rival explanations can be ruled out only by controlling all factors except the one in which they are interested, the independent variable, and allowing or making it vary and observing its effects. By observing the effects of the independent variable on the phenomena of interest, the dependent variable, scientists gain understanding about whether or not the independent variable is a "cause" of the dependent variable.

Manipulating an independent variable and observing its concomitant effects is not the only requirement of an experiment, however. A result on the dependent variable will almost always be observed. For the experimenter to determine if the result on the dependent variable is due to the independent variable or not, the researcher needs a comparison group. A comparison group is required to determine what happens to the dependent variable in the absence of the experimental treatment. With a comparison group, differences between experimental and comparison groups on the dependent variable can reasonably be attributed to the independent variable, assuming, of course, that all other variables have been controlled.

In addition to an independent variable, a dependent variable, and a comparison group, a true experiment also requires random assignment of subjects to groups. This is required if the experimenter is to equate the two groups on all person variables prior to the experiment. This requirement is relatively easy to accomplish in the laboratory, but more difficult in the field. In education, it is very difficult, although not impossible, to randomly assign students to groups because of the disruption to regular classroom assignments. More than likely, the field researcher must use intact groups. This has given rise to the concept of quasi-experimentation, where the experimenter still manipulates the independent variable but cannot randomly assign subjects to experimental and comparison groups. Because the experimenter no longer knows for certain whether the groups are the same prior to the independent variable, the experimenter is on shakier ground in attributing any differences on the dependent variable to the independent variable. Other extraneous variables might have had an effect as well. How to draw valid inferences from quasi-experiments has been discussed in detail by Cook and Campbell (1979).

We can see how this view of experimentation affects the analysis of data by examining a common model for data derived from an experiment. The purpose of the experiment is not merely to describe the sample providing the data (this can be done by examining the data). The purpose is to generalize beyond the sample to the population of individuals from which the sample was drawn and attempt to discover the general laws governing behavior. Inferential statistics has been developed to make this inference from the sample to the population, and models of data have been developed to help the researcher analyze the data. These models of data have had to deal with the fact that social science data are fallible, they contain error that must be handled in some way if valid inferences are to be made.

Consider the following example. Suppose a different method of teaching was used to teach each of three groups of students a unit on fractions for six weeks. At the end of six weeks, an achievement test on fractions was given. Further suppose we make certain assumptions about the scores (they were sampled at random from normal populations with equal variances), and use a basic linear model for the data as follows:

$$X_{ij} = \mu + \alpha_j + e_{ij}$$

where X_{ij} is score of the *i*th person in the *j*th group,

μ is a constant (the grand mean across all groups) and reflects the overall elevation of the scores on the dependent variable,

α_j is a constant for each person in a given group and reflects the increase or decrease in their scores as a result of being treated the way they were (e.g., they were taught with method A as opposed to method B or C), and

e_{ij} is the error score for person *i* in group *j*. It reflects that which is left over in X_{ij} after μ and α_j have been taken out.

Errors occur for many reasons, most notably because persons do not all react the same way to the same stimulus conditions. There are legitimate individual differences between people. In addition, there are momentary circumstances that produce error in scores. Conditions might be different between the groups as when one group was taught in the morning when they were fresh and another studied in the afternoon when they were less attentive.

It should be pointed out that the researcher only "sees" the X_{ij}s, the actual scores. The other components of the score are estimated based on the structure defined by the model. To see this, examine the fictitious data from our example in Table 3.4, first for the situation where there is no error in the data and then for the situation where there is error. Remember, the researcher really only has the X_{ij}s available for inspection. In the example, the overall elevation of the scores is 10, and the treatment effects for the three groups are 2 points, 0 points, and -2 points for methods A, B, and C respectively.

Research in Classrooms

TABLE 3.4

Fictitious Data With and Without Error

Group	Student	μ	$+\alpha_j$	$= X_{ij}$	μ	$+\alpha_j$	$+e$	$= X_{ij}$
			No error in scores				Error in scores	
1 (Method A)	1	10	+2	= 12	10	+2	+3	= 15
	2	10	+2	= 12	10	+2	+(−1)	= 11
	3	10	+2	= 12	10	+2	+(−3)	= 9
	4	10	+2	= 12	10	+2	+1	= 13
	5	10	+2	= 12	10	+2	+0	= 12
2 (Method B)	6	10	+0	= 10	10	+0	+0	= 10
	7	10	+0	= 10	10	+0	+(−1)	= 9
	8	10	+0	= 10	10	+0	+(−2)	= 8
	9	10	+0	= 10	10	+0	+(−1)	= 9
	10	10	+0	= 10	10	+0	+4	= 14
3 (Method C)	11	10	+(−2)	= 8	10	+(−2)	+0	= 8
	12	10	+(−2)	= 8	10	+(−2)	+2	= 10
	13	10	+(−2)	= 8	10	+(−2)	+1	= 9
	14	10	+(−2)	= 8	10	+(−2)	+(−3)	= 5
	15	10	+(−2)	= 8	10	+(−2)	+0	= 8

When no error is present (an impossible but illustrative situation), the data are quite clear: all the scores in group 1 are 12, in group 2 they are 10, and in group 3 they are 8. There is between group variance in the mean scores, variance that indicates that the method of instruction had an effect on the test performance of the students. Furthermore, within each group there is no variance in the scores; the variability is zero. This helps considerably in our ability to see the treatment effect since there is little "noise" in the data to obscure the treatment effect "signal."

Next consider the more realistic case, the case where error is in the scores. The average within-group score is still the same as before, but the scores now vary within each group. The data are "noisier" in that it is less obvious that the teaching methods had an effect on student learning. In fact, in a few cases, students in group 3 scored higher than students in group 2, and students in group 2 scored higher than students in group 1 even though group 1 had the highest mean score and group 3 the lowest.

Let us return now to our discussion of experimental control. The experimenter attempts to control within-group variation, variation among individuals within a group, and observe between-group variation in mean scores on the dependent variable. The ideal experiment is reflected in the no error situation in Table 3.4, where the within-group variation is at a minimum. This makes it easy to detect any between-group variability in mean scores, variability that we take to be the result of the independent variable.

In other words, the extent that the ratio of between-group variation is large relative to the within-group variation is an indication of the effect of the independent variable on the dependent variable. As mentioned above, these conditions are most easily observed in the laboratory, where conditions can be controlled, subjects can be randomly assigned to groups, and the experimenter can manipulate the independent variable. Of course, this is not always possible.

Correlational Psychology

We are now in a position to contrast correlational psychology with experimental psychology. If experimental psychology is characterized by examination of mean differences between groups, where within-group differences are viewed as sources of error in statistical models of data, then correlational psychology is characterized by examination of the very thing viewed as error by the experimentalists. Individual differences of a group are not a source of error but rather the phenomenon of interest to correlational psychologists. As Cronbach (1957) suggested, "While the experimenter is interested only in the variation he himself creates, the correlator finds his interest in the already existing variation between individuals, social groups, and species. . . . Nature has been experimenting since the beginning of time, with a boldness and complexity far beyond the resources of science. The correlator's mission is to observe and organize the data from Nature's experiments" (pp. 671–672).

Suppose we were interested in the relationship between student verbal ability (X_{ij}) and student achievement in reading comprehension (Y_{ij}). If we administered a 50-item verbal aptitude test and a 10-item reading comprehension test, and plotted each student's pair of scores on a graph, then our data might look something like that shown in Figure 3.1. The scatterplot shows a relatively strong correlation between verbal ability and reading comprehension, as we would expect, since high scores and low scores on one test tend to go with high and low scores on the second test. We can even "take out" the mean score on the tests and center the data by subtracted the mean score of each group from the individual scores. Since we are usually not interested in the elevation of scores, only their dispersion, this centering of the data has no effect on the position of the scores relative to the score scales. In the second part of Figure 3.1, the only thing that has changed is the location of the scale axes.

It is perhaps unfortunate that the term correlation came to be used to label this type of inquiry. Although the search for covariation between variables by the calculation of correlation coefficients is the underlying technique, experiments also look to establish covariation between variables (Cook and Campbell, 1979, p. 295). Non-experimental, in the sense that variables are not manipulated, or the Cook and Campbell "passive observation" is a more accurate description of this mode of inquiry.

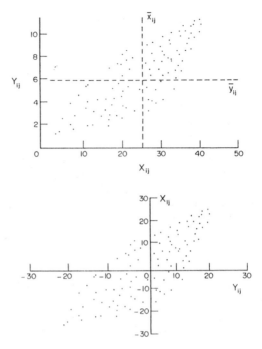

FIG 3.1   Examples of scatterplots.

Cronbach called for a cross-breeding of the two disciplines, one where both experimental and correlational modes were combined in single studies. His arguments generated a search of aptitude-treatment interactions (Cronbach and Snow, 1977), where within-treatment outcome on aptitude regressions are compared between treatment groups for possible inter-actions. We saw an example of this type of research in the work of Schneider and Treiber (1984) in the last chapter. Such interactions might suggest assignment policies for students, for example, to the treatment group most beneficial to the student. Although such interactions have been found, they account for relatively small amounts of variance, and as Cronbach (1975) observed almost twenty years after his initial plea for an integrated scientific psychology, "Once we attend to interactions, we enter a hall of mirrors that extends to infinity" (p. 119).

This is not to say that this line of research has not been successful. Such cross-breeding has yielded learning theory with individual difference para-meters and psychometric theory based in cognitive psychology. But Cronbach (1975) is less willing to believe that confirmatory inquiry will ultimately build the necessary store of knowledge:

> Our troubles do not arise because human events are in principle unlawful; man and his creations *are* part of the natural world. The trouble, as I see it, is that we cannot store

up generalizations and constructs for ultimate assembly into a network. It is as if we needed a gross of dry cells to power an engine and could only make one a month. The energy would leak out of the first cells before we had half the battery completed. So it is with the potency of our generalizations (p. 123).

Interpretive Inquiry

A second major mode of inquiry is interpretive, traceable to the German rationalists. In contrast to the British empiricists, Gottfried von Leibniz (1646–1716), Christian von Wolff (1679–1754), and Immanuel Kant (1724–1804) developed a view that emphasized mental activity and the structure of mind. Kant's view was of an active mind, with inborn capabilities to provide meaning to experience. Like Locke, Kant distinguished knowledge based on sensation from knowledge based in mental activity. But unlike Locke, Kant went on to describe mental activity that transcends experience altogether. In pure thought, ideas are possible that were never a product of external sensation and input. Furthermore, understanding was organized by certain, innate *a priori* categories that served to provide meaning to experience. The mind did not passively accumulate experience but actively molded it during acquisition.

Interpretive inquiry is more diverse than confirmatory inquiry, comprised of ideas not only from German rationalists, but also from the phenomenology of Edmund Husserl, the sociology of Max Weber, the psychology of Wilhelm Wundt, and the human science of Wilhelm Dilthey. A major feature of this mode of inquiry is a commitment to understand human social phenomena from the perspective of the individual. How do people define and interpret the world? The subjective meaning of action for humans is legitimate content for study, and indeed, much of work in this mode of inquiry focuses on understanding human meaning. Interpretive inquiry takes an idealist's point of view, the extreme form of which claims that there is no external reality independent of the cognition of the perceiver. Knowledge is not discovered, as the realist contends, but created by an active mind. Research often involves some form of participant observation, where the researcher undertakes long-term field work in the culture, group, or setting to better grasp the views of the members. In contrast to confirmatory inquiry, interpretive inquiry is more naturalistic than controlled, more qualitative than quantitative, uses "concretizing concepts" (to be discussed below) rather than operational definitions, is more subjective than objective, more rational than empirical, and is concerned more with context than replication.

Interpretive inquiry is typically more descriptive than confirmatory research. In part, this is because one of its purposes is to understand the inner perspective and meaning of actions and events of those being studied. It is also due to the fact that words are the primary form of data, and words can often convey more subtle and deeper meaning than can numbers.

As Bruyn (1966, pp. 28 ff) discussed, interpretive inquiry often uses "concretizing" procedures for defining concepts rather than operational procedures. Concretizing concepts identify and illustrate meaning by pointing to particular symbols in the culture or group being studied rather than defining concepts by pointing to how they are measured (operational definitions). Metaphors, analogies, and other devices are often used to convey the meaning of such symbols and how the researcher came to understand their meaning. Interpretive inquiry also uses "sensitizing concepts," a term coined by Herbert Blumer to refer to concepts that give a sense of reference or general orientation to a phenomenon rather than a precise definition. The meanings of sensitizing concepts are provided "by means of exposition which yields a meaningful picture, abetted by apt illustrations which enable one to grasp the reference in terms of one's own experience" (Blumer, as quoted by Bruyn, 1966, p. 32). Both concretizing and sensitizing concepts give rise to rich description. Coupled with the "thick description" of Geertz (1973)—contextually-rich and holistic accounts of social interaction and meaning—interpretive inquiry directs attention toward accurate and detailed description of meaning.

While it is easy to provide multiple contrasts between confirmatory and interpretive inquiry, and we do so later for pedagogical purposes, the truth of the matter is that interpretive inquiry is not an unified approach to the study of human phenomena; rather, interpretive inquiry is a number of different approaches which emerged in reaction to the dominant positivistic approach. Most interpretive approaches share, however, the view that positivistic science has neglected a significant part of human experience— the meaning humans given to social situations—because it was not amenable to study. Polkinghorne (1983) outlines five canons of interpretive inquiry (attributed to a paper by Kochelmans) that ensure social meaning is the focus of research:

1. Interpretive research needs to accept the autonomy of the object. The source of the articulated meaning is the phenomena themselves. The phenomena should not be forced into preconceived interpretive schemes, such as psychoanalytic or Marxian formats.

2. The researcher should search for an interpretation which makes the phenomena maximally reasonable or human. . . . The meanings have been covered over by secondary and tertiary layers of meaning so that their original significance is no longer available. The researcher must try to understand the phenomena in a more profound way than those who are involved in them or confronted with them.

3. The researcher must try to achieve the greatest possible familiarity with the phenomena—with the historical origin, with the various components of meaning which have been gradually attached to the original meaning, and with the various traditions which have influenced the origin and the future development of the phenomena.

4. This canon—which Kockelmans notes is most important—is the hermeneutic circle. This is the process of knowledge development that moves back and forth from understanding the parts to understanding the whole. The process is quasi-infinite on both sides, the parts and the wholes. Nevertheless, in most instances an interpretation can be reached which is adequate for the phenomena under consideration.

5. The researcher must try to show the meaning the phenomena have for the present situation. After the researcher has tried to understand the phenomena in their historical

origin and further development, he or she must look at them to determine their meaning for the present situation. This act involves a fusion of the researcher's situation and the phenomena (pp. 236–237). Reproduced with permission from Polkinghorne, D., Methodology for The Human Sciences (1983). State University of New York Press.

While Kochelmans' canons are not indicative of all approaches to interpretive inquiry, they do indicate the emphasis placed on the interpretation of social meaning that is characteristic of this mode of inquiry.

Jacob (1987) has outlined five qualitative research "traditions." These five schools or traditions are ecological psychology, holistic anthropology, ethnography of communication, cognitive anthropology, and symbolic interactionism. Jacob defines tradition along the lines of Kuhn's sociological definition of paradigm: "a group of scholars who agree among themselves on the nature of the universe they are examining, on legitimate questions and problems to study, and on legitimate techniques to seek solutions" (pp. 1–2). Jacob argues that most descriptions of interpretive inquiry confuse matters by treating it as a single approach rather than separating the multiple approaches and describing them separately.

We agree, and will briefly outline each of Jacob's traditions. The reader should consult Jacob's original article for references or examine the many books written on field methods in sociology (Bruyn, 1966; Denzin, 1970), anthropology (Pelto, 1970; Pelto and Pelto, 1978), and education (Bogdan and Biklen, 1982; Erickson, 1986; Goetz and LeCompte, 1984; Magoon, 1977; Smith, 1979; Spindler, 1982; Wilson, 1977).

Ecological Psychology

As mentioned in Chapter 2, Barker (1968) stated that the purpose of ecological psychology was to study "human behavior and its environment *in situ*" (p. 1), unaltered by laboratory constraints. Ecological psychologists study naturally occurring behavior and the coercive effects environments have on that behavior. Barker argued that psychology as a discipline had focused too much on attempting to establish laws of behavior through experimentation. He further argued that the "descriptive, natural history, ecological phase of investigation has had a minor place in psychology, and this has seriously limited the science" (p. 1). He went on to say:

> It is different in other sciences. Chemists know the laws governing the interaction of oxygen and hydrogen, and they also know how these elements are distributed in nature. Entomologists know the biological vectors of malaria, and they also know much about the occurrence of these vectors over the earth. In contrast, psychologists know little more than laymen about the distribution and degree of occurrence of their basic phenomena: of punishment, of hostility, of friendliness, of social pressure, of reward, of fear, of frustration (p. 2).

The early work of Barker and his colleagues involved the description of individual behavior and its immediate environment through the use of specimen records. But much of the later work shifted focus from behavior to the molar environments inhabited by humans. Barker suggested that when environments are uniform and stable, people are the primary source of behavioral variance, but when environments are more varied and unstable, as they are today, they contribute more to variance in behavior. Barker and his colleagues developed an elaborate theory and methodology for characterizing human molar environments through the use of the "behavior setting" concept introduced in the previous chapter (see Barker, 1968). Educational examples include the work of Berliner (1983), Gump (1967), and Stodolsky (1988).

Holistic Ethnography

Holistic ethnography is grounded in the cultural anthropology of Franz Boas and Bronislaw Malinowski working around the turn of the century. Boas believed that cultures should be studied by examining what the culture meant to the natives not what it meant relative to an outside or Western framework (Bogdan and Biklen, 1982, pp. 8–9). Malinowski established the ethnographic tradition of long-term field work and immersion in the culture being studied (Emerson, 1983, pp. 1–6). In general, ethnography means the study of culture.

The purpose of holistic ethnography is to describe the meaning, themes, and nature of the social and cultural worlds of a group of people and to describe how the cultural knowledge is interpreted and used by members of the group. In Malinowski's (1950) works, the goal of ethnography is to "grasp the native's point of view, his relation to life, to realize *his* vision of *his* world" (p. 25). Jacob outlines the basic methodological tenets of holistic ethnography, as espoused by Malinowski, as follows: (1) researchers gather evidence themselves through fieldwork, (2) the native's point of view should be documented, especially with verbatim statements, and (3) a wide range of data should be gathered using a variety of techniques. Techniques include observation, interviewing, and the use of key informants. An educational example can be found in Spindler (1982); Leacock (1969) presents an excellent example of classroom description and analysis.

Ethnography of Communication

Ethnography of communication, Jacob's label, also goes by the terms of constitutive ethnography or microethnography. Relying heavily on socio-linguistic methods and discourse analyses, a major purpose of ethnography of communication is to understand the rules, structures, and processes of social interaction. Critical of some field studies as being "too anecdotal," constitutive studies often use video and audiotaping to preserve much of the original phenomenon along with more conventional participant observation techniques (see Mehan, 1979). Erickson (1986), Green (1983), and

Wilkinson (1982) provide reviews and examples from classroom ethnographies.

Cognitive Anthropology

Cognitive anthropology is also known as ethnoscience or ethnographic semantics. It attempts to describe the cultural knowledge and categories used by members of a society to interpret events and actions and to behave acceptably in that society. Cultural knowledge is most easily studied by examining the language of the culture, and the cognitive anthropologists have developed standardized, formal procedures for eliciting cultural categories and rules and producing a thorough description of them (see Emerson, 1983, pp. 28–31).

There are few educational applications of cognitive anthropology. Perhaps the work best known to educators is the interview procedure outlined by Spradley (1979). He defines four types of ethnographic analyses that "uncover the system of cultural meanings that people use" and "lead to the discovery of cultural meaning" (p. 94). Domain analysis is a procedure for analyzing written transcripts and identifying the categories or "domains" used by interviewees to name things in their world. Domain analysis also suggests a procedure for outlining how the names are related in semantic relationships. The domain analysis, which occurs repeatedly during the ethnography, suggests hypotheses that can be tested with more formal interview questioning. Three additional techniques—taxonomic analysis, componential analysis, and theme analysis—allow the ethnographer to further explore the structure within and across domains and better understand cultural meaning.

Symbolic Interactionism

Symbolic interactionism, systematically presented by the sociologist Herbert Blumer (1969), assumes that "human beings act towards things on the basis of the meanings that the things have for them" (p. 2). It also assumes that the meaning of things is derived from the social interactions humans have with others. In other words, human action is mediated by the meaning given to each others' actions. A third and final assumption of symbolic interactionism is that the meanings are construed through an interpretive process. Humans do not simply react to each other, but interpret the action of others. Symbols, interpretation, and the derivation of meaning underly human interaction. To understand social interaction, then, requires direct examination of the social world. Researchers need to understand the meanings and interpretations of those involved. Symbolic interactionists attempt to understand these meanings and interpretations and how they mediate human interaction through participant observation.

As Blumer put it, "the empirical social world consists of ongoing group life and one has to get close to this life to know what is going on in it" (p. 38).

The Cusick study presented earlier in this chapter was based in a symbolic interaction framework. Bolster (1983) argues for ethnographic research based in symbolic interactionism as the model necessary to generate useful knowledge about teaching.

Contrasting Dimensions of Inquiry

· So far we have considered two broad systems of inquiry, confirmatory and interpretive, and outlined several of the more specific disciplines or traditions within each system that share some of the philosophical assumptions undergirding each mode of inquiry. As should be apparent by now, the methodology and research techniques of these two modes of inquiry are quite different. Confirmatory techniques include experiments, surveys, correlational procedures, and statistical analyses of quantitative data. Interpretive techniques include ethnographic field methods, participant observation, case studies, and sociolinguistic and semantic analyses of qualitative data.

Although the two systems are based on different assumptions about the world and human nature, focus on different aspects of reality, use different language systems for describing their subject matter, and suggest different roles for researchers, there is reason to believe that the two systems can coexist with each contributing unique information about phenomena (see, for example, Cook and Reichardt, 1979; Cronbach, 1975; Firestone, 1987; Howe, 1985; Soltis, 1984). Even Donald Campbell, one of the authors of the classic "Experimental and Quasi-experimental Designs for Research on Teaching" (Campbell and Stanley, 1963), who wrote in that article that case studies "have such a total absence of control as to be of almost no scientific value" (p. 176), is willing to concede that such studies can be "disciplined." After outlining the problems with drawing conclusions from case studies, Campbell (1975) writes:

> While it is probable that many case studies professing or implying interpretation or explanation, or relating the case to theory, are guilty of these faults, it now seems to me clear that not all are, or need be, and that I have overlooked a major source of discipline (i.e., of degrees of freedom if I persist in using this statistical concept for the analogous problem in non-statistical settings). In a case study done by an alert social scientist who has thorough local acquaintance, the theory he uses to explain the focal difference also generates predictions or expectations on dozens of other aspects of the culture, and he does not retain the theory unless most of these are also confirmed. In some sense, he has tested the theory with degrees of freedom coming from the multiple implications of any one theory (pp. 181–182).

In this section we further consider these two modes of inquiry by contrasting them on three fundamental dimensions, dimensions which are related to three important components of methodology: purpose, the conceptual framework, and the research plan. By outlining these dimensions we hope to highlight the fact that, even though the two modes of inquiry have been and are typically viewed as polar opposites, any given classroom research study varies along these three dimensions. Thus, while many studies can be clearly placed at one pole or the other on all three dimensions, other studies are not so easily classified and represent "hybrids." We believe that such "hybrids" are beneficial to the field of classroom research and we hope to support this belief throughout this book.

Purpose: Verification vs. Generation of Theory

One important dimension relates directly to the purpose of the research. Will the study attempt to verify propositions—hypotheses—derived from some theoretical framework, or is the purpose of the study to discover and generate new theory about the phenomena? Because the distinction between deductive and inductive reasoning is closely related to this question, it will be helpful to first define these two types of theory.

A deductive theorist, sometimes called a rationalist, typically works from the top down (general to the particular), developing logical theories that account for certain phenomena and then deducing hypotheses from the theory and testing those predictions with evidence. Although the theory is usually based in known observations about the phenomena being explained, much of the theory is speculative and in need of empirical verification. As hypotheses are tested and retained or discarded, the theory is constantly undergoing revision as more and more empirical work is completed. Hull's (1937) hypothetical-deductive theory of learning is perhaps the best known example of deductive theory in psychology, and his succinct description captures both the nature of deductive theory and positivistic thought from the mid-1930s:

> The essential characteristics of a sound scientific theoretical system, as contrasted with ordinary philosophical speculation, may be briefly summarized under three heads:
> 1. A satisfactory scientific theory should begin with a set of explicitly stated postulates accompanied by specific or "operational" definitions of the critical terms employed.
> 2. From these postulates there should be deduced by the most rigorous logic possible under the circumstances, a series of interlocking theorems covering the major concrete phenomena of the field in question.
> 3. The statements in the theorems should agree in detail with the observationally known facts of the discipline under consideration. If the theorems agree with the observed facts, the system is probably true; if they disagree, the system is false. If it is impossible to tell whether the theorems of a system agree with the facts or not, the system is neither true nor false; scientifically considered, it is meaningless (p. 5).

In contrast, the empiricist, an inductive theorist, works from the bottom up (the particular to the general), gathering data and developing theory to explain the evidence. As more evidence is gathered, the theory is revised or changed altogether to account for the new evidence. Perhaps B. F. Skinner is the best known empiricist in psychology, arguing that the hypothetico-deductive method is often inefficient and that research does not require theory to guide the collection of data (Skinner, 1950). "Theories are fun," according to Skinner, but unnecessary for research (p. 215).

Although researchers typically use both types of reasoning and theorizing in their work, the distinction is relevant to an extremely influential book written in 1967 by two sociologists, Barney Glaser and Anselm Strauss. The book, entitled *The Discovery of Grounded Theory: Strategies for Qualitative Research*, outlines procedures for generating theory *from* data rather than verifying theory *with* data. Their image of "grounded theory," theory that is close to and emerges from the events analyzed, struck a responsive chord among those sympathetic to interpretive inquiry and field techniques. Field data do not easily conform to the requirements of the hypothetico-deductive approach, and anyway, the purpose of interpretive inquiry to discover rather than confirm meaning. Their concept of theorizing also fit well with the emergent nature of design during field research:

> Generating a theory from data means that most hypotheses and concepts not only come from the data, but are systematically worked out in relation to the data during the course of the research. *Generating a theory involves a process of research* (p. 6).

We will have more to say in Chapter 7 about the specific strategies advocated by Glaser and Strauss for discovering grounded theory. Briefly, grounded theory involves the researcher developing theoretical categories to organize data and then revising the categories to fit new data. The process of continual checking and revising the conceptual system to fit the evidence virtually assures that the theory will be close to the data. It also blurs the separation of data collection and data analysis, since both occur at the same time. New collection of data is shaped by preceding analytic interpretations and further observations are more focused and directed at testing emerging concepts. Thus, the process of developing grounded theory dictates that data collection and analysis occur simultaneously and that both are ongoing while the researcher is in the field.

Grounded theorists also use theoretical sampling as opposed to statistical sampling. In theoretical sampling, the emerging theory determines what data to sample next during the study. Researchers often find that as they develop their initial theoretical categories, additional data are required to elaborate or test a category. Since the categories are derived from the data, it is impossible to know before data collection exactly what type of sampling will be required. Glaser and Strauss (1967) define it as follows:

> Theoretical sampling is the process of data collection for generating theory whereby the analyst jointly collects, codes, and analyzes his data and decides what data to collect next and where to find them, in order to develop his theory as it emerges" (p. 45).
> The basis question in theoretical sampling (in either substantive or formal theory) is: *what* groups or subgroups does one turn to *next* in data collection? In short, how does the sociologist select multiple comparison groups? (p. 47).

In contrast, research designed to verify theory uses statistical sampling of people. A population is defined, and individuals are selected from that population at random. If the sampling is carefully carried out, sampling theory allows the researcher to generalize findings based on the study sample to the population, the real interest of the experimenter. After all, the researcher is interested not in the behavior of the sample per se but in what the behavior of the sample informs the researcher about the population in general. Statistical sampling is used to make accurate inferences to populations with the goal of creating general, nomothetic laws.

The flexibility of design with grounded theory field methods is in sharp contrast to experimental procedures following the hypothetico-deductive logic. Hypothetico-deductive research uses fixed research designs and pre-specified hypotheses, and temporally separates data collection from data analysis. If new ideas or questions occur in the middle of the study, experimental researchers must typically wait and design a new study to examine the questions. In grounded theory approaches, new ideas and questions can be routinely examined and tested as they arise.

Figure 3.2 outlines these two approaches to theory construction and highlights their differences. First, the two approaches differ in their starting point, theory in the case of hypothetico-deductive research and data collection in the case of grounded theory research. Second, data collection and data analysis are separated temporally when the purpose of research is verification, but occur simultaneously when the purpose is to discover theory in the data. Third, the research design is predetermined and fixed in hypothetico-deductive research but flexible and evolving in grounded theory research. Finally, the end point is different in the two approaches. In

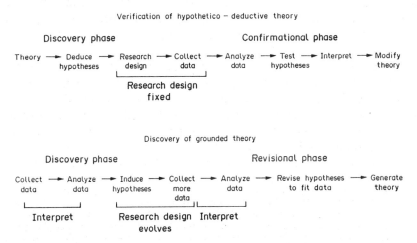

FIG. 3.2   Two approaches to theory construction.

hypothetico-deductive research, the product is a change in the theory, either because some or all of the hypotheses were confirmed or because some or all of the hypotheses were not supported and had to be revised or modified altogether. Thus, the end result is either confirmed hypotheses or speculation about why the hypotheses were not confirmed and suggestions for further research. In grounded theory, the product is new theory about the phenomenon that "fits or works" in the area studied because it has been derived from the data, not theory. Such grounded theory still needs further testing and clarification, however.

Conceptual Framework: Nomothetic and Idiographic Explanation

Polkinghorne (1983) attributes the distinction between nomothetic and idiographic approaches to phenomena to Wilhelm Windelband in an address he gave in 1894. In that address, Windelband suggested that the purpose of the natural sciences was nomothetic, from *nomos* meaning law, establishing general laws about phenomena. In contrast, the purpose of the historical sciences was idiographic, from *idio* meaning particular, focusing on the uniqueness of events and what the events meant.

It was the psychologist Gordon Allport who popularized the distinction in psychology. Nomothetic study of behavior attempts to study behavior in terms of universal laws and principles applicable to groups of people. Idiographic study of behavior focuses on the uniqueness of the individual and uses methods appropriate to explaining the behavior of particular individuals. Psychology, according to Allport, was caught between science's goal of discovering universal laws and human individuality:

> The individual, whatever else he may be, is an internally consistent and unique organization of bodily and mental processes. But since he is unique, science finds him an embarrassment. Science, it is said, deals only with broad, preferably universal, laws. Thus science is *nomothetic* discipline. Individuality cannot be studied by science, but only by history, art, or biography whose methods are not nomothetic (seeking universal laws), but idiographic (Allport, 1961, pp. 8–9).

Allport argued that the application of knowledge was always to the single case, and that nomothetic laws provided little assistance in making predictions about individuals. Only idiographic methods, focusing on the individual, are useful in making predictions about particular individuals. Allport did not reject nomothetic methods; he only argued that psychology was overwhelmingly nomothetic and in need of a more balanced approach to human phenomenon (see Franck, 1986, for an extended discussion of this issue).

Other concepts are closely related to Allport's nomothetic and idiographic approaches. One set of concepts is the dichotomy between explanation and verstehen (understanding). The verstehen doctrine was developed by the German sociologist Max Weber. Briefly, Weber distinguished between behavior and action, the former being the actual observable event and the latter being the behavior guided by meaning and values of the person performing the action. Social science, according to Weber, should focus on the meaning of human action, although meaning is not observable and can only be studied by interpretive understanding (verstehen). Understanding the meaning of an action by the researcher placing him or herself in the actor's situation and attempting to grasp the action's meaning, is required before a researcher can explain why the action occurs. Strike (1972) outlines the basic dichotomy as follows:

> The basic dispute clustering around the notion of *verstehen* has typically sounded something like the following: The advocate of some version of the *verstehen* doctrine will claim that human beings can be understood in a manner that other objects of study cannot. Men have purposes and emotions, they make plans, construct cultures, and hold certain values, and their behavior is influenced by such values, plans, and purposes. In short, a human being lives in a world which has "meaning" to him, and, because his behavior has meaning, human actions are intelligible in ways that the behavior of nonhuman objects is not. The opponents of this view, on the other hand, will maintain that human behavior is to be explained in the same manner as is the behavior of other objects of nature. There are laws governing human behavior. An action is explained when it can be subsumed under some such law, and, of course, such laws are confirmed by empirical evidence (p. 28).

Another set of concepts related to the nomothetic and idiographic dimension is that between objective and subjective points of view. To be objective means there is a common frame of reference to interpret experience to which some group of people can all agree. Typically, there is a set of ground rules, followed more or less by all members of the group, that allow the members to derive a common, generalizable meaning from experience. Subjectivity, on the other hand, implies that the experience of the person is often unique and that the derivation of common meaning by a group of people cannot be assumed. Because similar experiences are unique to different individuals, generalizability of meaning is difficult, if not impossible.

A final set of concept related to nomothetic and idiographic approaches is the one employed by the cognitive anthropologists for cultural description by using the cultural groups' own categories (see Pelto, 1970; Spradley, 1979, pp. 231–232). Kenneth Pike (1954) coined two terms, etic and emic, to characterize two ways that a human observer can describe behavior. Pike, a linguist, was interested in developing a "unified theory" of both human verbal and non-verbal behavior, of human action and human sound. He argued that human action and voice should not be sub-divided and studied as separate parts but rather that human activity was a structural whole and should be studied as such. Visual records separate from auditory records were incomplete and both were often fused into single events.

The etic approach (from phon*etics*, the study of the sounds made in spoken languages) attempts to describe data using a single system applicable to all languages and cultures of the world. The system of description is independent of any new language or culture in the sense it is *created* before gathering new data and the data are described in terms of this system. The system is classificatory in the sense that the observer uses logical categories to characterize different languages and cultures, categories derived prior to data collection. Thus, no attempt is made to capture the natural structuring of the language or culture. It is a point of view from outside the culture.

The emic approach (from phon*emics,* the study of sounds as they relate to the structure of a language), on the other hand, is valid for only a single language or culture (or dialect or homogeneous group within a culture). Emic description attempts to *discover* the elements of that language or culture and describe them in relation to each other as they are used in that culture rather than in terms of an outside system developed prior to description. It is a structural approach to description, according to Pike, because it assumes that human behavior is patterned and that the units of such patterned behavior are observable in the actions of the members of a culture, not "by the action of the analyst merely to obtain constructs which can be 'applied to' data to describe it" (Pike, 1954, p. 8). It is a point of view from inside the culture.

Research Plan: Experimental vs. Naturalistic Design

A fundamental question about any study is the role played by the researcher. Is it necessary to intervene in the phenomenon being studied or is it better to allow the phenomenon to occur without interference? In the former case, the researcher takes an active role and attempts to answer questions about a phenomenon by manipulating conditions antecedent to the phenomenon. In the latter case, the researcher interferes less with the phenomenon and attempts to answer questions by either observing or participating in the phenomenon, but not manipulating conditions antecedent to the phenomenon. The first case is characteristic of experimental research and the second case is often called naturalistic research (Guba, 1978; Willems and Raush, 1969).

Actually, the distinction between experimental and naturalistic research is more involved than described above. Willems (1969) identifies two ways a researcher may interfere with a phenomenon: does the researcher control the antecedent conditions and/or does the researcher impose units upon the phenomenon? In experimental terms, these two questions ask how much control does the researcher place on the independent variable (by manipulating it) or the dependent variables (by structuring them). Willems considers these two dimensions as forming a two-dimensional space that can be used to place researcher roles. Experimental research, for example, is defined as high-high on both dimensions while naturalistic research is defined as low-low in the two-dimensional space.

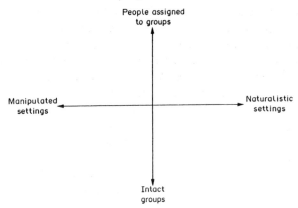

FIG. 3.3   Two dimensions for describing the role of the classroom researcher.

We would characterize this two-dimensional space differently, as shown in Figure 3.3. Our first dimension, running left-to-right, is the same as Willems: manipulation or lack of manipulation of the setting. Our second dimension, running top-to-bottom, is different from Willems. We see structuring of the dependent variable by the researcher an important but not critical dimension defining research design. Rather, whether the researcher assigns people to groups or studies existing, intact groups is more critical to the nature of the research design. Strict experimental designs are located in the upper left corner of our diagram, and naturalistic designs, where the researcher does not interfere with the setting nor the group of people being studied, is located in the lower right hand corner.

A related topic about design discussed by Willems (1969) was based on a major theme in the writing of Egon Brunswik (1955, 1956). Brunswik, a perceptual psychologist, was highly critical of laboratory factorial designs, which, "for their arbitrary orderliness and confinement . . . may be called 'systematic' " (Brunswik, 1955, p. 194). Brunswik noted an inherent asymmetry in systematic designs, which require, as we have seen, only one or perhaps a few independent variables to be manipulated while holding all others constant and observing the concomitant effect on the dependent variable. The asymmetry arises when subjects, who produce responses, are randomly sampled but the stimulus conditions of the experiment (the independent variable) are not. Not only are the stimulus conditions not sampled, they are artifically constrained in systematic design by either combining independent variables in ways not found in nature ("artificial tying of variables") or isolating independent variables (in factorial designs) found correlated in nature ("artificial untying of variables"). Brunswik argued for "representative design" which "separates variables to the extent to which they are separated in the particular ecology but no further, and

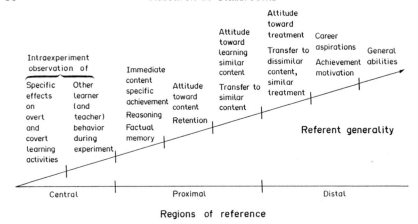

FIG. 3.4 Schematic scale of referent generality for outcome measure in
instructional experiments.

Source: Snow (1974).

does not tolerate any artificial perfect tyings (or untyings between variables"
(Brunswik, 1955, p. 202).

Richard Snow (1968, 1974) has applied some of Brunswik reasoning to
research on teaching, and offers many good suggestions for conducting
classroom research. Figures 3.4 and 3.5, taken from the more recent Snow
article, summarize how systematic designs can become more representative
by careful consideration of the generality of the outcome measures (Figure

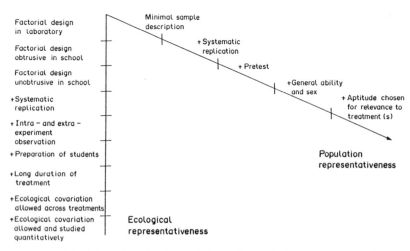

FIG. 3.5 Schematic scales of population and ecological representativeness in
instructional experiments.

Source: Snow (1974).

3.4), the population representativeness of the sample description, and the ecological representation of the independent variables (these latter two in Figure 3.5). The ecological representativeness dimension, for example, moves from the laboratory factorial experiment, with little ecological representativeness, down through a series of design features that allow the stimulus conditions of research on teaching and instruction to be more like the actual phenomenon.

Concluding Comments

In this chapter we have characterized research as "disciplined inquiry" and have attempted to present a balanced view of two forms of inquiry. In our view, both of these forms—confirmatory and interpretive—have value in classroom research. When these two forms of inquiry are examined along three key dimensions of methodology—purpose, conceptual framework, and research plan—the following distinctions emerge. Confirmatory inquiry seeks verification of theory and is nomothetic and experimental. In contrast, interpretive inquiry seeks to generate theory and is idiographic and naturalistic. As we shall see throughout this book, however, studies of classrooms do not fall neatly into these two extremes.

Regardless of the form of inquiry, then, the fact remains that classroom research is disciplined. Regardless of the mode of inquiry used by researchers, they must be careful in conducting their studies and equally careful in reporting what they have done. When care is not taken, we have no way of assessing the credibility of their findings. We are unable to judge whether their knowledge claims are derived from sound methodology or are simply their opinions. Because of the social nature of knowledge, methodological conventions must be followed if the field of classroom research is to advance. Opinion cannot be cloaked in methodological language that disguises the true source of the knowledge claim.

Unit II—Introduction
Designing Classroom Research

As a form of disciplined inquiry, classroom research is purposeful, systematic, and involves the collection, interpretation, and analysis of evidence. At the same time, however, classroom researchers have a number of options and must make several important decisions as they plan and carry out their research studies. These options and decisions are described in the four chapters contained in this unit.

In the first chapter, the three basic components of research design are described: the purpose of the study, the conceptual framework, and the plan of the study. Each of these components is discussed, some in detail and others briefly. The chapter ends with a discussion of the means by which researchers can make and defend knowledge claims based on their results of their studies.

In the second chapter, the variety of sources of evidence available to the classroom researcher is presented and discussed. These sources are divided into three general categories: observing, asking, or collecting. The strengths and weaknesses of each of these sources are described. Illustrations and examples of each source are presented. Recommendations for the selection, development, and use of each source are given.

In the third chapter, two fundamental issues concerning evidence are discussed. First, how is meaning derived from evidence? Second, how can the quality of the evidence be estimated or enhanced? The meaning of the evidence is derived primarily from the concepts that the evidence represents. These concepts are a part of the conceptual framework that underlies the study. The quality of the evidence depends primarily on the extent to which it is free from error. Several potential sources of error exist. Inappropriate sources of evidence may be used. The evidence as gathered may be biased. The evidence may not be dependable. Without meaningful evidence of high quality, research efforts are doomed to failure.

In the fourth chapter, issues surrounding the analysis of evidence are discussed. Since evidence exists in the form of words as well as numbers, issues in qualitative and quantitative analysis are described. Large amounts of evidence can cause numerous problems for the researcher. As a consequence, issues of aggregation and reduction are considered. Finally, analytic techniques range from the very simple to the highly complex. Examples of this range of techniques are included.

In many respects, this unit can be viewed as a bridge between the highly abstract chapters in the first unit and the very concrete studies to be reviewed and examined in the chapters included in the third unit. The reader who understands the concepts and principles presented in these chapters, then, will have a far easier time crossing that bridge.

4

The Nature of Classroom Research

In Chapter 2 we discussed classrooms and in Chapter 3 we focused on research. In this chapter we attempt to describe classroom research. Like all research, classroom research does not just happen; it must be planned and planned carefully. Studies of classrooms must be designed so that the evidence gathered has meaning in terms of the concepts represented by the evidence and is directly related to the purpose for which the study is being conducted. Once the evidence has been collected and examined or analyzed, researchers make knowledge claims based on the evidence. These knowledge claims are the true result of classroom research.

This chapter begins with a description of purpose, conceptual framework, and research plan, and ends with the making and defending of knowledge claims. In between, four major elements of the research plan are discussed: sampling of evidence, sources of evidence, the meaning of evidence, and analysis of evidence.

Purpose, Framework, and Plan

Before carrying out a classroom research study, a researcher needs three things: a question or set of questions that defines the purpose of the study, a conceptual framework that guides the collection and interpretation of the evidence, and a plan for collecting the evidence needed to address the question or questions being asked. Decisions that the researcher makes relative to each of these "needs" are informed by the paradigm or research program within which the researcher is operating (see Chapter 2) and, once made, may reflect an explicit or implicit choice of mode of inquiry (see Chapter 3). These decisions, then, frame the nature of the approach to research used to conduct the study. As a consequence, all of these decisions contribute to the overall research design.

Figure 4.1 represents schematically the three main components of the research design. Supporting the design is the paradigm or program. The purpose of the study and the conceptual framework guiding the researcher's

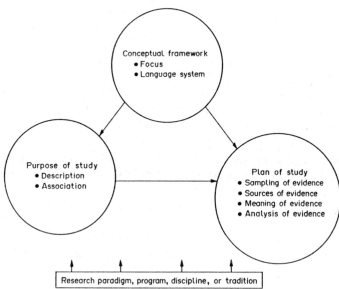

Fig 4.1   Basic components of research design.

thinking about the phenomenon both impact directly on the plan of study. We have indicated in the figure two fundamental purposes of research, description and association, which frame the kinds of questions asked in the study. We have also indicated two ways that the conceptual framework assists the researcher in developing the research plan: theory serves to focus the researcher's attention, and theory provides a language system for describing what is observed or inferred. And the plan of study is concerned with how the evidence bearing on the research questions will be sampled, gathered, interpreted, and analyzed. Each of these three components are discussed below.

Purpose of Research

When researchers conduct research, they attempt to answer questions in a systematic way. The answers they eventually find are as much a function of the questions asked as they are of the procedures used to collect, analyze, and interpret the evidence. Poorly formed questions will usually result in inadequate answers.

Social and behavioral scientists design their studies to answer one or both of two general questions. First, what the primary features of a phenomenon and how do these features vary? Second, what are the relationships between or among the features of a phenomenon (that is, how do the features co-vary)? In classroom research, the phenomenon of interest is the classroom. In any classroom a number of features can capture the researcher's attention: the physical and social arrangements, the equipment and materials, and the thoughts, feelings, and behavior of the participants (e.g., teachers, students) are but a few.

The first of the two questions is *descriptive*, with the researcher attempting to identify, categorize, or summarize the features and their variation. Goodlad (1984), for example, argued that the "first step in any program of examination and reconstruction [of schools and schooling] is to determine what now exists" (p. 5). His descriptive study of 38 schools provided data on many features of schools and classrooms including teachers and administrators, students and parents, and the curriculum that was presented and how it was taught.

The second question is *associational*, with the researcher attempting to relate certain features to others. Bennett (1976) was interested in the relationships among three features of the classroom environment: teaching style, pupil personality type, and pupil achievement. Both description and association are legitimate goals of classroom research.

Many researchers agree with Goodlad that one must describe the features of a phenomenon before one can examinate interrelationship among them. Description of phenomena has been considered the fundamental research activity. The primary features and their variation need to be described before more detailed examinations of the interrelationship among the features can be made. The quality of the concepts used to describe a phenomenon has a direct bearing on the theory that is developed or generated since it is concepts that are related to each other in theoretical propositions. Poor descriptive concepts will lead to fuzzy theorizing.

However, the two purposes of description and association are not mutually exclusive. Researchers conducting descriptive studies that attempt to answer the question, "What is the nature of this phenomenon?" usually make some attempt at explaining why the phenomenon is as it is. Similarly, researchers conducting associational studies concerned with the question "How or why does this phenomenon occur?" must typically describe what it is they are explaining. Nonetheless, most studies have a primary focus of either description or association, and it is usually easy to tell the difference.

In classroom research, a three-stage process involving the two purposes of research has been suggested (Nuthall and Church, 1973; Rosenshine and Furst, 1973; Gage, 1978). Termed the descriptive-correlational-experimental[1] loop, Rosenshine and Furst describe the process in the following manner:

1. development of procedures for describing teaching in a quantitative manner;

[1]In our terminology, both correlational and experimental studies are associational studies since their basis is relationships between or among the features of the phenomenon being studied.

2. correlational studies in which the descriptive variables are related to measures of student growth;
3. experimental studies in which the significant variables obtained in the correlational studies are tested in a more controlled situation (p. 122).

In this sequence of research activities, the early descriptive studies are thought to provide the concepts about teachers and teaching whose association with student learning could be examined in a series of correlational studies. Promising concepts from these latter studies could then be manipulated experimentally and the causal relationship between the concepts and student learning could be investigated. Much of the process-product research during the 1970s followed the descriptive-correlational-experimental loop (although more emphasis was placed on association than on description). Evertson and Green (1986) provide a nice example of this sequence, tracing the work done during the 1970s by Evertson and her collaborators. Another useful example is the decade of research conducted by Nuthall and his colleagues, based on the initial work of Smith and Meux (1962). The reader is encouraged to read *in order* Nuthall and Lawrence (1965), Wright and Nuthall (1970), Hughes (1973), and Nuthall and Church (1973). According to Gage and Needels (1989), this three-stage process has generated at least 13 experiments.

While we do not deny that this sequence of research activity has produced an impressive array of findings, we should caution the reader about one potential flaw in the descriptive-correlational-experimental loop. Only those teacher and teaching concepts on which teachers vary in naturally-occurring settings are selected for experimental manipulation and causal analysis. Concepts that do not differentiate among teachers for any number of reasons (e.g., infrequently occurring teaching practices or behaviors) cannot be associated with student learning in correlational research. [More will be said about this issue in Chapter 7]. It must be remembered that correlational studies do not tell us whether two features or concepts are related to one another; rather, correlational studies only tell us whether variability in one feature or concept is related to variability in another feature or concept.

A more appropriate use of the three-stage sequence of research activity, then, may be to spend more time on the descriptive stage. Remember that the purpose of descriptive studies is to examine features of a phenomenon *and their variation.* If sufficient natural variation is present, then correlational studies may be quite appropriate and useful. If not, however, a direct move from description to experimentation may be necessary, with experimental manipulation the vehicle for creating the needed variation.

Conceptual Framework

Conceptual frameworks are involved in one way or another in every study of classrooms. Embedded within the frameworks are general ideas concerning what and who will be investigated. The many models of classrooms described in Chapter 2 serve to illustrate the use of conceptual frameworks in focusing the researcher's attention. In addition, conceptual frameworks provide a point of view and a language system for describing the features of the phenomenon and their interrelationships. One of the most significant problems in classroom research is the plethora of concepts having essentially the same denotation. Different language systems aligned with different conceptual frameworks generate different concepts to describe the same phenomenon, making theory development difficult if not impossible.

Conceptual frameworks provide the means by which evidence is given meaning. Evidence has no meaning; meaning is provided when evidence is placed into categories and these categories, in turn, are related to other categories that are already "understood." All evidence in a particular category shares some attributes or features in common (e.g., evidence pertaining to the directives given to students by teachers) and the categories themselves are often referred to as concepts. In this sense meaning is relational, and it is the conceptual framework that provides the relationship network for "interpreting" and "understanding" the concepts imposed on or derived from the evidence. [This point will be discussed and illustrated in greater detail in Chapter 6.]

Conceptual frameworks, then, focus the attention of the research on certain features of the phenomenon under investigation and provide a language system for describing and interpreting the evidence gathered during the study. The conceptualization of classrooms is not a trivial problem, yet it has major implications for the way in which the plan of the study will be developed or is to evolve. At least three characteristics of classrooms make them especially difficult to conceptualize.

First, classrooms are complex settings in which physical, social, and behavioral features are intertwined. There is a lot of "action" that occurs and a great deal of "meaning" is subscribed to or derived from the action. Every day, teachers interact with many students in different arrangements for long periods of time. In order to conceptualize these complex settings a variety of ways of "unitizing" them have been developed. Evertson and Green (1986), for example, provide nineteen different "behavior units" and briefly describe each (see Table 4.1).

Second, classrooms are part of a larger, multi-leveled educational system, consisting of small units nested with larger ones (see Figure 4.2). Teachers and their students are nested within classrooms, classrooms within schools, schools within neighborhoods (or attendance zones), neighborhoods within administrative districts, districts within states (or provinces or regions), and so on. Outside of neighborhoods, this framework is structural in the sense that the boundaries of each level are clearly defined by organizational entities that influence the other organizational entities in the framework.

Research in Classrooms

TABLE 4.1

Terms for Behavioral Units

Type of Unit	General Definition
1. Natural units	Detected through the perceptual system and reflected in natural language (Barker & Wright, 1955). Perceived as breaks in streams of behavior.
2. Units of behavior	Can be described as a natural unit also. Laws of perceiving forms are also valid for behavioral forms. Just as there are forms in the world of objects, there are dynamic and temporal configurations (e.g., direction or speed of movement, position of the body).
3. Inductive vs. deductive	Refers to the process by which units are constructed. For inductive units, one starts with the behavior and attempts to classify (e.g., ethology). For deductive units, units are derived from theory, hypotheses, or logical propositions.
4. Directly observable vs. inferred	Two types are distinguished: those that are on principle invisible (e.g. a person's intentions, emotions, thoughts), and those that are invisible due to circumstances (e.g., instances when the observer cannot see the behavior because of an obstacle). Both instances require inference. The issues involved here are not so much whether inference should be used but at what stage in the data collection.
5. Descriptive vs. evaluative	The former notes concrete behaviors and suspends judgments. The latter summarizes and assesses a series of behaviors (e.g., one can observe a child for 30 minutes and conclude he is angry, or one can record the concrete behaviors which could lead to that judgment.)
6. Phenomenological	Behaviors that have the same form (Brannigan & Humphries, 1972).
7. Morphological	Similar to a phenomenological unit with emphasis on the formal or structural aspects of the behavior as criteria for constructing.
8. Units based on factor analysis	Units are based on dimensions emerging from the statistical analysis (see Emmer & Peck, 1973).
9. Discrete vs. continuous	This refers to the extent to which it is possible to count or measure behaviors. The issue of discreteness vs. continuousness arises with the use of rating scales.
10. Simple vs. complex	Two views exist of these types of units. The first views the uniqueness of the human cortex to analyze complex events and relies on ratings of complex concepts (Langer, Schulz, & Thun, 1974). The second is the construction of complex units out of already observed simple ones (Richards & Bernal, 1972).
11. Indices as units	Composed of various indicators drawn together. Mentioned more frequently in the sociological literature than in the psychological literature.
12. Reductionist	These are the result of finding the smallest unit of meaning, not necessarily the smallest observable unit. To be meaningful, it must have a particular meaning for the observer or evoke a particular response in a partner.
13. Causal	Behaviors with a common cause are regarded as identical.
14. Functional	A unit defined with respect to its effect or context. The emphasis is on the importance of the context.
15. Situations as units	If one is concerned with behavior which is to some extent rule bound and has recurrent elements, then situations can be viewed as units. More precisely such a unit should be comprised of both situation and behavior. Barker and Wright (1955) regard their "behavior setting" as such a unit.
16. Molecular	
17. Molar	Both terms are taken from Barker and Wright (1955). Molecular units are known as actones and molar units are actions (e.g., molecular: perspiration; molar: hurrying to school).
18. Time units	These refer to time intervals of time-sampling methods and to any time-derived measures used for behavior observation.
19. Action units or events	Conceptually similar to behavior unit and natural units, but is distinguished by its form and content.

Note. Adapted from *Theory and Practice of Observing Behavior* (pp. 76–81) by G. Fassnacht, 1982, London: Academic Press. Copyright 1982 by Academic Press. Reprinted by permission.

Substantively, what is important is that students are part of a class collective, which raises issues about what the proper unit should be; the individual, the group, or some other unit of analysis. We will have more to say about units of analysis shortly.

Third, classrooms endure for long periods of time. Most classrooms are open for 5–7 hours a day, five days a week, for much of the year. In the United States, the length of school years has been relatively standardized across states to about 180 school days. Other countries, notably Japan, have

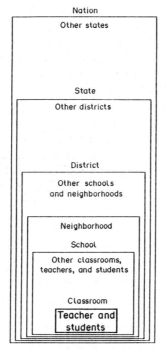

FIG 4.2   The "nesting" of the classrooms within larger organizational units

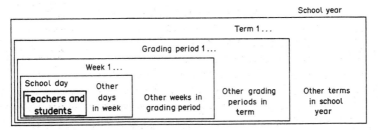

FIG 4.3   The "nesting" of the school day within the school year.

much longer school years. In any case, the question is how much of this classroom time will be studied and will it be enough time to examine the phenomena of interest. Figure 4.3 presents a temporal rather than structural view of the classroom based on typical United States school year. Classroom work occurs during daily lessons within a week during one of the four grading periods in one of the two terms during the year.

   The way time is usually treated in classroom research is to ignore it. Classroom observational data, for example, are usually collected on multiple occasions and then averaged over occasions. Yet such averaging ignores contextual influences on teacher behavior, and in effect, assumes that context does not matter. This assumption is often incorrect (see, for example, Mandeville, 1984). Figure 4.4, from Gump (1971), gives one example of how context is maintained. The figure depicts an entire day in a third-grade classroom from Gump's (1967) study described in Chapter 10. Each of the instructional segments for the day is indicated by brackets, a segment being a block of time with a definite concern and purpose. Note that a number of segments occur simultaneously, especially during the morning when the teacher works with reading groups and the remainder of the class does individual seatwork.

That classrooms are complex settings that exist in a multilevel organizational structure and extend over long periods of time make them particularly difficult to conceptualize. Because of the importance of conceptual frameworks in the development of sound research designs, we shall briefly mention a set of issues that educational researchers have raised about conceptualizing classrooms. These issues have typically been raised under the rubric "levels of analysis" or "units of analysis." An in-depth discussion of these issues is beyond the scope of the book. The interested reader may wish to consult Cronbach (1976), Burstein (1980, 1987), Treiber (1981), Oosthoek and Van Den Eeden (1983), and Bryk and Raudenbush (1987).

The issues surrounding levels or units of analysis arise from several sources and encompass complex methodological, theoretical, and statistical concerns. One source of concern arises from the problem of cross-level inference and aggregation bias; those situations where relations demonstrated at one level of analysis are used to infer associations at another level

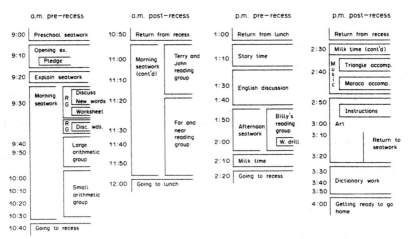

FIG 4.4   A day in Mrs. Carr's third-grade class: A segmental map (from Gump, 1971).
Reprinted by permission of the publisher from Gump, Paul V., 'What's Happening in the Elementary Classroom' in Westbury, I., & Bellack, A. A., *Research into Classroom Processes: Recent Developments & Next Steps* (New York: Teachers College Press, © 1971 by Teachers College, Columbia University. All rights reserved.), p. 160.

of analysis. Perhaps the simplest illustration of this problem is the well-documented fact that the correlation coefficient between mean scores on two variables (e.g., class averages on an aptitude test and an achievement test) is not usually equal to the correlation correction between the pairs of individual student test scores. Thus, there can be a bias involved in making individual-level inferences from class-level date (or vice versa).

In view of these known differences in results, a second concern has to do with choosing the "proper" unit for statistical analysis of the data. Should data collected across classrooms be analyzed using the class or the individual student as the unit of analysis? One approach to the problem is to use multiple units of analysis. Clark et al. (1979), for example, analyzed their data at both the student-level and the class- (or, more appropriately, half-class) level. Barr and Dreeben (1983) added another wrinkle by including "reading group" as a third unit of analysis in addition to the class and the individual student.

In contrast to conducting multiple analyses, arguments can be made for the inclusion of one unit of analysis rather than another (Burstein, 1980). These arguments can be made either on disciplinary or statistical grounds. Sociologists tend to study collectives of individuals and often suggest group-level units of analysis. They would argue, for example, that classroom treatments are applied to all students in a class or group, not to individuals. In contrast, psychologists often argue for individual students as units of analysis. They would argue that individual students respond to classroom treatments as individuals.

Traditional statistical procedures dictate that the unit of analysis be the "smallest divisions of the collection of experimental subjects that have been randomly assigned to the different conditions in the experiment *and* that have responded independently of each other for the duration of the experiment" (Glass and Stanley, 1970, p. 506). From this point of view, independence of response is crucial. Sampling theory requires that the units of analysis not be influenced by other experimental units, at least not in ways that will influence the dependent variable. Thus, the Glass and Stanley definition requires that treatments involving teaching methods applied to intact classrooms, for example, use class mean scores and not the individual student scores as the "proper" unit of analysis since students in a classroom are usually not treated independently. For example, a teacher who gives a confusing answer or provides a particular insightful example affects every student in the class. Of course, the loss of degrees of freedom (in the statistical sense) when the class rather than the individual is used as the unit of analysis is sometimes used as an argument for using the student as the unit of analysis.

Those following the multilevel perspective suggest that focusing on disciplinary or statistical rationales as opposed to substantive concerns is misleading. Burstein (1987), a leading proponent of the multilevel perspective, summarizes this issue well:

> A multilevel perspective shifts the investigative focus toward the development of
> adequate theories of educational processes and analytical strategies for assessing their
> effects. The multilevel structure of the data is not merely a nuisance; it reflects reality.
> What is needed is an appropriate model of the educational phenomena of interest and
> analytic strategies that disentangle effects from a variety of sources so that the interface
> of the individuals and the "groups" to which they belong and the implications of this
> interface for educational effects can be examined (p. 159).

From the multilevel perspective, then, the issue is not choosing the "proper" unit of analysis but rather how to best conceptualize the phenomena in ways that will answer the questions addressed. Burstein (1980), for example, presents an example of how individual-level, reading group-level, and class-level analyses can be done simultaneously and in a way that avoids aggregation bias. As another example, Barr and Dreeben (1983) present an analysis that conceptualizes schooling as consisting of four organizational levels—district, school, class, and instructional group—that are "nested, hierarchical layers, each having a conditional and contributory relation to events and outcomes occurring at adjacent ones" (p. 7). Their reanalyses of Barr's (1973/74, 1975) data on reading groups, instructional pacing, and student achievement attempts to relate these different levels of schooling and show how they influence student learning.

Plan of Study

It is commonly assumed that asking research questions is the creative part of the study and designing the plan is merely the technical part. This is simply not the case. While it is true that formulating the problem to study is an important and creative aspect of any research effort, the same can be said of the plan of the study. There are many ways to gather evidence on a question, and how a researcher decides to collect data is as much a creative act as the framing of the research questions in the first place. The diversity of research studies exhibited in this book attests to this observation.

A research plan is a blueprint for organizing evidence. The plan outlines how the evidence will be sampled, gathered, and analyzed. The plan will determine, in part, how well the questions under study will be addressed. The evidence gathered during a study is given meaning by the conceptual framework, but an existing conceptual framework can only do so much. The research plan must be such that the evidence gathered allows the researcher to modify existing frameworks and develop new ones.

A research plan, then, outlines the evidential base of a research study. An excellent example of such a plan, taken from a study by Bennett (1976), is shown in Figure 4.5. The primary questions under study were whether differences in teaching styles used by teachers were associated with differences in pupil achievement, and whether this association, if it existed,

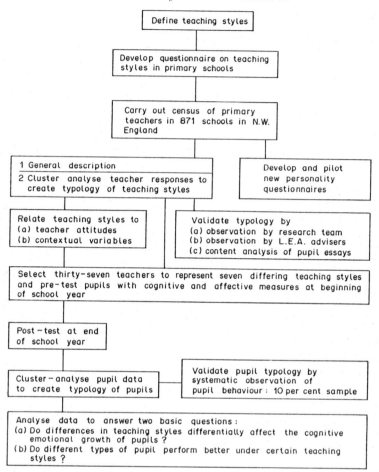

Fig 4.5 Simplified research design (from Bennett, 1976).

was the same for pupils of different personality types. In light of these questions, Bennett obviously had to first define, measure, and "validate" what was meant by "teaching style." This general activity takes us through the top half of Figure 4.5. Next, Bennett had to define, measure, and "validate" what was meant by "pupil personality type" and assess pupil achievement. Once all of the evidence was at hand, Bennett had to analyze the evidence relative to the two primary research questions. These activities complete Figure 4.5.

The Bennett study is an example of a research plan from a study following the confirmatory mode of inquiry (Chapter 3). In many ways, confirmatory studies are easy to "map out" schematically because they typically follow procedures sequentially. Their research designs are thought out in advance, and researchers seldom vary from the plan, if at all, as data are being collected. Interpretive studies, on the other hand, are not easy to schematicize. Their research designs are flexible, being modified as data are collected, insights gained, and questions formulated. The research plan evolves as the researcher learns about the phenomenon being studied. Even the research questions are often discovered during data collection rather than defined beforehand as they were in the Bennett study.

There is another reason it is difficult to schematicize research design in interpretive inquiry. Discussions of research design by interpretive researchers often employ analogy to characterize the design process. Thus, Bogdan and Biklen (1982) characterize the design of case studies as a *funnel*. The wide opening of the funnel is the beginning of the study as the researcher explores and discovers the phenomena and the design is continually being modified. Eventually, the questions develop a focus, the narrow end of the funnel, and data collection becomes more directive. Green (1983) uses the analogy of a *microscope*, where the power of the microscope is modified by changing lens. The interpretive researcher does the same, shifting lens, and "moving backward and forward across settings, bits of information, and in some instances, phenomena, exploring the part-whole/whole-part relationship between bits and larger patterns" (p. 192). Guba (1978) characterizes interpretive inquiry as a cyclic *wave* of alternating modes of discovery and verification, where researchers first allow the categories of the phenomenon to emerge from experience with the phenomena and then to develop hunches or hypotheses that can be tested in a more focused collection of data.

There are not many examples of research plans in interpretive inquiry comparable to that of Bennett. Figure 4.6 presents the design developed by Green (1983) to describe a study by Cook-Gumperz, Simons, and Gumperz (1981). Cook-Gumperz et al. were interested in exploring communication strategies in classrooms. The purpose of their "exploratory" study was to identify how differences in teachers and students' communication strategies affect the evaluation of student performance and student motivation to learn. A single classroom was studied for an entire school year by two researchers who participated as teacher aides in the classroom. They described their strategy as the "typical case method," divided into four stages:

1. gathering ethnographic information on the school setting, the classroom interaction, on students' cultural and family background and peer networks,
2. selection of key episodes,
3. conversational analysis of episodes,
4. search for further comparative ethnographic data and conversational data to test the assumptions about intent and findings of communicative stategies at work from the selection and analysis of key episodes. (p. 3).

While we have some misgivings about the actual Cook-Gumperz study, and the design depicted in Figure 4.6 seems overly rationalized given the

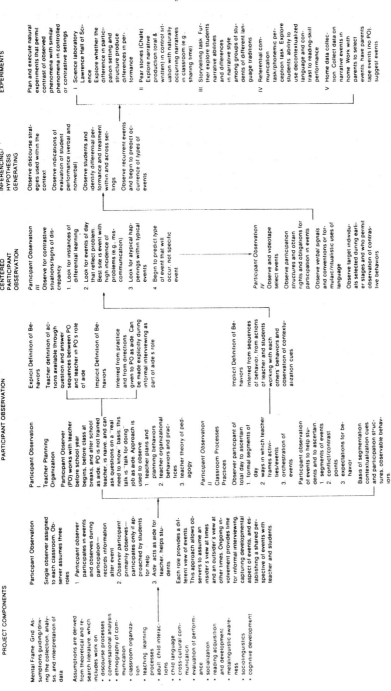

FIG 4.6 Design of the Cook-Gumperz et al. school/home ethnography project (from Evertson and Green, 1986).

relatively incomplete description of methodology in the actual final report, it does illustrate the "funneling" of observation and inquiry as the researcher becomes more familiar with the phenomenon under investigation. According to the figure, early observation of the teacher prior to the beginning of the school year and during instruction in Stage 2 gives way to more focused observation and the videotaping of selected events during Stage 3. The focused observation and videotape analyses yield hypotheses (Stage 4) that are then tested with "natural experiments" in Stage 5. The natural experiments were characterized by Cook-Gumperz et al. as "staged situations, which replicated naturally occurring behavior under more controlled conditions and which enabled us to test predictions from earlier ethnographic observation" (p. 17). Thus, in the "science laboratory" experiment, one fourth-grade student's behavior was observed in two settings—in the classroom and during a field trip to a local science center with a "biology discovery room." Based on their observations, they conclude that "the same behaviors defined in one setting as 'immaturity,' 'disruptedness' and 'inability to focus attention' are seen as 'curiosity,' 'creativity' and 'strong exploratory tendencies' in the other setting" (Schafer, 1981).

Elements of the Research Plan

The schematic representations of the Bennett and Cook-Gumperz et al. studies illustrate what is meant by a research plan. The plan outlines how the evidence will be sampled, what the sources of evidence will be, how meaning will be derived from the evidence, and how the evidence will be analyzed and ultimately interpreted relative to the research questions. In the following sections we describe briefly these four elements, with the sampling of evidence being discussed in somewhat greater detail. Separate chapters on sources of evidence, the meaning of evidence, and the analysis of evidence follow this chapter.

Sampling of Evidence

One of the important decisions that must be made by a researcher is what unit or units are to be sampled. As we discussed earlier in the section on conceptual frameworks, what units will be sampled largely depends on how the researcher conceptualizes the phenomenon and for what purpose the researcher samples.

Consider the Goodlad (1984) study of schools, mentioned above and discussed in detail in Chapter 9. The Goodlad study is one of the largest, if not the largest, observational studies ever done in classrooms. Observational data were obtained on 129 elementary and 887 secondary classrooms, an enormous undertaking. Here we are only interested in the sampling plan for selecting these 1,016 classrooms (see Overman, 1979).

The sampling plan included grade levels 1–12, where schools were selected in "triples." Classrooms were then selected for observation from the schools. A "triple" included a senior high school, the feeder junior high school with the largest number of students going to that high school, and the feeder elementary school with the largest number of students going to that junior high school. Original plans called for two "triples" to be selected from each of 12 states, the states selected to represent geographic regions in the United States. Four stratification variables, school size (large and small), socioeconomic status (middle and low), location (metropolitan and rural), and race/ethnicity (predominantly white, predominantly non-white, and mixed), created an idealized 24 cell sampling plan ($2 \times 2 \times 2 \times 3$) for selecting the 24 "triples," or 72 schools.

The plan was not realistic for two reasons. First, the sampling plan called for the selection of some schools that do not occur frequently in the population. Second, funding restrictions limited the number of "triples" that could be selected. Attention shifted to the selection of schools that were representative of *common types* of schools—school types based on size, location, and race/ethnicity.

As it turned out, five "triples" were studied in the spring, 1977, and an additional eight during the fall, 1977. Figure 4.7, taken from Goodlad, outlines the sampling plan of the study. The 13 "triples" were located in seven states representing seven major regions in the country, with two "triples" per state except for one state with only one "triple." At the secondary level, classrooms were selected so that eight subject areas were represented. At the elementary level, two classrooms were randomly selected from each grade level. All these classrooms were observed. Surveys were mailed to every family at each school. Questionnaires were administered to every teacher at each school. In addition, questionnaires were administered to all students in the selected classes. Interviews were conducted with the teachers of the sampled classrooms.

Now consider another study, that of Leacock (1969). The Leacock study was a descriptive, anthropological examination of "what is being imparted to children in ordinary, city school classrooms" as well as potential differences between white and black lower-income and middle-income classrooms. Initiated in the late 1960s when considerable attention was directed to the inequality of educational experiences of minority children, this study addressed the subtle ways in which differential expectations are held for students and how students are socialized for adult roles. A team of eleven anthropologists, educators, and psychologists collected observational, interview, and questionnaire data from second- and fifth-grade teachers and students at four schools.

The sampling plan in the Leacock study was *purposeful.* Purposeful

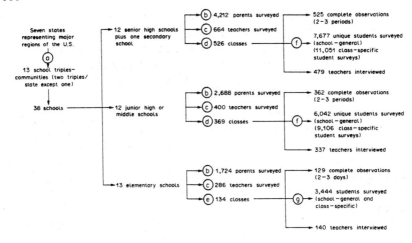

sampling is a deliberate attempt to sample specific groups or individuals so that the sample is representative of that group or type of individual. Purposeful sampling often allows the researcher to concentrate resources on a few cases when resources are limited. This occurred in the Leacock study, for example, because their decision to study the classrooms selected in detail prevented them from studying any more than the eight classrooms in the four schools. This also occurred in the Goodlad study, although it is less obvious because of the size of the sample.

Given Leacock's interest in comparing the educational experiences of black and white students, certain types of schools were required. Two major social groupings in the public schools were used to select the four schools of this study: low-income black, low-income white, middle-income black, and middle-income white. Schools serving these four populations were selected at random from the New York public schools. Schools that were at least 95 percent black or white were located on a map with neighborhood income levels, based on census data, marked as low, middle, or high. Free lunch data were also inspected to help match black and white schools on income level. Once the schools were selected (one school was rejected and only used for pilot work when it was found to practice heterogeneous classroom grouping), a second- and fifth-grade classroom at each school were picked for study. Since all the schools practiced homogeneous grouping or "tracking," as we now call it, the classrooms were selected from the "middle" classroom group at each grade level and school.

Both these examples, Goodlad and Leacock, are examples of purposeful sampling with relatively few schools. Both researchers were cognizant of the fact that random sampling or stratified random sampling would not be possible or would not help them answer their research questions. [Random sampling is the process of selecting units from a well-defined population in such a way that each unit has an equal probability of being selected. When random sampling is used, then sampling theory allows the researcher to generalize the findings from the sample to the population].

Both Goodlad and Leacock faced a crucial issue in their decisions about sampling. Given that resources are typically limited, the researcher is always faced with gathering fewer data on more "units" or more data on fewer "units." This breadth versus depth trade-off is one that most studies must confront (see, for example, Patton, 1980, pp. 97–99). Both Goodlad and Leacock felt it more important to gather extensive data about fewer schools, schools being the "sampling unit" in both studies. Both researchers sacrificed generalizability (breadth) for extensiveness (depth).

In classroom research sampling is often some combination of an initial non-random sampling of schools, classrooms, or teachers and a subsequent partitioning of the sample into contrasting groups. The initial non-random sampling is most often a function of convenience and reflects the difficulty of securing a random sample. The partitioning of the sample into contrasting groups is done so that the two groups can be compared on one or more variables of interest to the researcher.

A fairly typical approach to sampling is used in much of the teacher effectiveness research. A sample of teachers is identified in a non-random manner. Two contrasting groups of teachers are formed from this sample based on some indicator of their effectiveness (e.g., student test scores, nominations by supervisors). These two groups are then compared on any variety of personal or professional characteristics, beliefs and perceptions, or classroom behaviors and interactions.

A more concrete example of this approach to sampling can be found in

Phase III-A of the Beginning Teacher Evaluation Study (BTES) (Berliner, Filby, Marliave, Moore, and Tikunoff, 1976). The primary purpose of Phase III-A was to develop the methodology to be used during Phase III-B (which is described in some detail in Chapter 10). The emphasis in the study was on reading and mathematics.

The sampling process began by having teachers volunteer to participate in the study. Almost two hundred second- and fifth-grade classrooms taught by these teachers were included in the study. These classrooms were located in urban, suburban, and rural schools in eleven school districts. From this sample of approximately 200 teachers (and their classrooms), the researchers wanted to identify two groups of relatively more and less effective teachers. The problem was simply, "On what basis should the two groups of teachers be selected?"

To solve this problem, the researchers developed a set of four "Experimental Teaching Units" (or ETUs), one ETU for each of the grade level-subject matter combinations. ETUs were two-week instructional units to be taught by all 200 teachers. Each ETU contained a list of unit objectives, a set of instructional materials and activities, and pre- and posttests. The ETUs controlled the curricular content and overall instructional time, thereby permitting some experimental control in a naturalistic setting.

Each teacher taught the two ETUs appropriate for his or her grade level. Student test scores (actual posttest scores minus posttest scores predicted from the pretest scores) were used to identify the two groups of teachers. Twenty teachers whose students scored far better than expected based on their pretest scores were selected as more effective teachers. Likewise, twenty teachers whose students scored far more poorly than expected were selected as less effective teachers.

Closely related to purposeful sampling is the concept of theoretical sampling and the logic of grounded theory that was introduced in Chapter 3 (Glaser and Strauss, 1967). In theoretical sampling, the research plan emerges as the researcher learns more about the phenomenon under investigation and begins to ask more focused questions. As the questions crystallize, the researcher samples "units" from the phenomenon (e.g., the classrooms) so that additional information can be obtained and emerging hypotheses can be tested. This process of continually redirecting attention to various features of the phenomenon and modifying the sampling of units as the study progresses is termed "theoretical sampling."

Sources of Evidence

From one perspective, researchers are fairly limited as to what they can do to gather evidence about a phenomenon. They can observe persons, settings, or situations (that is, the interaction of persons and settings). They can ask people to be interviewed or to complete tests, surveys, or questionnaires. They can collect documents and artifacts. Observe, ask, and collect; these are the behaviors of researchers. But the apparent simplicity of these three means of gathering evidence belies their potential for complexity.

When researchers decide to use observation to gather their evidence, they have a number of systems and instruments at their disposal. They can use structured observation systems. Such systems include the concepts and categories on which to focus attention and ask the observer to note or record when instances of each concept or category occurs. Researchers can use rating scales. Rating scales also include concepts or dimension on which observers are expected to focus their attention. Rather than record the frequency or occurrence of instances of each concept, however, they are asked to make an overall rating about the concept on a five-point or seven-point scale (e.g., from apathetic to alert). Researchers can take audiotape recorders into the classroom, tape all of the verbal interaction between teachers and students, and have the tape transcribed. Researchers can take legal pads into the classroom and make extensive notes on objects or events in which they are interested. Once the researcher decides to observe, the next decision then is how to observe.

When researchers choose asking as their means of collecting evidence, they also have additional choices to make. They may conduct face-to-face interviews, or they may distribute questionnaires. They may choose to force people to select one of several options in response to their questions, or they may simply permit people to respond as they deem appropriate. They may choose to show a portion of a videotape recording and ask questions about it. They may choose to submit people to a formal testing situation.

Finally, when researchers choose to collect documents or exhibits (e.g., curriculum materials, lesson plans, photographs of classrooms, or instructional equipment), they also must make several decisions. How can I secure the documents or exhibits that I need? How do I know they are authentic? How do I classify or otherwise make sense of the documents I have acquired? A detailed discussion of observing, asking, and collecting existing evidence is presented in Chapter 5.

The Meaning of Evidence

Previously, we have suggested that meaning is a relational concept. This assertion implies that the meaning of a concept or proposition is derived from its relationships with other concepts or propositions. As Rychlak (1968) points out, the realistic interpretation of meaning "presumes that these relationships are ultimately to be found in nature, independent of the theorist's intellect" (p. 43). On the other hand, the idealistic interpretation of meaning "holds that such relations are provided more or less by a reasoning intelligence, and that reality need *never* have a set ordering of relations on which to base lasting and unchanging meanings" (p. 43).

The realistic-idealistic dichotomy—whether the world is composed of fixed and stable "objects" with inherent meanings independent of the perceiver or the world is composed of multiple realities "constructed" idiosyncratically by perceivers—raises fundamental issues concerning reality, truth, and the methodology best suited to deriving meaning (see, for example, Lincoln and Guba, 1985, Chapter 4; Patton, 1980, Chapter 8). Whether researchers discover or create meaning in the world, and how best to discover or create meaning, were basic issues separating the two modes of inquiry discussed in Chapter 3.

Regardless of where the researcher positions himself or herself in terms of the dichotomy, two points are essential. First, the connection of novel concepts and propositions—"real" or "imagined"—with familiar concepts and propositions provides meaning to the novel concepts and propositions. Second, and as a consequence of the first, evidence derives meaning from its connectedness to familiar concepts and propositions, the kind of concepts and propositions included in the researcher's conceptual framework. Whether a researcher engages in observation, question asking, or document collection, the evidence derived from these sources must be linked with the researcher's conceptual framework if it is to be meaningful.

Given that meaning is derived from the evidence in some fashion, we as researchers must have some assurance that the evidence is of sufficient quality to ascribe meaning to it. How do we know that the evidence obtained from observation represents what actually transpired in the classroom? How do we know that actual responses made by a teacher to a set of interview questions are congruent with the notes made by the interviewer? How can we be sure that the documents received from a school principal are authentic? These are all issues concerning the quality of the evidence. These issues must be addressed before any meaning is ascribed to the evidence.

Researchers have several strategies at their disposal for estimating or examining the quality of the evidence. Several of these strategies are associated with the time-honored measurement concepts of validity, reliability, and objectivity. Other strategies, such as triangulation, are attempts to examine the consistency of evidence derived from different sources (e.g., methods, instruments, perspectives). When corroborative evidence results from multiple sources, the quality of the evidence is enhanced. When the evidence is inconsistent or contradictory, the burden is placed on the researcher to deal with the inconsistencies and contradictions in such a way as to "construct meaningful propositions about the social world" (Mathison, 1988, p. 15).

For evidence to be useful in classroom research it must be meaningful and of sufficient quality. A more indepth discussion of the meaning and quality of evidence is presented in Chapter 6.

Analysis of Evidence

The last step in the research process is the analysis of evidence (or as it is more commonly labeled at this step, data). Just as meaning involves connecting the evidence to the conceptual framework, analysis is a means by which the evidence is linked to the purpose of the study. Thus, the results of analysis are descriptions of the features of the phenomenon and their variation, and estimates of the associations between or among features.

To many people, analysis is the part of the research process that most clearly differentiates confirmatory from interpretive inquiry. While in some ways this belief is valid, there are at least two reasons why it does not hold in all situations. First, while procedurally it is possible to separate confirmatory from interpretive modes of inquiry, as we did in Chapter 3, many studies mix elements of both modes of inquiry and thus blur the distinction between the two. Second, although analytic techniques can be neatly separated into those that pertain to words (qualitative data) and those that pertain to numbers (quantitative data), it turns out that words and numbers are not as different as they initially appear to be in terms of the information they convey. Let us elaborate on each of these two points.

In confirmatory studies, the collection and analysis of data are sequential steps. Data are first collected and then analyzed using statistical techniques determined before the studies begin. In interpretive studies, on the other hand, data collection and data analysis are often simultaneous activities, with analysis occurring as the data are collected and often influencing future data collection. In these studies it usually is impossible to say where collection ends and analysis begins. Thus, procedurally, in terms of research design, it is possible to distinguish confirmatory inquiry from interpretive inquiry.

In our discussion thus far, however, we have outlined "pure" forms of these two modes of inquiry. Researchers often mix elements of the two modes depending on their research questions. Patton (1980) uses a chart to illustrate this point (see Figure 4.8).

Patton uses different names for what we have termed the confirmatory and interpretive modes of inquiry. His hypothetical-deductive paradigm with an emphasis on experimental design is consistent with our confirmatory mode of inquiry, and his pure holistic-inductive paradigm with an emphasis on naturalistic inquiry is consistent with our interpretive mode.

Figure 4.8 illustrates how both qualitative and quantitative data can be collected within each paradigm and how qualitative data can be treated as words (using content analysis) or numbers (using statistical analysis). Quantitative data are numbers, by definition. Six types of studies can be derived from Figure 4.8 (e.g., a study in the hypothetical-deductive paradigm that begins with experimental design collects qualitative data, and performs a content analysis on the data). Only two of these six types of

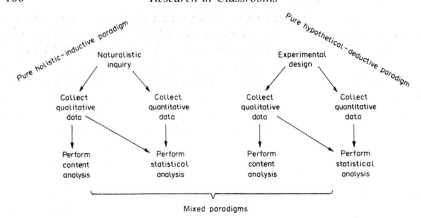

Mixed paradigms

Fig 4.8   Measurement, design, and analysis: Pure and mixed combinations.
From Patten (1980) *Qualitative Evaluation Methods,* pp. 115 © Sage
Publications. Reprinted by permission of Sage Publications Inc.

studies are "pure" studies of the two paradigms (i.e., naturalistic inquiry
with qualitative data and content analysis, and experimental design with
quantitative data and statistical analysis).

In addition to the mixing of elements from both modes of inquiry, it is
also true that numbers and words are not as different as they may appear
at first glance. It is often forgotten that words can and often do convey
quantity. Meehl (1986) makes this point forcefully:

> It is necessary to think clearly about words and to realize that many of the words—I
> would say most words—both in ordinary language and in scholarly discourse that
> purport to explain anything are quantity words intrinsically. . . . When a social scientist
> speaks of something—anything, a tribal custom or suicide tendencies or unconscious
> memories or a white rat's lever-pressing disposition—he typically uses words like
> "always," "frequently," "rarely," "never," "oddly," "weakly," "under special circum-
> stances," "mostly." Every single one of these words is a claim of the degree to which
> some force or entity exists or influences; every single one indicates a frequency or
> probability with which something happens or the magnitude of a disposition (propen-
> sity). It is foolish for social scientists to try to get away from this simple fact about the
> descriptive language of their disciplines. The question is, What are the circumstances
> under which it pays off at a given state of knowledge to re-express these quantity words
> of ordinary English in explicitly numerical form? (p. 320).

The analysis of the evidence is a critical part of the research process since
analysis links the evidence with the original research questions. In Chapter
7 we discuss in greater detail the options researchers have and the decisions
they must make in the analysis of data.

Interpreting Results: A Postscript

Classroom researchers can plan how they intend to sample evidence,
collect evidence, derive meaning from the evidence (in terms of its
relationship with the conceptual framework), and analyze the evidence (in

terms of its relationship with the research questions). Although they cannot technically plan their interpretation of the results of the study, they would be wise to give some thought to issues of interpretation at the outset. Interpretation is a complicated process which involves, directly, the credibility of the knowledge claims made by the researcher and the generalizability of these knowledge claims and, indirectly, the motivations of the researcher. In this final section of this chapter we shall outline some of the issues in interpreting the results of classroom research studies.

The "Fit" Between Hypotheses and Evidence

Either at the beginning of a study or during the conduct of the study researchers begin to speculate on what they expect to "find" as they examine the various features of the phenomenon they are studying. These speculations, which may be explicit or implicit, are technically termed "hypotheses." At the end of the study, they compare these speculations (the hypotheses) with their findings (the evidence) to determine the closeness or "goodness" of the "fit." In the confirmational mode of inquiry, the goodness of fit is typically determined by some test of statistical significance. In the interpretive mode, the fit is determined by a logical analysis of the evidence.

If the fit is considered to be a "good fit," the researcher can feel comfortable in making his or her knowledge claims. If the fit is considered to be a "poor fit," the researcher typically has several options to consider some of which still allow him or her to make knowledge claims. The options available to the researcher are displayed graphically in Figure 4.9. In order to help explain Figure 4.9, we shall use an example.

Suppose a researcher is interested in examining the relationship between the amount of structure that teachers provide to their students and the amount that the students actually learn. The researcher believes that more structure will result in greater learning. Six observations are made in each of 28 teachers' classrooms. Six different observers are used in the study, with each observer responsible for one observation in each of the 28 classrooms.

Prior to the observations, all of the students in these classrooms are administered the same achievement test. After the last observation, some eighteen weeks later, the same achievement test is readministered. Midway through the observations, the students are administered a questionnaire that includes a series of questions about their teachers (including the amount of structure the teachers provide). Furthermore, during their visits to the classrooms, observers collect copies of instructional materials used by the teachers and assignments given to the students.

A composite measure of structure for each teacher is formed based on the

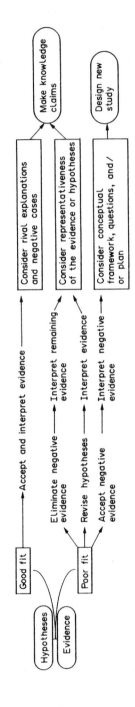

FIG 4.9   Examining and Interpreting the "fit" between the hypotheses and the evidence.

observers' reports and the students' responses to the questionnaire. The average pretest score and posttest score is computed for each teacher. The average posttest scores are then adjusted for differences in the pretest scores. Finally, a correlation between the composite measure of structure and the adjusted posttest scores is computed.

At this point in the discussion, let us return to Figure 4.9. The left-hand side of the figure represents the researcher's comparison between the hypotheses and the evidence and the determination of the degree of "fit" between the two. Suppose in the example the correlation between the composite measure of structure and the adjusted posttest scores was moderate and statistically significant. Thus, the researcher declared a "good fit" between his hypothesis and the evidence. As can be seen in Figure 4.9, the researcher then accepts the evidence (top row) and moves on to make his or her knowledge claim.

Before making the knowledge claim, however, the researcher should consider rival explanations (e.g., alternative hypotheses that also would fit the data) and examine negative cases (which may have produced a lack of a perfect fit). Again, using the example, suppose the researcher in examining the materials and assignments collected by the observers notices that much of the content included on the materials and assignments in some of the classrooms was directly related to the achievement test, while in other classrooms very little of the content was related to the achievement test. Furthermore, the teachers with the highest measures of structure also were those that taught more of the content aligned with the achievement test. A plausible alternative explanation for the result of the study is that the match between the content taught and content tested, not the amount of structure provided by the teacher, was the reason for the correlation between teacher structure and student achievement.

Similarly, in comparing the records made by the four observers in each of the classrooms, one observer's records are quite different from the records made by the other observers in 20 of the 28 classrooms. Furthermore, when that observer's records are eliminated and the composite measure of teacher structure is re-estimated, the correlation between teacher structure and student achievement is somewhat higher.

On the other hand, suppose that the researcher, when examining the scatterplot of the relationship between teacher structure and student achievement (see Chapter 3 for examples of scatterplots), notices that most of the teachers in the sample provided a great deal of structure. In fact, 25 of the 28 teachers cluster together on the teacher structure dimension. The remaining teachers, however, provided very little structure according to the composite rating of observers and students. Furthermore, these three teachers have students with very low adjusted mean posttest scores. If these three teachers are dropped from the analysis and the correlation coefficient is computed based on the other 25 teachers, the correlation between teacher structure and student achievement is virtually zero. In essence, the "moderate and statistically significant" correlation is the result of three quite deviant teachers (or "outliers," as the frequently are termed).

If researchers can rule out alternative explanations, provide reasonable accounts for negative cases that may have arisen during an examination of the evidence, or both, they have a stronger case for making their knowledge claims.

In contrast to the situation in which there is a good fit between the hypotheses and the evidence, where interpretation is relatively straightforward, the case of poor fit requires some elaboration. We can think of three possible reasons for the lack of fit. First, some of the evidence may be problematic (e.g., of questionable objectivity or validity). In the above example, suppose that the correlation between teacher structure and student achievement was initially non-significant (e.g., non-fitting). Eliminating the records made by the one observer may have resulted in a better fit (e.g., a fit that was statistically significant) which can then be interpreted. Quite obviously, however, the generalizability or representativeness of the knowledge claims is reduced.

Second, the hypotheses may need to be revised somewhat, although not totally discarded. In our earlier example, the definition of teacher structure may need to be expanded to include both *what* is structured (the content) as well as *how* it is structured (the behavior exhibited by the teacher). This expanded definition (which in fact results in a revision of the hypothesis) will likely increase the fit between the original hypothesis and the evidence.

Hypotheses can also be revised as the evidence is collected (rather than after it has been collected). Such revision is a typical qualitative strategy based on the notion of emergent research design mentioned previously. While proponents of these strategies argue that fitting hypotheses to the data is critical for the development of grounded theory, critics charge that such strategies capitalize on chance findings. More will be said about this issue in Chapter 7.

One final point should be made before moving to the next issue. If hypotheses are modified to fit the existing evidence, the representativeness (or, conversely, the context-specificity) of the knowledge claims is once again called into question. The hypotheses may well describe or explain the current evidence, but one cannot be certain that future evidence will support or confirm the hypotheses. As a consequence, modifications of hypotheses should lead to somewhat tentative knowledge claims and be the impetus for new studies or another round of data collection.

Third, the negative evidence and the lack of fit can be accepted as indicating a legitimate failure of the evidence to support the hypotheses. If, for example, the data indicate no relationship between teacher structure and student achievement, and attempts to eliminate negative evidence or to formulate alternative hypotheses are unsuccessful, the researcher may choose to simply accept the apparent fact that teacher structure and student achievement are independent. For many researchers this is a bitter pill to swallow since their original interest in the study stemmed from their belief that such a relationship did exist. Nonetheless, when a lack of fit is simply accepted, the researcher goes "back to the drawing board." The conceptual framework, research questions, and research plan are re-examined in an attempt to find a starting point for a new study or series of studies.

Once a knowledge claim has been advanced by a researcher, it becomes "public" and open to scrutiny by other members of the research community. Thus, the researcher must be ready to argue in support of his or her knowledge claims.

> Believing that one has found a pattern or relationship, one now seeks to interpret for others the evidence that the pattern or relationship exists and that, in contrast to plausible alternatives, the explanation being advanced in the best one. This is the confirmation phase; one has a claim one wishes to be considered true, to be fact, to be knowledge. There are conventions and expectations about how such a knowledge claim is made. One expectation is that as closely reasoned an argument as possible will be presented, including an examination of the cases for the strongest alternative explanations and the cases against them (Krathwohl, 1985, p. 31).

Krathwohl goes on to describe two sets of criteria by which closely reasoned arguments are to be judged, regardless of whether the arguments are confirmatory or interpretive in nature. He labels these two sets of criteria "linking power" and "generalizing power," building on the existing methodological concepts of internal validity and external validity.

Linking Power and Internal Validity

Outside of purely descriptive studies, Krathwohl argues that research studies attempt to establish the linkage between or among phenomena or the features of a phenomenon. Teacher effectiveness research, for example, attempts to establish relationships between teacher characteristics or teacher behaviors and some indicator of effectiveness. The extent to which a study convincingly demonstrates that the relationships exist is what Krathwohl terms the "linking power" of the study. Has the validity of the design of the study been sufficiently established to make knowledge claims? Are the data trustworthy? Does the researcher present a credible case for his or her interpretation of the evidence? Have rival explanations for the results of the study been considered and ruled out? Answers to these questions are needed to establish linking power.

Internal validity is the concept on which Krathwohl builds his notions of linking power. Campbell and Stanley (1963), in their classic paper on research design, defined internal validity in the form of a question. "Did in fact the experimental treatments make a difference in this specific experimental instance?" (p. 175). They suggested that design features such as the use of control groups, random assignment, multiple baselines, and time series would help a research eliminate rival explanations. More than anything else, the elimination of rival explanations has become the *sine qua non* of internal validity and research design.

Krathwohl (1985) outlines five specific criteria, written as a set of questions, to be used in judging the linking power or internal validity of a study. These questions are paraphrased below.

1. Are the relationships to be demonstrated plausible?
2. Does the study provide for true examples of the relationships?
3. Does the study actually demonstrate the relationships?
4. Are there other reasonable explanations to account for the results of the study?
5. Are the results credible in view of past research and the answers to the above four questions?

In planning studies and interpreting the results of the study, classroom researchers would be wise to remember these five questions.

Generalizing Power and External Validity

The generalizing power of a study refers to the extent to which the results are representative of the results found in other settings, with other people, and at other times. Usually the results of a particular study are important only in that they can be generalized to a broader class of results. Even those researchers who are interested in studying a single classroom tend to believe that what they learn about this classroom pertains or applies to some larger class of classrooms. Campbell and Stanley (1963) have used the term "external validity" to refer to the generalizing power of the study.

Krathwohl (1985) offers a second set of criteria for examining and judging the generalizing power of a study.

1. Is the level of generality in the explanation or theory being proposed reasonable?
2. Is the level of generality in the theory represented in the plan of the study?
3. Is the level of generality being claimed at least represented in the results of the study?
4. Are there alternative explanations of the results that would restrict or limit their generality?
5. Would the results likely be replicated in other settings and with other people?

Once again, classroom researchers would be well advised to consider these criteria when planning their studies and interpreting their findings.

Closing Comments

In this chapter we have outlined the major components of a research study. These components consist of a purpose (usually in the form of one or more research questions), a conceptual framework for deriving meaning from the evidence collected, and a research plan for sampling, collecting, interpreting, and analyzing the evidence. We have also painted, in broad strokes, the nature of the evidentiary base for generating and defending knowledge claims about classrooms, the events that occur within classrooms, and the people who live and work in them.

Throughout the discussion we have used the phrase "knowledge claims." As mentioned in the previous two chapters, knowledge claims become knowledge when they (1) have been made based on the results of studies conducted in accordance with an acceptable methodology, and (2) have been scrutinized and then accepted or endorsed by the research community. Unfortunately, there are two "presses" on us as researchers, one internal and one external, that may cause us to offer knowledge claims that are unlikely to achieve the status of knowledge.

The internal press is what Dunkin and Biddle (1974) have termed The Commitment. Although we have discussed this issue in Chapter 1, we would like to remind the reader of a recommendation offered by Dunkin and Biddle in regard to our commitments some fifteen years ago.

> Recommendation: *Investigators who hold Commitments to a given strategy for the improvement of teaching should take pains to recognize these Commitments and not allow them to color their research methods or interpretation of data* (p. 427).

The external press comes from the fact that classroom research creates almost a schizophrenic reaction on the part of researchers. On the one hand, researchers do not want to make false knowledge claims. Thus, they state that their knowledge claims are tentative, outline the limitations of their studies, and suggest the need to test their knowledge claims in other settings (i.e., the traditional call for "more research"). On the other hand, researchers seem somewhat compelled to explain the significance of their findings for understanding and improving classrooms, and if their studies have an improvement orientation, to suggest or demonstrate ways in which the improvements can be made.

Greenberg (1970), in her review of five well-known classroom studies conducted during the 1960s, describes this schizophrenic press on classroom researchers.

> Each researcher while, on the one hand, offering the reader assurances of the tentative nature of his findings and the exploratory nature of his study, at some point will, with equal firmness, assure the reader that his particular study has identified *the* critically important aspect of classroom behavior, and will often make observations and offer suggestions for teacher training and classroom practice for which no evidence has been presented and which are entirely independent of the design of the study (p. 149).

In this regard, we would like to close with a second recommendation, one intended as an addition to that made by Dunkin and Biddle.

> Recommendation: *When making suggestions for change or improvement, classroom researchers should stay as close to their evidence as is humanly possible. When forced or compelled to go beyond the evidence, classroom researchers should make it clear that they are doing so by offering their suggestions as professional opinions, not facts.*

5

Sources of Evidence

As was noted in Chapter 4, researchers tend to use three general approaches to gather the evidence they need to address the research questions they are asking. They either ask people who are able to provide the evidence, they visit settings in which the evidence they are seeking is likely to be manifest and observe in those settings, or they seek out evidence that already exists in some form (e.g., written records, photographs). In this chapter we shall examine these various "sources of evidence."

"Sources of evidence," as we use the term, refers to the means by which the evidence is gathered or collected (typically referred to in the research literature as "instrumentation") *and* the person or persons who provide the evidence (typically referred to as the "sample"). In the case of a variable such as student achievement, for example, the means by which the evidence is gathered is often a standardized achievement test and the persons responsible for providing the evidence are those students who respond to the test items. Similarly, in the case of a variable such as teacher praise, the means by which the evidence is gathered may be either a record made by an observer in a classroom or a self-report made by teacher. The means by which the evidence is gathered, then, may be an observation form or a videotape recording, or a questionnaire or class log, and the person providing the evidence may be a highly trained observer, a camera operator, or a teacher.

The choice of a source of evidence should be made carefully, with much attention paid to the type of evidence that is needed to support a particular knowledge claim. Too many educators, in our opinion, have become proponents of particular sources of evidence independent of the questions asked or the knowledge sought. In some cases, sources of evidence are chosen because of the inadequacies of other sources, not because of the adequacy or appropriateness of the source selected.

Bennett (1976), for example, selected questionnaires because of critiques of the observation instruments that were being used in classroom research made by Nuthall and Snook (1973) and Rosenshine and Furst (1973). Similarly, Dyer (1976) defended the use of interviews because they provide a way for researchers to examine "the many dimensions of the educational enterprise that are lurking below the surface of day-to-day operations [and, thus, presumably not amenable to observation]" (p. 14). In stark contrast, Webb, Campbell, Schwartz, Sechrest, and Grove (1981) argue that interviews and questionnaires

> intrude as a foreign element into the social setting they would describe, they create as well as measure attitudes, they elicit atypical roles and responses, they are limited to those who are accessible and will cooperate, and the responses obtained are produced in part by dimensions of individual differences irrelevant to the topic at hand (p. 1).

Webb and his colleagues go on to suggest that researchers consider using existing evidence (e.g., physical traces and archives) in their studies and, ultimately, begin to use multiple sources of evidence to increase the validity of the evidence.

The purpose of this chapter is to examine the various sources of evidence that are typically used in classroom research. Specifically, it is our intention to describe each source, consider the strengths and weaknesses, make recommendations for the development of instruments and procedures, and present examples and illustrations. The strengths and weaknesses we identify are the ones we consider to be primary or major. In this way, we hope to avoid long lists of strengths and weaknesses. Furthermore, the examples and illustrations we present are those that (1) have been used in studies of teachers, teaching, and instruction, and (2) appear to have been developed in accordance with our recommendations.

The chapter is organized around the three basic ways in which evidence can be gathered: asking, observing, and collecting evidence that already exists in some form. Asking is treated first since it is the oldest and most traditional means of gathering evidence about teachers, teaching, and instruction. Observation is treated second since it has gained popularity during the past two decades. Finally, the use of available evidence is treated last since it "has greatest utility *in consort with* other methodological approaches" (Webb et al., 1981, p. 5) (emphasis ours).

Asking

As researchers we ask people about a wide variety of things. We ask teachers to express their opinions on a variety of classroom practices in order to determine their teaching style (Bennett, 1976). We play audiotape or videotape recordings made in teachers' classrooms and ask the teachers why they said what they said or behaved the way they did at a particular point in the lesson in order to examine their interactive or "in flight" decision making (Calderhead, 1981). We ask teachers to sort cards or arrange concepts into a network of relationships in order to help us understand their knowledge of a particular subject matter, such as reading (Roehler, Duffy, Herrman, Conley, and Johnson, 1988) or mathematics (Steinberg, Haymore, and Marks, 1985).

We may ask these questions from afar (as when we mail questionnaires to our sample) or we may ask our questions face to face (as when we conduct an interview). But whatever questions we ask and however we ask them, two points are quite clear. First, we ask questions that are related to a specific and well-defined purpose, typically the purpose of the study. Second, as researchers we ask numerous questions. In behavioral terms, we provide the stimulus and expect people to respond. However, as can be seen in Figure 5.1, the nature of the stimulus and the range of options available to those responding to the stimulus (hereafter referred to as the respondents) can differ widely across studies.

The horizontal dimension of Figure 5.1 concerns the questions asked of the respondents and the prompts given to them to help them answer them. While everyone understands what questions are, prompts may need to be defined. As we use the term, prompts refer to any preparatory information or material given to the respondent that is either needed to answer subsequent questions or will assist the respondent in answering them. In the above examples, the set of cards given to teachers and the directions for sorting them, and the videotape recordings shown to teachers are prompts. Also, any statement made by an interviewer prior to asking questions is a prompt. Wineburg's (1986) opening statement to the social studies teachers he interviewed is a prompt.

> The purpose of today's interview is for you to walk me through your thinking about a unit or topic in U.S. history. One unit that is common in the high school curriculum is the unit on the American Revolution and the formation of the government, the period covering the dates of 1770–1800 (approximately) (p. 1).

Following the prompt, teachers are asked to tell first what they understand about this period that they would have their students understand and subsequently respond to several related questions.

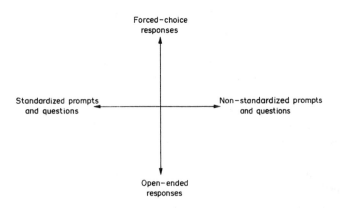

FIG 5.1   Stimulus and response: Two dimensions of asking.

As shown in the horizontal dimension of Figure 5.1, prompts and questions can either be standardized or non-standardized. Standardized prompts and questions are the same for all researchers and respondents. That is, all researchers using standardized prompts and questions are required to use the same prompts and ask the same questions in exactly the same order and in precisely the same way regardless of the respondents. Furthermore, questions may neither be added nor deleted. In Dyer's (1976) terms researchers are expected to follow a "standard set of procedures."

Non-standardized prompts and questions, on the other hand, permit individual researcher's to use whatever prompts or questions they deem necessary to collect the evidence they need in order to answer the research questions they have formulated. The evidence, rather than the particular prompts and questions used to collect the evidence, is paramount in the researcher's mind. If operating from an initial general set of questions, the researcher is free to delete questions, reword questions, or insert questions as needed. These "inserted questions" are typically referred to as "probes," and the process of asking these questions is termed "probing."

The middle of the horizontal dimension of Figure 5.1 is best termed "semi-standardized." Bussis et al. (1976) define a semi-standardized interview in the following manner:

> It specifies the overall sequence of questions, the initial wording of questions, and the probes (if any) for each question. In addition, however, a certain amount of informality in its presentation and flexibility of its use is essential (p. 44).

In essence, the primary difference between standardized and semi-standardized is whether the questions are *mandates* which researchers are expected to follow or *guides* that researchers may use to collect the evidence they need to address the research questions.

The vertical dimension of Figure 5.1 concerns the types of answers that respondents can give to the questions asked of them. At the one extreme, respondents have a limited number of alternative response options from which they are to choose (forced-choice responses). They can respond "yes or no," "agree or disagree," or that they have been teaching for between "10 and 15 years." At the other extreme, respondents are completely free to respond in any way they believe appropriate (open-ended responses). They can respond that they are not certain that the answer is yes or no. They can tell us why they agree or disagree. They can make it clear that they will have been teaching for eleven years in June. More importantly perhaps, they can offer their opinions or insights, or provide explanations for the answers they give.

To this point in the discussion, we have avoided the distinction between questionnaires and interviews. In our opinion, the primary difference rests on the horizontal dimension of Figure 5.1. Questionnaires tend to rely on standardized prompts and questions (since researchers are typically absent when the questionnaires are completed), while interviews tend to rely on less-standardized prompts and questions (either semi-standardized or non-standardized). In this regard, Dyer (1976) has defined an interview as

> a conversation between two people in which the aim is to generate information either about the person being interviewed or about other matters with which the respondent is presumably familiar (p. 1).

In the course of such a conversation, each person involved is expected, if not required, to react in some way to the comments made by the other.

With respect to the vertical dimension, both questionnaires and interviews can either restrict or extend the responses expected from the respondents. During an interview, teachers can be asked to indicate their age or experience by choosing one of several age or experience categories. Such a choice may relieve some of the anxiety associated with telling exactly how old one is or for how long one has been teaching. Likewise, the same set of response options can be included on a questionnaire.

Similarly, researchers can ask teachers to tell how they came to choose teaching as a career. The teachers can be asked to write their reasons on a sheet of paper (as in a questionnaire) or state their reasons orally (as in an interview).

It is probably safe to say that interviews are more likely to rely on semi-standardized or non-standardized prompts and questions and permit respondents to answer freely. In contrast, questionnaires are more likely to use more standardized prompts and questions and quite often restrict the response options available to the respondents. Our discussion of the two-dimensions shown in Figure 5.1 simply suggests that this *need not* be the case. At the same time, however, we would be the first to admit that using interviews consisting exclusively of standardized prompts and questions *and* forced-choice response options may be a waste of time and energy.

Strengths and Weaknesses of Asking

Asking people to provide the needed evidence has both advantages and disadvantages. There are general strengths and weaknesses, and more specific strengths and weaknesses associated with standardized questions, non-standardized questions, forced-choice responses, and open-ended responses. In this section, the strengths will be described first, then the weaknesses.

General Strengths. The major reason to ask questions of people is that the evidence needed by the researcher (1) does not currently exist, (2) exists but requires some corroboration or explanation, or (3) cannot be gathered using observation. When the needed evidence does not exist, but could be gathered either by asking or observing, simply asking people is likely to be more *cost-effective.* This is particularly true when standardized questionnaires are used to collect the evidence, but also is true when relatively short interviews are used (e.g., telephone surveys). When the needed evidence does exist (e.g., written records), asking can be used to corroborate the evidence or provide a *greater understanding* of it.[1] Asking teachers whether the posted classrooms rules remain applicable, or asking students whether the rules are enforced provides the researcher with a more complete understanding of the evidence. Finally, when the evidence being sought does not exist and is not directly observable (e.g., the beliefs, attitudes, or values of teachers), then asking becomes the *sole source* of evidence.

Strengths of Standardized Questions. Standardized questions have two major strengths and perhaps a third. First, standardization increases the efficiency with which the evidence is collected. Simply stated, more evidence can be gathered in shorter periods of time. Second, standardization reduces the knowledge and skill needed to use the instrument. Researchers using standardized questions during interviews, for example, require far less training than those using non-standardized or semi-standardized interview protocols. Third, proponents would argue that standardization makes it possible to compare the answers given by different people or groups of people. Without standardization, they argue, different answers may be given because the wording of the question is changed, the questions are asked in a different order, and other similar factors. Consequently, without standardization, the evidence obtained from responses given to the questions asked may not be comparable from one person or group to another. As we shall see, however, proponents of non-standardized or semi-standardized interviews will argue the issue of comparability quite differently.

Strengths of Non-Standardized or Semi-Standardized Questions

Proponents of the use of non-standardized or semi-standardized interviews would argue that those who suggest that standardization is necessary for comparability of responses across people or groups of people are assuming, incorrectly, that comparability of stimuli produces comparability of responses. They would argue that comparable understanding of or reactions to the stimuli are necessary if the responses given are likely to be directly comparable. In Dyer's (1976) words:

> The reliance on the interviewer's subjective judgments within the context of an elaborate set of specified procedures is usually justified on the grounds that, by adapting the conditions of the interview to the varying conditions of respondents, the comparability of their responses is maximized (p. 4).

In other words, the emphasis in non-standardized or semi-standardized interviews shifts from asking the "right" questions to getting the "right" (that is, most accurate, most informative) answers. And, once accuracy and

---

[1]The difference between the evidence per se and the meaning of the evidence is addressed in great detail in Chapter 8.

information are optimized, comparability of responses is maximized. Thus, increases in accuracy, information, and comparability represent the major strengths of non-standardized or semi-standardized interviews.

Strengths of Forced-Choice Responses

Forced-choice responses have two primary strengths. First, respondents are more likely to respond to instruments containing forced-choice responses. Somehow, making marks to indicate responses is less bothersome than having to write out the answer. As a consequence the return rates of forced-choice instruments are likely to be higher. Second, coding (that is, placing the responses in categories) or scoring (that is, assigning numerical values to the responses) is much more efficient with forced-choice responses. The scoring or coding can be done by computer or by minimally trained people with little knowledge of research.

Strengths of Open-Ended Responses

Open-ended responses also have two major strengths. First, such response opportunities permit the respondent not only to express an opinion, but to explain why that opinion is held; to not only give an answer, but to elaborate on why that answer seems reasonable. Thus, a "richer" set of evidence is available using open-ended responses. Second, the evidence gathered using open-ended questionnaires or interviews is in its "rawest" form. It has not been constrained by choices given to the respondent; neither has it been transformed by coding or scoring. As a consequence, this evidence can be re-examined or re-analyzed within various conceptual frameworks and using various methods or techniques of analysis.

General Weaknesses

Two general weaknesses have been associated with asking as a source of evidence. First, while the collection of the evidence may be very efficient, the preparation of "good" questionnaires and interviews is very time-consuming. Bussis et al. (1976) reflect on their experience in developing the interview they used in their study.

> The process of developing a final form of the interview for use in the study extended over an eight-month period prior to the beginning of data collection. During that time, several versions of an interview were tried out. . . . Various drafts were also discussed with advisors, workshop staff, and with other consultants (pp. 42–43).

Similar expenditures of time and effort can be expected for those developing most questionnaires or interviews to be used for research purposes.

Second, asking as a source of evidence requires that researchers rely on the honesty and truthfulness of those responding to the questions asked.

Several threats to honesty and truthfulness have been identified (Webb et al., 1981). To summarize, people are likely to give false, inaccurate, or inadequate answers when they:

1. assume a particular role that is different from whom they really are and respond in accordance with that role,
2. choose to respond consistently in a particular way, regardless of their true feelings, beliefs, or knowledge, or
3. are aware of being "tested" and believe that they must make a good impression.

These false, inaccurate, or inappropriate responses can be the result of the persons being asked the questions (e.g., numbers 1 and 2 above), or the persons asking the questions (e.g., number 3 above).

In addition to these threats to honesty and truthfulness, respondents may inadvertently provide false, inaccurate, or inappropriate responses. That is, they may give an answer they believe to be true, but is not. Or, they may give an approximation, when greater precision is required.

The real issue, then, is the credibility of the evidence provided by those who respond to the questions. They may not be credible sources or the evidence provided may not be credible. In either case, asking as a source of evidence has its limitations.

Weakness of Standardized Questions

The primary weakness of standardized questions was foreshadowed in the strength of non-standardized or semi-standardized questions. Researchers using standardized questions cannot adapt them to differences in the respondents' knowledge (including reading or listening comprehension) or their particular view of the world. As a consequence, researchers cannot ensure that the respondents fully comprehend the questions asked before they respond or, if they individually do comprehend the questions, this comprehension is shared by all who respond. Rather, researchers must assume or verify that the responses made are valid and reliable.

Weaknesses of Non-Standardized or Semi-Standardized Questions

Two weaknesses of non-standardized or semi-standardized questions can be identified. First, the use of non-standardized or semi-standardized interviews typically requires "special expertise of the sort one expects to find in an experienced clinical psychologist or social anthropologist" (Dyer, p. 1). Some researchers, particularly those who have recently completed their graduate degree programs, may not have the necessary experience. Stated simply, expertise, in addition to training, is needed to use non-standardized or semi-standardized interviews.

Second, despite the counter-claims made by proponents of non-standardized or semi-standardized interviews, direct comparisons of the responses made by the respondents to non-standardized or semi-standardized questions *may not* be possible. Asking completely different questions, asking questions whose answers may impact on the answers given to later questions, omitting some questions while adding others—all of these *can have* dramatic effects on the answers given. To the extent that any of these factors (and perhaps a dozen others) impact on the responses given by the respondents, the comparability of the responses must be questioned.

Weaknesses of Forced-Choice Responses

Two weaknesses of forced-choice responses are quite apparent. First, the choice that the respondent is either able or willing to make may not be among the choices that appear on the instrument. If not, the respondent in actuality has no choice (other than to offer no response or to falsify it).

Second, the respondent may feel a need to explain, justify, or qualify a response, but have no opportunity to do so. As a result, the respondent may write copious notes on the instrument (which typically are ignored), refuse to respond to the instrument, or provide less than accurate or adequate evidence (because of the nature of the response options available).

Weaknesses of Open-Ended Responses

The major weakness of open-ended responses is inefficiency. This inefficiency is manifest in at least two ways. First, some portion of the responses made by the respondent may be unrelated to the overall purpose of the study. Webb et al. (1981) refer to this proportion of irrelevant information provided by the respondent as the *dross rate*. The larger the dross rate, the less efficient the interview or questionnaire. Second, open-ended responses are not the most useable form of data. Lengthy written responses must be read and re-read to search out those elements or themes that are relevant to the study being conducted. Audiotape recordings must be listened to more than once for the same reason. Some researchers choose to have audiotape recordings transcribed; however, transcription is a very time consuming process (Galton, 1987).

Recommendations

Several recommendations can be offered for the development of useful and useable questionnaires and interviews. Several of these recommendations apply to both questionnaires and interviews; others pertain primarily to interviews. The more general recommendations are presented first.

1. Prepare a blueprint for the questionnaire or interview before writing any of the questions. The blueprint should be built around considerations

TABLE 5.1

Blueprint for Developing Questionnaire for Teachers in a Program Designed for Low Achieving Students

Evidence is Needed About:	Number of Questions Needed:
1. Demographic characteristics of teachers — Sex — Race/ethnicity — Educational background — Years of teaching experience	4
2. Availability and use of teachers' aides — Number of aides — Educational background — Hours per week in classroom — Tasks performed by aides	4
3. Teachers' preparation for teaching in the program — Formal coursework — Prior experience	2
4. Characteristics of students in program — Sex — Race/ethnicity — Ability levels	3
5. Objectives and assignments for students during a single week	5
6. Teachers' attitudes toward the program	12
	Total = 30

of the evidence that is needed in view of the purpose of the study (see Table 5.1). The blueprint shown in Table 5.1, used to develop a questionnaire for teachers teaching in a program designed for low achieving students, is simple and straightforward. The left-hand column asks researchers to consider what evidence they need in light of the purpose of the study and the research questions being addressed. The right-hand column asks for an estimate of the number of questions that would need to be included to obtain the evidence. This simple blueprint helps in the alignment of the questions on the questionnaire or interview with the evidence needed by the researcher to complete his or her study successfully.

2. Write questions that are short and to the point. If forced-choice responses are used, make sure that the response options are clearly differentiable and do not overlap. If more than one response option can be selected by the respondent, make this clear by indicating the respondent should "Check all that apply." Also, make certain that the response options

are "exhaustive." That is, each response that could be made by the respondent should be consistent with at least one of the response options included. Often a response option of "Other" is used to ensure an exhaustive set of options, with the respondent being asked to write in an open-ended response their reasons for choosing the "other" option.

If open-ended responses are used, questions with concrete references should be posed to the extent possible. Consider a question prepared by Bussis et al. (1976) which was eventually discarded: "On a general level, what do you think is the teacher's responsibility for children's emotional growth?" (p. 43). The question was discarded because it offered "no ready entry through personal experience" and "seemed to impede the formulation of coherent personal statements" (p. 43). Substitute questions such as the following were found to be far more useful in eliciting the desired responses.

> How about children who show little apparent interest in anything that you have in the room or who can't settle down and get involved? How do you deal with that situation? (p. 44).

Questions with concrete references to instructional materials, classroom practices, and student behavior appear to reduce the dross rate when using open-ended responses.

3. Prepare a draft of the questionnaire or interview. In the process of preparing the draft, directions should be written and concerns for sequencing the questions addressed. Directions are necessary for both interviews and questionnaires. In general, directions should include the purpose of the interview or questionnaire, something about the organization of the interview or questionnaire, and, particularly for questionnaires, the manner in which the person completing the questionnaire is to respond. Consider these directions, which are given orally to the respondent by the interviewer (Wineburg, 1987).

> The purpose of today's interview is for you to walk me through your thinking and teaching of mathematics at various levels, ranging from the entire year down to a single lesson. First, we'll talk, generally, about the topics that you cover throughout the year. Next, we will focus on fractions as a topic, and finally an individual lesson on equivalence of fractions (p. 1).

Both the purpose and organization are made clear to the respondent. The following excerpts from the directions included on Bennett's (1976) *Teacher Questionnaire* illustrate these same points.

> At present all too little is known about the way in which teachers adapt their methods to [school conditions and pupil characteristics]. In an attempt to obtain information which may be useful to [students training to be teachers], this questionnaire has been devised. . . . It is in three parts. . . . Part one asks for background information about the teachers, class and school; part two is designed to cover various aspects of classroom and curriculum organization, and part three asks for teachers' opinions on various educational topics. . . . Most of the items in this questionnaire ask you to choose one answer from a number of alternatives, by circling the appropriate CODE NUMBER (p. 164).

While the sequence of questions on interviews and questionnaires is no small matter, little has been written about it. An exception is the work of Bussis et al. (1976) who offer two suggestions. First, questions pertaining to topics or ideas with which the respondent is most familiar should be placed early in the questionnaire or interview. Questions related to less familiar topics and ideas should be placed later. Second, in interview protocols, more open-ended questions should precede more specific questions. With respect to interviews, both of these suggestions are intended to get the respondent talking as early in the session as possible so that any anxiety or tension may be reduced.

4. Conduct a small-scale pilot or field test. The pilot or field test provides much needed information as to the appropriateness of the *content* of the questions (that is, what is being asked) and the *format* the questions (that is, how the questions are being asked) (Bussis et al., 1976). Revisions in the questions suggested by the results of the pilot or field test should then be made. This process of trial, error, and revision is central to the development of sound questionnaires and interviews and may have to be repeated.

In fact, we would suggest that a two-stage approach to pilot or field testing be used. In the first phase, share your draft with your colleagues or members of the research team. They are more likely to be "kind" in their critique and to make suggestions that help you avoid embarrassment in the second phase (e.g., grammatical errors, simplistic questions). In the second phase, however, you must include people who are similar to those for whom the interview or questionnaire is designed. Remember that the phrase "source of evidence" refers to both the instrument *and* the sample. All interviews or questionnaires are targeted toward some population of respondents. It is essential that they understand the meaning of the questions (both in terms of content and format) so they can respond accordingly. Concerns for those who do not read or speak the language or whose vocabularies do include large numbers of the words in the interview or on the questionnaire can properly be addressed in the second phase of the pilot or field testing.

5. With respect to interviews, ensure that all of those who conduct the interview share a common understanding of the *purpose* of each question. [The type of blueprint mentioned in recommendation no. 1 is used in this regard]. A common understanding of the purpose is needed if those conducting the interview are to make decisions concerning when to reword a question, when to probe for more information (either searching for greater detail or higher levels of abstraction), when to clarify the intent of the question, and when to move on to the next question.

6. With respect to interviews, ensure that all of those who conduct the interview are trained to use the interview appropriately. This recommendation applies to both standardized and semi-standardized interviews. As Dyer (1976) points out, "there is implicit in the notion of standardiz-

ation that the interviewer shall have undergone rigorous training in the roles to be performed" (p. 4). With semi-standardized interviews, training is required so that the person conducting the interview becomes so familiar with the interview schedule that he or she is able to conduct each interview in an "easy, conversational manner" (Dyer, 1976).

One portion of the training session should address the issue of establishing rapport. Rapport is a subtle quality that has to do with the nature of the relationship between the person conducting the interview and the person being interviewed. Without rapport, the respondent "may answer questions reluctantly, untruthfully, or not at all" (Dyer, 1976, p. 4). Wineburg and Wilson (1986) have made a series of suggestions for those conducting interviews, many of which address the issue of rapport. These suggestions are shown in Table 5.2.

Examples and Illustrations

Asking people for evidence is a time-honored means of collecting it. As a consequence, examples and illustrations about. Sixty years ago, Charters and Waples (1929) asked pupils, school administrators, teachers, parents, professors of education, and representatives of teachers' agencies to respond to a series of questions.

1. What are the important qualities that a high-school teacher should possess? How are they shown?
2. (a) Think of the best teacher among all the high-school teachers you have ever known. Why is he or she the best teacher? (b) Did he (or she) have any bad qualities? What were they?
3. (a) Think of the poorest teacher whom you have known among your co-workers. Why was he or she so poor? (b) Did he (or she) have any good qualities?
4. Can you mention any traits that successful teachers need in high school more than in grade school work? (pp. 54–55).

TABLE 5.2

Suggestions for Conducting an Interview

1. Avoid confrontation at all costs. Asking respondents to justify or defend their answers is sometimes viewed as confrontational.
2. Avoid interrupting. Be patient and a good listener.
3. Avoid asking leading questions (that is, questions that have obvious correct or desirable answers).
4. Avoid asking two or three questions at the same time.
5. Avoid suggesting answers or "putting words into the respondent's mouth," either by tone of voice or by making explicit comments. Also, avoid making your value judgments explicit (e.g., Can you give me a *better* example?). Try to maintain a neutral stance toward the topics being discussed (e.g., Can you give me *another* example?).
6. Avoid mechanical establishment of rapport (e.g., Yes, I know just how you feel; Yeah, I really hear you).

Derived from Wineburg and Wilson (1986) and Dyer (1976).

Initially, then, Charters and Waples used standardized questions with open-ended responses. Eventually, they developed standardized stimuli in combination with forced-choice responses. The response options pertained to the importance of the traits or qualities and asked school administrators to "place each trait in one of three importance groups [most important, average important, and least important] and to place no less than eight traits in each group" (p. 71).

More recently, Bennett (1976) and Ashton and Webb (1986) have made extensive use of questionnaires in their studies of teaching styles and

PART 2. TEACHING METHODS ADOPTED			Card II
SEATING ARRANGEMENTS			1 - 5
1. Do your pupils decide for themselves where they sit in the classroom?			
	No	0	
	Yes	1	6
2. Are the seats usually arranged so that pupils sit			
	separately or in pairs?	0	
	in groups of 3 or more?	1	7
3. Are pupils allocated to places or groups on the basis of their ability?			
	No	0	
	Yes	1	8
4. Do pupils stay in the same seats or groups for most of the day?			
	No	0	
	Yes	1	9
CLASSROOM ORGANISATION			
5. Do you usually allow your pupils to move around the classroom			
	generally whenever they wish?	0	
	only during certain kinds of curricular activity?	1	10
6. Do you usually allow your pupils to talk to one another			
	usually whenever they wish?	0	
	only during certain kinds of curricular activity?	1	11
7. Do you expect your pupils to ask you permission before leaving the room?			
	No	0	
	Yes	1	12
8. Do you expect your pupils to be quiet most of the time?			
	No	0	
	Yes	1	13
9. Do you appoint monitors with responsibility for certain jobs?			
	No	0	
	Yes	1	14
ORGANISING THE CURRICULUM			
10. Do you regularly take pupils out of school as part of your normal teaching activities?			
	No	0	
	Yes	1	15
11. Do you use a timetable for organising the week's work?			
	No	0	
	Yes	1	16
12. For basic subjects do you more often use			
	text books?	0	
	specially prepared materials?	1	17

	Code Number	For Computer Use

13. Do you require that your pupils know their multiplication tables off by heart?

No 0
Yes 1   18

14. Teaching sometimes requires reference materials. Do you normally

supply most of this material for your pupils? 0
ask the pupils to find their own? 1   19

15. Do you regularly give your pupils homework?

No 0
Yes 1   20

16. In organising the work of your class, roughly what emphasis do you give to each of these five different approaches? Indicate approximately what percentage of time is spent on each approach. Your total should come to 100%, although this is not intended to imply that all the work necessarily fits into these five categories.   Percent

1. Teacher talking to the class as a whole. . . . . [ ] 21

2. Pupils working together co-operatively in groups, on work given by the teacher. [ ] 22

3. Pupils working together co-operatively in groups, on work of their own choice. . . . . [ ] 23

4. Pupils working individually, at their own pace, on work given by the teacher. . . . . [ ] 24

5. Pupils working individually at their own pace, on work of their own choice. [ ] 25

TOTAL [100%] 26-28

17. On which aspect of number work do you place *more* emphasis?

(i) Developing computational skills through graded exercises? . . . 0
(ii) Exploring concepts with materials or apparatus? 1   29

18. Do you encourage fluency and originality in written English, even if for many children this may be at the expense of grammatical accuracy?

No 0
Yes 1   30

TESTING AND MARKING

19. Do you put an actual mark or grade on pupils' work?

No 0
Yes 1   31

20. Do you correct most spelling and grammatical errors?

No 0
Yes 1   32

21. Are stars, or their equivalent given to pupils who produce the best work?

No 0
Yes 1   33

22. Do you give your pupils an arithmetic (mental or written) test at least once a week?

No 0
Yes 1   34

23. Do you give your pupils a spelling test at least once a week?

No 0
Yes 1   35

24. Do you have 'end of term' tests?   No 0
Yes 1   36

DISCIPLINE

25. Do you have many pupils who create discipline problems?

No 0
Yes 1   37

26. Do you find verbal reproof and/or reasoning normally sufficient?

No 0
Yes 1   38

27. For persistent disruptive behaviour, where verbal reproof fails to gain the pupils' co-operation, do you use any of the following disciplinary measures?

(i)   extra work   No 0
                              Yes 1   39

(ii) smack   No 0
                              Yes 1   40

(iii) withdrawal of privileges No 0
                                Yes 1   41

(iv) send to head teacher   No 0
                              Yes 1   42

(v)   sent out of room   No 0
                              Yes 1   43

ALLOCATION OF TEACHING TIME

28. When time has been deducted for registration and assembly, the number of hours per week left for teachers is 25. Estimate as accurately as possible how this is distributed among subjects and activities in the table below, by putting the appropriate number of hours in the boxes provided. Please use last week as your reference unless this was in some way unusual. (for example, Open day)

	Number of Hours
Number work	
English (including creative writing).	
Reading	44
History	
Geography	
French	
Science (including nature study) . .	
Scripture	
P.E.	
Music	
Art and Craft	45
Music and Movement	
Drama	
Environmental Studies	
Social Studies	
Project work	
Free choice activity	
Integrated studies	46

TOTAL 25(approx.)

FIG. 5.2 Excerpt from Bennett's *Teacher Questionnaire*.

teachers' sense of efficacy. A portion of Bennett's *Teacher Questionnaire* is shown in Figure 5.2, while a portion of Ashton and Webb's *High School Basic Skills Teacher Questionnaire* is displayed in Figure 5.3. Both questionnaires are excellent examles of the application of many of the recommendations made in the previous section.

Please indicate your degree of agreement or disagreement with each of the following statements.

25. When it comes right down to it, a teacher really can't do much because most of a student's motivation and performance depends on his or her home environment. (circle number)

1	2	3	4	5
Strongly agree	Agree	Neither agree nor disagree	Disagree	Strongly disagree

26. If I really try hard, I can get through to even the most difficult or unmotivated students. (circle number)

1	2	3	4	5
Strongly agree	Agree	Neither agree nor disagree	Disagree	Strongly disagree

Read each situation carefully. Consider similar situations from your own teaching experiences. Indicate how effective you would be in handling each situation by circling the appropriate number.

1	2	3	4	5	6	7
Extremely ineffective			Moderately effective			Extremely effective

27. One of your students misbehaves frequently in your class and often is disruptive and hostile. Today in class he began roughhousing with a friend in the back of the class. You tell him firmly to take his seat and quiet down. He turns away from you, says something in a belligerent tone that you can't hear, and swaggers to his seat. The class laughs and then looks to see what you are going to do. How effective would you be in responding to this student in a way that would win the respect of the class?

1	2	3	4	5	6	7
Extremely ineffective			Moderately effective			Extremely effective

28. Maria, an educable mentally retarded student in your class, has been working diligently but still performs below grade level in all subjects. At a conference the mother says that she doesn't expect much of the girl, because Maria is "dumb" just like herself. How effective would you be in talking to Maria's mother about her feelings and about the effect that parents' expectations can have on their child's school achievement?

1	2	3	4	5	6	7
Extremely ineffective			Moderately effective			Extremely effective

29. Your county has mandated that all teachers must restructure their course requirements to insure adequate development of students' basic skills by including these elements in each lesson plan. How effective would you be in incorporating achievement of basic skills objectives into your lesson plans?

1	2	3	4	5	6	7
Extremely ineffective			Moderately effective			Extremely effective

30. Half a dozen low-achieving female students are not getting much from your class. Lately they have begun to "hang around together" and to advertise that they don't like you or your class. They have begun to fool around, disrupt your lessons, and occasionally "talk back." When you attempt to involve them in class work they either make jokes or sit sullenly. How effective would you be in eliminating their disruptive behavior?

1	2	3	4	5	6	7
Extremely ineffective			Moderately effective			Extremely effective

31. This year your principal has assigned you to teach a class of low-ability students in your subject matter area. The teacher who taught this class last year tells you that it was the worst experience of her 20-year teaching career. How effective would you be in increasing the academic achievement of the students in this class?

1	2	3	4	5	6	7
Extremely ineffective			Moderately effective			Extremely effective

32. You have a student who never hands in assignments on time, seldom gets to class before the bell rings, and inevitably forgets to bring books or pencil to class. You have discussed this matter with his parents, but they don't seem to understand the importance of school achievement. How effective would you be in motivating this student to get to work?

1	2	3	4	5	6	7
Extremely ineffective			Moderately effective			Extremely effective

33. A new student has been assigned to your class. Her records indicate that she never does her homework and does not seem to care about her education. Her IQ score is 83, and her achievement scores have been below the 30th percentile. How effective would you be in increasing her achievement test scores?

1	2	3	4	5	6	7
Extremely ineffective			Moderately effective			Extremely effective

34. The student–teacher ratio in your class of compensatory education students is 20 to 1. You must plan your lessons to meet the individual needs of the students. How effective would you be in designing activities to match the individual interests and abilities of the students in your class?

1	2	3	4	5	6	7
Extremely ineffective			Moderately effective			Extremely effective

35. Because of repeated failure, one of your students confides to you that she has given up and will attend school only until she can find a way to drop out. How effective would you be in persuading her that she can be successful in school?

1	2	3	4	5	6	7
Extremely ineffective			Moderately effective			Extremely effective

36. A number of your students have been sleeping in class. They do poorly on in-class assignments and seldom turn in homework. You learn that they are taking drugs. How effective would you be in helping the students with their drug problem?

1	2	3	4	5	6	7
Extremely ineffective			Moderately effective			Extremely effective

37. A learning disabled student has been mainstreamed into your classroom. He has been described by his previous teachers as being extremely hyperactive and having severe reading problems. How effective would you be in teaching this student?

1	2	3	4	5	6	7
Extremely ineffective			Moderately effective			Extremely effective

Instructions: *Read each of the following paired statements and determine if you*
1. Agree most strongly with the first statement
2. Agree most strongly with the second statement

Indicate your answer by circling the appropriate number.

38. A. A teacher should not be expected to reach every child; some students are not going to make academic progress.
    B. Every child is reachable. It is a teacher's obligation to see to it that every child makes academic progress.
    Circle one:
    1. I agree most strongly with A.
    2. I agree most strongly with B.

39. A. Heterogeneously grouped classes provide the best environment for learning.
    B. Homogeneously grouped classes provide the best environment for learning.
    Circle one:
    1. I agree most strongly with A.
    2. I agree most strongly with B.

40. A. My skills are best suited for dealing with students who have low motivation and who have a history of misbehavior in school.
    B. My skills are best suited for dealing with students who are academically motivated and generally well behaved.
    Circle one:
    1. I agree most strongly with A.
    2. I agree most strongly with B.

41. A. Low-ability students should be encouraged to develop their vocational skills when they enter high school.
    B. Low-ability students should be encouraged to develop their academic skills when they enter high school.
    Circle one:
    1. I agree most strongly with A.
    2. I agree most strongly with B.

42. A. Students who are not interested in education and who continually misbehave should be expelled from school until their attitudes improve.
    B. Students who are not interested in education and who continually misbehave should be kept in school so that trained teachers can help such students to improve their attitudes.
    Circle one:
    1. I agree most strongly with A.
    2. I agree most strongly with B.

43. A. Most of my low-ability, poorly motivated students will eventually graduate from high school.
    B. Most of my low-ability, poorly motivated students will not graduate from high school.
    Circle one:
    1. I agree most strongly with A.
    2. I agree most strongly with B.

44. A. When I let myself think about it, I experience anxiety because I can't really know for certain that I am making a difference in the lives of students.

    B. When I evaluate my teaching, I have a feeling of professional confidence because I know rather certainly that I am making a difference in the lives of my students.
    Circle one:
    1. I agree most strongly with A.
    2. I agree most strongly with B.

FIG. 5.3   Excerpt from Ashton and Webb's *High School Basic Skills Teacher Questionnaire.*

From *Making a Difference: Teachers' Sense of Efficacy and Student Achievement* by Patrica T. Ashton & Rodman B. Webb. Copyright © 1986 by Longman Inc. Reprinted by permission.

A number of fairly recent studies have used interviews to collect evidence. An excellent example of a portion of an interview protocol is that of Bussis et al. (1976). (See Figure 5.4.) Both initial questions and probes to be used by the person conducting the interview are included. Shulman (1988) has used a number of interviews in his more recent studies of teacher knowledge.

CHILDREN IN THE CLASSROOM

9. In an open setting, children often work in small groups. What benefits do you see in such small groupings?

10. Do you think that children tend to express their needs and feelings more freely in an open setting as compared with the more conventional classroom?
    a. Does this (i.e., relatively free expression of needs and feelings) pose any difficulties for a teacher? What?
    b. Does it pose any difficulties for children? What?
    c. What benefits do you see in a more open expression of feelings?
    d. What about sensitive content—such as sex, death, birth, fears that children have? Do you think such content has any place in the classroom? How would you use it?

11. You hear a lot about "building on children's interests" in an open philosophy of education. But how does this work out in practice? How do you go about utilizing or building on a child's interests? Can you give me some concrete examples?
    a. How about children who show little apparent interest in anything that you have in the room, or who can't settle down and get involved? How do you deal with that situation?

12. In most every class there are times when some child or a group of children have a disruptive influence on the class. How do you generally handle this kind of problem?

13. "Opening up" a classroom usually means giving children some amount of choice in what they do. In your experience, how do young children handle choice situations? Can they make choices? On what basis do they choose?
    Probe for: - do you think most choices reflect genuine interest, a passing whim, or what? How do you tell the difference?
    - perceived reason why some children can't handle choice very well or don't make purposeful choices (e.g., age, home background, personality problem, etc.)
    - how do you help children make choices— or can you?
    - does it bother you when a child persistently sticks to one or two activities?

14. Aside from making choices, what other kinds of responsibilities do children have to learn to assume in this type of program?

15. There appears to be a good deal of debate about this next question, and I'd like your reaction. Do you think an informal approach is suitable for all children?
    Probe for: - what children can't or don't benefit in an informal approach?
    - if an informal approach is suitable for all (or almost all)—why do you think so? How do you help children who may have initial difficulties?

EVALUATING TEACHING AND LEARNING

16. Of all the various goals you have in mind as a teacher, which one (or ones) do you think you've made pretty good progress toward accomplishing this year?

    Probe for: - what clues led the teacher to believe that progress has been made?

17. With what goal (or goals) do you feel least satisfied—least sure that you have accomplished much progress?

    Probe for: - what clues led the teacher to question whether much progress has been made?

18. In general, do you consider judging individual children's progress to be more or less difficult in an informal setting?

    Probe for: - why? in what ways?
                  - why not?

PERCEPTION OF TEACHING REQUIREMENTS AND REWARDS

19. What about your own interests—do you have any personal hobbies or interests that carry over to the classroom?

20. Do you think your own general knowledge in a subject area affects your capabilities or style as a teacher? In what ways?

    a. Can an enthusiastic or accepting attitude toward a subject make up for lack of substantial knowledge in an area?

        Probe for: - can you give me an example from your own teaching of how:
                      enthusiasm carried you through?
                      enthusiasm wasn't enough?

    b. If you had the opportunity to take an extended period of time off for learning, what would you want to learn about? How would you go about it?

21. To what degree do you think your actual physical presence is necessary to the smooth functioning of the class? For example, how do your children typically react to a substitute teacher?

    Probe for: - if they act badly, why?

22. Do you find that your teaching now, in this program, is more or less personally satisfying than your previous experience—or is it about the same?

    Probe for: - what are personal satisfactions?
                  - are there rewards in what the teacher is doing?
                  - or in what she observes children doing?
                  - or in some combination of both?

23. If another teacher who was going to start an open classroom came to you for advice, what are some tips or ideas that would come to mind to tell her?

FIG. 5.4   Excerpt from interview protocol developed by Bussis et al. (1976)

Observing

Only a quarter of a century ago, Medley and Mitzel (1963) found it necessary to write:

> Certainly there is not a more obvious approach to research on teaching than direct observation of teachers while they teach and pupils while they learn. Yet it is a rare study indeed that includes any formal observation at all (p. 247).

During the years that followed, a number of researchers apparently took Medley and Mitzel's assertion to heart. By the late 1960s at least 120 different observation systems for use in classrooms had been identified (Simon and Boyer, 1967) and Rosenshine and Furst (1973) suggested that this number was clearly an underestimate of the number of observational systems that were available. Over the past two decades, observation has become a primary source of evidence for researchers as they study classrooms and a variety of different approaches to observation has emerged. The majority of these approaches can be differentiated along two dimensions as shown in Figure 5.5.

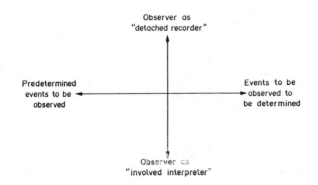

FIG. 5.5 Two dimensions on which approaches to observation can be differentiated (derived from Medley, 1982).

The horizontal dimension in Figure 5.5 concerns whether observers are expected to focus their attention on specific types or categories of events[2] (typically those included on a standardized observational form) or on any or all events as they so choose. Two approaches to observation focus the observer's attention on specific types or categories of events: structured observation systems (Medley, 1982) and rating scales (Remmers, 1963).

---

[2]Throughout the discussion of observation, an "event" is defined as any behavior, interaction, or activity that occurs within the perceptual field of the observer while in the classroom and captures his or her attention. Events may be small or "molecular" (e.g., teacher furrows her brow) or large or "molar" (e.g., teacher lectures) depending on the focal point of the observer. (See Wright, 1967, pages 12ff, for an excellent discussion of this distinction.)

Medley defines a structured observation system as a "scheme that specifies both the events that the observer is to record and the procedure to be used in recording them" (p. 1842). Many structured observation systems also include criteria to be used by observers to place the observed events into categories (Galton, 1987). As a consequence, the evidence from structured observation systems is typically in the form of either the frequency with which particular events or types of events occurred or the total length of time they occurred.

A rating scale is a set of characteristics or *dimensions* for which teachers, teaching, instruction, classrooms, or students receive a set of ratings. Good (1959) defines a rating as

> an estimate, made according to some systematized procedure, of the degree to which an individual person or thing, such as the classroom, possesses any given characteristic (p. 439).

The dimensions are specified in advance and the ratings are to be made based on evidence gathered during the observation. The evidence obtained from rating scales are numbers (e.g., 1 through 7) that represent the degree of each characteristic or dimension as determined by the observer based on the evidence.

Not surprisingly, criticisms of structured observation systems and rating scales typically emphasize the restriction imposed on observers by specifying the events, types of events, or dimensions in advance of the observation. Guba and Lincoln (1987), for example, contend that these approaches to observation constrain the inquiry

> to those elements recognized by the investigator as important, and may introduce biases (believing is seeing). In all events theory is more powerful when it arises from the data rather than being imposed on them (p. 149).

In contrast, proponents of these approaches, particularly of structured observation systems, contend that such systems are needed in order to

> carry the researcher beyond the initial, impressionistic level of observation into the formal, systematic, quantitative, replicable measurement that characterizes developed sciences (Hawkins, 1982, p. 21).

At the opposite end of the horizontal dimension, observers are not required to attend to specific events, types of events, or critical dimensions. Instead, they are free to make a written record of all the events that occur in the order in which they occur, or to attend to whatever events they believe important in order to address the questions guiding the research. In the first case, observers produce what are termed "specimen records" (Wright, 1967) or "classroom chronicles" (Gump, 1967). In the second case, they make what are termed "field notes."

Typically, observers using these approaches become "observation instruments" (Evertson and Green, 1986; Taft, 1987), although they are free to use mechanical recording devices such as audiotape recordings, videotape recordings, or still photography to help them record and remember the events that take place (e.g., Gump, 1967; Morine-Dershimer, 1985).[3] The point here is that observers using this approach *must make decisions* as to what to observe and what to ignore (within limits imposed by the conceptual framework and purpose of the study) and they have the full range of events occurring within the classroom from which to choose. In contrast, observers using structured observation systems have had these decisions made for them.

Critics of these approaches contend that since the criteria governing the selection of the events on which to focus ones attention are implicit and rarely available for consideration by others, the meaning of the evidence gathered during the observation may not be clear to anyone but the observer (Galton, 1987). Guba and Lincoln (1987) counter that the unique sensitivity and insights of observers are important to understanding the events that occur in classrooms. Similarly, Wright (1967) suggests that

> Freedom of the observer to make and record such synoptic judgments seems desirable; there is often accessible on the scene more or better data on which to base valid statements about events of any sort than can later be reproduced (p. 36).

The vertical dimension of Figure 5.5 concerns the role the observer plays in classroom observation. Two roles are depicted: "detached recorder" and "involved interpreter." Observers who assume the role of "detached recorder" are expected to remain somewhat distant from the people and events being observed; to "fade into the background" as soon as possible upon entry into the classroom. In addition, they are expected to record what they see and hear with as little inference, interpretation, and personal biases entering into their records as is humanly possible. Most frequently, explicit rules are used by observers to record their observations so that inference, interpretation, and personal biases are minimized. Medley and Mitzel (1963) summarize the "detached recorder" role.

> In any given study, between the record and the behavior it is supposed to represent should be interposed only the most primitive act of judgment or discrimination possible—the one needed to perceive whether the behavior has occurred or not (p. 253).

It should not be surprising that the records made by these observers are

[3]While some readers may consider mechanical devices observational instruments in their own right, we prefer to think of them as "memory aids." Someone has to decide in what direction the video camera should be aimed. Someone has to decide whether the microphone should be placed on or near the teacher or the students and, if the students, which students. Someone has to decide when to take the photographs, and whether a close-up or wide-shot is preferred. Quite clearly, these decisions influence what is recorded and, ultimately, what evidence is available, and some person (or persons) makes those decisions.

typically in the form of tallies, checkmarks, frequency counts, or time estimates.

In contrast, observers who assume the role of "involved interpreter" are encouraged to use their

> insightfulness, flexibility, and responsiveness, . . . take a holistic view, . . . utilize their tacit knowledge, . . . and simultaneously . . . acquire and process information (Guba and Lincoln, 1987, p. 149).

Both terms of the phrase "involved interpreter" are important. The use of the word "interpreter" means that the goal of the observers is to understand the events that occur, not simply record their occurrence. Observers are expected to go beyond the surface meaning of the events and capture the deeper meaning or the rather idiosyncratic "shared meanings" that have developed between the participants in the classroom (Walker and Adelman, 1975). Observers in this role are expected to be able to shed some light on questions such as "Why were so many of the questions asked by the teacher so difficult for so many students?" Quite obviously, simply raising this question suggests that the observer was aware the number of questions asked by the teacher answered correctly by the students (issues which are typically the focus of observers as "detached recorders").

The word "involved" in the phrase "involved interpreter" suggests that the level of understanding needed by observers in order to properly interpret the events that occur requires a great deal of involvement on their part. This involvement takes on two forms. First, observers may need to talk with teachers or students in the classroom or after class as they seek to understand the events they have observed. Looking at events from multiple perspectives (e.g., their own, the teacher's, the students') is likely to increase the observers' level of understanding.

Second, the use of the word "involved" means that observers have spent some extended period of time in the classrooms or with the participants (e.g., teachers, students). One way of looking at events from the multiple perspectives is for observers to become participants themselves (e.g., teacher's aides, students). This level of participation

> provides investigators with an understanding of the culture and the interactions between members that is different from that which can be obtained from merely observing (Taft, 1987, p. 151).

In contrast to the numerical records (e.g., tallies, frequency counts) made by observers using structured observation forms, observers in the role of "involved interpreters" make verbal records (e.g., recorded oral comments, written field notes). As we shall see in later chapters, however, these verbal records do not preclude quantification.

In summary, then, approaches to observation differ along two primary dimensions, each of which can be described in the form of a basic question.

First, are observers allowed to determine the events or types of events to which they attend? Second, are observers expected to remain apart from the events that occur in the classroom?

In some approaches to observation, typically those using structured observation systems (Medley, 1982), the events or types of events to be observed are determined in advance of the observation *and* observers are expected to serve as "detached recorders." Proponents of such systems would suggest that observers should not be allowed to determine the events to which they attend and should remain detached from those events that occur in the classroom. As we shall see, such approaches require a great deal of training on the part of observers.

In other approaches, typically those involving specimen records or classroom chronicles, observers operate without predetermined categories but are expected to describe as "fully as possible" (Wright, 1967) the events that occur. Observers are encouraged to make interpretations; however, at least two constraints are placed on observers in this regard. First, the interpretations are to be based on "elementary, garden variety, spur-of-the-moment notions and hunches about behavior that are common to man as a socialized being" (Wright, 1967, p. 38). Second, the interpretations should never "carry the burden of description" (Wright, 1967, p. 50). The events themselves, not the interpretations of those events, are subject to analysis. "Interpretative comments are of value principally as a means to the better understanding of what the observer describes" (Wright, 1967, p. 50). Finally, while the observers are expected to make interpretations, they are not expected to become involved with those being observed.

Other approaches, typically those that incorporate principles of ethnography (Taft, 1987) or naturalistic inquiry (Guba and Lincoln, 1987), allow observers to decide what events are worth noting, while at the same time *requiring* them to become "involved interpreters." That is, observers are expected to spend sufficient time in the classrooms to become truly knowledgeable of the people and the events and to move beyond simply recording the events to providing some interpretation of them. Observers using these approaches "construct meaning out of events to provide understanding to people who did not accompany [them] to the classroom" (McCutcheon, 1981, p. 3). As we shall see, ethnographic or naturalist approaches place the greatest burden of responsibility on the observers.

Finally, approaches to observation that include rating scales clearly specify the dimensions of the people or classrooms to which observers should attend. In this regard, they are similar to approaches that rely on structured observation systems. At the same time, however, they require that observers *interpret* what they have observed and make an overall judgment based on their observations (e.g., was the teacher partial or fair, or was the teacher apathetic or alert?). Thus, like those approaches using ethnographic or naturalistic observation, observers using ratings scales are expected to function as "interpreters" of the events that occur, although they are rarely as "involved" in the classrooms as those who use ethnographic or naturalistic approaches must be.

Figure 5.6 is intended as a visual summary to our verbal one. In this figure, structured observation systems, specimen records or classroom chronicles, ethnographic or naturalistic records, and rating scales are compared along the two dimensions shown in Figure 5.5. In the discussion that follows, we shall at times differentiate among structured observation systems, specimen records or classroom chronicles, field notes (which represent the records made by observers adopting an ethnographic or naturalistic approach), and rating scales. At other times, we shall refer to observation in general.

Strengths and Weaknesses of Observing

Observing, like asking, has its advantages and disadvantages. In this section we begin with the general advantages of observing and move to a discussion of the advantages of particular observational approaches. The disadvantages of observation are then described followed by a discussion of the disadvantages of specific approaches to observation.

General Strengths

Observing, as a primary source of evidence, has at least three advantages. First, observing permits researchers to study the *process* of education as it unfolds in the classroom. Evidence is gathered as the events are taking

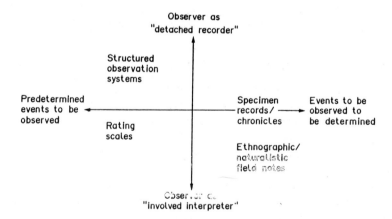

FIG. 5.6   Placement of Structured Observation Systems, Rating Scales, Specimen Records & Chronicles, and Ethnographic & Naturalistic Records Along Two Dimensions of Observation.

place, not before or after they have occurred. As a consequence, observation is far more likely than other sources of evidence to provide linkages between teachers and students, teaching and learning, or instruction and achievement. This advantage of observation has been recognized by educators and researchers alike for several decades. Barr and his colleagues, constituting the AERA Committee on the Criteria of Teacher Effectiveness, for example, stated that

> to secure bases for hypothesizing significant relationships [between teaching and learning], as well as for studying the relationships themselves, it would seem necessary to observe teachers operating in classrooms (Barr et al., 1953, p. 651).

Second, observing provides more detailed and precise evidence than any other source. Moment by moment records are possible. Sequences of events can be maintained. Insights and interpretations of observers can be noted [in brackets if desirable]. Neither asking nor examining available evidence provides the same degree of specificity as does observation.

Third, observation can be useful in stimulating change and verifying that the desired change has in fact occurred. Recommendations for changes in teaching or instruction appear to have more credibility among teachers when based on evidence gathered during observation, particularly observations conducted in individual teacher's classrooms. In this latter case, the suggestions for changes may come from the teachers themselves (Ghory, 1984). Furthermore, if instructional programs or teaching strategies are suggested to or prescribed for teachers, evidence collected from observation can be used to check on the "fidelity of implementation," that is, the extent to which the program or strategy is operating as desired or designed (Wang, 1984). The use of observation to monitor fidelity of implementation is an "excellent alternative to studies where one vague method is compared to another vague method" (Rosenshine and Furst, 1973, p. 153).

Strengths of Structured Observation Systems

Three strengths are associated with structured observation systems. First, the structure of the observation system increases the likelihood that everyone who knows or uses the system will share a common understanding of the events that are to be observed. As we shall see in Chapter 8, the meaning of the evidence gathered using structured observation systems is inherent in the structure of the system per se.

Second, the criteria used to define the types of events to be observed and the rules that govern the recording of events increase the likelihood that the same events will be recorded in the same way by everyone who uses the system. Furthermore, because of the explicitness of these rules, people with rather minimal knowledge of classrooms can be trained to use the system with reasonable degrees of accuracy.

Third, the nature of the evidence derived from structured observation systems (e.g., frequency counts, time estimates) makes quantitative analysis not only possible, but easily accomplished with the aid of computers. Thus, the evidence, once gathered, can be analyzed very efficiently.

Strengths of Specimen Records and Classroom Chronicles

Specimen records and classroom chronicles also are associated with three strengths. First, they preserve the continuity of the events. As a consequence, sequential analysis of the records—analysis seeking connections between antecedents and consequences, or causes and effects—is possible.

Second, specimen records or classroom chronicles are of a "theoretically neutral character." As described by Wright (1967), they are "biased only by the predilections of common sense in the meaning of sense that most of us have in common. [In addition], material in these records is often like behavior observed first-hand in the number and variety of the questions it raises and the answers it suggests" (p. 33–34). Because of the detail and "theoretical neutrality" of these records or chronicles, they can be examined and analyzed by a variety of researchers operating within different conceptual frameworks and from varying points of view.

Third, and related to the second strength, they produce permanent and stable records that are likely to be comprehensible to anyone who examines them. As a consequence, they can be examined at some later time as useful historical documents (Wright, 1967). An investigation of changes in classrooms over time becomes possible.

Strengths of Field Notes

The primary strength of field notes made by observers operating with the ethnographic or naturalistic tradition is that they provide the basis for gaining an understanding of the events that occur in the classroom from the point of view of the participants themselves. Smith, for example, used his notes as a basis for his daily discussions with Geoffrey, who was teaching the class being observed (Smith and Geoffrey, 1968). Based on the discussions (not the notes per se), Smith developed his conceptualizations of the teaching process. It is precisely because the notes are to be used to generate discussion and insights that complete, detailed written records are unnecessary.

A second strength lies in the nature of the field notes themselves. Taking field notes is not nearly as tedious as coding with structured observation systems or completing specimen records. The notes need to be sufficiently complete so that the observer is able to reconstruct the events that occurred and discuss them with one or more participants. However, as has been mentioned, they do not need to be as detailed as structured codings or specimen records.

Strengths of Rating Scales

Two major strengths of rating scales can be offered. First, rating scales have been used more often in classroom research than any other approach to observation (Remmers, 1963) and, as a consequence, numerous examples and critiques of rating scales are available. Despite the recent popularity of structured observation systems and ethnographic approaches, rating scales have continued to be used in recent years (Berliner and Tikunoff, 1976), particularly in studies conducted in higher education (Marsh, 1987).

Second, rating scales provide a more holistic portrait of the classroom than any of the other approaches to observation. The application of some of the other approaches to observation has resulted in an overabundance of evidence. So much evidence is gathered that the researcher is quickly overwhelmed. As a consequence, the researcher's emphasis often turns to sorting out the "trees," while at the same time forgetting about the "forest." Ten to fifteen key dimensions of the classroom and its participants included on a rating scale are more likely to keep the researcher's attention focused on the "forest."

General Weaknesses

Two general weaknesses are typically associated with observing as a source of evidence. First, observing is labor intensive and, hence, expensive in terms of both time and money. It is costly to place qualified, trained observers into large numbers of classrooms for any length of time. When mechanical recording devices are used, additional costs typically accrue. Both hardware and software must be purchased and maintained. If videotapes or still photographs are used, the camera operator or photographer may have to be paid. Furthermore, researchers must either watch videotapes, listen to audiotapes, or examine still photographs in order to glean the evidence needed to address the research questions asked. Medley (1982) suggests that it takes at least one hour for researchers to properly code the evidence included in one hour of audiotape or videotape. If typewritten transcripts of the audiotape or videotape are needed or desirable, the transcription of one hour of tape requires "nearly a week of an efficient typist's time" (Galton, 1987, p. 144).

Second, evidence collected using observation is susceptible to a variety of "errors." For example, observers may interject their biases into their records or unintentionally misinterpret events that were observed. In either case, the records may reflect what observers thought occurred more than they do what actually did occur. In addition, the records of different observers in the same classroom may be different not because of differences in the events that occurred, but because of differences in events to which they attended or differences in the particular aspects of the same events they noted (e.g., the teacher's role versus the student's role in the same event).

Weaknesses of Structured Observation Systems

Without a sound, defensible underlying conceptual framework, a structured observation system can result in "frequency counts of the minutiae of teacher and student behaviors" that have limited validity or utility (Nuthall and Snook, 1973). Unfortunately, with the proliferation of these systems during the 1970s, many such systems currently exist.

Furthermore, as has been mentioned earlier, structured observation systems tend to produce massive amounts of evidence, typically in some numerical form. Problems in readying these numbers for computer analysis (including their proper cleaning and editing) can easily become monumental (Anderson et al., 1989). Decisions concerning how to combine the records across time intervals (e.g., five minute scans of the classroom), occasions (e.g., three consecutive days of observation), or teachers or classrooms (e.g., twenty-five teachers using a particular instructional strategy) are neither easily made nor easily defended (Burstein, 1987).

Weaknesses of Specimen Records and Classroom Chronicles

Two primary weaknesses of specimen records and classroom chronicles have been identified. First, they require a great deal of time and effort; in a word, they are "demanding" (Wright, 1967). In light of the detail that is required, individual observers can be expected to become fatigued and teams of observers become necessary (Gump, 1967).

Second, they are known for their "sheer bulk" and have no "built-in provisions for quantification" (Wright, 1967). As a consequence, not only is the collection of evidence burdensome, but the analysis of the evidence is as well.

Weakness of Field Notes

The major weakness of field notes is related to their major strength. Only the observer is likely to be able to make sense of the notes that were taken, reconstruct their meaning, and use them to develop an understanding of the meaning of the events from the participants' point of view. Field notes are truly idiosyncratic; they tend not to be replicable. Some would argue they are not "scientific" (Hawkins, 1982). As a consequence, the validity of the evidence gathered using ethnographic or naturalistic approaches to observation depends almost entirely on the "expertise and interpersonal sensitivity" of the observer (Medley, 1982, p. 1846).

Weaknesses of Rating Scales

Two primary weaknesses of rating scales can be cited. First, rating scales rely on observers' impressions of events that occur in classrooms; they are not records of the events themselves (Fiske, 1978). The relationship of the events to the ratings is in the mind of the observer. As a consequence, a knowledge of the events that actually occurred within the classroom is not possible.

Second, rating scales tend to generate a large "halo" effect (Medley, 1987). Observers tend to form a general impression of the classroom, the instruction, the teacher, or the students'and to assign a rating consistent with that general impression to all of the dimensions included on the rating scale. Interestingly, if in a sample of classrooms some of the general impressions are positive and others are negative, the overall reliability (in the guise of internal consistency) is quite high. Clearly, this is a case in which "more" is not necessarily "better."

Recommendations

A number of recommendations can be made concerning the proper use of observation in research in classrooms. The first three recommendations apply to observing in general while the last four sets of recommendations pertain to the four specific observational approaches.

1. Choose an approach to observation that is consistent with the purpose for which the study is being conducted as well as the conceptual framework underlying the study, and whose demands do not exceed the capabilities of those who will conduct the observations or analyze the records made by the observers. There is a tendency among proponents of particular approaches to observation to denigrate other approaches or to advocate their non-use. Medley (1987), for example, suggests that researchers should completely abandon rating scales. Guba and Lincoln (1987) describe "axiomatic differences" underlying different approaches to classroom research and argue that the axioms of naturalistic inquiry "provide a better fit to most social/behavioral phenomena" (p. 147). As a consequence, Guba and Lincoln would likely argue that, in general, ethnographic and naturalistic approaches to observation should replace both structured observation systems and rating scales.

We would simply argue that suggesting the complete elimination of particular approaches to observation is akin to throwing the baby out with the bathwater. As we have attempted to point out, all approaches have their strengths and weaknesses. The issue, then, becomes how best to choose an observational approach within the context of a given research study so that the strengths are maximized and the weaknesses minimized.

If, for example, the purpose of the study is to provide a detailed, replicable description of classroom events, then structured observation systems, specimen records, or classroom chronicles are clearly preferable over rating scales or field notes. Similarly, if neophyte researchers are to be used as observers, structured observation systems are definitely preferable to field notes.

TABLE 5.3

Suggestions for the Design of an Observer Training Session

1. Prepare a manual for the observers. The manual should include:
   a. a statement of the general approach to observation,
   b. the role of the observer,
   c. complete and illustrated descriptions of the coding categories (with structured observation systems) or dimensions (rating scales), or general focus (specimen records, field notes),
   d. explicit procedures for recording what was observed, and
   e. written examples of classroom events and proper recordings of those events.

2. Select observers who, based on interviews and other sources of information, are likely to master the approach to observation in the time available for training. Ryans (1960a) suggests that such observers possess several traits and abilities. The following four traits and abilities seem to be very important. Observers should be:
   a. above average with respect to their ability to attend and perceive events that occur,
   b. familiar with classrooms and interested in the analysis of classroom events,
   c. able and willing to remain detached from and withhold judgment about the events they are observing,
   d. capable of making a good impression on the teachers being observed and putting them at ease.

3. Conduct the entire observation training session. In your outline of the session, consider the following points (adapted from Galton, 1987).
   a. Have the observers familiarize themselves with the manual.
   b. Concentrate on a few categories or dimensions at a time.
   c. Use excerpts from written examples of classroom events, audiotapes, or videotapes to illustrate categories or dimensions.
   d. Ensure observer "success" as early as possible.
   e. Allow ample opportunity for questions and answers.
   f. Arrange opportunities for "real-life" practice in classrooms, pairing up observers to the extent possible.
   g. Devote at least one day following each practice opportunity for "feedback and correctives."

4. Once the initial training has been completed, build into the study itself several short "refresher courses" to guard against "observer drift" and to deal with problems that emerge.

If, on the other hand, the purpose of the study is to gain an understanding of the classroom from the students' point of view, then field notes and possibly specimen records or classroom chronicles are essential. Likewise, if experienced researchers possessing high levels of expertise are used as observers, then field notes and possibly rating scales will likely result in more valid and useful evidence.

2. Whatever approach (or approaches) is chosen, a training session for observers should be designed and implemented. Several suggestions for the design of such a training session are displayed in Table 5.3. While most of the steps shown in the table should be self-explanatory, a few elaborations seem in order.

In step one, the preparation of the manual serves two purposes. Preparing the manual forces the researcher to plan. Such planning is crucial to the success of observer training sessions. Furthermore, the manual itself serves as a reference for observers. They can review portions of the manual as needed in order to enhance their understanding or increase their skill. A good example of a manual is that of Crocker, Brokenshire, Boak, Fagan, and James (1978).

The selection of observers is an often overlooked aspect of classroom research (see step two). Randomly choosing observers or selecting observers because they are available is likely to cause problems in the long run. Different approaches to observation require different qualifications of observers. Structured observation systems tend to require fewer qualifications than do the other approaches because the training is more rigorous and the criteria and rules are quite explicit. At the other extreme, field notes require highly qualified and experienced observers.

The actual training of observers requires that the designers of the training session attend to several issues (see step three). The general approach to training should follow a teach-test-feedback-reteach cycle. As early as possible, those training to be observers should experience success. Multiple opportunities for practice should be provided. Discussions between the trainer and "apprentice observers" should occur frequently, both before and after practice. It is important to remember that the goal of the training session is the development of competent observers. Within reasonable limits, any means by which this goal can be achieved should be pursued.

Finally, observers, like all of us, tend to forget what they have learned, or become tired or complacent (see step four). As a consequence, bringing observers together periodically for the purpose of discussing their experiences and resolving any conflicts is very useful.

3. Concerns for cost-effectiveness must be kept in mind as researchers decide on the most appropriate approach to observation. Since observing in general is costly, care must be taken to ensure maximum payoff in light of the time and effort expended. We admit that, for many researchers, raising the cost-effectiveness issue is similar to "hitting below the belt." After all, researchers are interested in seeking truth at all costs. Nonetheless, funding agencies are quite interested in cost-effectiveness and, as a consequence, researchers should be as well.

4. When structured observation systems are the preferred approach to observation, the following recommendations are offered.

   a. Functional rather than topographical categories should be included. Topographical categories focus on the events themselves, while functional categories address the intended or actual consequences of those events. While functional categories require that observers make inferences, they also are likely to provide more valuable information (Hawkins, 1982; Anderson, 1984).

b. The records made by observers should reflect the completion of events rather than the passage of time. That is, time should be viewed simply as a metric that measures the duration of events, rather than a factor which determines when records are to be made (Anderson, 1984). The use of time in this way leads to the formation of "naturalistic units" of classroom events (Galton, 1987). These naturalistic units have naturally-occurring, rather than artificially-derived, "beginnings" and "ends" (Wright, 1967). It is possible to approximate event-driven records from time-driven recordings, provided that the time intervals at which observers are expected to make their records is kept very short (e.g., 5 seconds, 30 seconds) (Medley and Mitzel, 1963).

c. Observation systems which permit or require the coding of a single event along multiple dimensions are preferred over systems that require the coding of a single event on a single dimension (Rosenshine and Furst, 1973). Most events that occur in classrooms are, in fact, multidimensional. That is, for example, a single event can be coded as to who said what to whom, in what context it was said (e.g., private or public), what was actually said, how was it said, and what were its actual or intended consequences. Coding systems such as those developed by Bellack, Kliebard, Hyman, and Smith (1966) and Stallings (1977) are examples of multidimensional coding systems.

5. When specimen records or classroom chronicles are the preferred approach to observation, the following recommendations are offered.

a. The length of each period of observation should be limited. The making of the records or chronicles is fatiguing, and no one can maintain the needed attention it requires for very long. Wright (1967) suggests that the maximum length for efficient observation is 30 minutes.

b. Specimen records require that observers focus on a single person (e.g., student, teacher). Observers are to record those events in which that person is involved, and those events that either impact or should impact on his or her behavior.

c. Specimen records and classroom chronicles emphasize not only the events that occur, but also how they occur. Teachers speak (what), but they also speak rapidly or cautiously (how). Students respond to questions (what), but they may respond eagerly or hesitatingly (how). Observers should note both the "what" and the "how."

d. Since the observer cannot faithfully record everything that has transpired, dictations or elaborations on the written records should be made as soon as possible. The dictation should be discussed with another person to guarantee the clarity of the records.

e. Interpretations should never carry the burden of description (Wright, 1967). Interpretative comments, when made, should be placed in brackets in the written records. Descriptive examples in support of the interpretations should be used whenever possible.

f. Attempt to maintain as continuous, unbroken records as possible. Understanding the sequence of events is essential to those making and analyzing specimen records.

6. When ethnographic and naturalistic approaches are preferred, the following recommendations are offered (Evertson and Green, 1986).

a. Observations must take place over a fairly lengthy period of time in the same classroom or school. In contrast to simply recording events, understanding the meaning of those events takes time. It takes time to get to know people and their unique ways of communicating with one another. The events observed today may only be understood within the context of the events that occurred yesterday and/or those expected to take place tomorrow.

b. Observers should formulate hypotheses based on the evidence gathered during an observation. However, they should consider these hypotheses to be tentative and subject to rejection, confirmation, or modification based on evidence collected during subsequent observations.

c. Observers must learn to converse with teachers and students in the classroom so that these participants talk freely and openly. At the same time, this conversation should not disrupt the classroom nor disturb the participants. Conversation before or after class, or at some other time, may be necessary.

d. Observers should use whatever instruments (e.g., observation schedules, questionnaires) and mechanical devises (e.g., camera, audiotapes, videotapes) they find useful in aiding them in the collection of the needed evidence.

7. When rating scales are preferred, the following recommendations should be considered.

a. The dimensions included on rating scales should be consistent with those identified in previous research (since rating scales have been so widely used) but should also be selected based on the expressed purpose of the study. Since innumerable dimensions *could be* included on rating scales, researchers once again must attend to issues of cost effectiveness. In this regard, the dimensions identified by Ryans (1960a) provide a useful "starter set" and those mentioned by Berliner and Tikunoff (1976) constitute perhaps the most complete set compiled to date.

b. Each dimension should be clearly defined and illustrated. The definitions should emphasize what is included and what is excluded. Furthermore, both positive and negative examples should be presented. An example of an appropriate definition, developed by Berliner and Tikunoff, is displayed in Figure 5.7.

c. Observers should be told to make as many independent judgments as they can with respect to each dimension. They should be informed that all of the dimensions are somewhat distinct, and that each is needed to provide additional evidence concerning the classroom, teachers, or students. In this way, the "halo" effect may be reduced somewhat.

ABRUPTNESS (T)
We mean:
—teacher changes from one activity or lesson to another without advising students
—unanticipated change without "tying up" what was in progress
—pupils surprised or confused by teacher's change in behavior
—teacher switches from instruction to behavior management and back again
Examples:
1. Teacher, "Okay, get out your readers and turn to page 195."
Students, "But we haven't finished our math work sheet."
Teacher, "Sorry, maybe you can find time to do it later."
2. During reading lesson, teacher is listening to students in a small group reading aloud. Several times she interrupts whoever is reading in order to administer discipline to someone in another part of the room.
3. Students have been working diligently, but noisily. After several warnings, teacher says, "All right. Put your books away. Since you already know the materials, it's quiz time."
We do not mean:
—smooth transition between work periods
—eases in from one activity to the next
Examples:
1. Teacher makes sure that students understand what they are to do before starting the activity.
2. Teacher systematically monitors work, gives assistance when or before it is needed.
3. Before math begins students may get a drink and relax for a moment. Then they get their math books and papers and begin their work.

FIG. 5.7   Example of appropriate definition of a dimension included on a rating scale (from Berliner and Tikunoff, 1976).

Examples and Illustrations

Observing in classrooms has come a long way since Goodlad, Klein, and their colleagues (1970) invited researchers to go *Behind the Classroom Door*. In this section, we present and discuss briefly specific tools that have been used by researchers in their attempts to respond to Goodlad et al.'s invitation.

A large number of structured observation systems have been developed over the past three decades. The system developed by Flanders (1960) has enjoyed a great deal of popularity and received a great deal of criticism (e.g., Walker and Adelman, 1975). As mentioned in Chapter 5, the system was developed for the purpose of differentiating between those teachers who were more "direct" and more "indirect" in their interactions with students. Because of the care that went into its development and the extensiveness of its use, the *Flanders Interaction Analysis System (FIAS)* is extremely useful pedagogically.

Flanders and Amidon (1981) describe the FIAS as follows:

> FIAS is a procedure for coding classroom interaction into ten categories. A trained observer records numerical code symbols to represent the communication events among pupils and between pupils and teacher. A code symbol is recorded at least once every three seconds . . . [producing] approximately 100 code symbols in five minutes, 600 in one-half hour, and 1,200 in an hour (p. 1).

The ten categories are: teacher accepts feeling, teacher praises and encourages, teacher accepts and uses ideas, teacher asks questions, teacher lectures, teacher gives directions, teacher criticizes or justifies, student responds, student initiates, and silence and confusion.[4]

Observers using the FIAC are to code observed events according to a series of four decision steps (see Figure 5.8). They are to decide first whether they can hear and understand what is being said in the classroom. If they can hear and understand, they next are to determine who said it, the teacher or a student. The third decision concerns whether the utterance represents an initiation or a response, while the final decision pertains to the nature of the initiation or response itself.

---

[4]It is both understandable and unfortunate that Flanders combined silence and confusion into a single category in the FIAS. The combination is understandable since the category has little to do with the primary purpose of the lines of inquiry developed by Flanders (that is, the investigation of direct versus indirect teacher-student communication). However, the combination is unfortunate since silence and confusion are quite distinct events with quite different meanings. As Dunkin and Biddle (1974) point out, "confusion is surely something to be avoided at most times in the classroom, while silence may at times be necessary for individual study" (p. 373).

Does an observer hear and understand what is said in the classroom ?

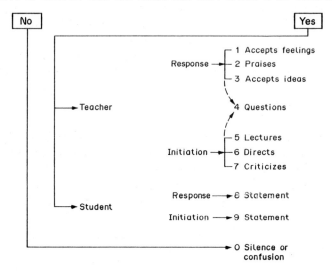

FIG. 5.8   Coding decisions for the Flanders Interaction Analysis System (from Flanders and Amidon, 1981).

Episode A			Episode B		
Category	Total	Percent	Category	Total	Percent
1	0		1	0	
2	0		2	0	
3 II	2		3 ℋℋ ℋℋ ℋℋ IIII	19	
4 ℋℋ ℋℋ ℋℋ I	16		4 ℋℋ ℋℋ III	13	
5 ℋℋ ℋℋ ℋℋ ℋℋ ℋℋ ℋℋ	30		5 ℋℋ III	8	
6 ℋℋ ℋℋ III	13		6 ℋℋ II	7	
7	0		7	0	
8 ℋℋ ℋℋ ℋℋ ℋℋ ℋℋ ℋℋ I	31		8 ℋℋ ℋℋ ℋℋ ℋℋ III	23	
9	0		9 ℋℋ ℋℋ ℋℋ ℋℋ II	22	
0 ℋℋ III	8		0 ℋℋ III	8	
Total	100		Total	100	

FIG. 5.9   Tally summary from two classroom observation episodes using the FIAS (from Flanders and Amidon, 1981).

As observers progress through these steps, they are to tally each time a particular type of initiation or response is made by a teacher or a student. At the end of a particular period of time (or episode), the total number of tallies made by the observer can be examined. Figure 5.9 illustrates the tally summary for two separate episodes.

One of the more popular structured observation systems is that developed by Stallings (1977). Stallings' system was used, with some modification, in the studies reported by Goodlad (1984) and Anderson et al. (1989). Stallings' system is different from Flanders' system in several respects.

First, the system provides general information about the classroom (e.g., general activities, seating arrangements, materials, and equipment) as well as more specific information about teacher–student interactions. Second, it is a multidimensional rather than a single dimensional system. For example, each observed interaction is to be placed into categories aligned with four dimensions: who initiated the interaction, to whom the interaction was directed, what the interaction was about, and how the interaction occurred. An example of the interaction coding is shown in Figure 5.10.

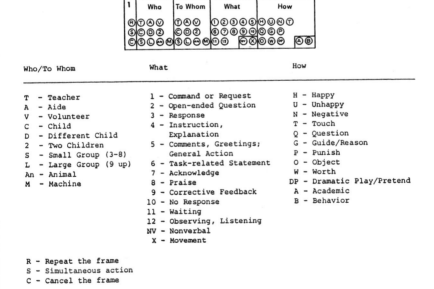

FIG. 5.10   One five-second frame from the Stallings' Five-Minute Interaction instrument (from Stallings, 1977). From *Learning to Look: A Handbook on Classroom Observation and Teaching Models* by Jane A. Stallings © 1977 by Wadsworth Publishing Company, Inc. Used by permission of the publisher.

Two other useful and useable observation systems have been developed: Galton, Simon, and Croll (1980) and Crocker et al. (1978). Both systems include separate forms for the observation of teachers and students. In addition, the system devised by Crocker et al. includes a separate form for coding the lesson. On the lesson form, a concise, four dimension rating scale is included (i.e., warmth, enthusiasm, clarity, and efficiency). Thus, like the Stallings' system, the Crocker et al. system emphasizes a concern for both teaching and instruction. Researchers would be wise to examine these existing systems before setting out to develop their own.

With respect to rating scales, Ryans (1960a) *Classroom Observation Record (COR)* is one of the oldest and best documented. The COR includes four pupil dimensions and eighteen teacher dimensions (see Figure 5.11). Each dimension is identified by two adjectives with opposite meanings. Events associated with each of the adjectives are included in a glossary.

CLASSROOM OBSERVATION RECORD
9-22-51
TEACHER CHARACTERISTICS STUDY

Teacher_____ No.____ Sex____ Class or Subject____ Date_____

City_____ School_____ Time____ Observer_____

PUPIL BEHAVIOR   REMARKS:

1. Apathetic	1	2	3	4	5	6	7	N	Alert
2. Obstructive	1	2	3	4	5	6	7	N	Responsible
3. Uncertain	1	2	3	4	5	6	7	N	Confident
4. Dependent	1	2	3	4	5	6	7	N	Initiating

TEACHER BEHAVIOR

5. Partial	1	2	3	4	5	6	7	N	Fair
6. Autocratic	1	2	3	4	5	6	7	N	Democratic
7. Aloof	1	2	3	4	5	6	7	N	Responsive
8. Restricted	1	2	3	4	5	6	7	N	Understanding
9. Harsh	1	2	3	4	5	6	7	N	Kindly
10. Dull	1	2	3	4	5	6	7	N	Stimulating
11. Stereotyped	1	2	3	4	5	6	7	N	Original
12. Apathetic	1	2	3	4	5	6	7	N	Alert
13. Unimpressive	1	2	3	4	5	6	7	N	Attractive
14. Evading	1	2	3	4	5	6	7	N	Responsible
15. Erratic	1	2	3	4	5	6	7	N	Steady
16. Excitable	1	2	3	4	5	6	7	N	Poised
17. Uncertain	1	2	3	4	5	6	7	N	Confident
18. Disorganized	1	2	3	4	5	6	7	N	Systematic
19. Inflexible	1	2	3	4	5	6	7	N	Adaptable
20. Pessimistic	1	2	3	4	5	6	7	N	Optimistic
21. Immature	1	2	3	4	5	6	7	N	Integrated
22. Narrow	1	2	3	4	5	6	7	N	Broad

FIG. 5.11   The Ryans' *Classroom Observation Record* (from Ryans, 1960a).
Reproduced by permission of the American Council on Education,
Washington, D.C.

Perhaps the most complete set of dimensions for inclusion on rating scales can be found in Berliner and Tikunoff (1976). Based on the results of their ethnographic study in conjunction with the Beginning Teacher Evaluation Study, Berliner and Tikunoff identified and defined 61 dimensions. Of these 61 dimensions, 52 pertained to the teacher, seven to the students, and two (adult involvement and conviviality) to the classroom. Researchers can develop their own rating scales by selecting those that are most appropriate in light of their purpose and conceptual framework. Observers using the rating scale are expected to rate each dimension on a seven-point scale, ranging from less (1) to more (7) (see Figure 5.12 for an example).

Specimen records, classroom chronicles, summaries of ethnographic field notes, and transcriptions of audiotape recordings all look very similar.

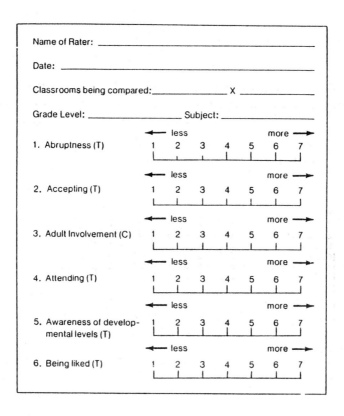

FIG. 5.12   A sample rating scale (from Berliner and Tikunoff, 1976).

Typically, classroom chronicles (see Figure 5.13) are somewhat more detailed than ethnographic field notes (see Figure 5.14). Furthermore, field notes typically include more of the observers' insights and impressions than do classroom chronicles. Both classroom chronicles and ethnographic field notes include descriptions of physical actions as well as verbal dialogue, whereas transcripts of audiotape recordings obviously include the verbal dialogue only (see Figure 5.15). Verbatim statements are needed in transcriptions, while paraphrases or summaries may be appropriate in classroom chronicles and field notes.

9:25 T says "All right now, we've talked about hard and

soft sounds. Again, I will go over the word, 'sit.'

The sound is hard or soft?"

So the students in this reading group say, "Soft." ...

[The explanation of worksheets continues four minutes.]

T says, "Who can put this word in a sentence?"

Billy raises his hand.

T asks Billy.

Bill uses the word in a sentence.

T says, "Good."

T then says, "Are there anymore questions?"

T continues, "All right go to work on these pages and

they'll be due this morning."

The students begin to work.

9:29 T comes over to her desk and says, "Children in the Red

Reader Group, why don't you just go back for a little bit

without your books and we'll practice our game."

The students begin to gather at the back of the room in the

reading circle.

9:30 T requests: "Move your chairs a little bit so that you can see

the board."

T says, "Who would like to be the leader? Becky?"

Becky comes up to the blackboard and points to a word on the

blackboard with a pointer.

Some of the students answer but none of them have done it

correctly yet.

FIG. 5.13   An excerpt from a classroom chronicle (Gump, 1969). [Note. T stands for teacher.]

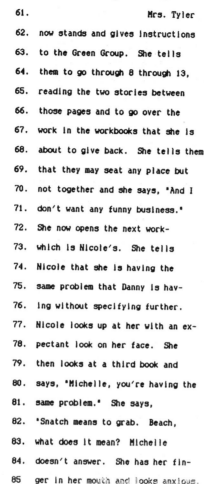

```
61.                    Mrs. Tyler
62.   now stands and gives instructions
63.   to the Green Group. She tells
64.   them to go through 8 through 13,
65.   reading the two stories between
66.   those pages and to go over the
67.   work in the workbooks that she is
68.   about to give back. She tells them
69.   that they may seat any place but
70.   not together and she says, "And I
71.   don't want any funny business."
72.   She now opens the next work-
73.   which is Nicole's. She tells
74.   Nicole that she is having the
75.   same problem that Danny is hav-
76.   ing without specifying further.
77.   Nicole looks up at her with an ex-
78.   pectant look on her face. She
79.   then looks at a third book and
80.   says, "Michelle, you're having the
81.   same problem." She says,
82.   "Snatch means to grab. Beach,
83.   what does it mean? Michelle
84.   doesn't answer. She has her fin-
85.   ger in her mouth and looks anxious.
```

FIG. 5.14   An excerpt from a protocol summary made from notes read into a cassette recorder (Berliner and Tikunoff, 1976). [Note. The line numbers are for easy recall and reference.]

Examining Existing Evidence

Sometimes the evidence needed to address the questions posed by researchers already exists and is available to them. When this is the case, researchers would be wise to examine these existing sources of evidence. In fact, before deciding to ask questions or observe events, researchers should determine whether the evidence exists, is accessible, and is useable. If so, much time and effort on the part of researchers can be saved.

T: However, to get back to our main point once more,
   in talking about the U. S. role in, in all this
   international trade. Our export trade is vital
   to us. Our import trade is vital to us, and it
   would upset and shake American economy to a
   tremendous extent if we were to stop importing
   or stop exporting. Let's turn to American in-
   vestments abroad. You suppose we do invest much
   money outside of the U. S.?

P: Yes.

T: In what ways, in what fields? How would it be
   done?

P: Well, a lot of the big companies here in the
   U. S. will set up companies over in other countries, and that way they can give the workers
   over there a chance to work and to sell their
   products and the foreign countries can get the
   tax off that.

T: I think you put the most important thing last,
   but that's true. The branch office in a foreign
   country, which involves the exportation of American capital, is so often done to avoid paying
   what?

P: Taxes.

FIG. 5.15 An excerpt from a transcript made from an audiotape recording
(Bellack et al., 1966). [Note. T stands for teacher; P for pupil]
Reprinted by permission of the publisher from Bellack et al., *The Language of
the Classroom*. (New York: Teachers College Press, © 1966 by Teachers
College, Columbia University. All rights reserved.), pp. 38–40.

Existing evidence typically comes in two forms: physical objects or
exhibits and written or visual records or documents.[5] Textbooks, desks,
projectors, computers, televisions, pencils and pens, and floor tiles or
carpeting are all examples of physical objects. Letters, memoranda, minutes
of meetings, lesson plans, audiotape or videotape recordings, and photo-

[5]Lincoln (1980) differentiates between a record and a document. A record is "any written
statement prepared by an individual or an agency for the purpose of attesting to an event or
providing an accounting" (p. 4). In contrast, a document is "any written (or filmed) material
other than a record . . . which was not prepared specifically in response to some request from
or some task set by the investigator" (p. 4). Thus, the primary difference lies in the purpose (or
lack of purpose) for which the material was prepared.

graphs are examples of records or documents. Each of these sources of evidence can be used to answer a variety of research questions. Consider the following two examples.

Suppose, first, we are interested in determining where those teachers who experiment with novel or innovative teaching practices get their ideas. Quite clearly, we may ask the teachers themselves. Many would say that this is the easiest way of getting the evidence we need. However, several other existing pieces of evidence may be equally or more useful in helping us make our determination. We can examine the journals and periodicals that are on the teachers' desks. We can read through correspondence sent to the teachers from publishing companies, the school principal, or personnel at the central office. We can examine notes taken during faculty meetings or staff development workshops. Each of these sources of evidence can shed some light on how teachers came to choose the novel or innovative practices they are using.

Suppose, next, we are interested in investigating the grouping practices in a school and how they have changed over time. Certainly, we can ask teachers about their current grouping practices and to recall how they have changed, if at all, during their tenure at the school. At the time, however, we may examine student records to see whether indications of ability grouping are present (e.g., levels of courses placed on their transcripts) or whether students assigned to a particular section of a course having similar or different scores on ability or achievement tests. Since grouping may occur within classrooms as well as between classrooms, we may walk into classrooms and note the physical arrangement of chairs and tables, or the opportunities for chair and tables to be moved (rather than bolted down). If our interest in grouping practices extends for longer periods of time, we may examine photographs that have been taken at different times.

These two examples illustrate the possibilities inherent in using existing evidence in studies of teachers, teaching, and instruction. Numerous other examples can be cited. Apparently, the only real limitation in the use of existing evidence is the lack of creativity of the researcher.

Strengths and Weaknesses of Examining Existing Evidence

As might be expected, examining existing evidence, like asking and observing, has its strengths and weaknesses. In this section, we discuss these strengths and weaknesses.

Strengths. Using existing evidence has at least two major strengths. First, the evidence was not produced for examination by researchers. As a consequence, reactivity on the part of those who produced the evidence (e.g., withholding evidence, misrepresenting the actual state of affairs) is minimized. In this vein, there is a certain anonymity inherent in the evidence. For example, a memorandum may come from the "Director of

Secondary Education." An historical document may have been prepared by someone who has since left his or her position.

Second, the evidence is available at minimum cost. Observers do not have to be selected or trained; questionnaires or interview protocols do not have to be prepared, distributed, or collected. The only real costs involved are the location of the sources of evidence and the analysis of the evidence once located (an issue to which we shall return in the next chapter).

Weaknesses. Two primary weaknesses are associated with the use of existing evidence. First, the available evidence may not adequately represent the range of evidence that currently exists or has existed. This lack of representation (or selectivity) may be due to the unintended loss of certain evidence (e.g., not all minutes of certain meetings were in a particular file) or the biased selection of evidence to be made available (e.g., a photographer in 1900 posed students to illustrate the "New Education" (Cuban, 1984)).

Second, the evidence as is may require verification or explanation if the researcher is to gain a full understanding of it. Researchers may not be sure of the accuracy or meaning of the evidence. Some corroboration may be necessary. With historical documents, comparisons with other relevant documents may be necessary. With contemporary documents, asking about the accuracy or meaning of the evidence may be necessary or useful.

Recommendations

Several recommendations concerning the use of existing and available evidence can be offered. Many of these recommendations are implicit in our analysis of the strengths and weaknesses of these sources of evidence.

1. Investigate the origins and usefulness of the exhibits and documents. Clark (1967) cited in Webb et al. (1981) provides a list of issues to which researchers should attend as they consider the value of existing evidence for their research purposes. This list is displayed in Table 5.4. Since Clark is a historian, not all of the entries on the list may be appropriate for researchers in education. Nonetheless, a careful perusal of the list would likely help those researchers concerned with the proper use of existing evidence in their own research.

2. Because of problems associated with selectivity and bias of the evidence, attempt to gather multiple and varied sources of evidence (e.g., photographs, written documents, physical artifacts) in different settings (e.g., urban vs. rural, elementary vs. secondary, traditional vs. open classrooms) and, if needed, at different time periods (e.g., ten years ago and today). Convergence across these sources of evidence, settings, and time periods increases the validity of the inferences made based on the evidence gathered. At the same time, however, divergence of the evidence points the

TABLE 5.4

Questions Researchers Should Ask When Examining Records and Documents

What is the history of the document?
How did it come into my hands?
What guarantee is there that it is what it pretends to be?
Is the document complete, as originally constructed?
Has it been tampered with or edited?
If the document is genuine, under what circumstances and for what purposes
  was it produced?
Who was/is the author?
What was he trying to accomplish? For whom was the document intended?
What were the maker's sources of information? Does the document represent
  an eyewitness account, a secondhand account, a reconstruction of an event
  long prior to writing, an interpretation?
What was or is the maker's bias?
To what extent was the writer likely to want to tell the truth?
Do other documents exist that might shed additional light on this same story,
  event, project, program, context?
If so, are they available, accessible? Who holds them?

Source: Webb et al. (1981).
Reproduced by permission of Webb, E. J., Campbell, D. T., et al. (1981) © Houghton Mifflin.

researcher to avenues of research in need of pursuit. The identification of the factors or conditions that tend to impact on the generalizability of the inferences is an important aspect of research in classrooms.

3. Consider the need for corroboration of the evidence. One of the major strengths of using existing evidence, anonymity, quite easily becomes a weakness. If the person who provided the evidence is unknown, that person's credibility also is unknown. As a consequence, the need to seek other sources of evidence (e.g., other people or other documents) becomes critical if existing evidence is to be considered reliable and valid.

Examples and Illustrations

In his study of the constancy and change in teaching methods over the past century, Cuban (1984) relied extensively on still photographs, many of which are reprinted in his book. These photographs of classrooms were analyzed in terms of five features: class arrangement, group instruction, classroom talk, class activities, and student movement. The nature of these analyses will be discussed in greater detail in the following chapter. Additional examples and illustrations are described in Webb et al. (1981).

Closing Comments

Classroom research requires that evidence be gathered to address the problems raised and questions asked by researchers. Researchers have at their discretion a variety of sources of evidence. None of the sources is likely to yield "perfect" or "error-free" evidence. Each has identifiable strengths and weaknesses.

In conducting classroom research, then, two points should be remembered. First, researchers should attempt to match the strengths of particular sources of evidence with the demands of the research study (while at the same time recognizing and attempting to minimize the weaknesses). Second, multiple sources of evidence are more likely to provide a level of understanding needed by the researchers to solve the problems they pose or answer the questions they raise. Placing the burden of responsibility on a single source of evidence is most likely to result in disappointment on the part of the researcher. In contrast, multiple sources of evidence are likely to provide the variety of evidence needed to understand the complexity of classrooms as they exist.

6

The Meaning and Quality of the Evidence

As discussed in the previous two chapters, classroom researchers have several sources of evidence from which to choose as they seek to answer their questions. As we saw in Chapter 5, examining the strengths and weaknesses of each source is a useful first step in deciding among the various alternatives. However, two other concerns must be addressed before the evidence collected can be used to arrive at answers to the research questions. First, is the evidence meaningful to the researchers and other people with whom they come into contact (e.g., colleagues, clients, practitioners)? Second, is the evidence of sufficient quality to ensure its credibility and accuracy? These two questions form the basis for this chapter.

The Meaning of Evidence

As defined in *The Random House College Dictionary* (Stein, 1984) meaning is "that which is intended to be, or actually is, expressed or indicated; signification; import" (p. 828). This definition immediately sets up a likely conflict between the person using a word or phrase and the person hearing or reading it. The speaker's or writer's intended meaning, and the meaning understood by the listener or reader may be quite different.

Linguists differentiate between denotative (primary) and connotative (secondary) meaning of words. While denotative meanings are widely accepted in a particular culture, connotative meaning are highly dependent on the specific audience to whom the word is being communicated. As Carroll (1964) points out:

> Rules of usage define the *denotative meaning* of a term. Thus, there is a rule of usage such that the noun *mother* can be used only for a certain kind of kinship relation. One thinks of denotative meaning as something that is socially prescribed. Connotative meaning, however, banks heavily on those aspects of concepts that are widely shared yet non-criterial and perhaps affective (emotional) in content. "Mother" as a noun might evoke various emotional feelings dependent upon one's experience with mothers (p. 186).

Psychologists define meaning primarily in terms of the listener or reader. Specifically, a word or phrase has meaning to someone when that person is able to form associations between the word or phrase and his or her mental representations of prior experiences (Neisser, 1967). Quite likely, some of these associations are made with representations of prior experiences that are shared with other people in the culture, while other associations are formed with representations or experiences that are unique to the individual.

Classroom researchers tend to live in a variety of cultures and attempt to communicate with members of each. They talk with and write for other classroom researchers who operate within the same paradigm. They talk with (but rarely write for) classroom researchers who operate within other paradigms. Finally, they talk with (and sometimes write for) non-researchers (e.g., policymakers, practitioners, and the lay public). Sadly, but perhaps unavoidably, these various groups speak very different languages and a common meaning of particular words, numbers, or symbols cannot be assumed.

Many of the terms and phrases used by classroom researchers do have the potential for multiple meanings. Other phrases are "coined" by researchers to add precision to their meaning or to differentiate them from more commonly used terms and phrases with similar though not identical meanings. "Pedagogical moves," "surface curriculum," "academic learning time," and "student-centered instruction" are but a very few examples of such phrases. Thus, it is incumbent upon classroom researchers to make clear their intended meaning; explicit conceptual frameworks are the primary vehicle for accomplishing this task.

Conceptual frameworks have an underlying structure. By structure, we mean the attributes that define each concept, the interrelationships among the concepts, and the source or sources of evidence associated with each concept. The structure of the conceptual framework gives meaning to the evidence that is gathered.

Several conceptual frameworks have guided studies of classrooms over the past several decades. Studies have been conducted within frameworks derived from fields as varied as social psychology (Flanders, 1960), linguistics (Bellack et al., 1966), phenomonology (Bussis et al., 1976), behavioral psychology (Fisher et al., 1978), sociolinguistics (Morine-Dershimer, 1985), and historiography (Cuban, 1984). In order to understand the impact of conceptual frameworks on the meaning of the evidence we shall consider four studies in some detail: Bellack et al. (1966), Bussis et al. (1976), Fisher et al. (1978), and Cuban (1984). Following our examination of the studies, we shall offer suggestions concerning ways in which the meaning of evidence can be enhanced.

Bellack et al. (1966)

An explicit conceptual framework underlies the Bellack et al. study.

Viewing classroom discourse as a kind of language game was a useful approach for purposes of this research, in that it suggested a framework of analysis within which we could identify verbal expressions that communicate various kinds of meaning. . . . Examination of the transcripts of classroom discourse suggested that the verbal actions of students and teachers could be classified into four major categories structuring, soliciting, responding, and reacting. We labeled these basic verbal actions *pedagogical moves* and classified them in terms of the pedagogical functions they perform in classroom discourse. . . . We were also interested in the dimension of meaning represented by the content of the messages communicated. Analysis of classroom discourse . . . revealed four functionally different types of meanings [substantive, substantive-logical, instructional, and instructional-logical] (pp. 3–6).

According to Bellack et al., then, verbal communication in the classroom can be defined in terms of two independent factors: "pedagogical moves" and the "content of communication." In actuality, the "content of communication" dimension consists of two independent factors: "substantive" and "instructional" (as shown in Figure 6.1).

Each of the factors or dimensions is divided into categories. The four

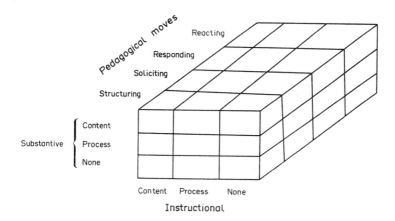

FIG. 6.1   The structure of verbal communication in classrooms as conceptualized by Bellack et al. (1966).

categories of "pedagogical moves" comprise the now-familiar sequence of structuring, soliciting, responding, and reacting. The "substantive" and "instructional" dimensions include two categories: content and process. The substantive-content category refers to the subject matter under study by the class, while the substantive-process category (labeled as "substantive-logical" by the authors) refers to the cognitive processes involved in dealing with the subject matter. Similarly, the instructional-content category refers to matters pertaining to classroom management, assignments, and procedures, while the instructional-process category (again labeled instructional-logical) refers to the cognitive processes involved in dealing with instruction. Each of the "substantive" and "instructional" categories were divided into a set of subcategories, some of which in turn were further subdivided. For example, the substantive-process category was divided into four subcategories (analytic, empirical, evaluative, and not clear). The analytic subcategory in turn was divided into four subcategories (defining-general, defining-denotative, defining-connotative, and interpreting). Bellack and his colleagues defined each of the categories shown in Figure 6.1 in somewhat general terms and then used examples of verbal interchanges taken from transcripts of classroom dialogue to complete the definitions.

Transcripts of audiotape recordings made in the teachers' classrooms constituted the primary source of evidence used to develop and examine this conceptual framework. The tapes were coded relative to the conceptual framework in the following manner. The first entry in each coding sequence represented the person who was speaking (that is, teacher, pupil, or audio-visual device). The next three entries represented the type of pedagogical move, substantive meaning, and substantive-logical meaning, respectively. The fifth entry represented the number of lines in the transcript pertaining to substantive and substantive-logical matters. The sixth and seventh entry represented the instructional and instructional-logic meanings, while the eighth entry represented the number of lines in the transcript pertaining to instructional and instructional-logical matters. The coding analysis of the excerpt shown in Chapter 5 (Figure 5.15) is displayed in Figure 6.2.

The first coding sequence indicates that the teacher (T) engaged in a reacting move (REA) by explaining (XPL) about imports and exports (IMX). The explanation lasted for five lines (5). Prior to the explanation, the teacher stated to the class (FAC) that it was time to get back to the main point (PRC). This statement required one line (1). Note that every coding sequence includes a pedagogical move. However, not every coding sequence includes a substantive or instructional code. When one or more of the substantive or instructional categories or subcategories is not appropriate, a hyphen is used. Thus, the sixth move P/RES/FOD/XPL/5/-/-/- indicates that neither the instructional nor the instructional-logical categories was appropriate in the analysis of this move. Rather, the pupil (P) simply

T: However, to get back to our main point once more,

in talking about the U. S. role in, in all this

international trade. Our export trade is vital

to us. Our import trade is vital to us, and it

would upset and shake American economy to a

tremendous extent if we were to stop importing

or stop exporting. |Let's turn to American in- T|REA|MX|XPL |5|PRC|FAC|1

vestments abroad. |You suppose we do invest much T|STR|FOR|-|-|PRC|FAC|1 /20|5|3/

money outside of the U. S. ?| ———————— T|SOL|FOR|FAC|1|-|-|-

————————— P|RES|FOR|FAC|1|-|-|-

P: Yes.|

T: In what ways, in what fields? How would it be /21 |18|7/

done?| ————————— T|SOL|FOR|XPL|1|-|-|-

P: Well, a lot of the big companies here in the

U. S. will set up companies over in other coun-

tries, and that way they can give the workers

over there a chance to work and to sell their

products and the foreign countries can get the

tax off that.| ———————— P|RES|FOD|XPL|5|-|-|-

T: I think you put the most important thing last,

but that's true. |The branch office in a foreign T|REA|FOD|-|-|STA|QAL|1

country, which involves the exportation of Amer-

ican capital, is so often done to avoid paying /22|14|4/

what?| ———————— T|SOL|FOD|XPL|3|-|-|-

P: Taxes.| ———————— P|RES|FOD|XPL|1|-|-|- /23 |14|2/

T: What kind of taxes?| ———————— T|SOL|FOD|FAC|1|-|-|-

P: Import.| ———————— P|RES|FOD|FAC|1|-|-|- /24 |14 |2/

T: Hm?| ———————— T|SOL|FOD|-|-|ACV|RPT|1

P: Import.| ———————— P|RES|FOD|-|-|ACV|RPT|1

T: Why would a company open up a branch in England, /25 |21|70/

or Germany or France or Italy?| ———————— T|SOL|FOD|XPL|2|-|-|-

P: Corporation won't have to pay tax?| ———————— P|RES|FOD|XPL|1|-|-|-

T: No, if it's an American corporation it's still

going to have a, have to pay corporation tax

over here. It might save a little bit on the

income earned by its branch office until it

brings that income back to this country it is

not taxed, but ultimately it would be. But

it's a different kind of tax. ⌐———————— T/REA|FOD|XPL|6|STA|NEG|1

P: The tariff. ⌐———————— P/RESOM3|FOD|XPL|1|-|-|-

T: The tariff. We're not the only country in the

world, you know, that has a tariff. If we want

to send our goods inside. . . Well, take tobacco,

for example. Most countries in the world have

placed a very, very high tariff on American

FIG. 6.2   Analysis of excerpt from protocol (from Bellack et al., pp. 267–268).

responded (RES) by explaining (XPL) about direct foreign investment (FOD).

The results of the coding analysis were summarized in terms of frequency counts and percentages. Two types of frequency counts were made. First, the number of lines in a transcript placed in each of the categories included in the conceptual framework provided one set of frequency counts. Second, the number of pedagogical moves was used as a second indicator of frequency. The excerpt displayed in Figure 6.2, for example, contains 24 lines and nine pedagogical moves (that is, coding sequences).

Both types of frequency counts were computed for each of the 36 cells in Figure 6.1. Furthermore, frequency counts were computed for each of the smaller cells not shown in Figure 6.1 (e.g., the number of structuring moves that included interpretation as a subcategory of the analytic process subcategory), each row of the figure, and each column of the figure. Percentages were computed based on the row totals, column totals, and overall total of lines and pedagogical moves. Furthermore, because of the structure of the conceptual framework, frequency counts could be summed (or aggregated) across the subcategories within the substantive and instructional dimensions. These aggregated frequencies also were transformed into percentages. Since the primary purpose of the study was to describe verbal interaction in classrooms these summary statistics were quite sufficient.[1]

Consistent with the main thesis of the chapter, the meaning of these frequency counts and percentages is heavily dependent on the conceptual framework developed by Bellack et al. The statement that four-fifths of the teachers' moves involved either soliciting or reacting is only interpretable when one understands the definition of soliciting and reacting, is aware of the other categories in the conceptual framework, and understands the concept of "pedagogical move." Similarly, the statement that teachers make relatively frequent directive statements concerned with instructional content, such as directing a pupil to speak or to perform some other classroom action must be understood in the context of the total number of utterances within the instructional-logical category (about one of every five of the total number of lines) as well as the total number of utterances within the overall conceptual framework (about one of every twenty of the total number of lines). Thus, the meaning of the evidence depends almost entirely on the conceptual framework underlying the study. Without a complete understanding of the conceptual framework, misunderstanding and misinterpretations are quite likely.[2]

Bussis et al. (1976)

Like the Bellack et al. study, the Bussis et al. study was conducted within the context of an explicit conceptual framework.

> The conceptual framework of this study does not rely heavily on assumptions about the actual occurrences of specific instances of behavior. Rather, it assumes that teachers' characteristic beliefs about children and learning have pervasive effects on their behavior, influencing the learning environment that they create for children and themselves. Teachers with similar characteristic beliefs may well foster similar kinds of growth and awareness in children, although they may differ markedly in behavioral specifics (pp. 15–16).

These characteristic beliefs were divided into several independent categories (see Figure 6.3).

---

[1]Ultimately, Bellack et al. examined the relationship between the verbal communication which occurred in the classroom and students' attitudes and achievement. In general, the relationship was nonexistent. However, in reading the report of the study, one gets the feeling that the investigation of this relationship was an afterthought. In the words of Bellack et al., "the test on international trade and the attitude scale used in this research represent very limited measures of learning outcomes" (p. 222). As a result, "no effort is made to present the results of these preliminary investigations in complex statistical terms, which are likely to mispresent the purpose of this study" (p. 222).

[2]Unfortunately, many practitioners get their information about research findings "second hand." Rather than read the original research reports, they read reviews of the research in professional journals or hear discussions of the research at professional meetings. Such "second hand" information rarely makes the connections between the conceptual framework and the eviddence that is needed. As Flanders and Amidon (1981) have pointed out, "knowledge of pedagogy is not so much imperfect as it is misunderstood and misused" (p. 14).

The first two general categories concern curriculum priorities and curriculum materials. Both of these categories are subdivided into subcategories. There are two subcategories of curriculum priorities: cognitive and person/social. Both these subcategories in turn are divided into "narrow," "middle-range," and "comprehensive" priorities. There are eight subcategories of curriculum materials, each pertaining to a different reason for using particular materials or types of materials (e.g., construing many possibilities, teaching a very specific outcome).

The remaining five general categories in the conceptual framework concern teachers' characteristic beliefs about children: the importance of their needs and feelings, the importance of their interests, the importance of choice of activities and materials, the ability of children to learn, and the importance of child-child interaction. The subcategories in each of these general categories are ordered from those most consistent with the principles of "open education" (i.e., the first subcategory under the general category) to those least consistent with these principles (i.e., the last subcategory under each general category). In certain cases, even smaller subcategories were developed to help those listening to the tapes to make proper coding decisions (see, for example, Bussis et al., p. 82, Table 5: 103–104, Table 11).

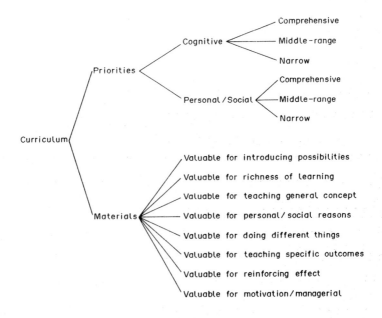

FIG. 6.3   The structure of teachers' characteristic beliefs about curriculum and children as hypothesized by Bussis et al. (1976).

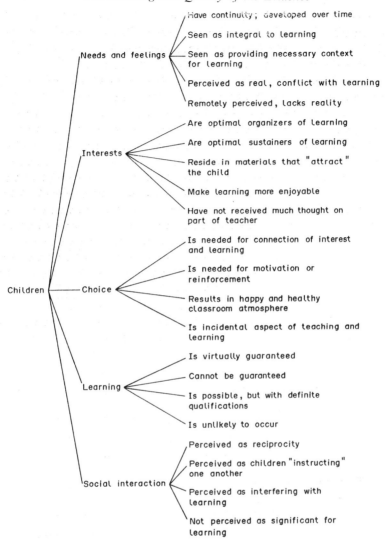

FIG. 6.3 (*continued*).

In many ways, the conceptual framework underlying the Bussis et al. study is the antithesis of that underlying the Bellack et al. study. Bussis et al. hypothesize that it is not the ways in which teachers and students communicate that is important to investigate; rather, it is the reasons that teachers have for communicating with students in the way they do that is important. As Bussis et al. state

A teacher may plan certain activities that are required of all children. . . . Because this is what an observer would see going on in the classroom, we have thought of this as the *surface content* (the perceptible form) of curriculum. At a deeper level, curriculum also has an *organizing content* that consists of the learning priorities and concerns that a teacher holds for children. . . . If surface content can be considered the *what* of curriculum, then organizing content is the *what for* (p. 50).

Audiotape recordings of open-ended interviews with the teachers served as the primary source of evidence. Researchers listened to the tapes and, based on the answers given and responses made by the teachers, assigned each teacher to a variety of coding categories. For the five categories associated with children, for example, teachers were first placed in as many of the smallest subcategories as the listener determined to be appropriate. Some of these subcategories were judged to be dominant in the teachers' responses; others were labeled "subsidiary." Based on their response patterns for these subcategories, teachers were assigned to one of the ordered categories associated with each of the five general categories shown in Figure 6.3. For the two categories linked to curriculum (that is, priorities and materials) no smaller subcategories were used. Rather, teachers were placed directly into one of the subcategories shown in Figure 6.3.

As in the Bellack et al. study, frequency counts and percentages were once again used to summarize the data. Unlike the Bellack et al. study, however, the frequency counts represented the numbers and percentages of teachers, not the number of lines of transcription or pedagogical moves. Also once again, the meaning of the evidence depends almost entirely on the conceptual framework and the general purpose of the study. To understand the statement that almost one-quarter of the teachers expressed a belief that child-child interaction is generally not significant for learning or can, in fact, interfere with learning, one must be aware of the definition of child-child interaction, the type of questions that teachers were asked concerning child-child interaction, and the other categories of teachers' reactions to child-child interaction that were included in the conceptual framework.

In an attempt to increase the meaning of the evidence, Bussis et al. used excerpts from teachers' interviews in combination with the frequencies and percentages. The following excerpts from interviews help us to understand what is meant by the belief that child-child interaction may interfere with learning.

Children can help each other when sometimes I don't realize they need help. Of course, in helping they also copy each other. I've discussed that with them (p. 105).

There's an awful lot of fooling around when children talk or work together, but you have to expect some of that (p. 106).

In addition to the conceptual framework, it is necessary to know something about the teachers who were interviewed if we are to understand the evidence gathered and presented. All 60 of the teachers interviewed were "attempting to implement open or more informal approaches to instruction" (p. 33). As a consequence, the evidence presented concerning teachers' characteristic beliefs about children (that is, the last five categories included in the conceptual framework) is likely to overestimate the percentage of teachers in the general population whose responses would place them in the more child-centered subcategories.

Fisher et al. (1978)

The Fisher et al. study differs from the previous two studies in three important ways. First, the primary purpose of the Fisher et al. study was to link what happened in classrooms with what students learned and achieved. The researchers were not particularly interested in what happened in classrooms (as in the case of the Bellack et al. study) nor in why it happened (as in the case of the Bussis et al. study). In our terminology, the Bellack et al. and Bussis et al. studies were *descriptive*, while the Fisher et al. study was *associational*. As we shall see later in this chapter, the difference between descriptive and associational studies is quite important as one struggles with issues concerning the quality of the evidence.

Second, Fisher et al. relied on a variety of sources of evidence. They used a structured observation system, a rating scale, and interviews with teachers. In contrast, both Bellack et al. and Bussis et al. used a single source of evidence, written transcripts of classroom dialogue and audiotape recordings of interviews, respectively.

Third, the categories included on the observation system and the dimensions included on the rating scales were derived from the conceptual framework (as was true of the two prior studies); in addition, however, these categories and dimensions focused the attention of the classroom observers on certain events at the exclusion of others. Thus, the categories were used to gather the evidence, rather than to analyze the evidence once gathered.[3]

Because of these differences, the conceptual framework underlying the Fisher et al. study is somewhat more complex than the frameworks underlying the two previous studies.

> The general goal of classroom research on teaching effectiveness is to identify classroom conditions and teaching acts which foster student learning. . . . Scores on achievement tests provide one index of student learning, but they do not constitute learning itself. . . . Student behaviors during instruction should provide a more immediate indicator of learning as it takes place. . . . The general model of instruction states that, for a given student, instructional processes (what happens in the classroom) lead to student learning behaviors and achievement test scores. [Student] aptitudes represent characteristics of the student which are "brought to" the learning situation (p. 2-2).

[3]This distinction between categories formed for the purpose of collecting the evidence and categories formed for the purpose of analyzing the evidence once collected has existed for some time. Perhaps the simplest way of differentiating between them is to label the first, "data collection" categories and the second, "data analytic" categories.

The conceptual framework underlying both the Bellack et al. and Bussis et al. studies had one primary, superordinate concept. For Bellack et al., this concept was the verbal communication which occurred in the classroom. The categories and subcategories included in their conceptual framework were intended to define this concept. For Bussis et al., this concept was the characteristic beliefs of teachers concerning the curriculum and children. Again, the categories and subcategories of the conceptual framework defined this concept. In general, the meaning of the results of descriptive studies depeneds on the structure of the primary concept or concepts being described. While relationships among the categories or subcategories that define the concept can be examined, accurate and credible descriptions of the primary concept remains the primary focus of descriptive studies.

Researchers conducting associational studies, on the other hand, should specify the relationships among the major concepts included in conceptual framework *as well as* the structure of each of the concepts. Fisher et al., for example, emphasize the hypothesized relationships among the concepts included in their conceptual framework, a graphical display of which is displayed in Figure 6.4.

The conceptual framework developed by Fisher et al. contains four primary concepts, not one. Furthermore, the expected relationships among the concepts are represented by arrows. Students' aptitudes are hypothesized to influence students' classroom behaviors and their achievement test scores. Instructional processes and the classroom environment are hypothesized to influence students' classroom behaviors, but are not believed to directly influence their achievement. Finally, students' classroom behaviors are believed to directly effect achievement test scores.

Each of the four primary concepts included in the conceptual framework has an explicit structure. In actuality, the concepts are best considered as "place holders." That is, evidence directly related to the concepts is never

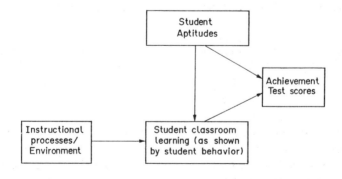

FIG. 6.4   Conceptual model underlying the Fisher et al. (1978) Study.

collected. Rather, the evidence is directly related to the "smallest" categories or subcategories included in the conceptual framework. Once the evidence is collected then either some computational or statistical technique is used to "move" the evidence to the next largest category or inferences about the larger categories are made by the researcher based on the evidence that exists relative to the smaller categories. Both options are used in the BTES.

Figure 6.5, for example, illustrates the structure of the concept, "instructional processes/classroom environment." The three major dimensions that define this concept are interactive teaching behaviors, setting, and the teacher and the classroom. These dimensions are subdivided into two, three, and five categories, respectively. And, as can be seen in Figure 6.5, most of these categories are further subdivided. The evidence gathered with respect to the smaller categories is never combined all the way to the level of the primary concept. Thus, any statement related to the "instructional processes/classroom environment" concept is based solely on inferences made by the researcher.

Figure 6.6 illustrates the structure of the concept, "student classroom learning (as shown by student behavior)." This concept is defined in terms of three critical dimensions: relevance of the instructional activities to a given academic outcome, student engagement in the activity, and student success in the activity. As we shall soon see, evidence pertaining to each of these dimensions is combined into a total value for the concept.

Finally, the concept "achievement test scores" also has an explicit structure, one consistent with the various subtests of reading and mathematics (such as word meaning and multiplication). Evidence on these subtests is not combined. Achievement test scores obtained *prior* to the study are used as indicators of the concept "student aptitudes." Again, the evidence is kept separate for reading and mathematics.

As has been mentioned, several sources of evidence were used in the study. Standardized tests were used as measures of student achievement and student aptitude. Structured observation systems were used as measures of instructional processes and student classroom learning. The

> observation system was a time-based rotating-sample procedure. [It] recorded detailed information on the instructional day for individual target students. An event for each student was sampled about once every four minutes. Each event was coded along several dimensions. These dimensions included content of instruction, setting, student behavior (engagement and error rate) and the instructional behavior provided by teachers and other instructors (pp. 5-1, 5-2).

In addition to the structured observation systems, observers on other occasions were asked to make notes on their observations and complete a series of rating scales, the majority of which pertained to "the teacher and the classroom" category of the "instructional processes/classroom environment" concept.

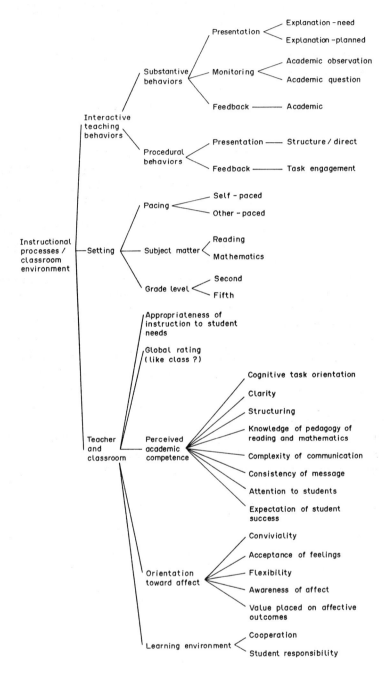

FIG. 6.5   Structure of Instructional Processes/Classroom Environment as
defined by Fisher et al. (1978).

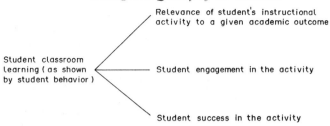

FIG. 6.6   The structure of Student Classroom Learning as defined by Fisher et al. (1978).
Note. Because this concept was measured in the time metric, it typically was referred to as Academic Learning Time (ALT). All three categories had to occur simultaneously for one minute of ALT to be coded.

Because of the large number of sources of evidence, a variety of types of evidence was produced. Achievement test scores were presented as residualized gains. Such gains represent the difference between the actual achievement score of a student and the achievement score for that student predicted from his or her prior year's test score (or aptitude) using a regression equation. These gains (or losses, as when a student scores less well than he or she was predicted to score) were averaged across all of the students in a particular classroom or receiving instruction from a particular teacher.

Evidence concerning the subcategories included on the structured observation system pertaining to the category "interactive teaching behaviors" was presented in terms of the "*percentages* of student instructional time in reading or mathematics" (p.5-5). These percentages, computed for teacher, were averaged across the observation occasions.

Evidence pertaining to the category "the teacher and the classroom" was gathered using rating scales. For each subcategory within this category, a numerical rating from 1 to 7 was assigned to each teacher on each observation occasion by the classroom observer. Once again, since multiple observations were made, average ratings were computed for each teacher.

Finally, evidence concerning the concept "student classroom learning" was summarized in terms of the *number of minutes* during which students in each classroom were given an activity related to an academic outcome, were engaged in the activity, *and* were successful in completing the activity. Because this concept was measured in terms of the number of minutes, it was referred to as academic learning time (ALT). It should be emphasized that all three of these conditions must have been in place before any amount of ALT was recorded. Once again, the minutes of ALT were averaged across observation occasions.

In addition to these various averages, correlations were computed between the various categories of each of the concepts included in the conceptual framework (see Figure 6.4). In addition, regression coefficients were computed to investigate the more complex relationships inherent in the framework.

Despite the increased complexity of the conceptual framework and the increased sophistication of the analytic techniques, the meaning of the evidence once again rests almost entirely in the conceptual framework. As Fisher et al. point out:

> All research is a combination of objective analysis and subjective interpretation. Although the image of science is that it is objective, in fact it is very difficult to separate the objective from the subjective. Whenever words are used to describe a phenomenon, subjective interpretation enters in to some degree (p. 11-2).

In order to understand the meaning of the conclusion that "more substantive interaction between the student and an instructor is associated with higher percentages of student engagement" (p. 11-14), one must know the meaning of "substantive interaction" and "student engagement," the place of these two categories in the overall conceptual framework underlying the study, the extent to which evidence was combined or inferences made, the range of substantive interaction within the sample of teachers (that is, the minimum and maximum amount of substantive interaction that occurred), and the range of student engagement with the classes of students (that is, the minimum and maximum percentage of student engagement).

Restriction of range typically results in lower correlation coefficients, thus confounding the interpretation. In addition, without an awareness of the range of "substantive interaction" and "student engagement," useful implications for educational practice are unlikely. If, for example, the upper limit of substantive interaction is 60 percent of the students' instructional time, it would make little sense to recommend that teachers currently engaging in substantive interaction for 58 percent of the students' instructional time increase the amount of their substantial interaction.

Cuban (1984)

Cuban set out to determine why certain teacher behaviors remained stable "decade after decade in the face of mighty efforts to move toward student-centered instruction" (p. 5). He identified five factors or dimensions that could be used to differentiate student-centered instruction from teacher-centered instruction: class arrangement, group instruction, classroom talk, class activities, and student movement. These dimensions, then, comprised his conceptual framework as shown in Figure 6.7.

Behavioral indicators that differentiated "teacher-centered," "student-centered," and "mixed pattern" classrooms on each of these dimensions were identified (see Table 6.1). In combination, the five dimensions and the associated indicators defined what Cuban meant by "teacher-centered," "student-centered," and "mixed patterns" of instruction.

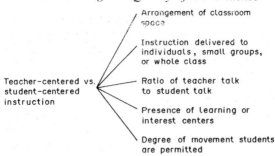

FIG. 6.7   Structure of teacher-centered and student-centered instruction as defined by Cuban (1984).

The primary sources of evidence used by Cuban included photographs of teachers and students in classrooms, textbooks and tests used by teachers, student recollections of their experiences in classrooms, teacher reports of how they taught, and reports from persons who visited classrooms (e.g., journalists, parents, and administrators). Evidence representing different time periods, school levels, and school locations was collected. Based on this wide variety of evidence, Cuban placed each of the classrooms for which evidence was available into one of three categories representing the three different types of instruction on each of the five dimensions.

The evidence then was summarized in terms of the number and percentage of classrooms in each of the three categories on each of the five dimensions. For example, 94 percent of the classrooms in Washington, D.C., during the period from 1920 to 1940 for which evidence was obtained had *class arrangements* (one of the five dimensions) associated with *teacher-centered* instruction (one of the three types of instruction). Six percent of these classrooms had class arrangements associated with student-centered instruction, while none of the classrooms had class arrangements associated with a "mixed pattern" of instruction.

Cuban collected the evidence from two time periods in order to increase the generalizability of his findings. Each of the time periods identified represented a recognized movement toward more student-centered instruction in the United States. Evidence pertaining to classrooms located in different cities and in rural areas was examined for the same reason.

Once again, the meaning of the evidence is derived primarily from Cuban's conceptual framework. The proper interpretation of the evidence depends on a knowledge of the five key dimensions that differentiate teacher-centered from student-centered instruction, the specific indicators used to differentiate these two types of instruction, and the specific sources of evidence examined (e.g., the particular pictures or reports consulted).

Research in Classrooms

TABLE 6.1

Dimensions, Types, and Indicators of Teaching

Classroom instruction was divided into five dimensions: classroom arrangements, group instruction, classroom talk, class activities, and student movement. For each dimension, there were specific behaviors that could be located in descriptions and photographs. If found, they were coded and counted. The patterns, classroom dimensions and specific behaviors follow:

	Teacher-Centered	Mixed Pattern	Student-Centered
CLASS ARRANGEMENT	• Movable desks and chairs in rows facing teacher's desk and/or blackboard	• Movable desks and chairs in hollow-square, horse-shoe, etc. • Up to half of class arranged at desks and chairs facing one another.	• Students sit at tables or clusters of desks facing one another • No rows
GROUP INSTRUCTION	• Whole class • Teacher works with individual student while rest of class works at desks	• Teacher works with small groups • Teacher varies grouping: whole, small, and individual.	• Class divided into groups • Students engaged in individual and small group activities
CLASSROOM TALK	• No one in class talking • Teacher talking • Teacher-led recitation/discussion	• Student reports, debates, panels, dramatizations • High frequency of both teacher and student instructional talk	• Student-led discussion or recitation • Students talking in groups or with individuals
CLASS ACTIVITIES	• Students working at desks • Teacher talking (lecture, explaining, giving directions, reading to class, etc.) • Teacher checking work • Students taking test, watching film, listening to radio, etc. • Teacher-led recitation/discuss.	• High frequency of activities that indicate both teacher- and student-centered behaviors	• Class in small groups • Students work individually and in small groups • Students lead discussions/ recitation • Students working on projects/centers
STUDENT MOVEMENT	• No movement at all • Student needs permission to leave seat	• Less than five students away from desks	• Six or more students away from seats at one time • Students move freely without teacher's permission

Enhancing the Meaning of Evidence

Based on our analysis of these four studies, five recommendations can be offered to those interested in enhancing the meaning of evidence collected during research studies. Each of these recommendations is stated and described briefly.

1. Recognize that conceptual frameworks reflect our beliefs about what is important and what is known. Stated somewhat differently, conceptual frameworks are not "value-free." Bussis et al. make this point quite succinctly.

> We have sometimes been asked where a particular coding scheme "comes from." . . . An easy answer, of course, is that the coding schemes "come from" our heads, but that is hardly the whole story. Basically, they represent a synthesis of our own theoretical predilections with what we have to come to understand about the aims of open education—aims that constitute a directional heading rather than a destination to be "arrived at" (p. 5).

The conceptual frameworks developed by Bellack et al. and by Bussis et al. are both excellent. They are well thought out, they are clearly defined, and the sources used to collect the evidence seem quite appropriate. Nonetheless, they are entirely different and rest on totally different assumptions concerning what is important to know about life in classrooms.

As a consequence, having the "right" conceptual framework is unimportant and impossible. Have *a* conceptual framework, however, is essential if the evidence gathered during the study is to be meaningful. This fact leads to our second recommendation.

2. Devise a conceptual framework to guide your study so that the meaning of the evidence once gathered will be clear to all concerned. As we have pointed out, conceptual frameworks provide the necessary structure within which evidence can be properly interpreted. There are, however, two types of structures that must be considered. The first type concerns the dimensions or categories used to define the primary concept or concepts included in the framework. These initial defining dimensions or categories can be further divided into subcategories, which in turn can be further subdivided, and so on. As was mentioned during our discussion of the BTES, the formation of increasingly concrete and precise subcategories allows us as researchers to move closer to the evidence that is collected. Once the evidence has been collected it can be summed or aggregated across all subcategories within each major category if *necessary*, and *appropriate*. Multidimensional figures (such as Figure 6.1) and structural diagrams (such as Figure 6.3) are useful ways of representing the structure of the primary concepts included in the overall conceptual framework. This type of structure is important for descriptive and association studies.

The second type of structure is useful for associational studies only. This structure includes the hypothesized relationship among the primary concepts included in the framework. In experimental studies this structure enables researchers to identify those extraneous variables that need to be estimated or controlled. In other associational studies this structure (in addition to the first type of structure) permits the researcher to select appropriate statistical techniques to use in analyzing the evidence once collected. Figure 6.4 is an example of this second type of structure.

As has been mentioned in Chapter 5, there is a useful distinction to be made between categories that guide or determine the collection of evidence (which we refer to as "data collection" categories) and categories that guide or determine the analysis of the evidence once collected (which we refer to as "data analytic" categories). Structured observation systems, forced-choice standardized questionnaires, and rating scales all rely on categories that guide or determine the collection of evidence. That is, the categories are in place prior to the time at which the evidence is collected. Open-ended interviews, specimen records, and ethnographic field notes tend to rely on categories to guide or determine the analysis of the evidence. That is, the evidence gathered is free from the constraints imposed by the categories included in the conceptual framework.

In this regard, it should be pointed out that the formation of explicit categories to guide or determine the analysis of evidence is not necessary. As Dyer (1976) points out one has three choices when confronted with open-ended or free-response material.

> One may simply smooth it into readable prose and let it speak for itself. One may take a phenomenological approach and try to figure out what typically goes on inside the respondent's or participant's head and present one's inference regarding the same. Or one may take an additional step and code the responses in accordance with the logical categories one finds in them. It is this coding operation that provides the basis for turning free-response material into measurable attributes (p. 10).

Consistent with Dyer's last comment, the vast majority of those classroom researchers who initially collect open-ended or free-response evidence typically use categories to guide or determine the analysis of the evidence. This approach has been so prominent that the bulk of the discussion in Light's (1973) chapter entitled "Issues in the analysis of the qualitative data" is concerned with the proper analysis of categorical data (which involves the proper application of fairly standard non-parametric statistics).

3. Use examples, excerpts, and indicators to enhance the meaning of the categories included in the conceptual framework. While different researchers use different methods to make their abstract definitions more concrete, most use some method. For example, Bellack et al. used excerpts from transcripts as examples to increase the meaning of the categories (see Table 6.2). Similarly, Bussis et al. used excerpts from the teachers' interviews to illustrate their categories (see Table 6.3). Finally, as has been mentioned,

TABLE 6.2

Using Definitions and Examples to Enhance Meaning

Interpreting (INT). To interpret a statement is to give its verbal equivalent, usually for the purpose of rendering its meaning clear.

Examples   *Code*

T: What does President Kennedy   T/SOL/TRA/INT/2/-/-/-
mean when he says, "We must
trade or fade?"

T: What does the slogan mean,   T/SOL/BAR/INT/3/-/-/-
"Buy American—the job you
save may be your own?"

Source: Bellack et al. (1966), pp. 23–24.
Reprinted by permission of the publisher from Bellack, A. A., et al., *The Language of the Classroom.* (New York: Teachers College Press, © 1966 by Teachers College, Columbia University. All rights reserved.), pp. 267–269.

TABLE 6.3

Using Explanations and Excerpts to Enhance Meaning

Orientation C teachers perceived the expression of needs and feelings to be a natural condition, and they welcomed such expression for its contribution to the creation of a warm and humane environment in which learning could take place.

"I hate the older way, because children just sat all morning—they couldn't move around and talk. How could they learn?"

"It's a much better way to learn. . . . It's only natural."

"They love school now. They hate to leave in the afternoon. If they get upset, they know that the teacher will listen or that their friends will help them. They have a good attitude about school."

Source: Bussis et al. (1976), p. 85.

Cuban used indicators to enhance the meaning of his categories and dimensions.

4. Make explicit the linkages between the concepts and categories, on the one hand, and the sources of evidence, on the other. These explicit relationships, often referred to as operational definitions of the concepts and categories, do in fact increase the meaning of the evidence. Tables and figures are once again useful as graphical representations of these relationships. Fisher et al., for example, used tables to explicate the relationships between the categories included in their conceptual framework and their sources of evidence (see Table 6.4) and between the categories and particular examples of the evidence (see Table 6.5).

5. Consider the nature of your sample when making interpretations of the evidence. As we pointed out in the previous chapter, the phrase "source of evidence" describes not only the means by which the evidence is collected

TABLE 6.4

Definitions of the General Variables

	Variable Label	Method of Data Collection	Description
A, AUN	Appropriateness of Instruction to Student Needs	Single rating based on interviews and observation (7-point scale)	Field workers were asked to rate "the extent to which the instructional program is appropriate to the level of readiness and needs of students." This includes the appropriateness of task difficulty and flexibility of pacing to allow for differential rates of learning.
G1	Global Rating (Like Class?)	Single rating based on interviews and observation (7-point scale)	Field workers responded to the question "Would you like your (hypothetical) child to be in this teacher's class?"
G2, G2UN	Perceived Academic Competence	A combination of 9 rating scales completed after each observation (each a 7-point scale; unit-weight combination)	Nine intercorrelated ratings were averaged to get an estimate of the field workers' perception of the quality of the academic instruction: Cognitive Task Orientation Clarity Structuring Knowledge of the Pedagogy of Reading and Math Complexity of Communication Consistency of Message Attention to Students Expectation of Student Success
G3, G3UN	Orientation Toward Affect	A combination of 3 rating scales completed after each observation and 2 ratings based on interviews and observation (each a 7-point scale; unit-weight combination within method and then across)	These intercorrelated ratings describe the classroom climate and the degree to which the teacher is aware of, encourages, and values the affective domain. Daily ratings: Conviviality Acceptance of Feelings Flexibility Interview-based ratings: Awareness of Affect Value Placed on Affective Outcomes
G4, G4UN	Learning Environment	A combination of 2 rating scales completed after each observation (each a 7-point scale; unit-weight combination)	These intercorrelated ratings describe the extent to which students take responsibility for classroom activities and work cooperatively with each other: Cooperation Student Responsibility

Source: Fisher et al. (1978).

TABLE 6.5

Definitions and Examples of Interactive Teaching Behaviors

General Function	Specific Behavior	Description	Example
		SUBSTANTIVE BEHAVIORS	
Presentation	Explanation-Need	The instructor explains academic content in response to a clear and immediate student need for help.	During a seatwork assignment on short vowels, the teacher notices that Sonia is having trouble, so she goes over the sounds with her.
	Explanation-Planned	The instructor explains academic content but not in response to a specific or immediate student need. This often takes the form of a lecture.	The class comes to a section in the reading workbook on compound words. The teacher introduces this concept and puts some examples on the board.
Monitoring	Academic Observation	The instructor looks at or listens to student academic responses, in order to see how the student is doing.	While Eric is doing seat-work, the teacher looks at his paper to make sure he understands what to do.
	Academic Question	The instructor asks the student for a written or oral answer in order to observe and assess academic performance.	During group discussion, the teacher asks Mary to give the meaning of a word from that day's reading lesson.
Feedback	Academic Feedback	The instructor tells the student whether his answer is right or wrong. Could involve giving the right answer. Does not involve explanation.	The teacher asks Johnny to read out loud to the class the answers to the arithmetic problems. In oral reading circle, Susan hears Jim reading out loud while she reads along silently.
		PROCEDURAL BEHAVIORS	
Presentation	Structure/Direct	The instructor states the goals of instruction or gives directions about the procedures and activities the student should carry out.	At the beginning of the math lesson, the teacher says "Today we are going to work on 10's and 1's like we did yesterday. Turn to page 20."
Feedback	Task Engagement Feedback	The instructor acts to control inappropriate behavior or to praise appropriate behavior. The focus is on the student's actions rather than the correctness of his answers.	Billy is out of his seat and standing by the pencil sharpener. The teacher tells him to "hurry up and get back to work."

Source: Fisher et al. (1978).

but the persons who are expected to provide the evidence. Simply stated, meaning is enhanced when we know something about the persons providing the evidence. This knowledge of the sample included in the study helps us understand to whom the results of the study may apply or can be generalized. Such knowledge also decreases the likelihood of misapplication or overgeneralization.

It is important to know, for example, that Bellack et al. included high school social studies teachers in their study. High school social studies teachers tend to talk a great deal and, more importantly, are more likely to carry on discussions with their students (Anderson, n.d.). Thus, the dialogue that occurs in social studies classes seems particularly appropriate for analysis using the coding scheme developed by Bellack et al. Several other subject areas, such as mathematics, art, or music, would have likely been more problematic since discussions with students are far less likely to occur (Anderson, n.d.). Thus, the results of the Bellack et al. study apply primarily to high school social studies teachers and only with extreme caution should the results be generalized to teachers of other subject areas and who teach at other grade levels.

As has been mentioned, Bussis et al. studied primary school teachers (Kindergarden through grade 3) interested in or intent on applying open education in their classrooms. One would expect (or one would certainly hope) that such teachers would respond to a series of questions concerning the curriculum and children in a manner reasonably consistent with the principles and practices of open education. As a consequence, the perceptions of the curriculum and opinions about children offered by this sample of teachers are not likely to generalize to teachers totally opposed to open education and may not apply to those teaching at upper grade levels in school.

The Quality of Evidence

Once we have an understanding of the meaning of the evidence, our attention turns to an examination of the quality of the evidence. Traditionally, investigation of the quality of evidence has centered around three basic concepts: objectivity, reliability, and validity. Occasionally, researchers have suggested other concepts, most of which tend to be different labels for basically the same concepts. Guba and Lincoln (1987), for example, suggest replacing objectivity with confirmability, reliability with dependability, and validity with credibility and transferability. We have no quarrel with these replacements. However, because of the familiarity of most researchers with objectivity, reliability, and validity, we shall use these terms. The discussion that follows is organized around three major issues: objectivity, the validity of description, and the validity of association. Issues concerning reliability are discussed within the context of validity rather than being included separately.

Objectivity

There are two different uses of the term "objectivity" in classroom research. The first use equates objectivity with agreement among observers or coders. Typically, some type of agreement index is computed (e.g., the percentage of data collection or data analytic categories in which the frequencies made by two researchers observing in the same classroom or coding the same audiotape or videotape are identical). This index may be adjusted to take into consideration the agreement that could be expected simply by chance (Scott, 1955).

If the index of agreement is high, the evidence or the meaning of the evidence is said to be objective. That is, the same evidence would be collected regardless of who collected it, or the evidence collected would have the same meaning in terms of the conceptual framework no matter who analyzed it. If the index is low, the evidence is said to be subjective. That is, the evidence or the meaning of the evidence is highly dependent on the person doing the collecting or coding of the evidence.

The second use of the term "objectivity" concerns the detachment of the observer or coder from the evidence collected or analyzed. This use of the term is consistent with Tyler's (1973) suggestion that the development of an "objective attitude" is a worthwhile goal of schooling. People with objective attitudes are able to separate or detach themselves from the phenomenon being studied; they are able to describe what they are studying without bias or prejudice (Galton, 1987; House, 1980). There is no index for this particular use of objectivity, as there is for agreement. Rather, concerns for detachment are typically addressed in the training received by observers or coders (see Chapter 5).

Observer agreement is the *sine qua non* of structured observation systems (Galton, 1987). Given a set of well-defined categories and proper training in the use of the system, all observers are expected to record the same event in the same way (Medley and Mitzel, 1963). In fact, most developers of structured observation systems as well as the researchers who use them report high levels of observer agreement (e.g., Stallings, 1977; Galton et al., 1980).

A similar argument can be made for what can be termed "coder agreement." Given a set of data analytic categories, proper training, and a classroom chronicle, transcript of an audiotape, or a video recording, everyone who analyzes the record in terms of the categories should place the same event in the same category. In the Bellack et al. (1966) study, for example, the following analytic procedure was used.

(1) each protocol of a single class session was first coded by one member of the coding team; (2) this initial coding was then reviewed by a second person, who noted his disagreements with the original analysis; (3) finally, these disagreements were arbitrated by two coders, who, whenever possible, were not involved in the initial coding of the protocol (p. 14).

Bellack et al. concluded that this procedure resulted in a high degree of intercoder agreement. Similarly, Gump (1967) reports that three independent analysts working from classroom chronicles were able to produce similar segment boundaries and titles.

Based on the discussion thus far, it is possible for the reader to conclude that observer or coder agreement is desirable. While not doubting this conclusion, we would like to address three questions concerning observer or coder agreement. First, under what conditions should observer or coder agreement be expected (or unexpected)? Second, to what extent is observer agreement necessary for high quality classroom research? Third, what is the relationship between objectivity-as-observer-or-coder-agreement and objectivity-as-detachment?

The answer to the first question is straightforward. Observers or coders who operate from a common framework or point of view, who have mastered the basics and nuances of a particular structured observation or coding system, and who possess a reasonable aptitude for observation or analysis should produce similar records or codings. The real value of this simple answer, however, rests with what it tells us about those observers or coders who *do not* exhibit high levels of agreement. For example, those persons who vary in their aptitudes for observation or coding, who differ in their knowledge of the observation system or coding scheme, or who possess different levels of skill in using the system or scheme *should not* be expected to agree with one other as to what they perceive, record, or code. Similarly those persons who operate from different frames of reference or points of view also *should not* be expected to agree (Evertson and Green, 1986).

In this regard, Anderson (n.d.) reports on a study in which school administrators were trained during a three day period to use a structured observation system. At the completion of the training, they were asked to watch a videotaped lesson and record on the instrument what they saw and heard. The videotape had already been coded by three individuals involved in developing the instrument and a "key" had been prepared based on consensus and majority rule. The records made by the trainees were then compared with the "key," and a percent correct score was computed for each trainee. These percent correct scores ranged from a low of just under 50 percent (with 50 percent being the score one would expect by chance) to a high of 85 percent. Quite clearly, the trainees differed in either their aptitude for observation, the extent to which they had mastered the structured observation system, and/or their frames of references or points of view. If two of these trainees were chosen at random and placed in the same classroom, their records of classroom events would likely show numerous disagreements.

A major implication of this discussion is that not all disagreements among observers or coders can automatically be considered as "error." This implication leads to our second question concerning objectivity, namely, "to what extent is observer or coder agreement necessary to conduct classroom research of high quality?" To some, particularly proponents of structured observation systems, this question borders on heresy. From their point of view, all disagreements among observers are considered to be errors. And, quite obviously, the smaller the error, the more accurate the observation.

To those who favor less structured, more informal methods of observation, however, the question concerning the necessity of observer or coder agreement is legitimate. Those holding this point of view would argue that multiple viewpoints are needed if accurate descriptions of classroom events are likely. When these viewpoints converge (that is, when agreement is high), the confidence that can be placed in the descriptions is enhanced greatly. If, on the other hand, different descriptions are given by those holding differing viewpoints, we, as researchers, cannot afford to:

> throw our hands up in despair because we cannot say anything about the phenomenon we have been studying. Rather, we attempt to make sense of what we find and that often requires embedding the empirical data at hand with a holistic understanding of the specific situation and general background knowledge about this class of social phenomena (Mathison, 1988, p. 17).

Like the person listening to the various descriptions provided by the blind men who confronted the elephant, we need to find means by which these apparently discrepant descriptions can be related in some meaningful way.

There are, then, legitimate disagreements among observers and coders that can provide classroom researchers with the information they need to provide more objective descriptions (objective here referring to the second use of the term). Suggesting that observer disagreement may lead to increased objectivity leads us to our third question, "What is the relationship between objectivity-as-observer-or-coder-agreement and objectivity-as-detachment?"

To proponents of structured observation systems and well-defined analytic schemes, these two uses of the term "objectivity" are typically seen as synonymous. We would disagree. Rather, we would suggest that observers or coders with similar personal biases (e.g., two lenient observers using a rating scale) will likely agree with one another. Nonetheless, the ratings made by these observers or the codings made by these coders are subjective in that they reflect the personal biases of the observers and coders and, hence, a lack of an "objective attitude" or detachment on their part.

On the other hand, two observers or coders with diametrically opposed personal biases (e.g., one lenient observer and one severe observer using the same rating scale) will likely agree less often. The records or codings made by these two researchers, then, will lack objectivity in both senses of the term. They are biased *and* they do not agree. Interestingly, and quite paradoxically, however, if these two researchers observe or code transcripts of a series of classrooms that are virtually identical in all respects, the internal consistency reliability estimates based on the dimensions being rated across classrooms will be substantial. The variability here, however, is caused by the observers or coders, not by the classrooms being observed or coded. This paradox helps us to explain in part the generally high internal consistency estimates of rating scales.[4]

In summary, then, the subjective-objectivity dichotomy is in many respects a false one. As mentioned by Fisher et al. (1978), the collection and/or analysis of evidence is partly subjective and partly objective. Those who use structured observation systems and formal coding schemes simply put their subjectivity "up front." This subjectivity is reflected in the underlying structure of the conceptual framework and the explicit definition of the categories included on the observation instrument or used to analyze the evidence. In contrast, those who use more naturalistic or ethnographic approaches simply permit their subjectivity to creep into the records they make while they observe and analyze the evidence (Hamilton and Delamont, 1974).

So where do we stand on the issue of objectivity? First, observer agreement is clearly desirable, particularly when structured observation systems or coding schemes are used. In other circumstances, expressed concerns for observer agreement may cause observers or coders to maintain the detachment they need to be "objective." Second, because of different points of view, aptitudes, and levels of training among observers or coders, this desired agreement may be difficult to achieve. In this regard, careful selection and training of observers and coders is necessary if substantial levels of observer agreement are to be attained.

Third, we recognize that there are two different uses of the term "objectivity" currently in vogue. Of the two, we believe the definition of objectivity-as-detachment to be the more important one. Differences in records or codings made by researchers may represent important distinctions among the researchers, rather than errors. In this regard, we would simply suggest that there may be some value in considering the *meaning* of these similarities and differences before we simply consider them to be errors. Some integration of these apparently different or conflicting reports may be necessary to enhance the validity of the evidence, an issue to which we now turn our attention.

---

[4]Another part of the explanation for high internal consistency estimates of rating scales is the so-called "halo effect" (Medley, 1982). This effect is present when the overall impression an observer or coder has of a teacher, student, or classroom influences the ratings assigned to all of the dimensions included on the rating scale. However, the reader should note that if there are no real differences in the classrooms being observed or coded and all observers or coders have an overall positive image of the classrooms, then the internal consistency reliability estimate would be near zero (since no variability among the classrooms was evident). Differences either attributed to classrooms or to observers or coders are necessary for these estimates to be large and positive.

The Validity of Description

Traditionally, validity has been defined as the extent to which an instrument measures what it is supposed to measure. Clocks tend to provide valid measures of time; thermometers tend to provide valid measures of temperature. If the evidence provided by these instruments is two minutes or three degrees different from the evidence provided by an impeccable source (e.g., Greenwich mean time), we question the reliability of the evidence not the validity.

Despite the apparent simplicity of this definition, two subtle aspects of validity must be explored before the meaning of validity can be fully understood. First, validity refers to the evidence, not the source of the evidence (e.g., an instrument). One cannot say, for instance, that Flanders' (1960) system is valid or invalid. Rather, the system is likely to yield more valid descriptions of certain classrooms and less valid descriptions of others. Walker and Adelman (1975), for example, point out that Flanders' system likely provides more valid descriptions of classrooms in which communication takes place in a "public dialogue form" and less valid descriptions of classrooms where "intimate conversations between teachers and children" occur frequently. Although this differentiation is intended as a criticism of Flanders' system, it is not. It is simply a statement of the settings in which the evidence provided by Flanders' system is likely to be more and less valid. Criticisms, if they are to be made, should be directed to those who use the system in settings in which it is unlikely to yield valid evidence.

Second, validity does not exist in the abstract, nor is it established once and for all. Rather, researchers must continually argue for the validity of the descriptions they make or the associations they infer. In general, the more credible the argument (coupled with the necessary supporting evidence), the more valid the description or association. There are some generally accepted ways in which arguments related to validity can be supported. In the two subsections that follow we briefly discuss some of these.

Descriptions Based on a Single Set of Evidence. Let us begin our discussion with the simplest case. Suppose a researcher is interested in describing the events that occurred in a single classroom during a single observation, the opinions voiced by a single teacher or student responding to an interview or questionnaire, or the activities or experiences mentioned in a written document. What arguments can be offered in support of the validity of his or her descriptions? There are several.

First, let us consider the matter of "face validity." The fundamental question in this regard is "Does the source of evidence appear likely to yield a valid description of the phenomenon under study?" Clocks are likely to yield valid measures of time; thermometers are likely to yield valid measures of temperature. Through the years, both of these sources of evidence have developed high degrees of face validity.

Observations, questionnaires, and interviews can derive their face validity from two sources: their structure and their development. As has been mentioned earlier in this chapter, the underlying structure of a source of evidence (e.g., observations, questionnaires, and interviews), or the coding system used to analyze the evidence once collected, allows the researcher to attribute meaning to the evidence. As a consequence, an examination of the underlying structure will likely support (or refute) the case for face validity. Structural diagrams which link concepts, categories, and sources of evidence provide a useful logical analysis of this structure.

The face validity of observations, questionnaires, and interviews is also increased when systematic procedures are used in their development. The formulation of blueprints to guide development, the use of reviews of early drafts, the revision of these drafts based on suggestions made during the review, and the conduct of field tests are stages of development that, when present, are likely to support an argument for face validity.

The equivalent of face validity with documents and exhibits would appear to be authenticity. Forgeries are obviously threats to face validity, as are "staged" photographs (see, for example, Cuban, 1984). Thus, some verification of the authenticity of the documents or exhibits is a minimal condition for validity.

While face validity is a useful first step, it is not sufficient (Galton, 1987). In this regard, high degrees of observer or coder agreement (as discussed in the previous section) can be supportive of the validity of the description. For such agreement to be supportive of validity, however, sufficient face validity must have been established. Specifically, the linkages between the source of evidence and the conceptual framework must be credible for agreement among observers or coders to contribute to the validity of the description. Face validity in combination with observer or coder agreement enhances the logic of the argument for the validity of description.

In addition, triangulation strategies (Webb et al., 1981) or cross-validation methods (Rosenshine and Furst, 1973) are very important in establishing the validity of description. Typically, such strategies and methods involve comparisons of the descriptions available from one source of evidence with those available from other sources of evidence. Suppose, for example, we are interested in describing the task-orientation of a particular classroom. Comparing notes made an observer with responses made by the teacher while watching a videotape of the classroom with answers given by students in response to a short questionnaire provides useful data related to the validity of the description of task-orientation. If the descriptions are consistent (or at the very least are not contradictory), they corroborate one another and enable the researcher to produce a single, valid description. If inconsistencies are evident, then attempting to construct a composite description may be appropriate. This composite can be shared with all parties to secure their reactions and suggestions for change. Eventually, some degree of validity of the description is quite likely.

In summary, then, explicit information concerning the underlying structure of a particular source of evidence and its development, the presence of reasonably high levels of agreement among observers or coders, and the use of cross-validation techniques and triangulation strategies are ways in which researchers can support their arguments that their descriptions based on a single set of evidence are valid.

Descriptions Based on Multiple Sets of Evidence. In most cases, classroom researchers are interested in a more general description of classrooms or teachers than are possible based on a single piece of evidence. They may conduct multiple observations in a single classroom or conduct multiple interviews with the same teacher over time (see Smith and Geoffrey, 1968). They may conduct single observations in multiple classrooms (e.g., Anderson, 1986) or they may use the same interview protocol with multiple teachers (e.g., Bussis et al., 1976). They may conduct multiple observations in multiple classrooms (e.g., Bellack et al., 1966). Each of these "multiples" (that is, occasions, classrooms, and teachers) increases the problem of the validity of the descriptions made by the researcher.

As might be expected, all of the issues pertaining to the validity of the description based on a single set of evidence apply to this more general case. In addition, however, researchers must concern themselves with the consistency of the evidence (or, perhaps more appropriate, the lack of consistency) across the occasions, classrooms, teachers, or students. Typically, the greater the inconsistency, the less likely it is that general descriptions of classrooms, teachers, and/or students can be made with any degree of certainty. On the other hand, high degrees of consistency across occasions, classrooms, teachers, or students, lends greater credence to our validity claims.

One obvious way of dealing with inconsistencies across classrooms, teachers, or students is to basically ignore them and describe the "average" classroom, teacher, or student, or "most classrooms," "most teachers," or "most students." This strategy is frequently encountered when one reads reports of classroom research.

A second, and potentially more useful approach, however, is to seek out factors that are associated with the inconsistencies and, based on these factors, to limit the descriptions to particular types of classroom settings or teachers. Stodolsky (1984), for example, suggests that descriptions of classrooms may vary according to the subject matter being taught, the goals and objectives being pursued, and the format used to deliver the instruction (e.g., lecture, laboratory, written seatwork). Thus, while descriptions of elementary classrooms in general are many and varied, descriptions of reading circles in elementary schools when word attack skills are being taught are likely to be far more consistent. What is being advocated here is placing proper restrictions on the settings or persons to which the descriptions apply so that the inconsistencies are reduced somewhat or eliminated.

A third way in which inconsistencies across classrooms or teachers can be handled is to describe the inconsistencies themselves. What are the major differences among teachers or classrooms? How many classrooms fit one description and how many fit another? How many teachers express a particular belief and how many express other beliefs?

In general, inconsistencies across occasions are more problematic than inconsistencies across classrooms or teachers, particularly when the purpose of the study is to describe classrooms, teachers, or students. Inconsistencies across occasions (that is, different days of observation, or different interview or testing sessions) are a primary source of error in such studies. Stated simply, if the descriptions of teachers, classrooms, or students vary from one day or week to the next, general descriptions of these teachers or classrooms (the primary reason for gathering multiple sets of evidence) are not particularly credible or useful.

When the evidence is in numerical form, these inconsistencies across occasions pose threats to what is termed the "generalizability" (Medley, 1982) or "reproducibility" (Rosenshine and Furst, 1973) of the results of the study. Using analysis of variance procedures (see, for example, Medley and Mitzel, 1963), the proportion of the variability in the evidence that can be attributed to classrooms, teachers, students, or occasions can be estimated.[5] In general, the greater the proportion of variance that can be attributed to occasions, the less valid the descriptions of the sample of classrooms or teachers.

The issue of the generalizability of non-quantitative descriptions (e.g., written or oral descriptions) is not nearly so straightforward. One technique is for researchers to share their descriptions with one or more audiences (e.g., other researchers, teachers, students) and listen to the extent to which these descriptions are accepted by or acceptable to various members of the audience (McCutcheon, 1981). In this situation, the audience rather than the researcher actually does the generalizing.

Similarly, Evertson (1986) recounts a story of her experience in sharing her research findings with a group of teachers. Following her presentation, a number of teachers came to her and said, "You've been in my classroom." Although she had not been in these teachers' classrooms, she had been in classrooms very much like theirs. Thus, some degree of generalization of her

---

[5]Concerns for objectivity can also be included within the analysis of variance. Observers, coders, or interviewers can be included as a third factor (along with classroom or teacher, and occasion). The larger the proportion of variability that can be attributed to this "objectivity" factor, the greater the error in the description of the classrooms, teachers, or students.

descriptions was possible by virtue of members of the audience accepting them as credible and appropriate.

In summary, before researchers make general descriptions about classroom events or teacher characteristics, they should examine the extent to which such generalized descriptions are appropriate. No descriptions apply to all classrooms, teachers, or students, but that is no reason to throw out the baby with the bathwater. Accurate and credible descriptions which apply to clearly-defined although limited types of classrooms, teachers, or students, are clearly preferable to either unwarranted overgeneralization or the total rejection of the validity of descriptions because they fail to apply to every teacher or student in every classroom on every occasion.

The Validity of Association

Besides description, the other primary purpose of classroom research is to identify those elements of teachers, teaching, and instruction that are associated, causally or otherwise, with student learning, behavior, achievement, or attitudes. As we shall discuss in this section, this purpose of classroom research requires different validity considerations from those discussed in the previous section.

The major emphasis in the section is on a set of conditions that must be in place before the validity of associations can be properly examined. In the discussion that follows we focus on student achievement as the primary outcome, simply because of the frequency with which it has been used in classroom research. This emphasis is not to suggest that student achievement is the only outcome, although we would agree that it is a very critical one. Four conditions that must be in place before associational validity can be examined properly are shown in Table 6.6.

TABLE 6.6

Conditions That Must Be Met Prior to Examining the Validity of Associations (With Classrooms or Teachers as Unit of Analysis)

1. The measures of student achievement (or other outcomes) must be sufficiently valid and reliable.
2. The evidence concerning the events or characteristics to be associated with student achievement must be sufficiently generalizable across occasions, observers, interviewers, and/or coders.
3. The evidence concerning the events or characteristics must differentiate reliably among classrooms and teachers.
4. In general, the classrooms should contain students who, on the average, are similar in terms of their aptitudes, prior achievement, and motivation. In those cases in which the classrooms are somewhat distinct, these differences should be considered in the analysis and interpretation of the evidence.

Valid and Reliable Measures of Student Achievement. If achievement tests are to be useful outcome measures in classroom research, they must be sufficiently valid and reliable. Perhaps the best indicator of the validity of an achievement test is an estimate of the opportunity students have had to learn the content or material covered by the test. Currently, three means of estimating opportunity to learn (OTL) exist. The first requires teachers, at or near the end of the study, to estimate the extent to which their students received instruction directly related to each item on the test. The percentage of items which include content or material that was taught to most or all of the students is an index of opportunity to learn (Anderson, 1987).

The second estimate of OTL requires that the same test be used as a pretest and posttest. In this situation, differences in the percentages of students answering the items correctly on the pretest and posttest are computed. Increases of some percentage of students (e.g., five, ten) are accepted as evidence that students had the opportunity to learn the content and material tested by that item. Again, the percentage of the items on which increases of this magnitude were found is accepted as an overall index of opportunity to learn. Achievement tests of comparable validity can be "manufactured" by selecting certain items (those that have similar OTL indices for all classrooms), while eliminating others (Anderson et al., 1989).

A third estimate of OTL requires that the lessons given to the students be audiotaped or videotaped. These tapes are then analyzed in terms of the presence or absence of content associated with the items included on the achievement test. Once again, the comparability of the content taught and content tested is estimated (e.g., Wright and Nuthall, 1970).

Rather than estimating the extent to which students have had an opportunity to learn, an alternative and perhaps preferable approach is to design instructional units that will be taught to all students and to match the achievement tests with the major content and objectives of those instructional units. Bellack et al. (1966) and Fisher et al. (1978) provide instructive examples of this approach.

In addition to validity estimates, some estimate of internal consistency reliability (e.g., KR-20, split half) should be computed for each achievement test. Estimates of internal consistency reliability for achievement tests used in observational research typically exceed 0.80. Lower reliability estimates suggest that modifications in the test are necessary before it can be used as an outcome measure.

Generalizability of Events or Characteristics Over Time. Although this issue has been raised earlier, we need to elaborate on it at this time. Most achievement tests used in classroom research measure student knowledge and skills acquired over some extended period of time (e.g., two weeks, one term, one school year). In contrast, evidence pertaining to classrooms or teachers is often obtained on only a few occasions. If an interview or questionnaire is used, for example, a single administration is the mode.

With evidence collected at one point in time the assumption must be made that the responses made will remain consistent over the duration of the study. If such an assumption cannot be made, weak relationships between the responses and student achievement should be expected. If several observations of classrooms are made, the consistency of the evidence over the occasions cannot be assumed; it must be examined. Inconsistency, as mentioned in the previous section, translates into error in most numerical estimates of generalizability. When the error associated with the measurement of achievement is combined with the error reflecting the inconsistency of classroom events or teacher responses over time, the low to moderate associations between classrooms or teachers and student achievement typically encountered in classroom research are, once again, expected.

There are at least two ways in which this problem of inconsistency over time can be minimized. Both require placing certain constraints on the classrooms under study. The first is derived from our earlier discussion of generalizability. The type of classroom or type of lesson can be delimited. That is, only particular types of classrooms or lessons can be included in the study. Generalizability of events within particular types of classrooms or during particular types of lessons is likely to be substantially higher.

The second strategy for dealing with this problem of inconsistency over time is to collect all of the evidence during a single lesson or class session. When this strategy is accepted, however, the achievement test used must be sensitive to the content or objectives taught during this relatively short period of time. Jayne (1945), in fact, conducted a study in which these conditions were met; that is, all of the evidence was collected during a single occasion, the content taught to all students in the different classes was essentially the same, and the achievement test was aligned with this content. Similarly, Nuthall and Church (1973) scripted lessons that lasted from one to three days. The short time period combined with the scripted lessons is likely to increase the consistency of classroom events over the duration of the study.

Reliable Differentiation Across Classrooms. Associations between classroom events or teacher characteristics and student achievement are most frequently investigated at the classroom level. That is, events observed on multiple visits to the classroom are combined into a general set of events that describes the classroom *qua* classroom. Student achievement scores are averaged at the classroom level. The relationship between classroom events and student achievement is then examined across the classrooms. Suppose, for example, a researcher was interested in the relationship between teachers' asking "higher level" (e.g., thought provoking) questions and students' problem solving. Suppose further that the researcher obtains evidence concerning the frequency with which each teacher asks these questions as well as the average achievement test scores of the students in each class. In examining the evidence, however, the researcher notes that the teachers do not differ a great deal in terms of the number of "higher order" questions they ask. As a consequence, the relationship between "higher order" questions and student achievement will be extremely small because the teacher behavior "asks higher-order questions" does not reliably differentiate among classrooms.

In more sophisticated designs, separate "average test scores" may be computed for groups of students (e.g., students assigned to reading groups in a single elementary school classroom). Subgroups, rather than classrooms, then become the appropriate unit of analysis. However, if teachers treat all of the groups the same, once again we are unable to reliably differentiate among groups.

Inclusion of Similar Classrooms and Similar Students. Classrooms that initially differ widely in average student achievement, aptitude, or other student characteristics pose additional problems for researchers interested in establishing associational validity. We know from years of research that the single best predictor of student achievement is prior student achievement or aptitude. Thus, if classes differ greatly in their initial achievement or aptitude, a large proportion of the differences in final achievement can be attributed to differences in initial achievement or aptitude. Differences in classroom events are likely to contribute very little to the differences in final achievement beyond that which can be predicted from initial achievement.

A similar problem may exist if wide differences among students in terms of their ability or motivation exist within the same classroom. In situations of this type the same classroom event may have quite different effects on different students. Explanations that are clear for some students, for example, may be confusing to others.

The traditional way of dealing with the first problem (that is, initial difference in classes) is to obtain measures of these initial differences using, for example, pretests. Using regression analysis, posttest scores are predicted for each student or each class based on the pretest scores. These predicted scores are then subtracted from the actual scores yielding what are termed residual gain scores. One solution to the second problem is to include the relationship between the pretest scores and the posttest scores in each classroom in the overall analysis of the relationship between classroom events and student achievement. These approaches will be discussed in greater detail in Chapter 7.

Our general reaction to these approaches is straightforward. They are methodological solutions to what is essentially a conceptual problem. Strategies such as those used by Nuthall and Church (1973) seem more directed toward the conceptual end of the dilemma.

Estimating Associational Validity. As should be evident to the reader, the difficulty with associational validity lies not in its estimation, but in putting in place the conditions that must be in place before the estimate is meaningful. Once these conditions are in place, the actual estimate of association validity is straightforward. A variety of correlational and regression techniques are typically used with numerical descriptions of classroom events and teacher characteristics. In contrast, non-parametric statistics are more frequently used with more qualitative descriptions (Light, 1973; Morine-Dershimer, 1985). (See Chapter 7.)

Concluding Comments

Classroom researchers have an arsenal of weapons at their disposal as they seek to understand and improve teachers, teaching, and instruction. As mentioned in the previous chapter, these sources of evidence all have strengths and weaknesses. The evidence once gathered is often subject to multiple interpretations; furthermore, it may be of questionable quality. In this chapter we have explored the meaning of evidence and made recommendations concerning the enhancement of meaning. We also have examined two major issues concerning the quality of the evidence: objectivity and validity. In the next chapter we examine a series of issues concerning the analysis of meaningful evidence of high quality.

7

Issues in the Analysis of Evidence

Classroom researchers need to organize their evidence in a manner that allows them to describe classrooms, those in the classrooms, and the events that occur within the classrooms, as well as the relationships that exist between and among classroom participants and events. The purpose of data analysis is to translate the evidence into a form which allows the researcher to make clear and concise statements of description and/or association.

In the previous two chapters we have examined the ways of collecting evidence, investigating the quality of the evidence, and deriving meaning from the evidence. Tests, survey questionnaires, interviews, structured observations, field notes, audio and video recordings, and collections of classroom materials generate what might be termed "raw data;" that is, data not yet subjected to a *major* analysis by the researcher. We stress major analysis since researchers operating within the interpretive mode often subject their "raw data" to preliminary analysis and interpretation at the time they are collected. As mentioned in Chapter 3, this "simultaneous" collection and analysis of data is in contrast to the sharply delineated steps of collection and analysis of the confirmatory mode.

As we saw in Chapter 5, researchers have three general ways in which they can gather evidence: observing, asking questions, and collecting documents or exhibits. Each way generates its own type of raw data. Conducting observations or asking questions can generate mechanical recordings (e.g., audiotape or videotape), written transcripts, written notes, written answers, tallies, checkmarks, circles, or darkened in "bubbles" on computer scan forms. Documents or exhibits can be in the form of memoranda, minutes of meetings, lesson plans, textbooks, and photographs.

All raw data require some organization before analysis can take place. In confirmatory analysis, "data screening," "data cleaning," and "data reduction" often must occur before analysis and summary of the evidence can begin. While data analyses are sometimes straightforward applications of statistical or other analytic techniques, more often than not the results of one analysis generate new questions and suggest other analyses not previously planned. Such "exploratory" analyses are certainly acceptable and even encouraged in some research circles.

In interpretive analysis, data must also be organized before final analysis and summary can begin. In some ways, the voluminous data often generated by field notes, interpretive memos, and documents collected over an extended period of time present greater data organization and preparation problems than do numbers. While techniques exist for selecting and reducing the sheer quantity of data, words are inherently more difficult to organize than are numbers.

In this chapter, we consider a number of issues related to the analysis of words and numbers. This chapter is divided into two major sections dealing with the analysis of words and the analysis of numbers. In each section, we address basic questions of data analysis and provide examples of how the questions have been addressed.

Issues in the Analysis of Words

Taylor and Bogdan (1984) divide qualitative data analysis into three phases or stages: discovery, coding, and discounting. These three phases present a nice overview, since they represent a sort of generalized methodology of the data analysis strategies presented in this section. The discovery phase involves reading the data, searching for emerging themes, developing concepts, and developing a story-line. The coding phase involves developing a coding scheme and sorting the data into categories. The final discounting phase involves checking the emerging concepts and theoretical propositions against possible biases and contamination.

How Do I Begin Data Analysis?

Qualitative data analysis blurs the distinction between data collection and data analysis. Here we will discuss issues related to early as opposed to late stages of data collection.

Miles and Huberman (1984), who have written one of the most extensive books on qualitative data analysis, conceptualize analysis as three concurrent activities: data reduction, data display, and conclusion drawing/verification. These three activities occur both during and after data collection.

According to Miles and Huberman, data reduction is "the process of selecting, focusing, simplifying, abstracting, and transforming the 'raw' data that appear in written-up field notes" (p. 21). It is not separate from analysis but rather part of it. Decisions about which data to select for summary are data analysis choices. We suggest that one can take this analysis step back even further, to the point of data collection. Observers can never write down everything; written field notes or specimen records must necessarily be selective. This selectivity determines what data are available for analysis, just as a structured observation instrument, for example, determines what data are available for analysis. One of the things that distinguishes the "observer as instrument" from the "observer using an instrument," in our view, is the timing of the decision about what to observe. The researcher writing field notes makes the decision at the time the phenomenon occurs; the researcher using the structured observation instrument makes the decision prior to observing the phenomenon. The implications of this timing issue are discussed below.

Miles and Huberman define data display as "an organized assembly of information that permits conclusion drawing and action taking" (p. 21). Such displays are important when organizing words because of the sheer volume of data generated by interpretive techniques. In fact, most of their book is about different ways of displaying words in tables, charts, and graphs.

The third data analytic activity is conclusion drawing and verification. Conclusion drawing occurs throughout data collection, as the patterns, regularities, and themes begin to emerge from the data. Data collection must be complete enough to allow for verification as well. As Miles and Huberman state, "the meanings emerging from the data have to be *tested* for their plausibility, their sturdiness, their 'confirmability'—that is, their *validity*. Otherwise we are left with interesting stories about what happened, of unknown truth and utility" (p. 22).

Miles and Huberman suggest six analytic methods during data collection. Arguing that such methods are critical to the success of a project, they suggest that analysis during data collection "lets the field worker cycle back and forth between thinking about the existing data and generating strategies for collecting new—often better quality—data; . . ." (p. 49). The six methods are contact summary sheets, first-level coding, pattern coding, memoing, site-analysis meeting, and interim site summary. Perhaps the only methods requiring explanation are the two coding methods and memoing.

The starting point of virtually all qualitative techniques, whether during or after data collection, is reading. While more reading will occur after than during data collection, it is still true that the researcher must become familiar with all the data, and the only way to do this is to read it, read it again, and continue to read it. First-level coding involves initial classification of a segment of words, be it a sentence, paragraph, a field note or memo, or a piece of transcription. There are virtually an unlimited number of ways to code or categorize the data, and the type of codes used will depend on the purpose and focus of the study. Much of what has been written about qualitative techniques involves the development of coding systems.

Through reading and thinking about the field notes, perhaps making interpretive comments about the notes and marking them as such, patterns or themes will begin to emerge. Pattern coding, the second coding technique of Miles and Huberman, involves this second-level coding of emerging explanation. If the emergence of patterns or themes in the data sounds somewhat mysterious, the reason is that it is mysterious. Not much is written about how such patterns emerge other than to suggest that the researcher read, code, compare, contrast, classify, integrate, and otherwise organize the data. The researcher must bring order to the data; how this occurs is left up to the researcher.

The writing of field notes, interpretive memos, reflective remarks, and the like is a fundamental and basic field activity. Such notes provide a major source of data for the researcher. Field notes, as we have seen, are written accounts of what the researcher has perceived about the phenomenon. Interpretive memos or reflective remarks are the written notes reflecting comments or interpretations of the researcher about what was observed or considered when the data was read. Table 7.1 presents an example of field notes with interpretive memos from a study of class size by Cahen, Filby, McCutcheon, and Kyle (1983).

TABLE 7.1

Example of Field Notes with Interpretive Memos

Miss Anderson's room

(The Teacher sits on the table in front of the room waiting for the class to settle down for spelling. Twenty students—several talking, moving around room, sharpening pencils, finding books, papers.)
1:05

T:	OK, page 36. Take your spelling books out so we'll all be ready. Everybody should be in their seats. Mike, what are you doing? Page 36.
Mike:	We did this.

T:	We haven't done the bottom part. Page 36. C'mon, Rachel Lee, Robert. Come on, Albert.
Albert:	What page?
T:	Shh, shh Robert. If you need to sharpen your pencils, sharpen them now, but one at a time, please. Roy, what are you doing? Keith, do you see somebody up there? Sit down. Come on, Clarence, that's enough. Quickly sharpen your pencils. Those in your seats need to get quiet. I'm waiting. I'm not going to talk over noise.

(Low murmuring still goes on; two out of their desks; about seven or eight look through books, papers, instead of being ready to start—six minutes have gone by.)

[Does it always take this long to start a lesson? The pencil-sharpening routine seems to be disruptive and takes so *long*—usual? What about other routines?]

1:13
T: Number one at the bottom of page 36. Turn around in your seat, Roy, Robert.
            What is picture A? Robert?
Robert: Black.
T: OK, spell *black*.
Robert: B-l-a-c-k
(T writes words on board as students spell them.)
T: Robert, how do you spell the *k* sound in *black?*
Robert: *ck*
(Repeats procedure for each picture. What is picture———? Spell it for me. How do you spell *k*
sound? Words: black, block, sock, lock, stick, kick.)

1:18
T: OK, Adelina, Mike, it's time for you to go to Mrs. Wilson. All right, I'm not going
            to talk over this noise. (Several have turned around to talk; others whisper to one
            another across the aisles.) What do these words have that's the same? Ronald?
Ronald: *ck*
T: Yes. Now, if I start with this word (writes *back* on board), and I want to change it
            to this word (draws a picture of a sack), what letter needs to change?
Gladys: Change *b* to *s*.
(Class goes through remaining four pictures in same way).

1:22
T: OK, I'm going to give you some paper. I want you to do what we've just gone over.
            Shh. Put your name and date on the paper. Start on page 36 with number 1 and go
            through page 37. (Noticing Rachel Lee's lost tooth), Rachel Lee, you can go rinse
            your mouth out in the bathroom.

        [Do they always go over the answers before doing the seatwork? Why? Does everyone do the
same spelling even if they're in different reading groups? True for other subjects? Rationale?]

T: Put your name and date on the paper where it should go. Please be quiet; some are
            trying to work. Valerie, come on.
(T moves around room, has erased answers from the board. Keith goes to get help.)
T: OK, you'll have to stay in your seats so I can come help you.
(As I move around, I find: Gladys finishes quickly then draws and erases smile faces. Randolph
finishes before most start and concentrates on drawing a truck. Ronald thinks stick picture is a
stem. He goes through all the other pictures and agrees they have *ck* sound, but not number 5
because it's stem. Vernon seems to be having great difficulty; Cynthia falls asleep.)

1:40
T: OK, if you've finished, put your papers on the front table neatly. I'll call rows to get
            coats to go outside.
(The noise level increases as students move to turn in papers, talk to one another, and get ready
for leaving the room.)
T: Shh. If you expect to go outside, you know what you should be doing.
(Ms. Lindley enters—needs reading folders for learning disabled students. Four students sent
to work on unfinished morning work instead of going outside. Students wait with heads down
to be dismissed.)

1:45
Spelling class over.

        [How often is not going outside used as time to finish morning work? Why couldn't the four
go outside? What will happen to the spelling work? Will the T find out why Ronald missed
stick?][1]

Source: Cahen, Filby, McCutcheon, and Kyle (1983).

In interpretive inquiry, then, a good deal of analysis occurs during observation as the research design is modified to fit the researcher's emerging conceptions about the phenomenon. One major strength of extended observation and emerging designs that blend data collection and data analysis is flexibility to pursue interesting questions that arise during data collection. This flexibility also places a great deal of responsibility on the observer to maintain adequate field notes and to clarify why certain features of the phenomenon were selected over others. "Literal description," where the observer simply records the "facts" of the phenomenon much like a video camera records action, is a myth. Emerson (1983) explains why:

> For example, it is impossible to observe everything that takes place in a particular scene, as there is simply too much happening on too many different levels. Perceptual matters aside, it is impossible—or more relevantly, without purpose—to describe everything that has been seen. These features mean that any and all description is inevitably *partial* and *selective*; descriptions include some traits, features, or aspects, and exclude others.
>
> What is included or excluded, however, is not determined randomly; rather, processes of looking and reporting are guided by the observer's implicit or explicit concepts that make some details more important and relevant than others. Thus, what is selected for observation and recording reflects the working theories or conceptual assumptions employed, however implicitly, by the ethnographer. To insist on a sharp polarity between description and analysis is misleading; description is necessarily analytic (p. 20).

As outlined by Emerson, the interpretive aspect of description raises two important implications for ethnographic description. First, an ethnographic description is never an exact picture of the phenomenon but a "re-presentation," to use Emerson's word, of the phenomenon. This is true whether the description is of observable action or the meaning imparted to that action by participants. Second, the ethnographic description depends on the conceptual framework of the observer. The ordering process begins with the observer's perception and follows all the way through to the eventual structuring and patterning of the phenomenon by the observer. It is the researcher's conceptual framework that first provides a language system that allows the researcher to describe the phenomenon and then provides the structure that allows the researcher to order the events in the phenomenon in one way as opposed to another. Ethnographers are well aware of these implications, and, as Emerson suggests, this issue forms the basis for differences between ethnographic traditions; for example, between cognitive anthropology and ethnomethodology in sociology (see Chapter 3).

The Cahen et al. study mentioned above provides a nice discussion of description and interpretation in field work. This study also provides a nice contrast between two approaches to classroom observation. They discuss three processes involved in classroom observation: description, interpretation, and appraisal. Description involves the familiar recording of events and action of the phenomenon. Interpretation involves the construction of meaning about the phenomenon by the observer. A third process, not necessarily done in a study, involves appraisal. Appraisal involves the researcher's judgment as to the worth of a behavior, event, or action. Obviously, such judgment depends on the researcher's point of view and values concerning the phenomenon. In the Cahen et al. study, where the phenomenon was classroom teaching and the appraisal was about the quality of lessons, they considered "its artfulness, its approximation of 'ideal' practice, given the situation, the setting, and the participants" (p. 30). Of particular interest in the Cahen et al. study was their discussion of three types of interpretation. Their discussion begins to outline the kinds of information processing done by an observer. Their three types of interpretation are patterning, interpreting social meaning, and relating phenomena to external consideration.

Patterning uncovers the interrelationships among features of the phenomenon. As they put it, "When patterning, we weave our observations into a fabric of interrelated facts" (p. 27). Patterns might involve the rules and customs for behaving or they might involve causal relationships. In either case, patterning gives coherence and meaning to action, without which description would simply be a set of unrelated facts. The second kind of interpretation is our familiar social meaning. As the reader might recall from Chapter 3, social meaning is a primary subject matter of interpretive inquiry and needs no further discussion here. The third type of interpretation is relating phenomena to external consideration. External consideration might involve the observer's past experience or conceptual framework. In either case, interpretation is made easier by relating the events to past events or theory.

One way to consider the selection and preparation of qualitative data is to understand potential problems that might arise later, after the researcher has left the field and is in the process of final analysis and write-up. An understanding of potential problems allows the researcher to avoid the problems in the first place. Erickson (1986) provides an outline of five potential deficiencies of qualitative data, and it is useful to consider them here:

1. *Inadequate amounts of evidence.* The researcher has too little evidence to warrant certain key assertions. . . .
2. *Inadequate variety in kinds of evidence.* The researcher fails to have evidence across a range of different kinds of sources (e.g., direct observation, interviewing, site documents) to warrant key assertions through *triangulation.* . . .
3. *Faulty interpretive status of evidence.* The researcher fails to have understood the key aspects of the complexity of action or of meaning perspectives held by actors in the setting. . . .
4. *Inadequate disconfirming evidence.* The researcher lacks data that might disconfirm a key assertion. Moreover, the researcher lacks evidence that a deliberate search was made for potentially disconfirming data while in the field setting. This weakens the plausibility of the absence of the disconfirming evidence and leaves the researcher liable to charges of seeking only evidence that would support favorite interpretations. . . .
5. *Inadequate discrepant case analysis.* The researcher did not scrutinize the set of disconfirming instances, examining each instance (i.e., discrepant case) and com-

paring it with the confirming instances to determine which features of the disconfirming case were the same or different from the analogous features of the confirming cases. Such comparative feature analysis often reveals flaws in the original assertion, which if rewritten can account for the discrepant cases as well as accounting for those initially thought to have been confirming instances (p. 140).

All five of Erickson's data deficiencies are faults that could be corrected in the field. The conscientious and disciplined researcher, who maintains good field notes of the phenomenon and a record of how he or she is studying the phenomenon, can avoid all five of these problems. In fact, several of the data analytic techniques suggested in the next section are designed to deal specifically with these problems.

There are activities that can occur during data collection that can help as well. The suggestions of Bogdan and Biklen (1982) about conducting analysis during data collection are useful reminders for overcoming some of these data deficiencies. Table 7.2 summarizes their suggestions.

How Do I Categorize Data?

When words are the data, the general data analytic strategy is to organize the data into categories representing characteristics, patterns, or themes of the phenomenon and then to illustrate and support the categories with quotes, vignettes, anecdotes, field notes, or narratives. The purpose of the data analysis is to understand the phenomenon as represented in the data and arrange the data in a way to convey that understanding to others. Data analysts works through the large set of field notes, narratives, interview transcripts, and documents and arrange it systematically.

One basic strategy for categorization is the development of typologies. The fundamental purpose of a typology is to describe the phenomenon as it is characterized in the data. Developing typologies is a basic form of theorizing (see Chapter 2). A typology is simply a classification based on a

TABLE 7.2

Suggestions for Qualitative Data Analysis During Data Collection

1. Force yourself to make decisions that narrow the study.
2. Force yourself to make decisions concerning the type of study you want to accomplish.
3. Develop analytic questions.
4. Plan data collection sessions in light of what you find during previous observations.
5. Write many "observer's comments" about the ideas you generate.
6. Write memos to yourself about what you are learning.
7. Try out ideas and themes on subjects.
8. Begin exploring literature while you are in the field.
9. Play with metaphors, analogies, and concepts.

Source: Bogdan and Biklen (1982).

TABLE 7.3
Data Based Descriptions of Activity Structures

Descriptions

Name: Reading Circle
Definition: An activity in which a small group of students read orally, usually in turn, and discuss the content of written materials under the direction and probing of the teacher.
Examples: Reading basal readers; reading weekly news magazines for children; reading workbook stories.

Name: Seatwork
Definition: An activity in which students make written responses to a variety of materials while working independently.
Examples: Doing workbook pages or dittos; writing a creative short story; tracing a series of geometric shapes.

Name: Two-way Presentation
Definition: Students and teacher communicate orally with each other, each having the opportunity to respond to the other.
Examples: Flashcards; drill exercises; discussion of social studies issue; tutoring; laboratory demonstration; interactive computer work.

Name: One-way Presentation
Definition: A teacher communicates orally to a small or large group of students. There is little or no chance for students to respond.
Examples: Giving a short explanation; presenting new material; demonstrating a new procedure such as regrouping in subtraction; lecturing.

Name: Mediated Presentation
Definition: An activity in which students listen, watch and/or read along with the presenter of information, who is not personally available to the student.
Examples: Automatic filmstrips and audiotape or slide and audiotape show on *The Living Desert*; movie on *Powers of Ten*; a television show that teaches a foreign language; record of story in story book played at the listening station.

Name: Silent Reading
Definition: An activity in which students read without any demands for a concurrent written or oral response.

Examples: Directed reading or free choice of books, magazines, or newspapers.

Name: Construction
Definition: An activity in which a student generates a product from a set of materials.
Examples: Baking a cake; performing a science experiment; building a model of a pueblo; creating a collage.

Name: Games
Definition: An activity designed to provide instruction or enrichment in an academic area that employs a set of rules or strategies that have a game-like quality.
Examples: Spelling bee; Around the World With Multiplication Facts; Ghost; Concentration.

Name: Play
Definition: An activity that has no obvious academic learning goals and in which students seem to have fun.

Examples: Jump rope; house; blocks; baseball; Parcheesi; Dungeons and Dragons.

Name: Housekeeping
Definition: Any activity in which students are informed of daily events and in which rituals are performed.

Examples: Picking the weekly traffic monitor; reciting the pledge; collecting milk money; announcing parent-teacher conference days; announcing the time and place of the swimming meet.

Source: Berliner (1983).
Reproduced by permission. Berliner, D., Developing Conceptions of Classroom Environments. *Educational Psychologist* **13**, 1–13 (1983), Lawrence Erlbaum.

set of rules. The typology can be developed using the concepts of the participants, the so-called *emic* description discussed in Chapter 3, or the typology can be developed using concepts from the researcher, what we called the *etic* description.

As one example, consider the taxonomy of eleven activity structures developed by Berliner (1983) and presented in Table 7.3. This typology was based on observations in seventy-five elementary classrooms. Berliner suggests that these eleven formats cover all possible formats: "We believe that if one looks at elementary school classrooms, everything that is observed can be classified as being one of these structures" (p. 10). Gump (1967) and Stodolsky (1988) have developed similar taxonomies of activity formats.

Another example comes from the study by Bussis et al. discussed in detail in Chapter 6. As you might recall, interview transcripts from sixty teachers implementing open education approaches to instruction were coded in a variety of ways. For example, in Chapter 6 we presented the coding categories used to characterize the teachers' curriculum and learning priorities for children. The next analysis by Bussis et al., using these curriculum priorities as a starting point, examined the one or two priorities that dominated the interview. They also looked for evidence of teachers' willingness to experiment with the curriculum. Table 7.4 presents the coding scheme that resulted. As is apparent, the coding scheme revolved around the "grade-level facts and skills" priority coding. These four categories cover all 60 teachers, and represent a taxonomy of teacher types.

TABLE 7.4

Coding Categories Developed for Classifying Teachers' Curriculum Priorities

Group 1. (12%)	"Grade-level facts and skills" is clearly the dominant priority, and there is little evidence of experimentation or change in the surface curriculum from what the teachers had been practicing previously.
Group 2. (22%)	"Grade-level facts and skills,' is clearly the dominant priority, but there is much evidence of change and experimentation with the surface curriculum.
Group 3. (39%)	"Grade-level facts and skills" is an expressed priority, but not the dominant priority. Middle-range priorities tend to be dominant, and there is evidence of a potentially rich surface curriculum.
Group 4. (27%)	A comprehensive or middle-range priority is dominant, and there is little evidence of pre-occupation with "grade-level facts and skills"—i.e., it is not codable as such. There is also evidence of a potentially rich surface curriculum.

Source: Bussis et al. (1976).

A more elaborate method of categorization comes from two sociologists, Glaser and Strauss (1967). Their influential book, and the concept of grounded theory developed in the book, is one of the most cited references and discussed concepts among qualitative researchers. The technique of constant comparison, along with theoretical sampling, are the bases for generating theory from the data at hand, theory "grounded" in evidence.

The technique of constant comparison is both a data collection and data analysis strategy. In fact, it is impossible to separate the two. Glaser and Strauss outline four stages in the constant comparison technique:

> 1. comparing incidents applicable to each category, 2. integrating categories and their properties, 3. delimiting the theory, and 4. writing the theory. Although this method of generating theory is a continuously growing process—each stage after a time is transformed into the next—earlier stages do remain in operation simultaneously throughout the analysis and each provides continuous development to its succesive-stage until the analysis is terminated (p. 105).

The starting point in the constant comparative technique is the coding of data into categories. The categories may emerge as data are examined or data may be coded into an existing category when it is collected or examined. As each new incident of data is compared to previously coded incidents in the same category, the constant comparison process "very soon starts to generate theoretical properties of the category" (Glaser and Strauss, 1967, p. 106). This coding process is quite fluid as theoretical concepts are employed to organize and understand the data, and new categories emerge or old categories are collapsed into others.

As coding proceeds, coding involves more and more the comparison of incidents to the properties of existing categories, and less to the other incidents of the category themselves. The properties of each category become more integrated and their relation to other categories start to become related as well. Glaser and Strauss suggest that, if data are collected using theoretical sampling, then it is easier for the interrelationships among the categories to emerge.

The goal of the analysis is, of course, to generate grounded theory. Two processes make this easier to happen, delimitation and saturation of categories.

As the theoretical relationships begin to come together, and more abstract concepts are used to account for more of the data, terminology is reduced. The reduction in terminology allows the researcher to begin achieving an integrated theory with wider applicability. Fewer categories are required for explanation, and the researcher can become more focused in the selection and analysis of incidents for coding. Such delimiting of categories makes it easier for the researcher to account for the data.

Categories can also become "theoretically saturated." This means that new incidents of the category do not add new properties to the category. Such data add more incidents but nothing new to the theory. Saturated categories help economize resources by narrowing the possible universe of additional data requirements and focusing future data collection on those data suggested by non-saturated categories.

Thus, the process of data collection and category generation are woven into one iterative process. As the process continues, the theoretical propositions and relationships begin to emerge, through insight, directly from the data, thus generating theory that is "grounded" in evidence. This is inductive theory development, and as Glaser and Strauss describe it, "To make theoretical sense of so much diversity in his data, the analyst is forced to develop ideas on a level of generality higher in conceptual abstraction than the qualitative material being analyzed" (p. 144). The technique of constant comparison is not a technique to verify theory, but to discover and generate theory.

Should I Quantify Data?

When data are categorized, as described above with typologies and the technique of constant comparison, the coding of data is done to arrange the data in categories. The purpose of the coding is to organize the data, making it easier for the researcher to discern regularities and patterns and discover what is important.

What may go unnoticed in this discovery and coding phase is the implicit "counting" that occurs. Even though the purpose of the coding is merely to organize the data one consequence of the categorization process is that some categories contain more coded data than others. The very fact that a category is formed at all means that multiple pieces of data were available to fill the category. "Recurrent" themes or patterns, by definition, mean that the theme or pattern occurred at least twice. Thus, other things equal, categories with more coded data are likely to be considered more or considered more important than categories with less data. The point is that the process of categorization involves a primitive quantification of data.

This quantification can be and sometimes is made explicit by interpretive researchers. In this case, a second purpose of the coding of data is to specifically examine frequencies of events or actions, or to compare frequencies of events or actions in different settings or between different participants. This is sometimes done informally, with tallies or frequencies reported, or more formally where specific hypotheses are tested statistically. In either case, words or units of words are coded and reported as frequencies.

It is important that the researcher characterize exactly what is being quantified and what the frequency of that code might indicate about the phenomenon. Smith and Geoffrey (1968, pp. 255–256), for example, discussed this issue as the "two-realities problem." The phenomenon represents the first reality, and the field notes of that phenomenon represent the second reality. They point out that quantification of the field notes rests on two assumptions. First, that everything in the notes represents events in the real world, and second, that the proportion of events in the field notes represent the proportion of events in the real world. Smith and Geoffrey had no problem with the first assumption but argued that the field notes they maintained did not provide the systematic sampling of events necessary to meet the second assumption. Field notes can provide rough tallies of events, but are difficult sources of data to use to generate comparative evidence about the frequency of categories of events in the phenomenon.

Other sources of evidence, however, such as interview data, narrative records, open-ended surveys, or characteristics of participants can be coded and analyzed statistically. When we quantify something, we do so by assigning numbers to instances according to a rule or set of rules. When the rule involves a simple classification of instances into categories, we have used the simplest form of measurement, and we usually call the result of this categorization process categorical data, discrete data, or nominal data.

Categorical data cannot be ordered. The numbers assigned to each piece of data merely name and separate instances of one category from instances of a second category. Once an instance has been categorized, it is considered just like all other instances in the category. For proper categorization to occur, categories should be exhaustive, mutually exclusive, and involve only a single classification rule. The categories should be exhaustive so that all instances can be categorized. They should be mutually exclusive so that the same instance is not categorized more than once on any given dimension or with respect to any one variable in the same analysis. Finally, each category should involve a single categorization rule so that all instances placed in the same category are at least similar in terms of one rule. When these three criteria are met, the frequencies, or number of instances, within each category can be interpreted in a relatively unambiguous manner.

Contingency tables are a common and useful way to view the frequencies of occurrence of two or more categorical variables. Contingency tables are typically represented by crossing two variables (i.e., the R rows of one variable, with each row representing a category, with the C columns of a second variable, with each column representing a category. The table, then, has $R \times C$ cells. A variety of analytic strategies are available for such a configuration, depending on how instances were assigned to the cells (see Light, 1973).

Certainly one of the most interesting ethnographic-like studies done in research on teaching is that of Tikunoff, Berliner, and Rist (1975). We call it "ethnographic-like" because observers were only in classrooms for one week, and thus, there was not the prolonged observation characteristic of ethnographies. Observers did, however, write narrative records of classroom events, and in this sense, data collection followed qualitative field techniques. It is included in this section on typologies because the purpose of the study was to generate categories that distinguished between relatively more and less effective classrooms, and, once identified, could be used in later research.

The study, known as Special Study A, was part of Phase III-A data collection of the Beginning Teacher Evaluation Study (BTES). This phase of the BTES study was discussed in Chapter 4 under the section on sampling of evidence, and the reader is referred there for a description of how the forty classrooms in Special Study A, twenty more effective and twenty less effective, were identified.

Trained ethnographers wrote narrative records, or protocols as the researchers characterized them, of what occurred during five consecutive days in both reading and mathematics. Pairs of these protocols, one from an effective classroom and one from an ineffective classroom, were read by a team of six experts whose task it was to generate as many student, teacher, and instructional characteristics as possible that discriminated between the pair of protocols. From a total of 211 characteristics, 61 dimensions were defined, each dimension characterized by positive and negative exemplars. The 61 dimensions are shown in Table 7.5, and an example of how one of the 61 dimensions was defined is given in Table 7.6.

In the second phase of data analysis, twenty trained raters evaluated pairs of protocols on a seven-point scale for each of the 61 dimensions, each pair having one more effective and one less effective classroom. Twenty-one of the 61 dimensions were found to discriminate between more and less effective classrooms across both grade level (second- and fifth-grade) and subject matter (reading and mathematics).

How Do I Test Propositions?

Analytic induction originated in sociology (Znaniecki, 1934; Robinson, 1951; also see Manning, 1983). In contrast to the constant comparison technique, the purpose of analytic induction is to test and verify theoretical propositions. Not only is the procedure intended to test propositions, it is designed to yield universal statements of the nature "All *S* are *P*" (Robinson, 1951). An attempt is made to develop propositions that apply to all cases of the problem under investigation. This is in sharp contrast to "enumerative induction," a name used to describe the statistical use of correlation coefficients that establish relationships by first collecting a set of cases from some population and searching for the relationship in those cases to generalize to the population. Analytic induction, on the other hand, proceeds from case to case, constantly testing each new case against initial hypotheses and definition of the phenomenon to be explained. If the case fits the hypothesis, a new case is examined. If not, the hypothesis is revised

TABLE 7.5

Dimensions for Comparing Classrooms

1. *abruptness (T):* unanticipated "switching" by teacher, e.g., from instruction to classroom management, to behavior management, to instruction, to behavior management.
2. *accepting (T):* teacher reacts constructively (overt, verbal, non-verbal) to students' feelings and attitudes.
3. *adult involvement (C):* adults other than the teacher are allowed to instruct.
4. *attending (T):* teacher actively listens to what a student is saying, reading, reciting.
5. *awareness of developmental levels (T):* teacher is aware of student's emotional, social educational needs and therefore assigns tasks appropriate for these.
6. *being liked (T):* teacher seeks approval from students in an ingratiating manner, often at expense of instruction.
7. *belittling (T):* teacher berates child in front of others.
8. *competing (T):* competition, outdoing others is emphasized by the teacher.
9. *complimenting (control) (T):* teacher's action reinforces student(s) whose behavior is in the right direction.
10. *consistency of message (control) (T):* teacher gives a direction or a threat and follows through with it.
11. *conviviality (C):* warmth, family-like quality to classroom interaction; good feelings between teacher–students, students–students.
12. *cooperation (S):* students cooperate with other students, teacher; willingness on part of students to help each other.
13. *defending (T):* teacher defends a student from verbal or physical assault by another.
14. *defiance (S):* a student's open resistance to teacher direction; refuses to comply.
15. *democracy (T):* teacher provides opportunities to involve students in decision making re class standards, instruction, procedures, etc.
16. *distrust (T):* teacher expresses doubt for validity of student's work or behavior.
17. *drilling (T):* teacher emphasizes regularization, rote memory, retrieval of facts on part of student learning.
18. *encouraging (T):* teacher admonishes student effort in order to motivate.
19. *engagement (S):* students express eagerness to participate, appear actively, productively involved in learning activities.
20. *equity (T):* teacher appears to divide time, attention equally among all students.
21. *ethnicity (T):* teacher expresses positive, informative comments about racial, class, ethnic contributions; encourages class discussion about cultural contributions.
22. *excluding (T):* teacher banishes student from class activity—to corner, cloakroom, out of room, etc.
23. *expectation (T):* teacher attributes scholastic problems or predicts success for student on basis of past information or student's "background."
24. *filling time (T):* teacher fills "empty" time periods with "busy work."
25. *flexibility (T):* teacher adjusts instruction easily to accommodate change in plans, time schedule, absenteeism, or change of students' behavior.
26. *gendering (T):* teacher assigns roles on basis of male or female (boy–girl) and reinforces these.
27. *harrassing (T):* teacher taunts, pesters, nags, hazes, "puts down," or physically hits a student.
28. *ignoring (T):* teacher appears to deliberately "not hear" or "not see" so as to treat a student as being invisible.
29. *illogical statements (T):* teacher makes a statement whose consequences would be ridiculous if carried out.
30. *individualizing (T):* teacher assigns to each student learning tasks designed to match his/her individual abilities and interests.
31. *job satisfaction (T):* *teacher seems to enjoy teaching.
32. *knowledge of subject (T):* teacher seems confident in teaching a given subject, and demonstrates a grasp of it.

33. *manipulation (S):* student is able to get on demand a desired response from the teacher.
34. *mobility (S):* students move freely and purposefully around the room; teacher allows students to work at places other than at their assigned seats.
35. *mobility (T):* teacher moves spontaneously about the room.
36. *modeling/imitation (S):* students copy teacher's behavior, and are encouraged to do so by teacher.
37. *monitoring learning (T):* teacher checks in on student's progress regularly and adjusts instruction accordingly.
38. *moralizing (T):* teacher emphasizes goodness vs. badness, verbally expresses ideal behavior model.
39. *oneness (T):* teacher treats whole group as "one" often in order to maintain peer control.
40. *openness (T):* teacher verbally acknowledges to students feelings of anger or frustration, admits mistakes, expresses need for self-improvement.
41. *open questioning (T):* teacher asks questions which call for interpretive responses and are open-ended.
42. *optimism (T):* teacher expresses positive, pleasant, optimistic attitudes and feelings.
43. *pacing (T):* teacher appears to perceive learning rate of students and adjusts teaching pace accordingly.
44. *peer teaching (S):* students help other students instructionally and are encouraged to do so, whether "olders" with "youngers" or students of same age group.
45. *personalizing (T):* teacher calls on students by name.
46. *policing (T):* undue emphasis on quietness, orderliness, good behavior, and teacher spends disproportionate time with monitoring student behavior and controlling for discipline.
47. *politeness (T):* teacher requests rather than commands, uses "please" and "thank you," encourages same in student–student interaction.
48. *praising (T):* teacher verbally rewards student.
49. *promoting self-sufficiency (T):* teacher encourages students to take responsibility for their own classwork.
50. *recognition-seeking (T):* teacher calls attention to self for no apparent instructional purpose.
51. *rushing (T):* teacher does not give students adequate response time, or answers for them; is tied to a pre-set time limit, and hurries students to finish work.
52. *sarcasm (T):* teacher responds in a demeaning manner, uses destructive/cutting remarks.
53. *shaming (T):* teacher instills guilt in students for their behavior in order to establish control.
54. *signaling (control) (T):* teacher uses body language, nonverbal signals to change students' behavior.
55. *spontaneity (T):* teacher capitalizes instructionally on unexpected incidents that arise during class time.
56. *stereotyping (T):* teacher labels and judges students by socioeconomic, ethnic, or racial characteristics.
57. *structuring (T):* teacher prepares students for lesson by reviewing, outlining, explaining objectives, summarizing.
58. *teacher-made materials (T):* teacher provides instructional materials other than textbooks, and arranges for their use by students.
59. *time fixedness (T):* teacher emphasizes promptness, begins and ends activities by clock rather than by student interest.
60. *waiting (T):* after asking a question, teacher waits in silence for student responses or waits in silence after student response before reacting.
61. *warmth (T):* teacher seeks contact with students, talks with them, shows affection toward them.

Source: Berliner and Tikunoff (1976).

TABLE 7.6

Description of the "Structuring" Dimension

STRUCTURING (T)

We mean:
— reviewing a lesson from the previous day or at the end of a lesson
— at the beginning of a lesson, the teacher tells the class what it will learn
— teacher outlines on board the main topics of a lesson
— teacher signals that one part of a lesson has been completed and another is to begin
— teacher underscores important points by pointing to them
— teacher summarizes a lesson by tying main points together

Examples:
1. "OK class, let's review what we talked about yesterday. First, we learned that ecology is a science; second we learned that ecology deals with both living and non-living things; and third we looked at some of the kinds of relationships between living and non-living things in the environment."
2. "After I review what you've read today, I'm going to ask you a few questions about ecosystems."
3. "Let's summarize the three kinds of relationships that we've been talking about: Predator–prey, benefit–no difference and mutual benefit."

We do not mean:
— beginning a lesson without organizing students thinking in that direction
— abruptly moving from one activity within a lesson to another without clarification
— picking up at a point in a lesson for the day before and plunging ahead without summarizing previous day's work

Examples:
1. "Okay. Get out your readers. Let's go! Tommy, you read first, please."
2. Teacher interrupts a student reading with, "That's enough. We're running out of time. Take out your workbooks and answer the questions for this story on page 32."
   Student says, "But we haven't finished reading it yet!"
3. At the beginning of a reading group's session with her, the teacher says, "I want you to fill out the ditto sheets for yesterday's story. Silently, please."

Source: Tikunoff et al. (1975).

or the phenomenon is redefined so that the case is accounted for. This continues until all cases are explained.

Thus, the general strategy is to state propositions that explain the phenomena under question, examine individual cases, and if a negative case is found, to either reformulate the hypothesis or redefine the phenomenon. The researcher then continues to examine cases until a universal relationship is established fitting all cases.

Robinson (1951) outlines the step-by-step procedures of this technique, taken from a dissertation by Donald Cressey:

> 1. A rough definition of the phenomenon to be explained is formulated. 2. A hypothetical explanation of that phenomenon is formulated. 3. One case is studied in light of the hypothesis, with the object of determining whether or not the hypothesis fits the facts in that case. 4. If the hypothesis does not fit the facts, either the hypothesis is reformulated or the phenomenon to be explained is redefined so that the case is excluded. 5. Practical certainty may be attained after a small number of cases has been

examined, but the discovery of negative cases disproves the explanation and requires a reformulation. 6. This procedure of examining cases, redefining the phenomenon, and reformulating the hypotheses is continued until a universal relationship is established, each negative case calling for a redefinition, or a reformulation (p. 813).

Researchers following this technique place great emphasis on the active search for negative cases, those cases that are counterexamples to the researcher's hypothesis. As Denzin (1970, p. 197) describes, the researcher must "state his theories in such a way as to indicate crucial tests of the theory and to permit the explicit search for negative cases."

We know of no examples of analytic induction being applied to classroom research. Most of the references to the technique in the literature point to a few classic sociological studies. A number of concepts from analytic induction, the search for negative cases and the systematic comparison of cases, for example, have made their way into the general interpretive methodology literature.

How Do I Present the Data?

The purpose of data presentation is to convince the reader that your knowledge claims are an accurate and plausible account of the phenomenon. To do this, knowledge claims must be accompanied with supporting evidence; otherwise, the knowledge claims become opinion and grounded not in evidence but inside the researcher's head.

The write-up of qualitative data is a difficult job. Not only must the researcher translate what has been learned from the study, but the researcher must convince the reader of the accuracy of the views by documenting descriptive statements or generalizations about the phenomenon. This is difficult because words are not easily summarized in tables or figures.

Data presentation can take many forms. Typically, one sees quotes from interviews, excerpts from field notes and interpretive memos, examples or anecdotes, or tabulations of observational data or words summarizing finding interspersed throughout the text to document and support statements or bolster arguments. Miles and Huberman (1984) present an excellent sourcebook on methods of data display.

Issues in the Analysis of Numbers

There is a wide array of statistical techniques available to classroom researchers. We have chosen to be selective in our presentation and focus on the more common techniques used in classroom research. These are by no means the only techniques nor necessarily the best. We have included these techniques to be illustrative of the kinds of analyses that have been used in past work and to illustrate the types of issues with which researchers have been confronted. As in the previous section on qualitative analysis, we organize the presentation around basic data analytic questions.

How Do I Prepare the Data?

Preparation of data for quantitative data analysis involves a number of complex decisions. First, the data must be examined for anomalies and missing data, and decisions must be made about how to handle the anomalies or missing data. Second, the data typically must be aggregated to form variables for analysis, across occasions in the case of observational data and across items in the case of achievement data. Third, once variables are formed, it is sometimes necessary to reduce the number of variables in a data set because there are too many variables to analyze at once or there are too many variables relative to the sample size. These three issues are usually intertwined, and decisions about one are often dependent on considerations of the other two. We will discuss each in turn.

Data Screening and Editing. Data screening and editing are seldom discussed in reports of research, but can involve large amounts of data preparation time. According to Anderson et al. (1989), "estimates of resources allocated for data editing tasks should be exceedingly liberal when engaging in international research" (p. 154). While the *IEA Classroom Environment Study* is perhaps the largest cross-national study ever conducted, this statement is well worth heeding.

In observational research, with literally hundreds of variables, students, and teachers to consider, examination of the raw data and editing of the data set can take more time than the actual analyses. Values outside the possible range of values for a given variable must be corrected if there is evidence to justify the correction (e.g., checking the original source of evidence, changing an obvious mistake) or deleted altogether if no correction is possible.

Decisions must be made about missing values and which cases to keep and which to drop. If missing data are to be estimated (rather than eliminated), decisions must be made as to which missing cases to estimate and which estimation procedures to use. Decisions must also be made about extreme cases (i.e., those vastly different from all other cases).

Missing values in a data set create particularly complex problems and require that researchers make some difficult decisions. To illustrate the magnitude of these problems, consider a study in which observational and questionnaire data are available on 75 variables on 50 teachers, with each teacher teaching in a classroom containing 30 students. Suppose further that observations were made on five occasions and that observational data were aggregated across those occasions. The situation is not unlike those studies in which relationships between teacher behavior and student achievement have been investigated. Missing data can and will occur for variables, for students, and for teachers. Variables will have missing data when they were not coded or coded properly. Students and teachers will have missing data when they were absent during the collection of the evidence or they did not respond to a question or an item.

Decisions must be made about how to handle the missing data. As one example, the authors of the *IEA Classroom Environment Study* established the following four rules for dealing with missing data: (1) a variable was eliminated from the data set if more than 15 percent of the data for that variable was missing; (2) a student was eliminated from the data set if (a) data on more than 20 percent of the variables for that student were missing, or (b) if the student was missing any of four different measures (that had been administered at different points in time, increasing the likelihood that at least one of the four would be missing due to student absences); (3) an entire class was eliminated when more than 20 percent of the variables aggregated to the classroom level were missing; and (4) a teacher (and the teacher's class) was eliminated if the teacher was missing either of two measures. Usually such decisions are made after careful assessment of the quality of the existing data and the effect of each decision rule on the data set. Obviously, data collection is expensive and the researcher wants to retain as much of the data as possible. But, in our opinion, the quality of the data is more important than the quantity.

Missing data is not the only editing issue. Decisions must be made about any outliers in the data, data points that are within the possible range of values for a variable but fall well outside the other data points. Such data points can have extreme and detrimental influences on correlational and/or regression statistics. Anderson et al. (1989) present a discussion of diagnostic statistics that can be used to screen for outlier cases. For example, Figure 7.1 presents the regression of residualized posttest scores on a teacher observation variable "teacher to student probes." Each data point represents a single teacher or classroom, and the solid line represents the unstandardized regression line. As can be seen, the one extreme case to the right severely affects the regression line. The correlation between the two variables is 0.26; with the outlier case omitted, the correlation coefficient is 0.50.

Outliers are not necessarily restricted to one deviant case. Figure 7.2 gives an example from the same study (but different country). In this scatterplot, "student questions" are related to posttest scores. Several features are noteworthy. First, the regression line is influenced by two pairs of outliers, both pairs lying to the right. Second, the frequency of occurrence of student questions was extremely low; in fact, two of the outlier classrooms were the only two classrooms where the percent of student questions was over one percent. The low frequency of occurrence, and resulting restriction in variance, will limit the potential of this variable to demonstrate relationships to achievement or other variables.

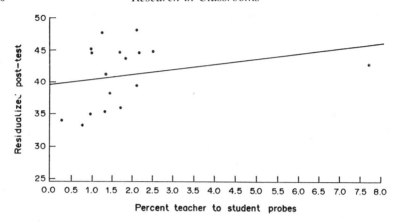

FIG 7.1   Plot for the regression of residualized posttest scores on the percent
of teacher to student probes*
*Canada Ontario-French, $N = 17$ classes

Source: Anderson et al. (1989).

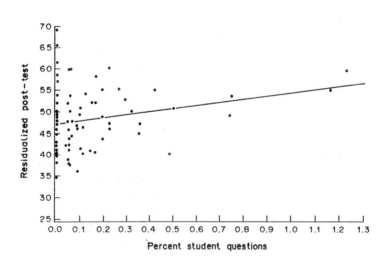

FIG 7.2   Plot for the regression of residualized posttest scores on the percent
of student questions*.
*Thailand, $N = 81$ classes.

Source: Anderson et al. (1989).

The identification of outliers is one thing, but how to deal with them is an entirely different matter. Anderson et al. (1989) discuss the pros and cons of *ad hoc* rescaling, non-linear scale transformation, and deletion of outlying cases as three possible options. Given their complicated and multiple data sets, none of these options were viable for them. However, in other studies, such options may be important to consider, especially with observational data distributed in restricted or unique ways.

Data Aggregation. Observational data are typically based on some small number of observation occasions, usually fewer than 10 occasions (with some studies including as few as two). Issues concerning the aggregation of observational data are illustrated in Table 7.7. In this hypothetical example, there were two observation occasions (days 1 and 2) and four cycles of observation during the study (1, 2, 3, and 4). Two coding categories were used (A and B) with the occurrence or non-occurrence of behaviors within each category recorded every 10 seconds or six times per minute. In Table 7.7, an occurrence of a behavior within a coding category is recorded as a "1," while a non-occurrence is recorded as a "0."

This observation procedure is an overly simplified but representative illustration of many time-sampling classroom observational instruments. Typically, more days would be observed, more cycles would be recorded, more coding categories would be required, each cycle would last longer, and codes would be recorded more frequently. The concept is the same, however. Frequencies of each coding category can be calculated, and then

TABLE 7.7

A Hypothetical Example of Observational Data

Day	Cycle	Coding Category	Minute 1 1	2	3	4	5	6	Minute 2 1	2	3	4	5	6	Frequency
1	1	A	1	1	1	1	1	0	0	0	0	0	0	0	5
		B	0	0	1	1	1	1	1	1	1	1	1	1	10
1	2	A	1	1	1	0	0	0	0	0	0	0	1	1	5
		B	1	1	1	1	1	1	0	0	0	0	1	1	8
2	3	A	0	0	0	0	0	0	0	0	0	0	0	0	0
		B	0	0	0	1	1	0	0	0	0	1	1	1	5
2	4	A	0	0	0	0	0	0	0	1	1	1	1	1	5
		B	0	0	1	1	1	0	0	0	1	1	1	1	7
TOTAL		A													15/48 = 31%
		B													30/48 = 67%

converted to percentages by dividing by a proper denominator. In our example, there were 48 10-second "frames" and thus 48 is a proper base with which to calculate the percent occurrence of the coded behaviors.

To provide a more realistic example, consider the massive observational study of Goodlad (1984), which included the collection of observational data in 129 elementary classrooms and 887 secondary classrooms. Each class was visited on three occasions, full days for elementary schools and full periods at the secondary level. One of the five observational instruments used, the Five-Minute Interaction (FMI) instrument, required the observer to record one frame every five seconds or so, a frame consisting of an interaction coded into each of five categories: *who* (nine possible codes) is doing *what* (12 possible codes) to *whom* (the same nine codes as for the who category), in what *context* (four possible codes), and *how* (eleven possible codes). Table 7.8 was adapted from their training manual and provides examples of how classroom interaction was coded using the FMI. Approximately sixty frames were completed in a five minute span, and, four cycles were completed each hour. Thus, approximately 48 FMI cycles (of 60 frames each) were completed for each elementary classroom, 12 at the secondary level. The code book for variable specification generates 127 variables from the FMI alone (see Giesen and Sirotnik, 1979). Needless to say, the scope of data aggregation illustrated in Table 7.7 pales in comparison to the scope of the Goodlad study.

Data Reduction. Once variables have been edited and aggregated to form variables, it is often the case in classroom research that there are too many variables for analysis. The major limiting factor is the number of classrooms that can reasonably be included in any given study. With classroom-level variables, sample size is determined by the number of classrooms. Past classroom observational studies have seldom included 100 classrooms in a study. Given one common (and minimum) rule of thumb for regression-based analyses is 10 cases for each variable in the study plus 50, the 50 to ensure sufficient sample sizes for data sets with few numbers of variables, 100 classrooms would be required to study only five predictor variables. Another rule of thumb sometimes seen is 30 cases per variable. One hundred classrooms would get you about three predictor variables.

One reason these variable-to-sample size ratios are suggested by statisticians is that the multiple R is regression is biased upwards due to capitalization on chance. That is, even when a particular predictor in a multiple regression has a zero correlation with the criterion in the population, the sample correlation, because of sample fluctuation, would rarely have a zero correlation and would thus make some contribution to the sample R-square. The expectation of the sample R-square when the population R-square is zero is $k/n-1$, where k is the number of variables and n is the sample size. Thus, when the number of variables is close to the

TABLE 7.8

Illustration of Coding Used in Goodlad Study (1984)

---

1. T: "I'm going to read a story to you now."

1. <u>TSm4i</u> The teacher (T) is introducing (4) to the small group (Sm) instructional material (i).

Who	Whom	What	Cx.	How
Ⓡ ● Ⓐ Ⓞ	Ⓣ Ⓐ Ⓞ	① ② ③ ●	● Ⓡ	ⓃⓋ Ⓣ Ⓧ Ⓜ Ⓗ
Ⓢ Ⓢ Ⓓ ②	Ⓢ Ⓓ ②	⑤ ⑥ ⑦ ⑧	Ⓑ Ⓢ	Ⓩ
Ⓒ Ⓢ Ⓜ Ⓛ	● Ⓜ Ⓛ	⑨ ⑩ ⑪ ⑫		Ⓖ Ⓓ Ⓡ ⊕ ⊖

2. T: "Sit down very quietly in a circle."

2. <u>TSm5R</u> The teacher (T) has given the small group (Sm) a routine (R) command (5).

Who	Whom	What	Cx.	How
Ⓡ ● Ⓐ Ⓞ	Ⓣ Ⓐ Ⓞ	① ② ③ ④	ⓘ ●	ⓃⓋ Ⓣ Ⓧ Ⓜ Ⓗ
Ⓢ Ⓢ Ⓓ ②	Ⓢ Ⓓ ②	● ⑥ ⑦ ⑧	Ⓑ Ⓢ	Ⓩ
Ⓒ Ⓢ Ⓜ Ⓛ	● Ⓜ Ⓛ	⑨ ⑩ ⑪ ⑫		Ⓖ Ⓓ Ⓡ ⊕ ⊖

3. All the children sit down quietly.

3. <u>SmT3RNVX</u> The small group (Sm) responds (3) non-verbally (NV) to the teacher's (T) command regarding routine (R) with movement (X).

Who	Whom	What	Cx.	How
Ⓡ Ⓣ Ⓐ Ⓞ	● Ⓐ Ⓞ	① ② ● ④	ⓘ ●	● Ⓣ ● Ⓜ Ⓗ
Ⓢ Ⓢ Ⓓ ②	Ⓢ Ⓓ ②	⑤ ⑥ ⑦ ⑧	Ⓑ Ⓢ	Ⓩ
Ⓒ ● Ⓜ Ⓛ	Ⓢ Ⓜ Ⓛ	⑨ ⑩ ⑪ ⑫		Ⓖ Ⓓ Ⓡ ⊕ ⊖

4. T: "That was very nice, thank you."

4. <u>TSm7R+</u> The teacher (T) praises (7+) the small group (Sm) regarding routine matters (R).

Who	Whom	What	Cx.	How
Ⓡ ● Ⓐ Ⓞ	Ⓣ Ⓐ Ⓞ	① ② ③ ④	ⓘ ●	ⓃⓋ Ⓣ Ⓧ Ⓜ Ⓗ
Ⓢ Ⓢ Ⓓ ②	Ⓢ Ⓓ ②	⑤ ⑥ ● ⑧	Ⓑ Ⓢ	Ⓩ
Ⓒ Ⓢ Ⓜ Ⓛ	● Ⓜ Ⓛ	⑨ ⑩ ⑪ ⑫		Ⓖ Ⓓ Ⓡ ● ⊖

5. T: "Once there was an old man who had hundreds of cats. He lived in a little house in the country.

5. <u>TSm4i</u> The teacher (T) begins reading (4) to the small group (Sm), which is considered instruction (i).

Who	Whom	What	Cx.	How
Ⓡ ● Ⓐ Ⓞ	Ⓣ Ⓐ Ⓞ	① ② ③ ●	● Ⓡ	ⓃⓋ Ⓣ Ⓧ Ⓜ Ⓗ
Ⓢ Ⓢ Ⓓ ②	Ⓢ Ⓓ ②	⑤ ⑥ ⑦ ⑧	Ⓑ Ⓢ	Ⓩ
Ⓒ Ⓢ Ⓜ Ⓛ	● Ⓜ Ⓛ	⑨ ⑩ ⑪ ⑫		Ⓖ Ⓓ Ⓡ ⊕ ⊖

6. T: "There were cats on the chairs and the bed and in the windows."

6. <u>R</u> The teacher continues reading, so this frame is coded repeat (R).

Who	Whom	What	Cx.	How
● Ⓣ Ⓐ Ⓞ	Ⓣ Ⓐ Ⓞ	① ② ③ ④	ⓘ Ⓡ	ⓃⓋ Ⓣ Ⓧ Ⓜ Ⓗ
Ⓢ Ⓢ Ⓓ ②	Ⓢ Ⓓ ②	⑤ ⑥ ⑦ ⑧	Ⓑ Ⓢ	Ⓩ
Ⓒ Ⓢ Ⓜ Ⓛ	Ⓢ Ⓜ Ⓛ	⑨ ⑩ ⑪ ⑫		Ⓖ Ⓓ Ⓡ ⊕ ⊖

7. Ann hits another child, Jonathon (T watches).

7. <u>T212SNVT-</u> The teacher (T) observes (12) two students (2) fighting (-) and touching (T) without exchanging words (NV) in a social context (S).

Who	Whom	What	Cx.	How
Ⓡ ● Ⓐ Ⓞ	Ⓣ Ⓐ Ⓞ	① ② ③ ④	ⓘ Ⓡ	● ● Ⓧ Ⓜ Ⓗ
Ⓢ Ⓢ Ⓓ ②	Ⓢ Ⓓ ●	⑤ ⑥ ⑦ ⑧	Ⓑ ●	Ⓩ
Ⓒ Ⓢ Ⓜ Ⓛ	Ⓢ Ⓜ Ⓛ	⑨ ⑩ ⑪ ●		Ⓖ Ⓓ Ⓡ ⊕ ⊖

8. T: "Leave Jonathon alone!" (T angry).

8. <u>TS9B-</u> The teacher (T) corrects (9) one student's (S) behavior (B) with negative affect (-).

Who	Whom	What	Cx.	How
Ⓡ ● Ⓐ Ⓞ	Ⓣ Ⓐ Ⓞ	① ② ③ ④	ⓘ Ⓡ	Ⓝ Ⓣ Ⓧ Ⓜ Ⓗ
Ⓢ Ⓢ Ⓓ ②	● Ⓓ ②	⑤ ⑥ ⑦ ⑧	● Ⓢ	Ⓩ
Ⓒ Ⓢ Ⓜ Ⓛ	Ⓢ Ⓜ Ⓛ	● ⑩ ⑪ ⑫		Ⓖ Ⓓ Ⓡ ⊕ ●

9. Ann sits down quietly, complying with the teacher's wishes.

9. <u>ST3BNV</u> The student (S) responds (3) non-verbally (NV) to the teacher's (T) behavioral (B) correction.

Who	Whom	What	Cx.	How
Ⓡ Ⓣ Ⓐ Ⓞ	● Ⓐ Ⓞ	① ② ● ④	ⓘ Ⓡ	● Ⓣ Ⓧ Ⓜ Ⓗ
Ⓢ ● Ⓓ ②	Ⓢ Ⓓ ②	⑤ ⑥ ⑦ ⑧	● Ⓢ	Ⓩ
Ⓒ Ⓢ Ⓜ Ⓛ	Ⓢ Ⓜ Ⓛ	⑨ ⑩ ⑪ ⑫		Ⓖ Ⓓ Ⓡ ⊕ ⊖

10. T: "There were cats on the roof and cats in the garden."

10. <u>TSm4i</u> The teacher (T) resumes reading (4i) to the small group (Sm).

Who	Whom	What	Cx.	How
Ⓡ ● Ⓐ Ⓞ	Ⓣ Ⓐ Ⓞ	① ② ③ ●	● Ⓡ	Ⓝ Ⓣ Ⓧ Ⓜ Ⓗ
Ⓢ Ⓢ Ⓓ ②	Ⓢ Ⓓ ②	⑤ ⑥ ⑦ ⑧	Ⓑ Ⓢ	Ⓩ
Ⓒ Ⓢ Ⓜ Ⓛ	● Ⓜ Ⓛ	⑨ ⑩ ⑪ ⑫		Ⓖ Ⓓ Ⓡ ⊕ ⊖

11. Two children begin giggling as teacher pauses (T watches).

11. <u>T212SNV+</u> The teacher (T) stops and observes (12) two children (2) giggling (+) in a social context (S).

Who	Whom	What	Cx.	How
Ⓡ ● Ⓐ Ⓞ	Ⓣ Ⓐ Ⓞ	① ② ③ ④	ⓘ Ⓡ	● Ⓣ Ⓧ Ⓜ Ⓗ
Ⓢ Ⓢ Ⓓ ②	Ⓢ Ⓓ ●	⑤ ⑥ ⑦ ⑧	Ⓑ ●	Ⓩ
Ⓒ Ⓢ Ⓜ Ⓛ	Ⓢ Ⓜ Ⓛ	⑨ ⑩ ⑪ ●		Ⓖ Ⓓ Ⓡ ● ⊖

12. T: "Be quiet so the other children can listen to the story."

12. <u>T29BNV</u> The teacher (T) corrects (9) the two students' (2) behavior (B) by giving them a reason (G).

Who	Whom	What	Cx.	How
Ⓡ ● Ⓐ Ⓞ	Ⓣ Ⓐ Ⓞ	① ② ③ ④	ⓘ Ⓡ	● Ⓣ Ⓧ Ⓜ Ⓗ
Ⓢ Ⓢ Ⓓ ②	Ⓢ Ⓓ ●	⑤ ⑥ ⑦ ⑧	● Ⓢ	Ⓩ
Ⓒ Ⓢ Ⓜ Ⓛ	Ⓢ Ⓜ Ⓛ	● ⑩ ⑪ ⑫		Ⓖ Ⓓ Ⓡ ⊕ ⊖

13. The two children stop giggling and prepare to listen.

13. <u>2T3BNV</u> The two students (2) respond (3) non-verbally (NV) to the teacher's (T) correction of their behavior (B).

Who	Whom	What	Cx.	How
Ⓡ Ⓣ Ⓐ Ⓞ	● Ⓐ Ⓞ	① ② ● ④	ⓘ Ⓡ	● Ⓣ Ⓧ Ⓜ Ⓗ
Ⓢ Ⓢ Ⓓ ●	Ⓢ Ⓓ ②	⑤ ⑥ ⑦ ⑧	● Ⓢ	Ⓩ
Ⓒ Ⓢ Ⓜ Ⓛ	Ⓢ Ⓜ Ⓛ	⑨ ⑩ ⑪ ⑫		Ⓖ Ⓓ Ⓡ ⊕ ⊖

Source: Adapted from Giesen and Sirotnik (1979), pp. 78–80.

number of the cases the sample R-square approaches unity even when the population R-square is zero.

It goes without saying that most classroom observational studies collect more data than can be used in correlational or regression analyses; descriptively there is no problem. But if the goal of the study is to establish relationships between teacher or instructional variables and student achievement, evidence on fewer variables need to be collected or the number of variables must be reduced in some manner.

Reducing the number of variables can be done in several ways. First, variables that are logically similar, are highly correlated, or are shown to go together through cluster analysis, can be composited to form a single variable. Cluster analysis is a set of techniques for classifying people or objects into relatively homogeneous groups. Bennett (1976), for example, used cluster analysis to group 468 teachers into 12 different teacher styles based on questionnaire responses. Table 7.9 presents descriptions of seven of these teacher types. The seven types, which were used in the second phase of the study (see Chapter 10), were combined into three categories of teacher styles: informal, mixed, and formal. Although cluster analysis was only used to form the 12 initial styles, it could have been used to further group the teachers into the three categories illustrated in Table 7.9. The point here is that cluster analysis permitted Bennett to classify over 400 teachers into a reasonable number of types or groups.

Factor analysis is a second technique for reducing the number of variables in a data set. Beginning with the covariance among a set of variables, factor analysis actually "clusters" variables rather than people. Those variables that are moderately or strongly related with one another, but are unrelated to other variables in the original data set, are placed on a single factor. As a consequence, factor analysis typically results in a smaller number of superordinate variables (or constructs or factors) that accounts for the covariance that exists in the original set of variables. Ryans (1960a) presents a very complete discussion and illustration of the use of factor analysis in classroom research.

How Do I Deal with Non-equivalent Groups?

When groups have been formed randomly, data analysis and interpretation are relatively straightforward. Random assignment of individuals to groups provides a sound basis for arguing that the groups are equivalent on a variety of characteristics and behaviors. In experimental research, if the groups are equivalent prior to the treatment, but unequal on the dependent variable or variables after the treatment, and if other than the treatment all other experiences of the two groups during the experimental are virtually identical, then the researcher has good reason to believe that the treatment has caused the differences in the dependent variable or variables.

However, as mentioned in Chapter 4, classroom researchers seldom have the luxury of random assignment. Classroom researchers must normally use existing, intact classrooms in their research and assign classrooms, not students, at random to experimental groups. One issue raised by this approach is the equivalence of the experimental groups prior to the treatment. Invariably, the use of intact classrooms produces pre-treatment differences between the groups. These pre-treatment differences are a major

TABLE 7.9

Primary Types of Teachers Identified Using Cluster Analysis

Informal Teachers

Type 1

These teachers favor integration of subject matter, and, unlike most other groups, allow pupil choice of work, whether undertaken individually or in groups. Most allow pupils choice of seating. Less than half curb movement and talk. Assessment in all its forms—tests, grading, and homework—appears to be discouraged. Intrinsic motivation is favored.

Type 2

These teachers also prefer integration of subject matter. Teacher control appears to be low, but the teachers offer less pupil choice of work. However, most allow pupils choice of seating, and only one third curb movement and talk. Few test or grade work.

Mixed Teachers

Type 3

The main teaching mode of this group is class teaching and group work. Integration of subject matter is preferred, and is associated with taking their pupils out of school. These teachers appear to be strict, most curbing movement and talk, and offenders are smacked. The amount of testing is average, but the amount of grading and homework below average.

Type 4

These teachers prefer separate subject teaching but a high proportion allow pupil choice of work both in group and individual work. None seat their pupils by ability. They test and grade more than average.

Type 7

This group are separate subject orientated, with a high level of class teaching together with individual work. Teacher control appears to be tight, few teachers allow movement or choice of seating, and offenders are smacked. Assessment, however, is low.

Formal Teachers

Type 11

All members of this group stress separate subject teaching by way of class teaching and individual work. Pupil choice of work is minimal, although most teachers allow choice in seating. Movement and talk are curbed, and offenders smacked.

Type 12

This is an extreme group in a number of respects. None favor an integrated approach. Subjects are taught separately by class teaching and individual work. None allow pupils choice of seating, and every teacher curbs movement and talk. These teachers are above average on all assessment procedures, and extrinsic motivation predominates.

Source: Bennett (1976).

problem for researchers because they are an excellent rival explanation to the treatment for any observed differences on the dependent variable. The argument is that the reason the groups are different on the dependent variable is not because of the treatment but because the groups are different to begin with and those differences are reflected in the dependent variable. In other words, we do not know whether differences on the dependent variable are due to the independent variable or whether differences are due to the groups being different prior to the independent variable. Such quasi-experimental designs are common place in education and have generated an enormous amount of attention (see Cook and Campbell, 1979).

Researchers have attempted to handle this problem in a number of ways, none of them satisfactorily. Four of the most common procedures have been analysis of variance (ANOVA), the use of gain scores, the use of residualized scores, and the use of analysis of covariance (ANCOVA). For fuller discussion of these methods, see Bryk and Weisberg, 1977; Cook and Campbell, 1979, Chapter 4; and Pedhazur, 1982, Chapter 13.

The most elemental model for the structure of data involving one independent variable and one dependent variable is a model we first saw in Chapter 3 in the section on experimental psychology. This linear model, a one-way fixed effects model, is as follows:

$$Y_{ij} = \mu + \alpha_j + e_{ij},$$

where Y_{ij} is the score for the ith person in the jth group;
  μ is the grand mean of all the scores;
  α_j is the effect of treatment j; and
  e_{ij} is the error term.

This model assumes that the treatment is the only cause of differences between the j groups. For experiments, this assumption is reasonable and ANOVA can be used. As described above, however, when random assignment has not occurred, pre-treatment differences are a possible cause of posttest differences between groups. When such pretreatment differences exist, the ANOVA model cannot take them into account.

Rather than use the posttest scores for analysis, researchers have sometimes included pretests in their design. This enables them to calculate gain scores, the posttest minus the pretest, and perform ANOVAs on the gain scores rather than the raw scores. Gain scores represent a common sense (and unbiased estimate of true change) notion of student growth. Gain scores, or change scores as they are sometimes called, have been much maligned in the literature on growth (Rogosa, Brandt, and Zimowski, 1982). Their primary weakness is that they are often correlated with initial pretest, producing different expected amounts of growth for students starting at different initial levels and biasing the estimate of the effect of the treatment on change. To eliminate this problem, researchers have calculated residual gain scores.

Residual gain scores are obtained by regressing the posttest scores on to pretest scores and using the regression equation to predict posttest scores. The residual gain score is the difference between the predicted posttest score and the actual posttest score. These residual scores are uncorrelated with initial pretest scores. In effect, whatever relationship that existed between pretest and posttest has been removed from the posttest score. What is left over are residual scores, uncorrelated with initial status.

Residual gain scores, while adjusting for initial differences between groups in pretest scores, do not adjust for other differences that might exist between the groups. Consequently, they may still provide biased estimates of treatment effects. Furthermore, Burstein (1980, pp. 185ff) argues that when residual gain scores are calculated from classroom-level mean pretest and posttest scores, they suffer from aggregation bias that provide misleading estimates of student-level effects.

A fourth technique, ANCOVA, does make within-group adjustments for pretest, or covariate differences. Suppose one residualized the dependent variable as described above, but did so within each group, using some pretest or covariate thought to be important to the dependent variable. The resulting residuals would have zero correlations with the covariate, and statistical analyses on the residuals would show whether the groups differ after the scores have been adjusted for differences on the covariate. In effect, the mean scores on the dependent variable for each group are adjusted to reflect the differences between the groups on the pretest or covariate. Pedhazur (1982, p. 504) gives the formula for the adjustment as

$$\overline{Y}_j(\text{adj}) = \overline{Y}_j - b(\overline{X}_j - \overline{X}),$$

where $\overline{Y}_j(\text{adj})$ is the adjusted mean in group j;
$\overline{Y}_j$ is the mean of group j prior to adjustment:
b is the common regression coefficient for regressing Y on X;
$\overline{X}_j$ is the mean of the covariate for group j; and
$\overline{X}$ is the grand mean for the covariate.

Two important features of ANCOVA are illustrated in this formula. First, if the groups are equal on the covariate, then $\overline{X}_j = \overline{X}$ and no adjustment would occur since the $b(\overline{X}_j - \overline{X})$ term would be zero. However, the inclusion of the covariate would reduce the error term in the overall analysis. Second, the covariate must be related to the dependent variable or no adjustment will take place. If $b = 0$ (indicating no relationship between the covariate and the dependent variable), again $b(\overline{X}_j - \overline{X})$ would be zero. There are a variety of assumptions that must be made to use ANCOVA properly. Unfortunately, these assumptions are rarely met, yet the technique is used (and abused) anyway. Two assumptions are mentioned here. One assumption is that there is random assignment of students to groups, an assumption that is not often met in classroom research. A second assumption is that the within-group regression coefficients are not significantly different. If they are, ANCOVA should not be used. In fact, ANCOVA was originally developed to control for extraneous variables in experiments, not to make posttest adjustments in non-equivalent control groups and equate the groups. Although often used for this purpose, ANCOVA is not a substitute for random assignment. Pedhazur summarizes the problems in ANCOVA by quoting Anderson (1963, p. 520): "One may well wonder what exactly it means to ask what the data would look like if they were not what they are" (p. 170).

How Do I Establish Relationships?

Without control groups, it is difficult to establish causal relationships between variables. Nonetheless, there are techniques that allow researchers to explore associational relationships among variables. These correlation-based techniques are often used in single group designs and form the primary mode of analysis in such designs. They are also used in quasi-experiments to examine relationships between teacher variables and student achievement when treatments consist of clusters of teacher behaviors.

Suppose we are interested in two variables where one variable (X) is suspected of influencing or causing the other variable (Y). If we gather data on these two variables, we can represent the scores in a scatterplot like the one in Figure 7.3. We can draw a line through the data in such a way that it comes as close as possible to as many of the data points as possible, the least squares criterion. The equation for the line is

$$Y = a + bX,$$

where a is the point on the Y axis that the line intersects and b is the slope of the line, or the rate of change in Y given a one unit change in X.

Several features of our regression of Y on X are indicated in the figure. First, both the mean of X and the mean of Y lie on the regression line. Second, the line intercepts the Y axis at point a. Third, the slope of the line, b, is given by the ratio c/d, or the amount of change in Y given a one-unit change in X. Finally, the predicted Y score for X_i, using the regression line, is given as Y_i', and the difference between the actual Y_i and the predicted Y_i', that is, $Y_i - Y_i'$, is the residual. It is also true that $a = \overline{Y} - b\overline{X}$ and that $b = r_{xy} * s_y/s_x$. In this latter equation, r_{xy} is the correlation coefficient between X and Y and s_x and s_y are the standard deviations of X and Y respectively. Another way to represent the correlation coefficient is by

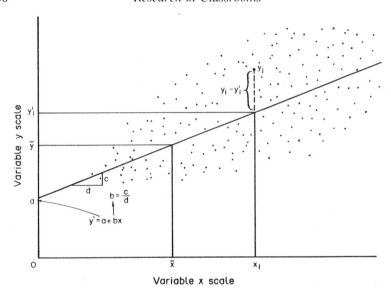

Fɪɢ. 7.3   Example of regression analysis and residual gain score.

$r = s_{xy}/s_x * s_y$, where s_{xy} is the covariance between X and Y and s_x and s_y are as described above.

Correlation coefficients are ubiquitous in educational research. Warnings about spurious correlations and the potential dangers of drawing causal conclusions from correlation coefficients are equally ubiquitous among researchers. And for good reason. Many examples of inappropriate conclusions have been cited in the literature. Perhaps the simplest example of a spurious correlation between two variables is when both are caused by a third variable. Partial correlations are correlations between two variables controlling for the influence of a third variable. In effect, a partial correlation is the correlation between two residual variables, where each original variable is residualized on the third variable.

Process-product research has generated an enormous number of correlation coefficients over the years. Outside of a few exceptions (e.g., McDonald and Elias, 1975/76), most research on teaching following the process-product paradigm has avoided the more complex multiple regression and path analytic regression techniques discussed below and chosen instead to examine, in exploratory studies, simple correlations between teacher process measures and student achievement, usually residualized student achievement. For example Good and Grouws (1979) report the correlations given in Table 7.10 between teacher process measures and residualized student achievement. These correlation coefficients come from

TABLE 7.10

Variable	Correlation in Low SES	p Value	Correlation in High SES	p Value
Classroom Climate[1]	0.42	0.01	0.28	0.11
Managerial[1]	0.10	0.57	0.00	0.97
Total Class Time	0.10	0.56	0.18	0.32
Transition Time	−0.27	0.12	0.11	0.55
Time Going Over Homework	0.26	0.14	0.02	0.91
Review Time	0.09[3]	0.60	0.29	0.10
Development	−0.14[3]	0.41	−0.13	0.50
% of Students Probably Involved	0.45	0.01	−0.07[1]	0.68
Student Asks Question	0.13	0.46	0.09	0.60
Discipline Type Question	−0.04[2]	0.79	−0.30[2]	0.08
Direct Question	0.16	0.34	−0.08	0.65
Open Question	0.15	0.39	0.17	0.64
Student Calls Out Answer	0.01	0.95	0.32	0.06
Process Question	−0.16[3]	0.34	−0.15	0.60
Product Question	0.15[3]	0.39	−0.02	0.89
Choice Question	0.14	0.42	0.15	0.59
Self-Reference Question	−0.07[2]	0.66	0.20[2]	0.25
Opinion Question	−0.25[2]	0.14	0.05[2]	0.76
Correct Response	0.11	0.51	−0.03	0.85
Partially Right Response	−0.09	0.60	−0.13	0.51
Wrong Response	0.16	0.36	−0.20	0.26
"Don't Know" Response	0.02[2]	0.88	−0.22[2]	0.20
No Response	−0.12	0.47	−0.19	0.28
Praise	0.35	0.04	−0.18	0.67
Affirm	0.04	0.80	0.15	0.57
Summarize	−0.39[2]	0.02	−0.13[2]	0.50
No Feedback	0.26[2]	0.13	0.03	0.84
Negate Wrong	0.15	0.39	0.04	0.80
Criticism	−0.09[2]	0.58	0.02[2]	0.91
Process Feedback	−0.11	0.53	0.27	0.12
Gives Answer	−0.09	0.59	−0.02	0.90
Ask Another Student	0.30	0.08	−0.07	0.70
Another Student Calls Out Answer	−0.20[2]	0.26	−0.15[2]	0.59
Repeats Question	−0.25	0.15	−0.07	0.68
Gives Clue	−0.06	0.73	0.03	0.87
Asks New Question	−0.28	0.10	0.12	0.51
Expands Student's Response	−0.32[2]	0.06	0.02[2]	0.92
Student Initiated Work-Related Contact—Teacher Praise	0.12[2]	0.47	0.28	0.11

Variable	Correlation in Low SES	p Value	Correlation in High SES	p Value
Student Initiated Work-Related Contact—Teacher Gives Process-Type Feedback	−0.25	0.15	0.14	0.56
Student Initiated Work-Related Contact—Teacher Gives Feedback	0.00	0.99	0.37	0.03
Student Initiated Work-Related Contact—Teacher Criticizes	−0.37^2	0.02	−0.11^2	0.55
Student Initiated Work-Related Contact—Teacher Type Feedback Unknown	0.04^2	0.78	−0.21^2	0.24
Right Response Followed by Teacher Praise	0.35	0.04	0.09	0.62
No Response or "Don't Know" Response Followed by Sustaining Feedback	−0.22^2	0.20	−0.21	0.24
No Response or "Don't Know" Response Followed by Terminal Feedback	0.01	0.93	−0.22	0.23
Wrong Response Followed by Terminal Feedback	0.22	0.21	−0.19	0.29
Wrong Response Followed by Sustaining Feedback	−0.16	0.36	−0.10	0.56
Part Right Response Followed by Terminal Feedback	−0.02^2	0.88	0.11	0.58
Part Right Response Followed by Sustaining Feedback	−0.18^2	0.29	0.30	0.12
Total Response Opportunities	0.16	0.36	0.14	0.55
Total Teacher Initiated Work-Related Contacts	0.28	0.10	−0.33	0.06
Total Teacher Initiated Behavior-Related Contacts	0.00	0.97	−0.21	0.23
Total Teacher Initiated Contacts	0.22	0.20	−0.33	0.06
Total Student Initiated Work-Related Contacts	−0.06	0.70	0.37	0.03

Variable	Correlation in Low SES	p Value	Correlation in High SES	p Value
Total Student Initiated Procedure-Related Contacts	0.10^2	0.55	−0.03	0.87
Total Student Initiated Contacts	−0.05	0.75	0.35	0.04
Total Dyadic Contacts (Student Initiated, Teacher Initiated, and Response Opportunities)	0.04	0.79	0.17	0.66
Direct Question / Direct, Plus Open Question	0.00	0.98	0.05	0.76
Direct Question / Response Opportunities	0.12	0.48	0.02	0.91
Open Questions / Response Opportunities	0.09	0.61	−0.09	0.62
Call Outs / Response Opportunities	−0.07	0.69	0.00	0.98
Student Initiated Work-Related Contacts / Total Student Initiated Contacts	−0.01	0.93	0.01	0.96
Teacher Initiated Work-Related Contacts / Total Teacher Initiated Contacts	0.32	0.06	−0.26	0.13
Total Teacher Initiated Contacts / Total Student Initiated Contacts	0.11	0.53	−0.34	0.05
Process Questions / Total Questions	-0.31^3	0.07	−0.19	0.28
Choice Questions / Total Questions	−0.06	0.70	−0.25	0.15
Opinion Questions / Total Questions	−0.16	0.35	−0.03	0.84
Product Questions / Total Questions	0.25^3	0.14	−0.10	0.60
Correct Responses / Total Responses	0.00	0.96	0.25	0.15.
Wrong Responses / Wrong Responses Plus No Response	0.21	0.22	0.19	0.27
"Don't Know" / "Don't Know" Plus No Response	0.04	0.81	−0.16	0.61

Variable[1]	Correlation in Low SES	p Value	Correlation in High SES	p Value
% of Responses Teacher Gave No Feedback	0.08	0.64	−0.07	0.71
Student Initiated Procedure-Related Contact—Teacher Praise	0.16^2	0.35	0.18^2	0.30
Student Initiated Procedure-Related Contact—Teacher Gives Feedback	0.10^2	0.56	−0.05	0.76
Student Initiated Procedure-Related Contact—Teacher Criticizes	-0.02^2	0.87	-0.10^2	0.57
Teacher Initiated Work-Related Contact—Teacher Gives Praise	0.18^2	0.29	-0.14^2	0.56
Teacher Initiated Work-Related Contact—Teacher Gives Process Feedback	0.24	0.16	-0.29^2	0.10
Teacher Initiated Work-Related Contact—Teacher Gives Feedback	0.22	0.20	−0.25	0.15
Teacher Initiated Work-Related Contact—Teacher Criticizes	-0.06^2	0.70	-0.19^2	0.30
Teacher Initiated Work-Related Contact—Teacher Type Feedback Unknown	0.16^2	0.36	-0.28^2	0.11
Teacher Initiated Behavior-Related Contact—Teacher Gives Procedure Feedback	-0.10^2	0.57	0.02	0.88
Teacher Initiated Behavior-Related Contact—Teacher Praises	0.05^2	0.78	0.05^2	0.79
Teacher Initiated Behavior-Related Contact—Teacher Warns Student	0.02	0.89	−0.30	0.08
Teacher Initiated Behavior-Related Contact—Teacher Criticizes Student	-0.18^2	0.30	-0.05^2	0.76

Variable	Correlation in Low SES	p Value	Correlation in High SES	p Value
Wrong Response Followed by Teacher Criticism	-0.11^2	0.51	-0.15	0.61
Process Feedback Response Opportunities	-0.01	0.95	0.24	0.17
Process Feedback Product Feedback	-0.01	0.93	0.25	0.15
Expands Feedback Total Feedback	-0.24	0.16	-0.15	0.57
Process Feedback in Student Initiated Work Related Contacts Total Student Initiated Work	-0.17	0.34	-0.19	0.30
Process Feedback in Teacher Initiated Work Related Contacts Total Teacher Initiated Work Related Contacts	0.14	0.43	-0.20	0.25
Total Process Feedback	-0.10	0.54	0.16	0.61

1. High-inference variable.
2. Correlations based on variables with a low frequency of occurrence.
3. Correlations that might be contaminated by the treatment.
4. Most of the variable descriptors are self-explanatory; however, some may need additional clarification as provided below.

DIRECT QUESTION: Teacher calls on a child who is not seeking a response opportunity.

OPEN QUESTION: The teacher creates the response opportunity by asking a public question, and also indicates who is to respond by calling on an individual child, but chooses one of the children who has indicated a desire to respond by raising his/her hand.

PROCESS QUESTION: Requires students to explain something in a way that requires them to integrate facts or to show knowledge of their interrelationships. It most frequently is a "why?" or "how?" question.

PRODUCT QUESTION: Product questions seek to elicit a single correct answer which can be expressed in a single word or short phrase. Product questions usually begin with "who?", "what?", "when?", "where?", "how much?" or "how many?"

CHOICE QUESTIONS: The child does not have to produce a substantive response but may instead simply choose one of two or more implied or expressed alternatives.

SELF-REFERENCE QUESTION: Asks the child to make some non-academic contribution to classroom discussion ("show and tell," questions about personal experiences, preferences, or feelings, requests for opinions or predictions, etc.).

OPINION QUESTIONS: Much like self-reference (except no one correct answer) except that they seek a student opinion on an academic topic (e.g., Is it worth putting a man on the moon?).

NEGATION OF INCORRECT ANSWERS: Simple provision of impersonal feedback regarding the incorrectness of the response, and not going further than this by communicating a personal reaction to the child. This can be communicated both verbally and nonverbally.

From Active Mathematics Teaching by Thomas L. Good, Douglas A. Grouws & Howard Ebmeier. Copyright © 1983 by Longman Inc. Reprinted with permission.

two separate studies involving about 40 teachers each, one study observing predominantly middle and high socioeconomic status classrooms and one study observing predominantly low socioeconomic classrooms.

To get a better sense of the difficulty of interpreting so many correlation coefficients, Figure 7.4 presents a stem-and-leaf display of the correlations for the low SES study. With 40 degrees of freedom, a correlation coefficient of 0.30 is significant at the 0.05 level. As can be seen in Figure 7.4, 10 of the 91 correlation coefficients are significant, only about twice as many as expected by chance. The correlations seem to be randomly distributed about 0.00, with only slightly more positive correlations than negative correlations. With only 40 classrooms, it would be difficult to handle these data in any other way. This example illustrates what was said earlier, that most observational studies on teaching obtain more variables than they can handle in any one analysis.

Multiple regression techniques are designed to handle multiple independent variables. The basic regression equation above can be extended to include multiple independent variables:

$$Y = a + b_1X_1 + b_2X_2 + \cdots b_KX_K,$$

where b_1, b_2, and b_K are partial regression coefficients for the independent variables X_1, X_2, and X_K, respectively. Partial regression coefficients indicate the expected change in the dependent variable for a unit change in an independent variable holding all other independent variables constant. A multiple correlation coefficient can also be calculated between Y and the X_1, X_2, up to X_K, and the square of the multiple correlation coefficient, R^2 would indicate the proportion of variation in Y shared with or predicted from the set of independent variables.

One of the major uses of multiple regression is to partition the variance of Y among the independent variables in some meaningful way so as to assess the relative importance of each independent variable to the dependent variable. Unfortunately, when the independent variables are intercorrelated,

```
 .5

 .4    2 5

 .3    0 2 5 5

 .2    1 2 2 2 4 5 6 8

 .1    0 0 1 1 2 2 3 4 4 5 5 5 6 6 6 6 6 8

 .0    0 0 0 0 0 0 1 1 2 2 4 4 4 4 5 8 9 9

-.0    1 1 1 2 2 4 5 6 6 6 6 7 7 9 9 9

-.1    0 0 1 1 2 4 6 6 6 7 8 8

-.2    0 2 3 4 5 5 5 6 7

-.3    1 2 7 9

-.4

-.5
```

FIG. 7.4 Stem-and-leaf diagram for the correlation coefficients for lower SES students shown in Table 7.10.

as in the case of non-experimental designs, there are no agreed upon approaches for accomplishing this goal. Indeed, as Pedhazur (1982, p. 219) concludes, "If the situation appears hopeless, it is because it is indeed so in the context of variance partitioning." Pedhazur argues strongly that theory must guide the use of multiple regression techniques.

One multiple regression technique that has received considerable attention in recent years among educators is structural regression or path analysis (see Pedhazur, 1982, chapter 15). Path analysis requires that the researcher specify a model relating variables to each other prior to the estimation of regression coefficients. Researchers typically express their models in terms of path diagrams, a schematic that shows the hypothesized causal relationships among a set of variables. When a set of assumptions are met, especially the strong assumptions that the residuals of variables are not intercorrelated and that each variable is measured without error, then path analysis can be completed as a series of one or more multiple regression analyses, the number depending on the actual model being tested.

Figure 7.5 gives an example of a path analysis completed in the study by Barr and Dreeben (1983). The variables specified in the figure are of two kinds: endogenous variables, whose variability is hypothesized to be explained by other variables in the model, and exogenous variables, whose variability is hypothesized to be explained by variables not included in the model. For example, Aptitude, SES, Age, and Sex are all exogenous variables in the model specified in Figure 7.5. All other variables are hypothesized to be endogenous variables. The numbers in the figure are standardized regression coefficients or beta weights obtained from regression each endogenous variable on all other endogenous or exogenous variables hypothesized to influence it. To obtain these coefficients, a series of multiple regressions are carried out. Working backwards from the right, each endogenous variable is regressed on to all prior variables in the model hypothesized to cause it; in other words, on any variable that has an arrow drawn to it. In Figure 7.5, this means that seven multiple regressions occurred, one for each of the seven endogenous variables in the model. The results of these seven multiple regressions are given in Table 7.11.

The beta weights in Figure 7.5 provide an indication of the pattern of relationships among the variables given the model specified. It is important to note that path analysis is predicated.

Closing Comments

Evidence collected during classroom research comes in two general forms, words and numbers. Quite obviously, the approach to data analysis and the specific techniques used to analyze the data are quite different for these two forms of evidence. In this chapter we have raised a number of questions that must be addressed by classroom researchers and suggested options that these researchers have when addressing the questions.

Classroom researchers whose data are in the form of words are in the realm of qualitative data analysis. Questions that should be asked by these researchers include: How do I begin data analysis? How do I categorize data? Should I quantify data? How do I test propositions? How do I present the data?

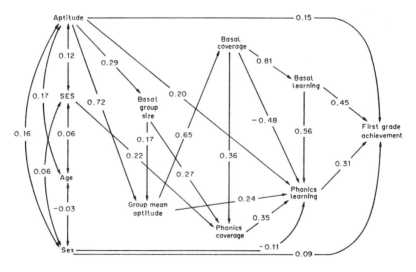

FIG. 7.5   Path analysis of children's characteristics, instructional conditions, and learning (*n* = 147) (from Barr and Dreeben, 1983).

TABLE 7.11

Beta Coefficients Showing the Contributions of Children's Background Characteristics and Group Conditions to Successive Dependent Variables (n = 147)

Independent Variables	Dependent Variables (Variable Numbers)						
	5	6	7	8	9	10	11[a]
1 Children's Aptitude	0.29*	0.72**	0.01	−0.01	0.08	0.20*	0.15*
2 Children's SES	−0.04	0.04	0.04	0.22*	−0.01	0.07	0.02
3 Children's Age (months)	0.13	−0.00	−0.08	−0.02	−0.01	0.02	0.04
4 Children's Sex (m = 0; f = 1)	−0.07	0.08	0.03	−0.09	0.00	−0.11*	0.09*
5 Basal Group Size		0.17*	0.07	0.27*	0.03	0.11	−0.01
6 Group Mean Aptitude			0.65**	0.09	0.09	0.24*	0.08
7 Basal Coverage				0.36*	0.81**	−0.48*	−0.00
8 Phonics Coverage					0.00	0.35**	0.06
9 Basal Words Learned						0.56*	0.45*
10 Phonics Learning							0.31*
R	0.34	0.80	0.69	0.63	0.93	0.80	0.91
R^2 (percent)	11	65	48	40	87	64	83
Adjusted R^2 (percent)	9	64	46	37	87	62	82

[a] Measure of standardized first grade reading achievement.
*Unstandardized coefficient is 2 to 4 times as large as the standard error.
**Unstandardized coefficient is 5 or more times as large as the standard error.

Source: Barr and Dreeben (1983).

In contrast, those researchers whose data are numerical are likely to perform quantitative data analysis. They too have a number of questions to answer. How do I prepare the data (which includes issues of data screening and editing, data aggregation, and data reduction)? How do I deal with non-equivalent groups? How do I establish relationships?

In view of the large amount of evidence typically collected during any given classroom research study and the wide variety of techniques available for analyzing the evidence, the most important lesson to be learned from this chapter is that the techniques are only as good as the use to which they are put by the researcher. They can be used or abused, and it is the responsibility of the researcher to choose appropriate techniques and demonstrate their proper application. Without proper application credibility diminishes and the knowledge claims made by the researcher become suspect.

Unit III—Introduction
Illustrative Classroom Research

In this unit we shall examine in some detail several studies of teachers (Chapter 8), teaching (Chapter 9), and instruction (Chapter 10) that have been conducted during the past sixty years. As mentioned in the Preface, our hope is that the reader will learn about the conceptualization, design, and conduct of research in each of these areas by reading about how the research *has been and is being* conducted, rather than by reading about how research in these areas *should be* conducted.

The final chapter in this unit contains a review of the various reviews of classroom research that have been written over the past three decades. Like the three chapters preceding it, the review is organized around studies of teachers, teaching, and instruction.

The structure of the first three chapters in the unit is virtually identical. Each chapter includes summaries of six studies conducted during the past sixty years. The initial study in each chapter was conducted during the late 1920s, the second study was conducted sometime during the 1950s or 1960s, and the final four studies were conducted from the mid-1970s to the present time. Because of the extremely large numbers of studies of teaching and instruction that have been conducted over the years, brief synopses of several additional studies are included in Chapters 9 and 10. After all of the summaries have been presented, comparisons of the purposes of the studies, the views of the researchers concerning the improvement of student learning, and the plans that guided the researchers in collecting and analyzing the evidence are made. Finally, recommend- ations for those interested in the study of teachers, teaching, and instruction are offered.

Two additional points must be made before we embark on our investigations of teachers, teaching, and instruction. First, the studies included in these chapters have been selected for both their importance as studies of teachers, teaching, and instruction, as well as for their peda- gogical value. The earliest study in each chapter provides an important benchmark as we examine research in each area, while the other studies are examples of the variety of research conducted during the past three decades. Many of the studies are large-scale studies, with several having received funding from government, foundation, or other sources.

Second, the summaries of these studies focus exclusively on the purpose of the studies, the conceptual framework underlying the studies, and the procedures by which the studies were conducted. Based on our experiences in the field, the results of the studies too often take precedence over the studies themselves in the minds of many readers. That is, there is a tendency to be more intrigued with the "findings" than with the conceptual framework that guide their interpretation or the research procedures that produced them. Consistent with this belief, findings and results will not be included in the first three chapters of this unit. Summaries of findings and results will be included in the final chapter.

8

Studies of Teachers

Teachers have been studied for decades. Searches for the characteristics and qualities that define good teachers have occupied the time and energy of a large number of researchers for generations. Studies geared toward an understanding of who teachers are, what beliefs they hold, and how they make decisions in their classrooms are a more recent addition to the field. Over the years we have learned a great deal about teachers; however, as is evident from the recent re-emphasis on the study of teachers, we still have much to learn. In this chapter, we shall review six studies of teachers that have been conducted over the past sixty years. Following this review, we shall examine the similarities and differences among the studies. Finally, we shall offer a set of recommendations for research on teachers based on our analysis of these studies.

Analysis of Six Studies of Teachers

The Charters and Waples' (1929) and Ryans' (1960a) studies are considered classics in the field. The studies reported by Bussis et al. (1976), Ashton and Webb (1986), Leinhardt and Greeno (1986), and Shulman (1988) are useful examples of the current research on teachers being conducted.

The Commonwealth Teacher-Training Study (Charters and Waples, 1929)

In response to a perceived need for a "radical reorganization of the curricula of teacher-training institutions" (p. v), the authors of this report secured a grant of $42,000 for a three-year study. The expressed purpose of the study was to "define criteria for teacher-training curricula so as to eliminate much of the present duplication and supply many of the deficiencies" (p. 4). The study (see Box 8.1) was to produce master lists of teacher traits, illustrative trait actions (that is, actions indicative of the presence of those traits), and the activities that teachers did perform or were expected to perform in the classroom, school, and community.

Purpose

"To define criteria for teacher-training curricula so as to eliminate much of the present duplication and supply many of the present deficiencies" (p. 4).

Framework/Model

The study was motivated by a perceived need for a "radical reorganization of the curricula of teacher-training institutions." Like other curricula, teacher-training curricula had "developed without clear definition of objectives and with no logical plan or procedure." As a consequence, "sponsors of the project have based their support on the hope that a comprehensive description of the duties and traits of teachers might provide the necessary basis for determining systematically what should be taught" (p. vii). Information gained from this study, then, was to be used by those responsible for teacher-training to revise and restructure teacher-training curricula and programs. These curricula and programs would result in better prepared teachers who, in turn, will have a more positive influence on their students. Graphically,

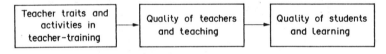

Research Method

PHASE 1

1. Conduct open-ended interviews with administrators, teachers, parents, students, and others to identify (1) the traits that characterize excellent teachers, and (2) observable manifestations of the traits.

2. On the basis of the results of these interviews, design a questionnaire, including 25 "trait families," that can be used to examine the perceived importance of each trait family in terms of teacher excellence.

3. Distribute questionnaire to samples of teachers and administrators. The sample of teachers was stratified by level of schooling (senior high school, junior high school, intermediate, and kindergarten-primary) and location of schools (rural, non-rural).

4. Correlate ratings of importance across subsamples of teachers (school levels and locations) and administrators.

PHASE 2

5. Distribute open-ended survey to experienced teachers to identify those activities that teachers do or should perform "on the job."

6. Based on the results of this survey (plus considerations of prior research and recommendations of professors of education), design a questionnaire including just over 1,000 activities to determine (1) the frequency with which each activity is performed, (2) the importance of performing each activity, (3) the difficulty of learning to perform each activity, and (4) whether each activity is best learned in college or "on the job."

7. Distribute questionnaire to sample of teachers ($n = 425$), critic teachers ($n = 50$), professors of education ($n = 50$), city supervisors ($n = 50$), and principals ($n = 50$). Only teachers were asked to estimate frequency with which each activity was performed. All were asked about importance, difficulty, and location of learning.

8. Summarize teacher ratings of difficulty, and correlate ratings of importance, difficulty, and location of learning across samples.

PHASE 3

9. Combine all ratings to determine the "curriculum value" of each activity. Each rating above the median for any sample was assigned a numerical value of one point, and the numerical values were summed across groups. The greater the numerical value, the greater the curriculum value.

10. Compute the "depth of treatment" in existing textbooks. Five levels of comparisons were noted: (a) merely mentioned, (b) described in sufficient detail to make meaning clear to students unfamiliar with it, (c) discussed to the end of defining difficulties commonly met in performing it, (d) discussed to show methods of overcoming difficulties, and (e) discussed with sufficient thoroughness to define the principles or informational statements that support accepted methods of performing it.

11. Compare "curriculum value" with "depth of treatment" for each activity.

Box 8.1 Summary of the Charters and Waples (1929) Study.

The assumption of the authors was that these master lists would be used by those responsible for teacher training in colleges and universities to revise and reorganize the existing teacher-training curriculums. As a result, prospective teachers would be more adequately prepared for their responsibilities as teachers and the job of teaching. Ultimately, students would benefit from the study by virtue of the improved preparation and increased quality of their teachers.

The study began with a set of open-ended interviews of administrators, teachers, parents, students, college professors, and representatives of teachers' agencies. These individuals were asked to identify those traits they considered to be the most essential for success in teaching, regardless of the grade level of the students and the community in which the school was located. They also were asked to identify those actions whereby each of these traits was expressed.

Based on the results of these interviews, a list of 25 generalized traits (or "trait families") was compiled. Each trait on the list was defined both conceptually (that is, using a dictionary definition) and operationally (that is, using the aforementioned trait actions). The traits and their definitions formed the basis for a questionnaire which was administered to groups of administrators and teachers representing different school levels (e.g., kindergarten-primary, senior high) and different school locations (e.g., urban, rural). Each respondent was asked to indicate the extent to which each trait was important for teaching success. The responses made by various groups of administrators and teachers were compared.

Next, an open-ended survey was distributed to experienced teachers. The teachers were asked to identify those activities they either performed or thought they should perform "on the job." These responses formed the basis for the development of a structured questionnaire which included over 1,000 activities. The questionnaire was administered to samples of teachers, "critic teachers," principals, city supervisors, and college professors.

Each teacher in the sample was asked to estimate the frequency with which they performed each activity. All respondents, including teachers, were asked to indicate (1) the importance of each activity, (2) the difficulty of learning how to perform each activity, and (3) whether each activity was best learned in college or "on the job." These estimates of importance, difficulty, and "location of learning" were then compared across the groups of respondents.

Once the data were compiled, the "curriculum value" of each activity was determined by summing the responses across the various groups of respondents. Simply stated, the higher the summed score, the greater the curriculum value. Next, the common textbooks used in undergraduate courses were examined to determine the "depth of treatment" each activity received. Five categories of "depth" were identified: merely mentioned, described in sufficient detail to make the meaning clear to students who were unfamiliar with it, discussed in terms of the difficulties commonly met in performing the activity, discussed to show methods of overcoming the difficulties, and discussed with sufficient thoroughness to define the principles that support accepted methods of performing the activity. Ultimately, comparisons between the "curriculum value" and the "depth of treatment" were made.

Several of the components of the Commonwealth Teacher-Training Study seem particularly noteworthy. First, there is the basic assumption that evidence gathered from research can and will inform practice through its impact on practitioners. Second, responses to open-ended interviews and surveys were used to design structured questionnaires. Thus, the traits and activities included on the questionnaires were empirically derived, rather than "conjured up" by the researchers themselves. Third, traits were defined in dictionary terms and illustrated using a series of trait actions. Thus, a more complete understanding of the traits was available to researcher and respondent. Fourth, the use of multiple groups of respondents made it possible to examine the similarities and differences in their perceptions of the importance, difficult of learning, and "location of learning" of the various activities. Finally, discrepancies between "what is" (e.g., the depth of treatment of topics in textbooks) and "what ought to be" (e.g., the curriculum value of the various activities) were apparently intended to create a sense of need on the part of those responsible for the development of the curriculum of undergraduate teacher-training programs.

The Teacher Characteristics Study (Ryans, 1960a)

The Teacher Characteristics Study actually consisted of a set of approximately 100 studies carried out over a seven-year period from 1948 to 1955 under the auspices of the American Council of Education (see Box 8.2). Eventually, some 6,100 elementary and secondary school teachers in 1,700 schools participated in various phases of the study.

Purpose
> "To compile information on significant teacher characteristics and to develop objective measures that might be used in evaluating and predicting teacher behavior" (p. 369)

Framework/Model
> "Teacher behavior is a function of situational factors and characteristics of the individual teacher" (p. 16). Both situational factors and individual teacher characteristics exist at a variety of levels ranging from the most specific to the most general. The more general teacher and situational characteristics influence the

more specific teacher and situational characteristics which, in turn, influence specific teacher and pupil behavior (see Figure 8.1).

Graphically,

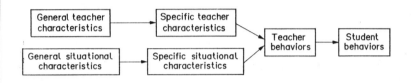

Research Method

PHASE 1

1. Develop the *Classroom Observation Record* (COR) based on a list of generalized teacher behaviors derived from a review of research on effective and ineffective teaching. Conduct field test of COR and make revisions consistent with the results of the field test.

2. Conduct observations of a sample of teachers, each teacher being observed on two occasions by different observers. [If a major discrepancy is found, use a third observer on a third occasion to resolve it.]

3. Perform factor analyses separately for elementary and secondary teachers and students. Three factors, consistent across both groups of teachers, are identified:

    X_o Understanding, friendly, and responsive vs. aloof and egocentric.

    Y_o Responsible, businesslike, and systematic vs. evading, unplanned, and slipshod.

    Z_o Stimulating, imaginative, and original vs. dull and routine.

    [A single pupil factor is also identified (P_o).]

4. Administer battery of attitude scales, forced-choice questionnaires, and verbal intelligence measures to teachers. The battery provides information on six teacher characteristics:

    Q.   Attitude toward administrators and other personnel,

    R.   Attitude toward pupils,

    R1.   Attitude toward democratic classroom procedures,

    B.   Educational viewpoint on learning-centered, traditional vs. child-centered, permissive dimension,

    I.   Verbal understanding,

    S.   Emotional stability.

PHASE 2

5. Develop an omnibus self-report instrument referred to as the Teacher Characteristics Schedule (TCS). The purpose of the TCS is to "identify teacher traits and behaviors indirectly from *correlates,* or 'symptoms,' of these behaviors and traits" (p. 162). Based on the results of field tests, design three forms of the TCS: one each for elementary teachers, English-social studies secondary teachers, and mathematics-science secondary teachers. Field test TCS and make revisions based on the results of the field test.

6. Develop scoring keys for TCS that permit the most accurate predictions of the nine teacher characteristics (X_{co}, Y_{co}, Z_{co}, Q_{co}, R_{co}, $R1_{co}$, B_{co}, I_{co}, and S_{co}) to be made. Compute scores on the subscales of the TCS which correspond to these nine characteristics.

PHASE 3

7. Compare teachers differing in sex, grade level, subject matter, age, experience, marital status, amount of college training, teacher-principal agreement of educational viewpoints, and selected personality variables in terms of their scores on these characteristics.

8. Compare teachers scoring at least one standard deviation above the mean on all three behavior patterns—X_{co}, Y_{co}, and Z_{co}—with those scoring below the mean on all three in terms of their scores on the nine TCS subscales.

9. Conduct biographical interviews of 20 female elementary school teachers. These teachers were chosen from a pool of 60 teachers as being rated in the top 5 percent on X_{co}, Y_{co}, and Z_{co}. Describe the qualities that characterize these teachers.

Box 8.2 Summary of Ryan (1960a) Study.

The motivation for the study emanated from a lack of research data on noncognitive characteristics of teachers and the desire to include measures of such characteristics on the National Teacher Examinations. The expressed purpose of the study was to "compile information on significant teacher characteristics and to develop objective measures that might be used in evaluating and predicting teacher behavior" (p. 369). Consistent with this general purpose, three specific objectives were identified:

1. to identify patterns of classroom teacher behavior, attitudes, viewpoints, and intellectual and emotional qualities;
2. to develop objective instruments which might aid in predicting these patterns; and
3. to compare characteristics of teachers classified according to personal factors such as age, experience, sex, and situational factors such as size of school or type of community.

The primary assumption underlying the study was that "teacher behavior is a function of situational factors and characteristics of the individual teacher" (p. 16). Both situational factors and individual teacher characteristics were believed to exist at a variety of levels, ranging from very global to very specific. The more global factors and characteristics influence the more specific factors and characteristics which, in turn, influence the ways in which both teachers and students behave in the classroom (see Figure 8.1).

The study began with the development of an observation instrument called the *Classroom Observation Record* (COR). The initial development of the COR was based on a review of studies that had examined differences between more and less effective teachers. Modifications were made in the COR based on the results of a field test.

Using the revised COR, a series of observations was made on a sample of teachers by various observers. Initially, two observers made ratings in each classroom on two different occasions. If discrepancies between the observers' ratings were evident, a third observer went into the classroom on a third occasion. Thus, the ratings represented either consensus among observers or a majority view.

These ratings were submitted to a set of factor analyses and three factors were identified. These factors were defined in terms of bi-polar dimensions, namely,

1. Understanding, friendly, and responsive vs. aloof and egocentric,
2. Responsible, businesslike, and systematic vs. evading, unplanned, and slipshod, and
3. Stimulating, imaginative, and original vs. dull and routine.

Next, a battery of standardized attitude scales, forced-choice questionnaires, and verbal intelligence tests was administered. This battery yielded scores on six teacher characteristics:

1. Attitude toward administrators and other personnel,
2. Attitude toward pupils,
3. Attitude toward democratic classroom procedures,
4. Educational viewpoint on learning-centered, traditional vs. child-centered, permissive dimension,
5. Verbal understanding, and
6. Emotional stability.

Thus, data on a total of nine characteristics (three derived from classroom observations and six derived from the standardized inventories and tests) were available for each teacher.

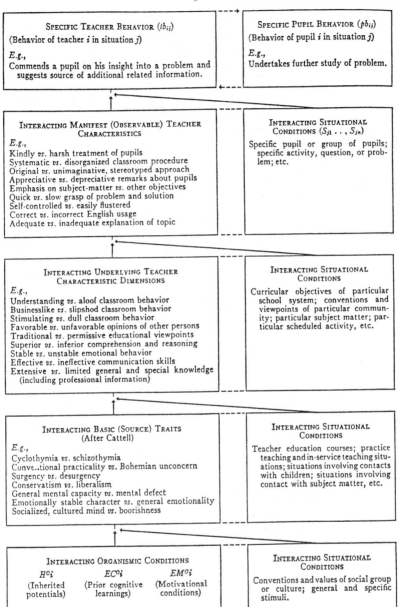

FIG. 8.1   Paradigm illustrating the integration of teacher behavior (from Ryans, 1960a).

In an attempt to increase the efficiency and practicality of the data collection, a battery of inventories and scales, collectively referred to as the *Teacher Characteristic Schedule (TCS)*, was developed. The expressed purpose of the TCS was to "identify teacher traits and behaviors indirectly from *correlates,* or 'symptoms,' of these behaviors and traits" (p. 162). Separate forms were developed for elementary teachers, English-social studies secondary teachers, and mathematics-science secondary teachers. Scoring keys that permitted the most accurate predictions of the initial measures of the nine characteristics to be made from the corresponding nine subscales of the TCS were developed.

Teachers differing in their sex, grade level, subject matter, age, experience, marital status, amount of college training, teacher-principal agreement of educational viewpoints, and selected personality variables were compared on each of the nine characteristics. In addition, teachers who were above and below the mean on the classroom rating scales were compared on each of the nine TCS subscales. Finally, biographical interviews of 20 female elementary school teachers were conducted, and the qualities that characterized those teachers were described.

Several aspects of the Teacher Characteristics Study are worthy of comment. First, while the interaction of situational factors and teacher characteristics is made explicit in the underlying conceptual framework, situational factors are not a major component of the study. The primary situational variable is school level; that is, the evidence was examined separately for elementary and secondary school teachers. Second, one of the major activities in the study was the development of a battery of indirect measures of teacher characteristics that could be used to predict direct measures of those same characteristics. One question raised in the study was whether ratings derived from observations could be reliably predicted from self-report measures. The issue of the comparability of direct and indirect measures of teacher characteristics remains an interesting one. Third, empirical interrelationships were examined using factor analytic techniques in order to reduce the sheer magnitude of the evidence. Thus, an awareness of the need to include a reasonable number of characteristics or variables in studies of teachers is evident in the Ryans' study.[1]

Beyond the Surface Curriculum (Bussis et al., 1976)

The purpose of the study was to "gain a better understanding of the constraints, problems, and supports that teachers perceive" as they work toward the implementation of "open education" (p. 2) (see Box 8.3). The investigation focused on three general areas: curriculum, children, and the working environment.

[1]This need was also recognized by Charters and Waples (1929) who suggested that one of the most important technical problems was how to steer a middle course between general classes of activities so broad as to be indefinite and detailed activities so numerous to be unmanageable.

Purpose

"To gain a better understanding of the constraints, problems, and supports that teachers perceive in their beginning years of 'opening up' " [that is, implementing open education] (p. 2), and "to investigate understandings and perceptions [of teachers] regarding curriculum, children, and the working environment" (p. 33).

Framework/Model

"Internal mental processes (such as understandings, beliefs, and values) are major determinants of behavior and of the environments that people create. Translated to teaching, this means that the most significant educational variation exists at the level of the individual practitioner—not at the level of instructional materials, packaged programs, or the like" (p. 1). Furthermore, "the conceptual framework of this study does not rely heavily on assumptions about the actual occurrences of specific instances of behavior. Rather, it assumes that teachers' characteristic beliefs about children and learning have pervasive effects on their behavior, influencing the learning environment that they create for children and for themselves. Teachers with similar constructs may well foster similar kinds of growth and awareness in children, although they may differ markedly in behavioral specifics" (p. 16).

Graphically,

Research Procedure

1. Develop interview protocol. Protocol contains two portions: the curriculum/child portion (which examined teachers' understandings of curriculum and the use of children's resources in learning and instruction) and the working environment portion (which examined teachers' perceptions of support from advisors and workshop experiences as well as their perceptions of other significant influences in the school setting).

2. Identify 60 elementary school teachers in four states who are attempting to implement open or more informal approaches to instruction. Forty-six teachers were in Advisory Programs

(with advisers who visited their classrooms periodically); 14
teachers attended workshops at Teacher Centers.

3. Conduct interviews with teachers; record complete interviews on audiotape. Each interview lasts from two to three
hours.

4. Develop sets of categories to use in coding the responses to
the interviews. These coding schemes were derived both
from the theoretical considerations underlying the construction of the interview and from the actual content of
teachers' reponses to the interview.

5. Have several people listen to the audiotapes of the interviews and code the responses relative to the coding schemes.
Have each interview coded by two people and maintain
formal records of interjudge agreement. Resolve any discrepancies either by mutual agreement or by judgment of
third person.

6. Summarize results in terms of the percentages of teachers
who are placed into the various coding categories.

7. Examine the results. Look for the one or two concerns
expressed most emphatically or frequently by each teacher.
Also, look for evidence that a teacher was experimenting in
ways intended to be responsive to the interests of individual
children.

8. Combine coding categories into larger categories and report
the percentages of teachers in the larger categories.

Box 8.3   Summary of the Bussis et al. (1976) Study.

The researchers believed that the behaviors exhibited by teachers and the
activities of the classroom constituted the "surface curriculum." They
perceived a need to move research beyond this surface curriculum by
examining teachers' "characteristic beliefs about children and learning"
(p. 16). These beliefs were thought to have "pervasive effects on [teachers']
behavior, influencing the learning environment that they create for children
and for themselves" (p. 16).

The study began with the development of an interview protocol. The
protocol included questions pertaining to the teachers' understandings of
the curriculum, their perceptions of children, and their working environment. Once the interview was developed, 60 primary school teachers (that
is, kindergarten through grade 3) who were attempting to implement open
or more informal approaches to instruction were identified and interviewed.
Each interview lasted from two to three hours and was recorded on
audiotape.

Sets of categories to be used in coding the interviews were developed. These categories were derived in part from theoretical considerations and in part from the actual content of the responses. Several members of the research team listened to the audiotape recordings and coded the responses into the predetermined categories. Each interview was coded by at least two researchers. Discrepancies in codings were either resolved through mutual agreement or by a third researcher.

The results of the study were summarized in terms of the percentages of teachers placed in each of the coding categories. In addition, combinations of categories were used to form larger, more superordinate classifications of teachers. Once again, the percentages of teachers placed in these larger classifications were reported.

Several features of the Bussis et al. study are noteworthy. First, open-ended interviews were used to collect the evidence. The interviews required approximately eight months to develop and refine. This careful development lends credibility to the evidence. Second, because the interviews were open-ended, an analytical framework (or coding scheme) was developed to aid in the analysis of the responses made by teachers to the interview questions. Some of the categories in the coding scheme were theoretically-derived, while others were empirically-oriented. The theoretically-oriented categories "would have appeared in the schemes even if they had failed to describe a single teacher who participated in the study" (p. 46). The empirically-derived categories, on the other hand, were intended to "serve the express purpose of describing the variation that exists among this particular sample of teachers on certain matters" (p. 46). Third, the categories included in the analytic framework were ordered from those most consistent with the principles and practices of open education to those least consistent with these principles and practices. Thus, the relationship between the analytic framework and the purpose of the study is quite clear. Fourth, the study stands in stark contrast to both the previous studies in one very important way. Charters and Waples assumed that information pertaining to both teacher traits and teacher activities was needed to properly reorganize the curriculum of teacher-training institutions. Similarly, Ryans assumed a direct relationship between teacher traits (e.g., their attitudes, intellect, and emotional stability) and teacher behavior in the classroom. In contrast, Bussis et al. contend that the characteristic beliefs of teachers and their behavior in the classroom are largely unrelated. In the authors' words, "Teachers with similar [characteristic beliefs] may well foster similar kinds of growth and awareness in children, although they may differ markedly in behavioral specifics" (p. 16).

A Study of Teachers' Sense of Efficacy (Ashton and Webb, 1986)

The authors of this report were interested in "the degree to which teachers' beliefs about teaching and chidren affected their classroom performance and accomplishments" (p. vii). They were concerned with this issue because of an apparent decline in teachers' beliefs that they could have an impact on their students' learning and lives. A parallel decline in teachers' motivation to teach also was cited. The belief that teachers, individually or collectively, can make a difference is referred to as a "sense of efficacy." The expressed purpose of the study, then, was to "investigate (1) the nature of teachers' efficacy attitudes, (2) factors that facilitate and inhibit the development of a sense of efficacy, (3) teacher behaviors associated with teachers' sense of efficacy, and (4) the relationship between teachers' sense of efficacy and student achievement" (p. 25).

The study began with the selection of two schools that were believed to differ on organizational dimensions that might influence a teacher's sense of efficacy (see Box 8.4). The first school was a middle school; the second was a junior high school. Both schools were similar in grade level configurations, student enrollment, home background of students, and location (that is, both were urban schools). All teachers in both schools were administered a questionnaire which contained items associated with nine variables. Several items measured the teachers' sense of efficacy. The responses made to all of the items by the teachers in the two schools were compared.

Purpose

"To investigate (1) the nature of teachers' efficacy attitudes, (2) factors that facilitate and inhibit the development of a sense of efficacy, (3) teacher behaviors associated with teachers' sense of efficacy, and (4) the relationship between teachers' sense of efficacy and student achievement" (p. 25).

Framework/Model

The multidimensional construct, teachers' sense of efficacy, lies at the heart of the conceptual model. The four efficacy dimensions are (1) generalized beliefs about response-outcome contingencies, (2) generalized beliefs about perceived self-efficacy, (3) sense of teaching efficacy, and (4) sense of personal teaching efficacy. Teachers' sense of efficacy is influenced by a wide variety of situational and setting factors (e.g., class size, school norms, legislative and judicial mandates). Teachers' sense of efficacy, in turn, influences the ways in which teachers behave in their classrooms and the amount their students learn.

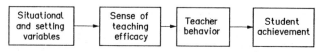

Research Method

PHASE 1

1. Select two schools (one a middle school, the other a junior high school) differing on organizational dimensions believed to influence teachers' sense of efficacy.

2. Administer a questionnaire to teachers in both schools. Questionnaire measures nine variables: teachers' sense of efficacy (specifically, sense of teaching efficacy and sense of personal teaching efficacy), teacher expectations, collegial relations, student conflict, job satisfaction, stress, interest in teaching, importance of teaching, and role responsibilities.

3. Compare responses of teachers in the two schools on items related to each variable using multiple statistical tests (analysis of variance, Wilcoxin test).

4. Select two teachers from each school and conduct series of classroom observations (at least 12) and interviews with each. Transcribe field notes made during observations and interviews.

5. Analyze the transcripts using a "cultural theme analysis." As defined by Spradley (1979), a cultural theme is "any principle recurrent in a number of domains, tacit or implicit, and serving as a relationship among domains; any system of cultural meaning" (p. 141). Identify those themes that differentiate the teachers at one school from those at the other.

PHASE 2

6. Select 48 high school teachers of mathematics and communication who are responsible for teaching lower socio-economic status students.

7. Administer a questionnaire to each teacher, observe each teacher's classroom several times during a four-month period, and conduct a one-hour interview with each teacher. The questionnaire measured five variables: teaching efficacy, personal teaching efficacy, stress in teaching basic skills, stress in teaching in general, and degree of responsibility for students' learning. The observations yield fifteen "process

scores": teacher negative affect, teacher positive affect, pupil
negative affect, pupil positive affect, teacher strong control,
teacher moderate control, pupil disorder vs. control, pupil
follows routine, teacher central and directs activity, differentiated activities, guided discovery, narrow one-answer interaction, guess or hypothesize, interest-attention rating, and
engagement.

8. Obtain from students' records their scores on the reading,
    language, and mathematics subtests on the Metropolitan
    Achievement Test for two consecutive years. The MAT was
    administered to the students during the Spring prior to the
    **study and during the Spring following the completion of
    the study.**

9. Using the class as the unit of analysis, compute partial
    correlations between each questionnaire and observational
    variable and the end-of-study MAT subtest scores (par-
    tialing out the prior-to-study MAT subtest scores). Also
    compute zero-order intercorrelations among all question-
    naire and observational variables.

Box 8.4   Summary of the Ashton and Webb (1986) Study.

Two teachers from each school were identified and several observations
were made in each teacher's classroom. In addition, each teacher was
interviewed. Both the notes made during the observations and taken during
the interviews were transcribed and the transcriptions were subjected to a
"cultural theme analysis" (Spradley, 1979). Several themes that apparently
differentiated the teachers in the two groups were identified.

A second sample, this one consisting of 48 high school teachers, was
selected for the second phase of the study. Each teacher was administered a
questionnaire, observed on several occasions over a four-month period, and
interviewed for one hour. Evidence pertaining to a total of 20 variables was
collected, with evidence on fifteen of the variables derived from the
classroom observations and evidence on the other five derived from the
questionnaire. Students' scores on reading, language, and mathematics
subtests of the Metropolitan Achievement Tests for two consecutive years
were obtained from the students' records. Correlations among the entire set
of observational and questionnaire variables were computed, as were partial
correlations between each of the 20 variables and second-year test scores
(holding first-year test scores constant).

Several components of the Ashton and Webb study are worthy of
consideration. First, schools differing on important organizational dimensions, but similar in terms of other potentially extraneous variables, were

selected. Thus, the validity of the interpretations relating school organization and sense of efficacy was increased. Second, different sources of
evidence (e.g., questionnaires, observations, and interviews) were used for
the purpose of developing a more complete understanding of the teachers
being studied. Unlike the Ryans (1960) study in which the results obtained
from different sources of information, both direct and indirect, were
expected to be correlated, each source of information in the Ashton and
Webb study was expected to add something to furthering the researchers'
understanding of the nature and function of the phenomenon being studied,
namely, teachers' sense of efficacy. Third, a balance between the intensive
study of small numbers of teachers and a more extensive study of larger
numbers of teachers was maintained. This balance reflects concerns for both
qualitative and quantitative research traditions. Finally, student test scores
are included in the conceptual framework, and the relationship between
teacher characteristics and these test scores is examined. Thus, test scores
have replaced expert opinion (Charters and Waples) and teacher classroom
behavior (Ryans) as evidence of teacher effectiveness.

A Study of Teachers' Cognition (Leinhardt and Greeno, 1986)

Consistent with their view that teaching is a complex cognitive skill which
requires "the construction of plans and the making of rapid on-line
decisions" (p. 75), the authors conducted a study which focused on the
knowledge structures that teachers need to be successful in their classrooms.
Referring to these knowledge structures as schemata, they identify two types
of schemata that are required for successful teaching: routines and
informational schemata.

Routines are activities that teachers perform fluently. They "reduce
cognitive load and expand the teacher's facility to deal with unpredictable
elements of a task" (p. 76). In contrast, informational schemata include
provisions for acquiring the information that teachers need in order to
decide what activities they should perform and how they should perform
those activities. Both routines and information schemata are incorporated
into agenda which guide the activities that actually take place in the classroom. In light of this discussion, the purpose of the study was to "elucidate
the activity structures and routines of skilled teachers by (a) describing what
they are, (b) analyzing their frequency and duration, (c) analyzing the
functions that routines serve for the cognitive processes of teachers, and
(d) contrasting the activity segments of novices and experts" (p. 83).

The study began with the identification of a group of expert and novice
teachers, all of whom were teaching mathematics to fourth grade students
(see Box 8.5). Each teacher was observed several times during a $3\frac{1}{2}$ month
period. Some of the observations were recorded on videotape, while others

were preceded and followed by interviews with the teachers. The interviews pertained to a number of issues: the teachers' plans for their upcoming lessons, their reflections of lessons recently completed, and their perceptions of their own and their students' knowledge of mathematics.

Purpose

"To elucidate the activity structures and routines of skilled teachers by (a) describing what they are, (b) analyzing their frequency and duration, (c) analyzing the functions that routines serve for the cognitive processes of teachers, and (d) contrasting the activity segments of novices and experts" (p. 83).

Framework/Model

Teaching is a complex cognitive skill which requires the construction of plans and the making of rapid on-line decisions. Skill in teaching rests on two fundamental systems of knowledge, lesson structure and subject matter. A skilled teacher has a complex knowledge structure composed of interrelated sets of organized actions called schemata. Two types of schemata exist: routines and informational schemata. Routines are activities that are performed with little effort because they have become automatic through practice. They reduce the cognitive load and, as a result, expand a teacher's facility to deal with unpredictable events. Informational schemata are used to decide (1) which information is needed for future activities, and (2) how to secure the needed information. The conduct of a lesson is based on an operational plan, or agenda. This agenda includes a "lesson plan," operational routines, activity structures, and decision elements (that permit continuous updating and revision of the agenda itself).
Graphically,

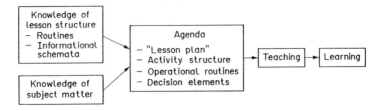

Research Methods

1.   Identify a group of expert teachers, defined as those whose students' growth scores (over a five-year period) were in the

top 15 percent of teachers at that grade level. Select from this group of teachers, those whose students' scores during the most recent year was in the top 20 percent. Fifteen were identified; eight agreed to participate.

2. Identify a group of novice teachers from a pool of 20 student teachers in their last semester of undergraduate training. Select from this group four who were considered the best student teachers and who taught fourth grade.

3. Observe each teacher several times during a $3\frac{1}{2}$ month period. The pattern of observations was as follows:
   a. observation of 3 class sections with open-ended notes,
   b. observation of one week of continuous class sessions, with an all-day observation taken once during the week,
   c. observation of 3 class sections in which pre- and post-interviews were conducted to ask teachers about their plans, and
   d. videotapes of three to five class sessions, for which there also were pre- and post-interviews as well as stimulated recalls based on these videotapes.

4. Conduct interviews with teachers concerning their own and their students' knowledge of mathematics (the subject being taught). Transcribe the notes made during observation and the interviews.

5. Segment the notes into "action records" that list the "durations, actions of student, actions of teacher, and a name for each teacher's action. Each action was defined, and the definitions were used as the basis for analyzing additional transcriptions or videotapes" (p. 83).

6. Compute medians and ranges of time spent in each activity.

7. Compare expert and novice teachers in terms of time spent on each activity (using box plots of medians and ranges).

8. Select two expert and one novice teachers for in-depth analysis. The most competent of the novice teachers was selected. For the expert teachers, the "tapes were selected for recording quality and teachers' comfort with the session" (p. 83).

9. Analyze teaching episodes of these teachers in terms of the goals, actions, functions, and outcomes. Results of analysis are presented visually as protocols.

10.   Compare protocols of teaching episodes of expert and novice teachers in terms of (1) homework check, (2) lesson presentation, and (3) guided practice.

Box 8.5   Summary of the Leinhardt and Greeno (1986) Study.

The majority of these responses and reflections were transcribed and these transcriptions were segmented into "action records." These action records listed the "durations, actions of student, actions of teacher, and a name for each teacher's action" (p. 83). Based on these analyses, summary statistics for each activity were computed and comparisons between expert and novice teachers were made. Two expert teachers and one novice teacher were then selected for more in-depth analysis. The transcripts of videotapes made in these teachers' classrooms and the interviews conducted with these teachers were analyzed in terms of the goals, actions, functions, and outcomes for each particular lesson. Comparisons were made of the ways in which expert and novice teachers (1) checked homework, (2) presented the lesson, and (3) provided for supervised student practice.

Several components of the Leinhardt and Greeno study are noteworthy. First, the emphasis in this study is on teachers' characteristic ways of operating in their classrooms *and* the reasoning behind their actions. One of the major findings of the study, in fact, was that expert teachers were more consistent in the activities they performed than were novice teachers. In other words, expert teachers had developed characteristic ways of operating in their classrooms which were controlled by their internalized mental representations of the way in which classrooms should operate. Second, observation was used to gather information about the activities in the classroom, but also as a stimulus for use in collecting information about the teacher's thinking and decision-making. The use of observational data as "means" as well as "ends" is an excellent way of linking actions with underlying thought patterns. Third, the sample of teachers was very small. However, this small number of teachers permitted the collection of large amounts of information concerning each teacher. Finally, the primary comparisons involved expert teachers (as determined by consistently high student performance on tests over several years) and novice teachers (who were engaged in student teaching). Both verbal prototypes of lessons as well as time estimates of teaching activities were used in the comparisons. That is, differences between expert and novice teachers both "in kind" and "in amount" were examined.

A Study of Knowledge Growth in Teaching (Shulman, 1988)

The study was designed in response to what the author refers to as the "missing paradigm" problem. Shulman contended that few studies of teacher effectiveness had examined the extent to which differences in subject matter knowledge were associated with differences in teacher effectiveness. Rather, numerous studies had investigated generic teacher behaviors or decision-making capabilities that were hypothesized to transcend the subject matter being taught and learned. Thus, researchers operating within the context of the "missing paradigm" would include teacher knowledge as a primary concept in their conceptual framework. Initially, the study was to be a general examination of how teacher knowledge develops over time (see Box 8.6). Over the three and one-half years of the study, however, the study became more focused, emphasizing the ways in which "teachers learn to transform their own understanding of subject matter into representations and forms of presentation that make sense to students" (p. 1).

Purpose

"The investigation has evolved from a general examination of how knowledge in teaching develops in general to a more focused study of how teachers learn to transform their own understanding of subject matter into representations and forms of presentation that make sense to students" (p. 1).

Framework/Model

A variety of types of knowledge (substantive and syntactic subject matter knowledge, pedagogical understanding of the subject matter, general pedagogical knowledge, knowledge of educational aims, knowledge of curriculum, knowledge of other content, and knowledge of the learner) influences a teacher's pedagogical reasoning. Improved pedagogical reasoning (which is cyclical in nature—see Figure 8.2) results in better teaching and increased learning.

Graphically,

Research Method

1. Based on initial speculations and hypotheses about the knowledge base of teaching, develop tentative research design and drafts of instruments to be used in data collection.

---

2. Conduct pilot study of twelve prospective teachers in four teacher education institutions in order to try out initial design, instruments and procedures.

3. Based on results of pilot study, make modifications in design (e.g., decrease number of teacher training institutions) and instruments (e.g., include structured tasks and interviews). Also begin to formulate conceptual framework.

4. Identify 20 prospective secondary school teachers who are in their final year of their teacher education program. Seven of these teachers were English teachers, five were science teachers, four were social studies teachers, and four were mathematics teachers.

5. Using document analysis and interviews, collect data on the education programs in which these teachers were enrolled. The intention was to collect data concerning the intended and actual content of the teacher education program.

6. Use instruments to collect data on these teachers over a two-year period. [In point of fact, 12 of the 20 teachers were followed into their initial year of teaching.] During the first year, stimulated recall techniques vignette-guided interviews, and structured tasks and interviews were used. During the second year, teachers were observed as they taught in their classrooms. Before and after each observation, interviews with the teachers were held.

7. On the basis of the available data, prepare a series of case studies. Each case study includes (a) an intellectual biography, (b) a description of the teacher's professional preparation and its reported effects, (c) a description of the teaching context within which each teacher taught, and (d) a description of the instruction provided by the teacher.

8. Perform cross-case analyses which focus on (1) consistencies across teachers (e.g., initially, beginning teachers refer back to the way their high school teachers taught their subjects in thinking about teaching) and (2) relationships among training, knowledge, and practice (e.g., subject matter training and the character of teachers' knowledge affect both style and substance of instruction).

Box 8.6   Summary of the Shulman (1988) Study.

Prior to the major study, a small-scale pilot study was conducted. The pilot study was intended to examine the appropriateness and feasibility of the initial design, instruments, and research procedures. Based on the results of the pilot study, minor modifications in design and instrumentation were made. In addition, a conceptual framework which included numerous categories of teacher knowledge as well as a model of pedagogical reasoning (see Figure 8.2) was formulated. And, as has been mentioned, the purpose of the study was modified.

The major study began with the identification of 20 prospective secondary school teachers (English, social studies, mathematics, and science) who were in their final years of their teacher education programs. Documents collected from the teacher-training institutions and interviews with members of the faculty and administrative staff provided the initial sources of data.

A variety of instruments were used to collect data on the prospective teachers over a two-year period. During the first year, stimulated recall techniques, vignette-guided interviews, and structured tasks and interviews were employed. During the second year, classroom observations of twelve of the teachers were made. Before and after each observation, the teachers were interviewed.

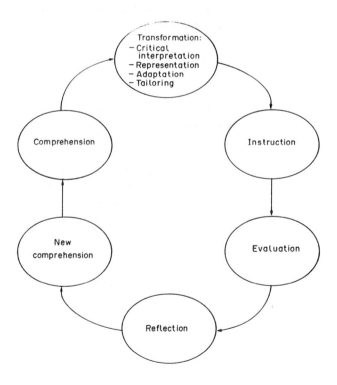

FIG. 8.2   Model of pedagogical reasoning (from Wilson, Shulman, and Richert, 1987).

Based on the available data, a series of case studies was prepared. Each case study included an intellectual biography of the teacher, a description of the teacher's professional preparation and its reported effects on the teacher, a description of the teaching context within which each teacher taught, and a description of the instruction provided by the teacher. Ultimately, several cross-case analyses were performed, with an emphasis placed on the consistencies across teachers and relationships of teacher education, knowledge, and practice.

Several components of the Shulman study are worth noting. First, teacher knowledge is seen as multifaceted, rather than unidimensional. Teachers have a variety of types of knowledge from which to draw as they practice their craft. Second, a pilot study was conducted to make adjustments in the design, instrumentation, and procedures, as necessary. The use of a pilot study is consistent with Shulman's belief in the "iterative nature of research, in which the initial findings can help refine and inform later stages of data collection and analysis" (pp. 5–6). Third, although a minor part of the study, existing documents were analyzed to glean information needed to understand the teacher-training programs in which the prospective teachers were enrolled. Document analysis, like content analysis (Kerlinger, 1973), is often a forgotten method of analyzing existing evidence. Finally, as was also true of the Ashton and Webb study, multiple sources of evidence were obtained and examined. Observations and a variety of structured interviews provided a diverse set of evidence for the researchers' consideration.

Comparisons of the Studies

The six studies reviewed in the previous section are similar in several respects and different in others. In this section we examine both these similarities and differences. In order to facilitate such a comparison among the studies Table 8.1 has been prepared. In this table the studies are compared relative to seven dimensions, ranging from the general purpose of the study to the analysis of evidence collected during the study. These dimensions form the subheadings for this section.

Purpose of the Study

The purpose of all but one of the studies was descriptive. That is, the researchers were interested in describing the characteristics of teachers. Despite this apparent similarity, however, the nature of the characteristics being described has changed dramatically over time. The two earlier studies focused on general and generalized teacher characteristics. Intelligence, verbal understanding, adaptability, breadth of interest, and human relations are examples of characteristics included in the Charters and Waples' and Ryans' studies. Quite different characteristics are examined in the more recent studies: beliefs about the curriculum and about children, beliefs about their ability to influence children's learning, and the structure of their subject matter and pedagogical knowledge. These characteristics are different in two fundamental respects. They are far more specific than those studied earlier. They also are more directly related to teaching strategies and practices. Similar changes in research on teacher characteristics have been noted by Doyle (1987) and Levis (1987).

Keys to Improving Student Learning

Quite different assumptions concerning the ways in which studies of teachers can impact on student learning are made by the various researchers. Charters and Waples, for example, suggested that improved

TABLE 8.1

A Comparison of Studies of Teachers Along Seven Dimensions

	Studies		
Dimensions	Charters & Waples	Ryans	Bussis et al.
Purpose of the Study	Descriptive	Descriptive	Descriptive
Key(s) to Improving Student Learning	Improving teacher-training programs	Understanding teaching as a function of both situational factors and teacher characteristics	Changing teacher beliefs about children and learning
Extent of Manipulation	None	None	None
Sampling	PRPS ($n=650$) [Types of educators]	CONV ($n=6,100$)	CONV ($n=60$)
Sources of Evidence	QUES INTR DOEX	RATE QUES INTR TEST	INTR
Nature of Evidence	FREQ/% MEANS	MEANS FREQ/% EXCRPT	FREQ/% EXCRPT
Analysis of Evidence	COMPARE CORR	FACTOR COMPSTAT	COMPARE

| | Studies | | |
Dimensions	Ashton & Webb	Leinhardt & Greeno	Shulman
Purpose of the Study	Associational	Descriptive	Descriptive
Key(s) Improving Student Learning	Enhancing teachers' sense of efficacy	Increasing teachers' knowledge of subject matter and lesson structure	Increasing teachers' knowledge and pedagogical reasoning
Extent of Manipulation	None	None	None
Sampling	**PRPS** (*n* = 49); [Types of schools] **CONV** (*n* = 48)	**PRPS** (*n* = 12) [Types of teachers]	**CONV** (*n* = 20)
Sources of Evidence	QUES NOTES INTR TEST	NOTES VIDEO INTR TRANS	INTR NOTES DOEX
Nature of Evidence	MEANS EXCRPT	MEDIAN GRAPH EXCRPT	CASE
Analysis of Evidence	CORR	OTHR (Protocols)	OTHR (Cross-case analysis)

Key to abbreviations used in Table 8.1

Sampling
CONV = convenience
PRPS = purposeful

Sources of Evidence
DOEX = documents/exhibits
NOTES = field notes
INTR = interviews
QUES = questionnaires
RATE = rating scales
TEST = tests
TRANS = transcripts
VIDEO = videotapes

Nature of Evidence
FREQ/% = frequencies, percentages
MEANS = means (and/or standard deviations)
MEDIAN = medians (and/or ranges)
EXCRPT = written excerpts from observations or interviews
GRAPH = graphical displays
CASE = case studies

Analysis of Evidence
CORR = correlations
COMPARE = comparisons between groups using human inference
COMPSTAT = comparisons between groups using statistical inference (e.g., *t*-test, ANOVA, chi-square, ANCOVA)
FACTOR = factor analysis
PATH = path analysis
OTHR = other

teacher training programs are the key to enhancing student learning, since such programs will improve the type of teachers and teaching that students encounter. Ryans, on the other hand, believed that "a major drawback to the improvement of teaching [and, hence, learning] has been the lack of understanding of teacher characteristics and of ways of estimating them" (p. 9). Furthermore, the effectiveness of teachers depend on the "social or cultural group in which the teacher operates" and "the grade level and subject matter taught" (p. 4). All of these "suggestions for improvement" reside somewhat outside of the teachers themselves.

In contrast, the more recent studies place the locus of improvement within the teacher. Bussis et al., for example, assume that student learning will improve when teachers change their beliefs about the students and the curriculum. Similarly, Ashton and Webb assume that student learning will increase when teachers began to understand that they can make a difference. Leinhardt and Greeno, as well as Shulman, assume that student learning will improve when teachers possess proper structures of knowledge and see the connection between those knowledge structures and their classroom strategies and practices.

Extent of Manipulation

In none of the studies did the researchers manipulate any of the conditions surrounding the teachers. Rather, they studied teachers in naturally occurring settings. In examining the relationship between school organizational structure and teachers' sense of efficacy, for example, Ashton and Webb could conceivably have assigned teachers to schools with different organizational structures. This assignment of teachers would have constituted an act of manipulation on the part of the researchers. They chose instead to study teachers who already were employed in such schools.

Sampling

Three of the studies included convenience samples (CONV), while the other three used purposeful samples (PRPS). Charters and Waples included various types of educators (e.g., administrators, teachers), Ashton and Webb, as mentioned, included teachers from two types of schools, and Leinhardt and Greeno included two types of teachers (i.e., expert and novice). In none of the studies were random samples selected. Ryans' comment on the issue of random sampling in research on teachers is worth remembering.

> Obviously the educational system in this country does not permit the use of a random sampling design or even a modification thereof for which adjustments for systematic error may be made with any great assurance. The cooperation of a school system, a school, or a teacher in a research project must remain voluntary in any decentralized system of education (p. 58).

Because of the lack of random sampling, researchers have had to find alternative ways of generalizing their results to samples broader than the one they have included in their studies. Ryans, for example, compared his relatively large sample with samples used in other studies on a variety of demographic characteristics (e.g., age, sex, marital status, type of college attended). Based on this comparison, he was able to conclude that the teachers participating in his study constituted a sample which was not very different from the population of teachers in the United States.

Sources of Evidence

As might be expected, interviews and questionnaires are the major sources of evidence used in studies of teachers. Examining teachers' traits, beliefs, and knowledge, it appears, requires that researchers ask questions. Observation was used in four of the studies, although it is of interest to note that in no studies were structured observation systems used. Rating scales (Ryans), field notes (Ashton and Webb, Leinhardt and Greeno, and Shulman), and videotapes (Leinhardt and Greeno, and Shulman) were the primary means of observing. Videotapes typically either were transcribed (Leinhardt and Greeno), used as part of the stimulated recall technique (Leinhardt and Greeno, Shulman), or both.

Nature of the Evidence

Numerical evidence in the form of frequencies, percentages, means, and standard deviations was primary in the initial two studies. Ryans did include some excerpts from interviews with teachers, but did so late in the volume. A combination of quantitative and qualitative evidence was used in the Bussis et al., Ashton and Webb, and Leinhardt and Greeno studies. In general, quantitative evidence was used as summaries, while qualitative evidence provided useful examples and illustrations to enhance the meaning of the summaries. Finally, Shulman used exclusively qualitative evidence in the form of case studies of individual teachers.

Analysis of the Evidence

High powered statistical analysis is the exception, not the rule, in these studies. In three of the studies (Bussis et al., Leinhardt and Greeno, and Shulman), in fact, no inferential statistical techniques were used. Bussis et al. computed frequencies and simply discussed the frequencies they had computed, using excerpts from the interviews for emphasis and illustration. Leinhardt and Greeno calculated medians and ranges, but did not use statistical tests to compare the groups of novice and experienced teachers (perhaps because of the very small sample sizes). Shulman avoided numerical evidence altogether.

Ryans, and Ashton and Webb, did make use of more traditional statistics. Ryans used factor analysis as a data reduction technique, and analysis of variance to compare various typologies of teachers on a variety of measures. Ashton and Webb computed correlations and partial correlations (partialling out previous achievement from subsequent achievement).

Finally, Charters and Waples relied heavily on numerical comparisons of the various groups of educators (administrators, college professors, teachers). They also computed correlations of the ratings made by the various groups (e.g., the correlations between the rankings of the importance of traits for senior high school teachers and for junior high school teachers).

Recommendations for Research on Teachers

In view of both the similarities and differences that exist among the six studies reviewed in this chapter, several recommendations for research on teachers can be offered. These recommendations are discussed below.

1. Since teachers are complex individuals and many of their characteristics appear to be multifaceted rather than unidimensional, the complexity of the characteristics to be investigated should be explicated in the conceptual framework. These characteristics should be defined both conceptually (in terms of their meaning) and operationally (in terms of the evidence that will be gathered). Connections between characteristics and behaviors (e.g., between the thoughts and actions of teachers) would seem to be an important aspect of the conceptual framework.

2. Regardless of the complexity of the conceptual framework, a reasonable number of teacher characteristics should be included in any given study. Either limitations should be imposed in advance on the number of characteristics or empirical means such as factor analysis should be used as a data reduction technique to limit the number of characteristics. The inclusion of too many characteristics in a single study is likely to produce results that are very difficult to understand and interpret.

3. Pilot studies (i.e., preparatory small scale studies) are very useful in improving the conceptualization, design, instrumentation, and procedural requirements of the primary studies. For example, the responses made to open-ended interviews or questionnaires included in a pilot study can be used to develop standardized questionnaires for inclusion in the primary study. Initial plans for the conduct of research should not be viewed as cast in concrete. Rather, the iterative nature of classroom research (Shulman, 1988) should be recognized and acted upon.

4. Studies investigating the situational nature of teacher characteristics should be conducted. Virtually all of the researchers involved in the studies reviewed in this chapter assumed that certain conditions or situations favored certain characteristics, while other conditions or situations inhibited

those characteristics. The relationship between situations and teacher characteristics is most explicit (although not explicitly tested) in the Ryans' study. According to Ryans' model there is a continual interplay of teacher characteristics and situational factors. Charters and Waples found that different characteristics are believed to be of different importance in different types of schools. Ashton and Webb suggested that different organizational structures are associated with differences in teachers' sense of efficacy. Initially, Shulman suspected that the characteristics of perspective teachers graduating from different educational institutions would differ. Certain situations, then, may require certain characteristics, may influence the development of certain characteristics, or may interact with particular characteristics to produce different effects. Because of the vast array of relationship between situations and teacher characteristics, research directed toward explicating these relationships is sorely needed.

5. Typically, multiple sources of evidence and multiple perspectives should be used to increase our understanding of the teacher characteristic(s) under study. Observations of teachers can be used to document the characteristic actions of teachers or to stimulate teachers to reveal and reflect on the beliefs that underlie those actions. Questionnaires distributed to teachers coupled with examinations of existing evidence can provide insights unavailable from either source of evidence alone. If discrepancies among these various sources of evidence are evident, ways must be found to resolve them. At present, four approaches seem worthwhile in this regard. First, the extent of the disagreement among the sources can be simply stated. If the disagreement is minor, it typically is ignored. Second, disagreements can be resolved through consensus. That is, those involved in the disagreements can be brought together in an attempt to discuss their differences and arrive at consensus. Third, disagreements can be resolved by bringing in a "third party" who adjudicates or mediates the disagreement. Typically, this third party initially strives for consensus and then simply casts her or his vote in one direction or the other. Fourth, a single person (typically the researcher) can be asked to incorporate the disagreements into a single cohesive statement. The ideal statement is said to be parsimonious (that is, it is the simplest statement that incorporates most available evidence).

6. Researchers intent on investigating teacher characteristics in the context of teacher effectiveness should be aware of the different indicators of effectiveness. Effectiveness is often assumed. Teachers with beliefs consistent with open education (Bussis et al.) or who are able to articulate a more complete, complex, or informed knowledge of subject matter or pedagogy (Shulman) are assumed to be more effective in their classrooms. Effectiveness also is determined by the teachers' reputations. Charters and Waples assumed that teachers who are nominated as being effective are more effective than those who are not nominated. Effectiveness is equated

with teachers' classroom behavior. Thus, teachers who behave in certain ways in their classrooms are presumed to be more effective (Ryans). Finally, effectiveness is equated with student achievement. That is, teachers who have students who achieve more during a particular year (Ashton and Webb) or over time (Leinhardt and Greeno) are believed to be more effective.

These varying definitions of effectiveness represent value orientations on the part of researchers (see Chapter 1). As a consequence, researchers must be aware of the various definitions if they are to properly design, conduct, and interpret research on teachers.

Closing Comments

In this chapter, six studies of teachers conducted over the past 60 years have been reviewed. These reviews are intended to help researchers understand the nature of research on teachers that has been conducted over this time period. With this increased level of understanding, researchers are more likely to conceptualize, plan, and implement studies of teachers that add to our current body of knowledge.

9

Studies of Teaching

What do teachers say and do in their classrooms? How is what is said and done by teachers related to how students behave and what they learn? These are the primary questions confronting classroom researchers who choose to study teaching. Observational studies of classrooms, the primary means by which teaching is studied, have been conducted for at least 60 years. Large scale observational studies of classrooms, however, are a product of the past decade (Fisher et al., 1978; Galton et al., 1980; Goodlad, 1984; Anderson et al., 1989). In this chapter we shall review six studies of teaching. The organization of this chapter is similar to that of the previous one. We began with an analysis of each study, then examined the similarities and differences among the studies, and, finally, offered a set of recommendations for research on teaching based on our analysis of the studies.

Analysis of Six Studies of Teaching

After 60 years the Barr (1929) study remains the classic in the field. The Bellack et al. (1966) study also has achieved classic status. The Nuthall and Church (1973) study is one of the few true experimental studies of teaching. The Galton et al. (1980) study is the first of a series of studies conducted as part of a larger research program, Project ORACLE. The Morine-Dershimer (1985) study represents a prototype of a shift in methodology sponsored by the United States National Institute of Education in the early 1980s. Finally, the Anderson et al. (1989) study is the largest, cross-national observational study of teaching conducted to date.

Characteristic Differences of Good and Poor Teachers (Barr, 1929)

The study was motivated by a concern for the poor quality of the supervision of teachers. Barr argued that the supervisory methods used at the time were of "doubtful validity, reliability, and objectivity" (p. 11). He contended that the reliability of supervisors' ratings of teachers was so low that "if these supervisors had closed their eyes, stopped up their ears, and then had rated these recitations at random upon the twelve items which composed the recitation score card . . ., their ratings would have been only five percent poorer than they were when rated according to conventional standards of classroom supervision" (p. 10). As a partial response to this problem Barr designed a study to determine whether observable activities and classroom conditions could be "objectively described" and whether the teaching performance of good and poor teachers could be differentiated based on these objective descriptions (see Box 9.1)

Purpose

To test the assumption that there exist in classrooms "observable activities and conditions" in terms of which teaching can be "objectively described:" to determine the "characteristic differences in the teaching performance of good and poor teachers of the social studies;" and to inquire into "the causes of success and failure in teaching" (pp. 11–12).

Framework/Model

The study was framed in the context of the supervision of teachers. Barr argued that supervisory methods were of "doubtful validity, reliability, and objectivity" (p. 11). Barr's solution to the problem was to train supervisors to "observe, analyze, and describe teaching in terms of specific teacher and pupil activities" (p. 11). In this way, an "objective terminology" can be substituted for the "subjective phraseology ordinarily used in supervision" (p. 1). Ultimately, this objective terminology coupled with systematic procedures would improve the quality of teaching.

Graphically,

| Objective terminology and systematic procedures | → | Quality of supervision | → | Quality of teaching | → | Quality of learning |

Procedures

1. Select samples of good and poor teachers. The selection occurred in three steps. First, superintendents were asked to nominate "outstandingly" good or poor teachers. Second, each nominated teacher was checked against the ratings made by state inspectors, eliminating those who did not fall into the two extreme groups. Third, Barr visited the teachers

and eliminated those who did not seem to be either "strikingly" successful or "strikingly" poor. Eventually, 47 good and 47 poor teachers were included in the sample.

2. Conduct unannounced observations in each of the teachers' classrooms. Each teacher was observed at least once (with some being observed two or three times) and each observation lasted about four hours.

3. During each observation, make the following record of classroom events and teaching activities:
   a. General observations (written work on blackboard, materials and equipment, copies of outlines, study directions, and assignments).
   b. Morrison's Attention Chart (which recorded the number of students who were paying attention).
   c. Time Chart (which recorded the common activities that occurred in the classroom in increments of 10 seconds).
   d. Stenographic Record and Check List (not well described).
   e. Miscellaneous notes (made by researcher).
   f. Rating scale (12 dimensions plus "General Merit Rating").

4. Also collect the following materials.
   a. Time distributions (a log kept by each teacher for a period of one week).
   b. Superintendent's letter (a letter from the superintendent indicating the teacher's strengths and weaknesses).
   c. Teacher's letter (a self-analysis of his or her teaching).

5. Organize the information collected during the observations into quantitative data (e.g., frequency distributions, mean scores) and qualitative data (e.g., verbal comments made by teachers, notes made by researcher).

6. For the qualitative data, report differences between good and poor teachers in terms of expressions used by teachers in one group, but not the other. Also report these differences in terms of the notes made by the researcher about teachers in one group, but not the other. Differences are organized into categories (e.g., techniques for motivating work, provision for individual differences, appraisal of pupil responses) to facilitate presentation of qualitative data.

7. For the quantitative data, report and compare the mean time allocations for the two groups of teachers. Also report and compare the number of teachers in each group who engaged in various types of activities, used particular types

of materials, and so on. These analyses were organized around the categories mentioned above. Finally, compute correlations between the various time allocations and a composite rating of the quality of the teachers made by the researcher.

8. Combine the results of the study with findings from three other sources (a survey of 200 experts in the field of social studies education, an analysis of 229 articles of methods of teaching in the social studies, and a similar analysis conducted by another researcher of 339 articles on the teaching of history) into a listing of the "minimum essentials of teaching success."

Box 9.1   Summary of the Barr (1929) Study.

The study began with the selection of samples of good and poor teachers. The selection occurred in three stages. Superintendents were asked to nominate good and poor teachers; the nominated teachers were checked against ratings made by state inspectors; and Barr himself visited the teachers' classrooms to verify the nominations and ratings. As a result, 47 good teachers and 47 poor teachers were identified.

Barr conducted observations in each teacher's classroom at least once for a period of approximately four hours. During this time, he made general observations, recorded the numbers of students who were paying attention, noted the sequence of classroom activities and the time spent on each, and made miscellaneous notes. He also asked each teacher to keep a log of the amount of time spent on the various classroom activities for a week, and to write a letter containing a self-analysis of his or her own teaching. The superintendent who nominated the teacher was also asked to write a letter on the teacher's strengths and weaknesses.

Following the observations, Barr summarized the evidence collected in terms of frequency counts within particular coding categories, mean time estimates for various activities, and written notes or comments. He then examined the differences between the good and poor teachers in terms of the expressions they used in talking with their students, the ways in which they performed a number of important functions (e.g., motivating students, providing for individual differences), the frequency with which they performed these functions, and the ways in which they used the time available to them in the classroom. Barr combined his results with those from other studies to derive a list of the "minimum essentials of teaching success."

Several of the components of the Barr study are quite noteworthy, particularly in light of the studies of teaching being conducted today. First, Barr used reputational evidence of teaching quality to identify his "good"

and "poor" teachers. In order to increase the credibility of this classification, however, he used three different sources of evidence to identify the
teachers: the school superintendent, the state inspectors, and his impressions. Second, Barr used extreme groups in his study, excluding those
teachers who fell in the middle of the distribution of teacher quality. The
use of extreme groups increases the likelihood that differences in classroom
conditions or teaching behaviors will be identified if they exist. At the same
time, however, the use of extreme groups reduces somewhat the generalizability of the findings of the study. Third, Barr used almost every
observational instrument or approach that is used to study teaching today.
He used Morrison's Attention Chart to estimate the percentage of students
"paying attention." In today's terminology, "paying attention" is referred
to as being on-task or engaged in learning (Fisher et al., 1978). He used his
Time Chart to estimate the amount of time spent on various classroom
activities. The emphasis on activities (or activity segments or lesson formats)
continues today (Stodolsky, 1988). Furthermore, time is the metric most
frequently used in reporting on these activities (Goodlad, 1984). Barr also
used a rating scale (composed of 12 dimensions plus a "General Merit
Rating") and made miscellaneous notes (which today may be termed "field
notes"). The only observational tool not used by Barr is the teacher-student
interaction system (e.g., Flanders, 1960; Stallings, 1977). Fourth, as a result
of this vast array of observation tools and approaches, Barr was able to
include both quantitative and qualitative evidence in his study. He was
concerned not only with time estimates and frequency counts, but with the
particular expressions teachers used in communicating with their students
and the notes and comments he made as he observed in the classroom.
Fifth, and finally, Barr found it necessary to use categories to organize the
vast array of evidence that he collected during the observations. Interestingly, many of his categories (e.g., organization of subject matter, provision
for individual differences, appraisal of pupil response, and disciplinary
activities) remain in use today.

The Language of the Classroom (Bellack et al., 1966)

Because language plays such an important role in teaching, Bellack and
his colleagues chose to examine in some detail the "language game" in the
classroom. They contended that "teaching is similar to most games in at
least two respects. It is a form of social activity in which the players
(teachers and students) fill different but complementary roles. Furthermore,
teaching is governed by certain ground rules that guide the actions or moves
made by the participants" (p. 4). By studying the language game, then,
Bellack et al. intended to identify the various types of verbal moves made
by teachers and students and the rules they followed in making these moves.
As a result, they could investigate the functions these verbal moves served

and examine the meanings that were being communicated.

A four-day unit on international trade intended for use with high school students was developed (see Box 9.2). An achievement test aligned with the major concepts and principles included in the unit was prepared as was a scale measuring students' attitudes toward the study of economics. Fifteen teachers who taught high school social studies and who agreed to teach the unit participated in the study.

Purpose
"To gain understanding of the special world of the classroom rather than to identify the 'good' teacher or the 'best' teaching methods" (p. v). Furthermore, "to study the teaching process through analysis of the linguistic behavior of teachers and students in the classroom. . . . Our major task was to describe the patterned processes of verbal interaction that characterize classrooms in action; a subsidiary aim, viewed primarily as an exploratory phase of the general line of research, was to study linguistic variables of classroom discourse in relation to subsequent pupil learning" (p. 1).

Framework/Model
The communication which occurs in classrooms is part of a "language game" in the sense that the "linguistic activities assume different forms and structures according to the functions they come to serve in different contexts" (p. 3). Viewing classroom discourses as a kind of language game was useful in that it suggested a framework for analysis. "Teaching is similar to most games in at least two respects. It is a form of social activity in which the players (teachers and students) fill different but complementary roles. Furthermore, teaching is governed by certain ground rules that guide the actions or moves made by the participants. . . . If we could identify the various types of verbal moves teachers and students make . . . and the rules they implicitly follow in making these moves, we would be in a position to investigate the functions these verbal actions serve in classroom discourse and hence the meanings that are communicated" (p. 4). If these rules, functions, and meanings can be determined, they can be communicated to the teachers themselves. The communication of these findings to teachers is important because "only as teachers have available knowledge of the teaching process gained through research will they be able to exercise effective control over the process" (p. v).

Graphically

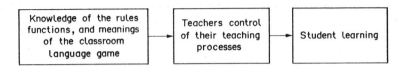

Procedures

1. Prepare a four-day unit on international trade and an achievement test directly related to the basic concepts and principles included in the unit. Also prepare a scale measuring students' attitudes toward the study of economics.

2. Select 15 teachers to participate in the study. Each teacher must teach high school social studies, agree to teach the four-day unit on international trade, and agree to have her lessons on this unit audiotape recorded.

3. Administer the achievement test, attitude scale, and a verbal intelligence test to all students.

4. Tape record the verbal transactions in each teacher's classroom for four consecutive days or lessons. Thus, a permanent record of all of the lessons related to the instructional unit was available.

5. After the last lesson has been taught, re-administer the achievement test and attitude scale.

6. Prepare written transcriptions of all sixty audiotapes (that is 15 teachers × 4 lessons). Analyze the transcripts within the context of the coding scheme developed by the researchers. [Note: The coding scheme was described in great detail in Chapter 6.]

7. Have each transcript coded first by one coder, then by a second. Disagreements in coding are arbitrated by two additional coders.

8. Following the coding of the transcripts, compute the frequencies of the number of lines and pedagogical moves (see Chapter 6) within each coding category across all 15 teachers.

9. Examine the sequences of pedagogical moves (termed teaching cycles) using Markov chain analysis.

10. Adjust each student's posttest score by subtracting from that score the posttest score predicted for that student based on his or her pretest score. Compute mean adjusted posttest scores for each class. Identify three classes whose students

achieved higher than expected posttest scores and five classes whose students achieved lower than expected posttest scores.

11.   Compare the two groups of classrooms (higher and lower than expected) on the frequency of occurrence of the various coding categories.

12.   Present and discuss the results pertaining to the frequency distributions of all teachers and the comparisons of these frequency distributions for the two groups of classes mentioned in step 11.

Box 9.2   Summary of the Bellack et al. (1966) Study.

Before the unit was taught, the achievement test, the attitude scale, and a verbal intelligence test were administered to the students in the fifteen classes. On each of the four days on which the unit was taught, the lesson presented by each teacher was audiotape recorded. Following the last lesson, the achievement test and attitude scale were re-administered.

Written transcripts were made of all audiotaped lessons. Each transcript was then analyzed by two members of the research staff, with disagreements in coding arbitrated by two additional research staff members. As was mentioned in Chapter 6, the codes were written directly on the written transcripts. Following the coding of all transcripts, the number of lines and pedagogical moves for each of several categories was computed. Sequences of pedagogical moves were examined using Markov chain analysis.

Based on mean adjusted posttest scores, three high achieving classes and five low achieving classes were identified. Comparisons of the frequencies of occurrence of each of the coding categories between the two groups of classes were made.

Several aspects of the Bellack et al. study are worthy of comment. First, the purpose of the study is quite different from that of the Barr study. Bellack and his colleagues make it clear at the outset that their study was not intended to identify the "good" teacher or the "best" teaching methods. Despite this clear statement of purpose, however, Bellack et al. did investigate the possibility that differences in verbal communication may be related to differences in student achievement. Second, all of the teachers included in the study taught the same instructional unit for the same period of time. Furthermore, the achievement test was tied directly to the content and objectives taught to the students. In this way, the impact of differences in content on both teaching and learning was minimized. Third, like Barr, Bellack and his colleagues felt it necessary to develop a set of categories that could be used to organize the large amounts of information included on the transcripts. In addition, however, Bellack et al. believed that it was necessary to ensure that different coders used the coding scheme in the same way. Thus, concern for agreement among coders is evident in the Bellack et al. study. Fourth, and finally, Bellack and his colleagues chose to use achievement test data rather than reputational data in differentiating among teachers in terms of their teaching effectiveness. In this regard, the posttest scores were adjusted by subtracting the scores that students were expected to achieve based on their pretest performance from their actual posttest scores. These "residual gain scores" (that is, actual scores minus expected scores) have become a common part of research on teaching effectiveness.

The Canterbury Experimental Studies of Teaching Behavior (Nuthall and Church, 1973)

Nuthall and Church conducted a series of experimental studies in their search for answers to two questions. First, how do students learn in classrooms? Second, what is the relationship between teacher behavior and student learning? Only the most comprehensive of the three studies is described in Box 9.3.

Purpose

To address two questions: "how do pupils learn in classrooms?" and "how are observable teacher behaviors related to that learning?" (p. 11). "Our concern is primarily with the discussion-type of lesson in which teachers and pupils interact verbally, and in which the object of that interaction is some relatively self-contained unit of subject matter" (p. 12).

Framework/Model

"Classroom teaching is worth studying, as it exists, for its own sake. . . . While we have a deep-felt concern for the improvement of teaching, we have attempted not to let this concern distort the nature of our research. In the long run, the interests of education are best served by developing a comprehensive understanding of classroom teaching, rather than by finding immediate solutions to topical questions" (p. 10). At the same time, however, the research is directed toward understanding the "moment-by-moment chaining of teacher and pupil acts" (p. 11). ·

Graphically, the model can be displayed as shown in Figure 9.1.

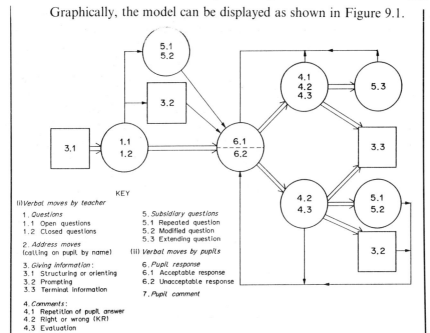

KEY

(i) *Verbal moves by teacher*

1. *Questions*
1.1 Open questions
1.2 Closed questions

2. *Address moves*
(calling on pupil by name)

3. *Giving information*:
3.1 Structuring or orienting
3.2 Prompting
3.3 Terminal information

4. *Comments*:
4.1 Repetition of pupil answer
4.2 Right or wrong (KR)
4.3 Evaluation

5. *Subsidiary questions*
5.1 Repeated question
5.2 Modified question
5.3 Extending question

(ii) *Verbal moves by pupils*

6. *Pupil response*
6.1 Acceptable response
6.2 Unacceptable response

7. *Pupil comment*

FIG. 9.1   A flow-chart of common verbal move sequences in classroom (from Nuthall and Church, 1973).

Procedures

1. Develop a series of scripts designed to introduce the principles of elementary electricity to ten-year-old children. The scripts consisted of a set of question-initiated episodes with predetermined rules guiding the teacher's handling of pupil responses. For each question, the maximum number of pupil responses that might be used was fixed. Appropriate prompts were standardized as were equipment and materials. A summary of the content to be covered by pupil responses was also provided.

2. Vary the scripts in such a way that 10 treatments are produced. The first three treatments differ according to the thoroughness with which the content is covered (A, B, and C). The next three treatments differ according to the way in which teachers are to react to students' answers to questions. In treatment D, teachers are to give the answers. In treatment E, teachers are to let the discussion continue until an appropriate answer is given. In treatment F, teachers are to probe and prompt the students so as to lead them to appropriate responses. The remaining four treatments em-

phasize different aspects of teaching: G, teacher informing rather than questioning; H, reduced pupil opportunity to respond to the questions; I, reduced feedback to students; and N, no instruction given at all (see Table 9.1).

TABLE 9.1

Abbreviated Descriptions of Experimental Treatments

Treatment:

A. *Single Standard:* Covers as briefly as possible posttest content, using highly structured closed questions. Single reference is made to each concept name, concept definition, concept example, and principle. Reference is made to two problems illustrating each of the three principles. One 50-minute lesson, 54 episodes. Questions addressed by random non-replacement procedure, average of five responses per pupil.

B. *Double Standard:* Same procedure as for Single Standard, but content is doubled, i.e. two references to each concept name, definition, example, and each principle. Four references to problems illustrating each principle. Two 35-minute lessons, 111 episodes. Questions addressed by random non-replacement procedure, average of nine responses per pupil.

C. *Triple Standard:* Same procedure as Single Standard, but content is tripled, i.e. three references to each concept name, definition, example, and to each principle. Six references to problems illustrating each principle. Three 40-minute lessons, 179 episodes. Questions addressed by random non-replacement procedure, average of 15 responses per pupil.

D. *Open Question: terminal comment:* Same content and number of moves as Double Standard. Questions are opened (less structured, vague) and addressed to pupils who volunteer. Wrong answers handled by redirecting questions to further pupils, and content coverage controlled by terminal information moves (giving answers). Two 35-minute lessons, 86 episodes.

E. *Open Question: evaluation only:* Same content and number of moves as Double Standard. Questions are opened as in above treatment. Wrong answers are handled by redirecting to further pupils, by evaluation, KR, and repetition comments. Number of pupil responses is allowed to increase to level of Triple Standard treatment. Control of length of episodes exercised by directing questions to pupils of differing ability. Three 35-minute lessons, 90 episodes.

F. *Open Question: prompting moves:* Same content and number of episodes as Double Standard. Questions opened as for above treatment. Number of responses as for Triple Standard (see above treatment). Control of content coverage through use of prompting (additional information during episode) moves, and through redirection of questions to pupils of differing ability levels. Three 40-minute lessons, 97 episodes.

G. *Infrequent Questions:* Same content as Triple Standard, number of questions as for Single Standard treatment. Two-thirds of questions in Triple Standard treatment turned into information moves, either structuring or terminal. Three 25-minute lessons, 52 episodes.

H. *Infrequent Responses:* Same content and procedures as for Triple Standard treatment, but almost all questions addressed to non-experimental subjects. Three 40-minute lessons, 180 episodes.

I. *Infrequent Feedback:* Content as for Triple Standard, but number of feedback comments reduced to number as for Single Standard treatment. Pupils were asked to write down answers to two-thirds of questions, and not told whether they were correct. Three 40-minute lessons, 180 episodes.

N. *No Instruction:* Classes which received the same testing programme as other classes but no instruction.

Source: Nuthall and Church (1973).

3. Develop an achievement test directly related to the content included in the scripts. Achievement tests include two sets of items; those assessing prerequisite knowledge, and those assessing the content included in the scripts.

4. Administer pretest several weeks before study begins to students in several classes. Based on the results of the pretest and a culture-fair intelligence test, identify those pupils in each class whose ability and prior knowledge fall within an "average" range. Only those classes in which at least 20 "average" students were enrolled were included in the primary analysis of the study. Other students in the classes were considered separately.

5. Assign treatments to classes. Each treatment has a minimum of three classes, with four treatments having four classes.

6. Have teachers perform treatments according to their scripts. Depending on the treatment, from one to three lessons are presented to the students.

7. Administer posttest four days after the last lesson. Compute residual gain score for each student.

8. Compare differences in mean residual gain scores for the "average" students both within treatments (that is, from class to the next) and across treatments.

9. Present and discuss the results of study.

Box 9.3   Summary of the Nuthall and Church (1973) Study.

Nuthall and Church suggest that the "practice of teaching in most Western countries is a relatively stable, self-contained and repetitive set of behaviors" (p. 10). Sequences of these commonly occurring behaviors can be identified (see Figure 9.1). Once such sequences have been identified, variations in these sequences can be formulated to create a series of experimental conditions or treatments. The effects of these various treatments on student achievement can then be examined.

The study began with the development of a series of scripts designed to introduce the principles of elementary electricity to ten-year-old children. The scripts consisted of a set of question-initiated episodes with predetermined rules pertaining to the maximum number of student response opportunities and the types of reactions and prompts that the teacher could use. The scripts were varied in such a way that ten treatments were produced. The differences among the treatments are summarized in Box 9.3, while the treatments themselves are outlined in Table 9.1. An achievement test was prepared, which included two sets of items; those assessing students' prerequisite knowledge and those assessing the content included on the scripts.

The achievement test was administered as a pretest to students in 34 classes several weeks before the study began. Based on the results of the pretest and an intelligence test, students whose ability and prior knowledge fell within an "average" range were identified in each class. Only those classes which contained at least 20 "average" students were included in the study.

The ten treatments were randomly assigned to the remaining classes, resulting in a minimum of three classes per treatment. Four of the treatments contained four classes. Depending on the treatment, from one to three lessons were taught to the students. Following the last lesson, the achievement test was re-administered as a posttest. A residual gain score was computed for each of the "average" students (as well as for each of the other students in the classes). A mean residual gain score for the "average" students in each class was calculated. Finally, statistical comparisons of the mean residual gain scores both within and across treatments were made.

Several components of the Nuthall and Church study are important to consider. First, the study is an experimental study. Thus, Nuthall and Church are concerned with manipulating the conditions in which teaching and learning occur and examining the impact of that manipulation on student achievement. Second, because it is an experimental study, they are concerned with minimizing the impact of several potentially important extraneous variables. Four of the most important extraneous variables attended to by Nuthall and Church are (1) the type of lesson (which is a discussion-type lesson with an emphasis on the mastery of particular subject matter), (2) the content taught and tested (which is equivalent for all students), (3) other teaching factors (which are minimized by scripting the teachers), and (4) the students to whom the lesson is taught (who are restricted to so-called "average" students). Third, and finally, because the effects of treatments may not necessarily be uniform across teachers or classrooms, a minimum of three classes per treatment are included. Because of this aspect of the design, differences which can be attributed to the treatments can be separated from those that can be attributed to classrooms, teachers, or students.

Inside the Primary Classroom (Galton et al., 1980)

The study was being planned at about the same time that the results of Bennett's (1976) study of formal and informal teaching methods were being released. In contrast to Bennett's contention that more formal methods were superior, Galton and his colleagues argued for a "combination of individual, group, and class work; a highly complex, dynamic 'system' which permits, and in fact encourages, differentiated treatment for individual children" (p. 48). This "system" includes aims, strategic decisions, tactics (that is, teacher behavior and teacher-student interactions, pupil behavior), and products (that is, learning outcomes) (see Figure 9.2). The purpose of the study was to describe the complexity of this "system" in operation in the classroom and to gain an understanding of "why certain teachers do one thing while others do something else" (p. 4).

Prior to the study, two structured observation systems were developed; one focusing on the teacher, the other on the students. Table 9.2 includes the observation categories of the teacher-focused system, the Teacher Record.

Once the observation systems had been developed, a sample of schools and classrooms was selected (see Box 9.4). Each of the 58 classrooms was visited for three days each term. During each visit six observation sessions were completed using the two structured observation systems. In addition, observers collected evidence pertaining to the physical layout of the classroom, the curricular content, and the class timetable. They also recorded their impressions and asked the teachers about their grouping policy and their classroom management orientation.

As might be expected, a large amount of evidence was collected. The evidence gathered using the structured observation systems was summarized in terms of the percentages of all of the codings that were placed in each of the categories included on the two systems. Comparisons of different types of classrooms were made in terms of these percentages. Furthermore, the percentages were incorporated in a series of cluster analyses which led to the identification of four teaching styles and four pupil types. Finally, the relationships between the teaching styles and pupil types were explored.

Purpose

"To describe, using the information gathered during systematic observation, some of the richness and variety of what goes on in a modern primary classroom. Second, to search for patterns from among these events in order to help explain why certain teachers do one thing while others do something else" (p. 4).

Framework/Model

The study was being planned at the same time that the results of the Bennett study (see Chapter 10) were being published. The results of the Bennett study suggested that "pupils taught by so called 'formal' methods (classes taught, in silence, with regular testing and plenty of competition) were, on the average, four months ahead of those taught by 'informal' methods on tests in the basic skills of mathematics and English" (p. 7). In contrast, Galton and his colleagues proposed a "combination of indivi- dual, group and class work; a highly complex, dynamic 'system' which permits, and in fact specifically encourages differentiated treatment for individual children" (p. 48). This system includes three overall strategic decisions: how to manage the learning environment (organizational); what to teach (curriculum); and how to teach it (instructional). Once in the classroom, the teacher uses tactics (that is, minute by minute exchanges between the teacher and the students) to implement the overall strategy developed by making these three types of strategic decisions. When properly executed these tactics are expected to impact on pupil behavior which, in turn, are expected to impact on pupil achievement (or pupil products).

Graphically, the relationships among the various elements of the teaching-learning process are shown in Figure 9.2.

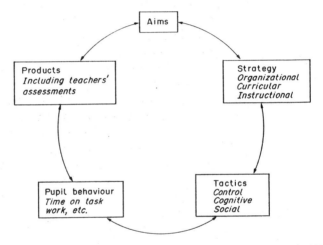

FIG. 9.2 A description of the teaching process (from Galton et al., 1980). Reproduced by permission of Galton et al., *Inside the Classroom* (1980) Routledge.

Procedures

1. Develop structured observation instruments. Two instruments were developed: the Pupil Record (used to examine the nature and frequency of children's classroom activities when working alone and interacting with adults and with other pupils) and the Teacher Record (used to examine the statements made and questions asked by the teacher as well as nonverbal behaviors of the teacher) (see Table 9.2).

2. Select a sample of classrooms and schools. Fifty-eight classes located in 19 schools were selected. Pupils ranged in

TABLE 9.2

The Observation Categories of the Teacher Record

Conversation	Silence
Questions	*Silent Interaction*
Task	Gesturing
Q1 recalling facts	Showing
Q2 offering ideas, solutions (closed)	Marking
Q3 offering ideas, solutions (open)	Waiting
Task supervision	Story
Q4 referring to task supervision	Reading
Routine	Not observed
Q5 referring to routine matter	Not coded
Statements	*No Interaction*
Task	Adult interaction
S1 of facts	Visiting pupil
S2 of ideas, problems	Not interacting
Task supervision	Out of room
S3 telling child what to do	
S4 praising work or effort	*Audience*
S5 feedback on work or effort	*Composition*
Routine	*Activity*
S6 providing information, directions	
S7 providing feedback	
S8 of critical control	
S9 of small talk	

Source: Galton et al. (1980). Reproduced by permission of Galton et al., *Inside the Classroom* (1980). Routledge.

    age from 8+ to 10+ years. Almost three-fourths of the classrooms arranged in "box plan;" the remainder were "open plan."

3.   Conduct observations in classrooms. Each classroom was visited for three days *each term* with a total of six observation sessions across the three days. For the Pupil Record eight previously selected target pupils were observed in a predetermined order. Pupils were selected by prior achievement (by quartiles) and by sex.

4.   While in the classrooms secure the following additional information:

    a. physical layout of the classroom and equipment,

    b. outline of curricular content,

    c. class timetable and outline of organization of all activities, whether observed or not,

    d. prose account of impressions of the observer,

    e. grouping policy and rationale, and

    f. teacher reports of classroom management orientation.

5.   Summarize findings in terms of the percentages of total number of codings that were placed in each of the categories

on the Pupil Record and Teacher Record.

6. Examine differences in these percentages in terms of several other factors:
   a. "box" type versus "open plan" classrooms,
   b. single age versus multi-age classrooms,
   c. boys versus girls, and
   d. high, medium, and low ability students.
   From time to time incorporate "additional information" (see step 4 above) into discussion of differences.

7. Use cluster analysis to identify teaching styles based on observational data. Describe each teaching style in terms of the observational data and assign a label to each style.

8. Use cluster analysis to identify pupil types based on observational data. Describe each pupil type in terms of observational data and assign a label to each style.

9. Examine the relationship between teaching styles and pupil types (that is, determine whether particular pupil types are more or less likely to occur in classrooms of teachers with particular teaching styles).

10. Draw conclusions based on composite set of results.

Box 9.4   Summary of the Galton et al. (1980) Study.

Several components of the Galton et al. study are worthy of consideration. First, separate observation systems were used for teachers and for students. The use of two systems with different foci permitted a number of comparisons to be made concerning the classrooms as seen from two different points of view (that is, the teacher's and the student's). Second, similarities and differences of the results across different classroom arrangements (e.g., single-age and multi-age classrooms) and categories of students (e.g., high, middle, and low ability students) were examined. As a result, Galton and his colleagues were able to investigate the extent to which their findings generalized across different types of classrooms or students. Third, the notes made by observers while in the classrooms were used at times to enhance the meaning of the quantitative evidence. That is, Galton et al. used qualitative evidence in support of the quantitative evidence which was the primary emphasis of the study. Fourth, and finally, cluster analysis (a fairly sophisticated quantitative data analytic technique) was used to identify typologies of teachers and students based on the observational evidence. The use of cluster analysis with observational evidence allows the typologies of teachers and students to be defined in behavioral terms.

Talking, Listening, and Learning in Elementary Classrooms (Morine-Dershimer, 1985)

The primary purpose of the study was to investigate teachers' and students' conceptions of the verbal communication that takes place in the classroom. Morine-Dershimer hypothesized that students' success in school was influenced greatly by the conceptions and misconceptions of language held by students and the extent to which they participated in the discussion and dialogue that took place in the classroom. Furthermore, these conceptions, misconceptions, class participation, were influenced by the complexity of the verbal communication that occurred in the classroom and the students' classroom status (both academic and social).

The study began with the selection of the sample of teachers for inclusion in the study (see Box 9.5). Six teachers (and 165 elementary school students) in a single school were selected. Using sociometric techniques with students and questionnaires with teachers, evidence as to each student's status within the classroom was gathered. Evidence pertaining to the student's sex, race, and reading achievement was also collected.

Purpose

To "investigate participant (pupil and teacher) perspectives of the nature of communication in the classroom, describe pupil conceptions of the differences between discourse in the classroom at home, and at play, examine the correspondence between pupil and teacher conceptions of the rules of classroom discourse, and compare participant concepts to those of a sociolinguistic specialist in analysis of classroom discourse" (p. 6). Furthermore, the study was designed to identify the "possible causes of pupil misunderstanding of the rules and processes of classroom discourse, and the identification of possible effects of such misunderstanding on school achievement" (p. 39).

Framework/Model

Pupil conceptions of the language spoken in the classroom (or, conversely, their misconceptions of the language) and the extent to which they participate in the class discussions are the primary determinants of their success in school. Their conceptions and the extent of their participation in turn are influenced by their status in the classroom (both academic and social) and the complexity of the language actually spoken. Furthermore, the pupil conceptions of language may differ in different settings (home, school, and play) and may differ from the conceptions of language held by teachers and sociolinguists. Graphically,

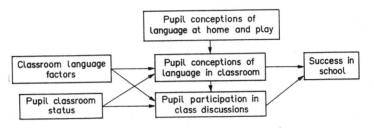

Procedures

1. Identify subjects to include in study. Sample consisted of 165 second, third, and fourth grade pupils and six teachers in a single elementary school.
2. Determine classroom status of pupils in terms of sex, race, entering reading achievement, status with teachers, and status with other pupils.
3. Videotape segments of 30-minute lessons conducted by each of the six teachers. Teachers were asked to plan lessons that directed to the whole class and involved verbal interaction.
4. Select three four-minute segments of each lesson for analysis.
5. Videotape segments of conversations in the homes of the third grade pupils.
6. Select three four- to five-minute segments for analysis.
7. Videotape segments of play among six students in an unstructured indoor setting, playing with construction toys.
8. Select a single 12-minute segment for analysis.
9. Replay the seven selected videotaped segments to pupils, teachers, and three researchers who operate within different conceptual frameworks. Ask pupils and teachers rather general questions concerning what they had seen and heard. Have researcher analyze the taped segments in line with their particular frameworks.
10. Develop coding categories for analyzing the answers to the questions given by pupils and teachers. Compute the frequencies of responses made by students and teachers in each of the coding categories.
11. Present and discuss the results of analyses separately for pupils and members of the research teams. Use excerpts from pupils' and teachers' responses to questions to enhance the meaning of the quantitative evidence.

12. Use a variety of non-parametric statistical techniques to compare pupils' responses with those of teachers and members of the research teams.

Box 9.5   Summary of the Morine-Dershimer (1985) Study.

Each of the six teachers was asked to plan a lesson that was directed to the whole class and involved verbal interaction. These 30-minute lessons were videotaped. Three four-minute segments of each videotaped lesson were selected. Videotape recordings of conversations in the homes of several of the third grade students were made. Three four- to five-minute segments of these recordings were selected. Finally, a videotape recording of six students playing with construction toys in an unstructured indoor setting was made. A single 12-minute segment from this recording was selected. These seven segments of videotape recordings, then, became of the focus of the analysis.

The videotaped segments were replayed to groups of students, teachers, and researchers. Following the viewing of each segment, students and teachers were asked rather general questions concerning what they had seen and heard. The researchers were asked to analyze the segment based on the frameworks that guided their research.

A set of coding categories was developed to aid in analyzing the responses made by the students and the teachers. The frequencies of responses made within each category were computed separately for students and teachers. Excerpts from the interviews with the students and teachers were used to enhance the meaning of the quantitative evidence. The researchers' analyses of the taped segments also were discussed. Finally, a variety of non-parametric statistical techniques were used to compare the students' responses with those made by teachers and researchers.

Several aspects of the Morine-Dershimer study are noteworthy. First, while Morine-Dershimer agrees with Bellack and his colleagues about the importance of language in the classroom, she disagrees in terms of whose conceptions of language are crucial to study. Stated simply, Morine-Dershimer believes that the participants' views of language, not an "outsider's" view of language, must be understood if the study of classrooms is to increase children's success in school. Second, understanding children's conceptions and misconceptions of classroom language requires that several comparisons and contrasts be made. Examining these conceptions in different settings—home and play as well as school—provides insights as to the conceptions of children's language that are unique to the school setting. Examining these conceptions relative to the conceptions of adults—both teachers and researchers—permits a greater awareness of the nature of differences in the conceptions of language held by members of these three groups that may lead to "misconceptions" on the part of children. Third, while not formally tested, the underlying framework of the study is in the form of a causal model. That is, relationships among the major concepts are viewed as causal in nature. Causal models are typically more complex than other models, since they require the explicit specification of the relationships between and among the primary concepts included in the model. At the same time, however, causal models have the somewhat unique potential of enabling researchers to develop plausible explanations of their findings.

The IEA Classroom Environment Study (Anderson et al., 1989)

Researchers in nine countries located on five continents participated in the study. The study began by reviewing the research on teaching and learning in order to identify those classroom activities, teacher and student behaviors, teacher-student interactions, and teacher and student beliefs and perceptions that were associated with student achievement. Because a vast array of activities, behaviors, interactions, beliefs, and perceptions were identified, an organizing framework was developed. Initially, this organizing framework included six generalized concepts that served primarily as placeholders for this vast array of variables. Eventually, the organizing framework evolved into a causal model which included fifteen concepts and their hypothesized interrelationships (see Figure 9.3). Within the context of the organizing framework and causal model, the study had two primary purposes. First, similarities and differences in teaching practices and conditions of classroom learning were to be examined. Second, relationships of these practices and conditions with student achievement and attitudes were to be investigated.

The study began with the selection of a structured observation system and the development of several questionnaires and interviews to be used by researchers in all participating countries (see Box 9.6). Achievement tests were developed by the researchers in each participating country. The questionnaires and interview protocols were translated as necessary. Several training sessions for observers were held.

Purpose
"To identify the similarities and differences in teaching practices and the conditions of learning as they occurred in a variety of countries" and "to identify those particular aspects of the classroom environment (e.g., general classroom activities, teacher and student perceptions of the classroom environment and specific behaviors exhibited by teachers and students) that likely influenced student achievement and attitudes" (Anderson, 1987, p. 70).

Framework/Model

   Researchers in nine countries located on five continents participated in the study. In order to organize the multitude of
activities, behaviors, interactions, opinions, and perceptions
about which evidence was to be collected in the various
countries, fifteen general concepts (termed constructs) were
identified by this group of researchers. Furthermore, in order to
prepare the evidence for the analysis needed to address the
second purpose of the study (that dealing with the possible
influence of classroom variables on student achievement and
attitudes), a causal model was designed which specified the
relationships among the fifteen primary concepts or constructs.
This model, referred to as the core model, is shown in Figure
9.3. As can be seen in the figure, more than thirty cause-effect
relationships between the concepts are hypothesized, with the
arrows indicating the direction of the relationship (that is, which
of the two concepts is believed to influence the other).

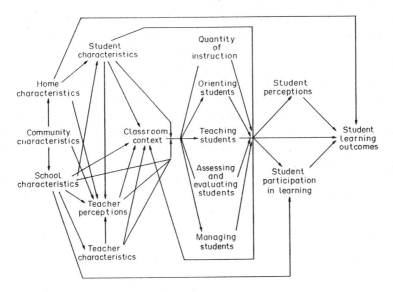

FIG. 9.3   The causal model underlying the IEA Classroom Environment
Study (from Anderson et al., 1989).

Procedures

   1.   Select or develop instruments to be used in the study. In all,
        fifteen instruments were either selected or developed. These
        included questionnaires, interviews, a structured observation
        system, a rating scale, student aptitude tests, and student
        achievement tests. The use of some of the instruments were

required in all countries; others were optional.

2. Select samples of classrooms (and by virtue of their selection, teachers and students) to include in the study. The number of classrooms differed across countries; all were selected by virtue of their convenience.

3. Administer student achievement tests (or aptitude tests) and student and teacher questionnaires prior to conducting any observations.

4. Conduct from 4 to 10 observations in each classroom (the number depending on the country). Prior to each observation interview the teacher concerning the type of lesson to be observed (e.g., new content, review material) and the objective of the lesson (e.g., recall of information, problem solving).

5. After the final observations are conducted, readminister the student achievement tests and additional student and teacher questionnaires.

6. Summarize the evidence collected using the structured observation system in terms of frequencies and percentages. Summarize the evidence collected using the questionnaires and interviews in terms of frequency distributions and mean scores. Summarize the evidence collected using student aptitude and achievement tests using mean scores.

7. Compare the countries in terms of the major concepts included in the core model.

8. Compute the residual gain scores for all students in each classroom and the mean residual gain score for the students in each classroom. Also, for each classroom, compute average percentage of students who were observed to be on-task.

9. Within each country, calculate correlations between the evidence gathered from the questionnaires, interviews, and structured observation system, and residual gain scores and time-on-task.

10. Within those countries having the largest numbers of classes, use path analytic techniques to estimate the magnitude of the relationships among the concepts included in the core model.

Box 9.6   Summary of the Anderson et al. (1989) Study.

Samples of classrooms were selected. The number of classrooms varied from country to country as did the age level of the students and the subject matter. Achievement tests (or, in some cases, aptitude tests) were administered as pretests; questionnaires were administered to both teachers and students.

In each classroom from four to 10 observations were conducted (with a median number of observations of eight). During each observation three structured observation systems were used in a fixed sequence. The first focused on classroom activities and the extent to which the students in general were paying attention or on-task. The second focused on teacher-student interactions. The third focused on classroom activities and the extent to which selected students were paying attention or on-task. Prior to each observation teachers were interviewed briefly concerning the lesson to be observed.

After the final observations were completed, student achievement tests were administered (or in several countries, re-administered). A different questionnaire was administered to the teachers and a portion of the initial questionnaire was re-administered to the students.

The evidence from the observations was summarized using frequencies and percentages, while evidence from questionnaires, interviews, and tests was summarized in terms of frequency distributions, mean scores, or both. Comparisons across the countries were made in terms of the fifteen primary concepts included in the causal model. Correlations between activities, interactions, behaviors, beliefs, and opinions, and student time-on-task and residual achievement gain were computed. Finally, in those countries with the largest number of classes, path analysis was used to investigate the causal model.

Several aspects of the Anderson et al. study are worth mentioning. First, the causal model served two purposes. It organized the large number of activities, behaviors, interactions, beliefs, and opinions that were included in the study. In addition, it specified the relationships among the primary concepts that were to be examined using the evidence collected during the study. Second, multiple observations of each classroom were conducted. Thus, the consistency of the evidence across classrooms and across observation occasions could be examined. Third, both questionnaires and observations played a major role in the study. Evidence pertaining to eight of the concepts included in the model was gathered using questionnaires, while evidence related to six of the concepts was collected using the structured observation system. Evidence on the final concept, student learning outcomes, was gathered using both achievement tests and questionnaires. Fourth, and finally, the evidence was analyzed using path analytic techniques, which are some of the most sophisticated quantitative analytic techniques available. Using such techniques both direct and indirect relationships among the concepts included in the model can be examined.

Synopses of Other Studies

As mentioned in the introduction to this second unit, numerous studies of teaching have been conducted during the past 60 years. Thus, the choice of the six studies to review in some detail was not an easy one. Three other studies of teaching are important and worthy of consideration. Brief synopses of these studies are presented in this section.

Flanders (1960)

The primary purpose of this two-year study was to investigate the effects of teacher directness (direct versus indirect) and clarity of the learning task (clear versus ambiguous) on the learning of gifted, average, and slow students, as well as independent and dependent students. Only the second year of the study is described in this synopsis. The variable "clarity of the learning task" was included only in the first year of the study.

Two-week long mathematics and social studies units prepared by the research team were taught to eighth-grade students by 16 mathematics and 16 social studies teachers (with one of the social studies teachers eventually dropped from the study). Based on observations made in the teachers' classrooms using the Flanders Interaction Analysis System (FIAS), teachers were classified as "most direct," "average," and "most indirect." For some of the analyses, two classifications were used: "direct" and "indirect" (with two of the "average" teachers placed in the "indirect" classification and three placed in the "direct" classification).

Prior to the beginning of the study, students were administered an intelligence test, a dependence proneness measure, and an achievement test directly related to the content of one of the units. Based on the results of intelligence test students were classified as high, average, or low ability. Based on the results of the dependence proneness measure students were classified as high, average, or low relative to dependence proneness. During the study observers were to note the teachers' planning, work arrangements, evaluation, attention to administrative matters, and routine procedures. Based on these notes, two types of planning and work arrangements were identified: expanding (those activities possessing greater potential for stimulating student participation) and restricting (those activities with less potential).

At the end of the units and four to six weeks after the units had been completed, the achievement tests were re-administered. Posttest scores were adjusted for differences in pretest scores. Differences between groups of teachers (direct versus indirect), types of activities (expanded and restricted) and typologies of students (ability levels, categories of dependence proneness) on the adjusted posttest scores were examined. Relationships between teacher directedness and the extent of use of "expanded" activities also were examined.

The Flanders study is important for at least two reasons. First, the study was concerned with the differential impact of teacher directedness on different types of students. As such it represents a movement away from the more traditional "teaching method" studies (see Chapter 10) and toward studies of the "aptitude-treatment interaction" variety (Cronbach and Snow, 1977). Second, it brought the Flanders Interaction Analysis System to the attention of classroom researchers in the United States. Since that time the system has been used in numerous studies of classrooms across the world (Flanders and Amidon, 1981).

Smith and Geoffrey (1968)

The purpose of the study, as the title of the report makes clear, was to understand the complexities of the urban classroom. In their words their "primary intent was to describe the silent language of a culture, a classroom in a slum school, so that those who have not lived in it will appreciate its subtleties and complexities" (p. 2). Smith was the observer, Geoffrey was the teacher.

Smith observed in Geoffrey's classroom every day for an entire semester and kept extensive field notes. Smith used these notes as the basis for his daily discussions with Geoffrey. Together, they attempted to clarify the intentions and motives behind Geoffrey's behavior in the classroom. Based on these discussions a series of models was prepared (one of which was included in Chapter 2). Each model had to meet two criteria before it was accepted. First, did the model make sense to Geoffrey and feel intuitively "right?" Second, was the model consistent with Smith's carefully taken field notes? Overall, some 36 models on a wide variety of topics and containing several hundred variables were produced.

The Smith and Geoffrey study is important because it brought to the study of classrooms the methodology of anthropological field studies. The need for both extensive and intensive observation in classrooms, dialogues with teachers and students, and models that focus on practical problems and reflect what really goes on in the classroom is made explicit in the study.

Goodlad (1984)

The primary purpose of the study was to describe the conditions currently in place in schools and classrooms in such a way that efforts to reform the schools would be informed by the descriptions. As Goodlad asserted, "If we are to improve [the school], we must understand it" (p. xvi). The study was a massive undertaking, examining both schools and classrooms. In this synopsis, we focus solely on the study of classrooms.

Triplets of schools were selected, with each triplet including a senior high school, a middle or junior high school, and an elementary school. Students in the elementary and middle or junior high school eventually would attend the senior high school in the triplet. The triplets were selected based on a purposive sampling of schools that varied according to school size, school location (urban or rural), and composition of the study body in terms of socioeconomic status, race and ethnicity.

Observations were conducted in 129 elementary school classrooms, 362 middle or junior high classrooms, and 525 senior high school class-rooms. All observations were made using a modification of Stallings' (1977) observation system. For the elementary schools, a randomly selected class at each grade level was observed for approximately four hours. For the secondary schools, randomly selected classes representing eight subject areas were observed for three class periods of roughly 40 to 55 minutes each.

The vast array of evidence was summarized in terms of frequency counts and percentages. Comparisons were made across the three levels of schooling on a wide variety of classroom activities and teacher-student interactions.

The Goodlad study is important for at least two reasons. First, it is the largest observational study of classrooms ever conducted. As a consequence, the problems involving the aggregation and summarization of the evidence were quite acute. Second, by virtue of the sampling plan, the results of the study quite likely apply to large numbers of classrooms in the United States. Few classroom researchers can make this claim.

Comparisons of the Six Primary Studies

The six studies reviewed in some detail earlier in this chapter are similar in some respects and different in others. Table 9.3 contains an analysis of the studies in terms of the same seven dimensions that were used in the previous chapter (see Table 8.1).

Purpose of the Study

The studies are evenly divided between the two major purposes of classroom research. The Bellack et al. and Morine-Dershimer studies are both descriptive studies that investigate the language of the classroom. As has been mentioned, the primary difference between the two studies is that Morine-Dershimer is primarily interested in students' conceptions of language, while Bellack et al. approaches the problem from a more theoretical perspective. The Barr study as well as the Nuthall and Church are associational studies. Barr focuses on differences in classroom activities and verbal expressions of good and poor teachers. Nuthall and Church examine differences in student achievement that may result from differences in the ways in which teachers teach. Finally, the Galton et al. and Anderson et al. studies are both descriptive and associational. Associationally, Galton and his colleagues are interested in the relationship between teacher styles and pupil types. Anderson and his colleagues explore the relationships among a large number of concepts included in a causal model.

Keys to Improving Student Learning

A single theme runs through the majority of the studies reviewed in this chapter. Simply stated, understanding is the key to the improvement of student learning. This theme is particularly strong in the studies of Bellack et al. and Nuthall and Church. Bellack et al. contend that "only as teachers have available knowledge about the teaching process gained through research will they be able to exercise effective control over the process. We have depended too long on unexamined 'conventional wisdom' about

TABLE 9.3

A Comparison of Studies of Teaching Along Seven Dimensions

	Studies		
Dimensions	Barr	Bellack et al.	Nuthall & Church
Purpose of Study	Associational	Descriptive	Associational
Key(s) to Improving Student Learning	Improving supervision of teaching (by increasing is objectivity, systemization)	Providing teachers with knowledge of the teaching process, particularly rules, functions, and meanings of language	Promoting a real understanding of classroom teaching rather than finding immediate solutions to topical questions
Extent of Manipulation	None	Teachers had to teach the same instructional unit	Varying scripts to be used by teachers to create 10 treatments
Sampling	PRPS ($n = 94$) [Type of teachers]	CONV ($n = 15$)	CONV ($n = 34$) RNDM (Teachers to treatment)
Sources of Evidence	SOBS NOTES OTHR (Self-evaluation by teacher)	AUDIO TRANS TEST	TEST
Nature of Evidence	FREQ/% EXCRPT	FREQ/% MEANS	MEANS
Analysis of Evidence	CORR	COMPARE OTHR (Markov chain analysis)	COMPSTAT

| | Studies | | |
Dimensions	Galton et al.	Morine-Dershimer	Anderson et al.
Purpose of Study	Descriptive & Associational	Descriptive	Descriptive & Associational
Key(s) to Improving Student Learning	Increased use of "balanced" set of strategies and tactics; avoid extremes of formal and informal	Increased understanding of pupils' conceptions of language and increased pupil class (overt and covert) participation	Increased understanding of the myriad of factors that impact directly and indirectly on student learning
Extent of Manipulation	None	Teachers asked to plan lessons for whole class and which involved verbal interaction	None
Sampling	CONV ($n=58$)	CONV ($n=6$)	CONV ($n=450+$)
Sources of Evidence	SOBS NOTES	VIDEO RATE OTHR (Sociometry)	SOBS QUES INTR TEST
Nature of Evidence	FREQ/% EXCRPT	FREQ/% EXCRPT	FREQ/% MEANS
Analysis of Evidence	COMPSTAT OTHR (Cluster analysis)	COMPSTAT	COMPARE PATH

Key to abbreviations used in Table 9.3

Sampling
CONV = convenience
PRPS = purposeful
RNDM = random

Sources of Evidence
AUDIO = audiotapes
NOTES = field notes
INTR = interviews
QUES = questionnaires
RATE = rating scale
SOBS = structured observation
TEST = tests
TRANS = transcripts
VIDEO = videotapes
OTHR = other

Nature of Evidence
FREQ/% = frequencies, percentages
MEANS = means (and/or standard deviations)
EXCRPT = written excerpts from observations or interviews

Analysis of Evidence
CORR = correlations
COMPARE = comparisons between groups using human inference
COMPSTAT = comparisons between groups using statistical inference (e.g., t-test, ANOVA, chi-square, ANCOVA)
FACTOR = factor analysis
PATH = path analysis
OTHR = other

teaching in pre-service and in-service training of teachers" (p. v). Nuthall and Church echo this sentiment. "In the long run, the interests of education are best served by developing a comprehensive understanding of classroom teaching, rather than by finding immediate solutions to topic questions" (p. 10). Morine-Dershimer believes that researchers and teachers need a more complete understanding of students' conceptions of language (since language is the primary communication device in classrooms). Anderson et al. suggest that a better understanding of the myriad of factors, both factors internal and external to the students, is needed before we can substantially improve learning.

Extent of Manipulation

Manipulation is present in three of the studies. Bellack et al. required all teachers in the study to teach the same instructional unit. Nuthall and Church required all teachers to teach according to scripts that differed along several key experimental dimensions. Finally, Morine-Dershimer asked teachers to prepare lessons for the whole class which involved verbal interaction.

The purpose for the manipulation is quite different in these three studies. Bellack et al. use manipulation to control differences in the content being taught. Thus, differences in teaching are not contaminated by differences in curriculum. Nuthall and Church use manipulation to examine the effect of varying clusters or patterns of teaching behaviors on student achievement. Like Bellack et al., Nuthall and Church also control for differences in content. Morine-Dershimer uses manipulation simply to create classroom conditions in which talking and listening will occur frequently and will occur loudly enough so that videotape recordings will be of sufficient sound quality for analysis.

Sampling

The vast majority of studies used convenience samples. Observational studies require that researchers travel to the sites at which they conduct their observations. Distance, then, becomes a constraint in planning studies of teaching. As an extreme example of this point, schools and classrooms in one of the countries participating in the Anderson et al. study were selected because of their location near railroad lines. Barr used a purposeful sample of identified good and poor teachers, while Nuthall and Church used a convenience sample. However, within this sample they randomly assigned teachers to treatments (or treatments to teachers).

Sources of Evidence

A variety of approaches to observation are included in the studies. Structured observation systems tend to be more prevalent than the others (particularly if one includes the Flanders (1960), Fisher et al. (1978), and Goodlad (1984) studies). Audiotape and videotape recordings are represented. Field notes were used by Barr and by Galton et al. (and extensively by Smith and Geoffrey, 1968). Achievement tests were included in three of the studies.

Nature of the Evidence

Quantitative evidence tends to predominate in all six studies. Evidence from structured observation systems is typically presented in the form of frequencies and percentages. In those studies in which the evidence was preserved in its raw form (e.g., transcripts of audiotape recordings, segments from videotape recordings), coding categories were used to analyze the evidence. Typically, frequency counts of the occurrences of events within each of the coding categories were computed and presented. Means and standard deviations were reported in three of the studies (Bellack et al., Nuthall and Church, and Anderson et al.). The predominance of quantitative evidence in studies of teaching is obvious in the Flanders and Goodlad studies. With the exception of Smith and Geoffrey, qualitative evidence is treated as supplementary to the quantitative evidence. That is, written excerpts from field notes, classroom transcripts, or responses to interview questions are used primarily to enhance the meaning of the quantitative evidence (Barr, Galton et al., and Morine-Dershimer).

Analysis of the Evidence

In view of the quantitative nature of the evidence, it is not surprising that a variety of statistical techniques are used to analyze the evidence. Fairly traditional techniques such as correlations (Barr) and analysis of variance (Nuthall and Church) are evident. Non-parametric techniques are used by Galton et al. and Morine-Dershimer. More sophisticated techniques such as Markov chain analysis (Bellack et al.), cluster analysis (Galton et al.), and path analysis (Anderson et al.) are also used to analyze the evidence.

Recommendations for Research on Teaching

In view of the dual purpose of research on teaching—description and association—separate sets of recommendations will be offered for each purpose.

Recommendations for Descriptive Studies

1. Descriptions of classroom teaching are likely to be enhanced when multiple sources are used to collect evidence over fairly lengthy periods of time. We would discourage the "quick and dirty" one-shot approach to the study of teaching and support a move toward achieving a balance between the extensive (breadth) and intensive (depth) study of classroom teaching. Observations supplemented with dialogues between researchers and classroom participants are likely to yield greater understanding on the part of the researchers. Similarly, the use of multiple observation systems with different foci (e.g., teachers and students, individual students and groups of students) is likely to provide a more complete understanding of classroom events (Galton et al.). Finally, multiple classroom visits are likely to provide researchers with the insights they need to understand both the form and function of teaching. Counting questions, for example, is one thing; understanding the significance and meaning of the questions is quite another.

2. An understanding of classroom teaching is more likely when other factors that may influence teachers and students are controlled. The Nuthall and Church study is particularly instructive in this regard. Differences in the content and students being taught and the type of lesson being conducted by the teacher may result in quite different teaching. As a consequence, when these factors are controlled we gain an understanding of teaching in its "purest" form. When these factors are allowed to vary, however, the teaching we are observing is likely to be confounded with these other factors. Thus, our descriptions of teaching are likely to be somewhat misleading and may lead to misunderstanding or overgeneralization.

3. Field notes appear to be a valuable source of evidence in descriptive studies, even when the primary sources yield purely quantitative evidence. Written comments and excerpts from transcripts or interviews help the reader understand the meaning of the quantitative evidence. Knowing how frequently a particular activity occurred or a behavior was demonstrated provides us with a certain level of understanding. Reading examples of the activity or examining illustrations of the behavior provides an additional level of understanding which seems essential in descriptive studies. For this same reason, using behavioral data in cluster analysis provides a deeper understanding of various typologies of teachers or students than do data gleaned from responses to questionnaires.

4. In attempting to describe classrooms, more evidence is not necessarily better. Too much evidence is more likely to confuse than to enlighten. Almost all researchers who study teaching find it necessary to form categories in order to organize the evidence they collect. If these categories are a part of an organized conceptual framework, they also provide the scaffolding necessary to properly interpret the evidence. Thinking through

the amount of evidence needed and the methods that might be used to reduce and/or aggregate the evidence is a useful step in planning studies of teaching.

Recommendations for Associational Studies

1. The majority of associational studies of teaching are conducted within the context of teacher effectiveness. As a consequence, concerns for proper indicators of effectiveness must be addressed. Two suggestions can be offered in this regard. First, if student achievement is used as an indicator of effectiveness, controlling for differences in content covered, students taught, and, perhaps, lesson type is critical (Nuthall and Church; Fisher et al., 1978). Additionally, selecting teachers who have produced consistent levels of achievement for several years is worthwhile (Leinhardt and Greeno, 1986; Good and Grouws, 1979). Second, if reputational indicators are used, some corroboration of the teachers' reputations is necessary. Barr provides an excellent example of one approach to this problem.

2. Causal models appear to have great value in planning studies of teaching *regardless* of how the evidence is analyzed. Causal models enable researchers to think through the concepts that may impact on teaching and learning. The causal model developed by Morine-Dershimer, for example, helps us understand the logic behind the study. Causal models also suggest proper analytic techniques to use with the evidence once collected. If the evidence is quantitative, path analytic techniques provide great statistical power. Finally, causal models are necessary if we are to move beyond description to explanation. Explanation requires that we understand not only what happened, but why it happened. Without understanding why something occurred, attempts to change or improve it are quite likely to be unsuccessful.

Closing Comments

We have reviewed six studies of teaching and have considered others. Once again, these reviews are intended to help researchers understand the studies of teaching that have been or are being conducted. Such understanding is needed if researchers are to plan and conduct studies of teaching that provide us with the knowledge we need to improve student learning.

10

Studies of Instruction

Because instruction as we have defined it includes six components, studies of instruction do not constitute as homogeneous a set as do studies of teachers and teaching. In fact, few studies of instruction include all six components. Rather, most studies have focused on either instructional format, grouping arrangement, time, pacing and content coverage, or some combination of these components. Some studies of instruction include teacher-student interaction, while others do not. For classroom studies to be considered studies of instruction, then, at least one component of instruction other than teacher-student interaction must be included. In this chapter six studies of instruction are reviewed. Following the review of these studies, we compare them on several important dimensions. We conclude the chapter with a set of recommendations concerning research on instruction.

Analysis of Six Studies of Instruction

Early studies of instruction focused primarily on teaching methods (i.e., instructional format plus grouping arrangement). The Johnson (1928) study is a prototypical example of such a study. The Gump (1967) study remains a classic in the field. Gump, in fact, was among the first to identify the primary components of classroom instruction. The Bennett (1976) study represents a new twist on an old theme. He replaces teaching methods with teaching styles. The Good and Grouws (1979) study is interesting since the plan for the study was derived from research on teaching. As a consequence, the study includes teacher-student interactions as a primary component of instruction. The Barr and Dreeben (1983) study examines the relationships among several of the components of instruction. Finally, the Cuban study (1984) represents a return to concerns for teaching methods or teaching styles, but uses historical evidence to examine the stability of certain teaching methods or styles over time.

An Experimental Study of the Teaching of Science
(Johnson, 1928)

Johnson's motivation for the study was remarkably similar to that of Charters and Waples (1929) (see Chapter 8) and Barr (1929) (see Chapter 9). In all three cases, the authors believed that objective evidence was needed to improve teaching and learning. Charters and Waples asserted that such evidence should form the basis for teacher education programs. Barr contended that such evidence was needed to improve the quality of supervision of teaching. Johnson suggested that "various methods of teaching science have had from time to time ardent supporters and inflexible opponents. It is only recently that attempts have been made to evaluate these claims on an objective basis" (p. 104). The purpose of the Johnson study then was to "try out under ordinary school conditions the relative efficiency of three different methods of laboratory instruction" (p. 104). (See Box 10.1.)

Purpose

To "try out under ordinary school conditions the relative efficiency of three different methods of laboratory instruction in high school biology: the lecture-demonstration, the group experimentation, and the individual experimentation methods" (p. 104).

Framework/Model

"Various methods of teaching science have had from time to time ardent supporters and inflexible opponents. It is only recently that attempts have been made to evaluate these claims on an objective basis. Hitherto, the prevailing criteria have been teachers' judgments and *a priori* reasoning" (p. 104). "If progress in methods is to be made there must be substituted for this state of conditioned emotional response the scientific attitudes of the open mind and a willingness to try out different procedures" (p. 104).

Graphically, the model is:

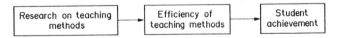

Procedures

1. Select sample of three classes of high school biology students located in a single school. A total of 50 students were included in the sample.

2. Administer an intelligence test to students twice during a two-month period. Use average score as measure of intelligence.

3. Identify 48 separate biology experiments and divide them into 24 experiments per semester.

4. Develop a series of achievement tests, each directly related to one or more of the experiments. Also develop more cumulative retention tests.

5. During the first semester, teach eight of the experiments to each class of students using one of the three teaching methods, teach another eight of the experiments using a second teaching method, and teach the final eight experiments using the third teaching method. Vary the order in which the teaching methods are used with the three classes. Class 1 received "group," "individual," and "lecture/demonstration." Class 2 received "individual," "lecture/demonstration," and "group." Class 3 received "lecture/demonstration," "group," and "individual." Outside readings and time (40 minutes per period, five times a week) were the same for all students.

6. Administer the achievement tests at the appropriate time in the sequence of experiments. Administer a set of retention tests one month after completion of the last experiment.

7. Replicate the study with the other 24 experiments during the second semester.

8. Combine the test scores across classes for each of the three treatments (using percent of items answered correctly).

9. Compare the scores across the three treatments.

10. Present and discuss the results of the study.

Box 10.1   Summary of the Johnson (1928) Study.

The study began with the selection of three classes of high school biology students located in a single school. The students were administered an intelligence test twice during a two-month period and their scores were averaged to produce an initial estimate of ability. A total of 48 separate biology experiments were identified; 24 experiments were assigned to each semester. A series of achievement tests was developed with each test directly related to one or more of the experiments. Tests covering more experiments were designed as retention tests.

Three treatments were designed. The first was the more traditional "lecture/demonstration" method. The teacher would conduct and discuss each experiment with the class, while the students watched and listened. The second was termed the "group experimentation" method. In this method, groups of students worked together on the various experiments. The third method was the "individual experimentation" method. As its name implies, students in this method worked on each experiment on their own.

During each semester, each class of students received each treatment but in a different order. One class, for example, received the "group experimentation" treatment for the first eight assignments, the "individual experimentation" treatment for the next eight assignments, and the "lecture/demonstration" method for the final eight assignments. The order for the second class was "individual experimentation," "lecture/demonstration," and "group experimentation." For the third class, the order was "lecture/demonstration," "group," and "individual." Outside readings and time allocated for instruction were the same for all classes. The entire study was replicated during the second semester.

The achievement tests and retention tests were administered at the appropriate times in the sequence. A final set of retention tests was administered one month after completion of the last experiment. All test scores were converted to the percentage of items answered correctly. An average "percentage correct" score was computed for each of the three treatments across classes. Differences in test scores across the three treatments were examined using standard statistical procedures.

Several of the components of the Johnson study are noteworthy. First, several potential extraneous variables are controlled in the study: content covered, time spent on instruction, and student ability. Furthermore, all three classes of students received all three treatments (in varying orders). As a consequence, the internal validity of the study is enhanced. Second, tests of immediate achievement and retention were included. As mentioned in Chapter 1, concern for student learning or achievement over time is an important aspect of studies of instruction. Third, the study was replicated on two separate occasions. Comparisons of the results across the replications could be made. If the results on both occasions were similar, their generalizability would be enhanced.

The Classroom Behavior Setting (Gump, 1967)

Gump remains one of the few researchers who set out to study classrooms; not teachers, nor students, but classrooms. Classrooms are viewed as behavior settings in which participants act in accordance with expected patterns of behavior. Understanding classrooms requires an understanding of the "ecological 'wholes' which, in turn, bind and organize the event details" (p. 8). "Activity segments" are such "ecological 'wholes.' " The purpose of the study, then, was to develop methods by which these classroom segments could be identified, design a set of concepts that could be used to characterize these segments, and to investigate the relationship between various segment characteristics and teacher and pupil behavior.

The study actually began with a small pilot study of two classrooms (see Box 10.2) to try out the system to be used to collect evidence in the classroom. Basically, the system involved the observer dictating notes into a Stenomask (which provided for silent dictation) and using a camera that took still photographs at 20 second intervals.

Purpose

To 1) develop "classroom chronicles" as a means of describing classroom activity, 2) develop methods for defining classroom "segments" as units of classroom activity, 3) develop concepts for characterizing segments, 4) develop methods for recording and analyzing teacher and student behavior, and 5) determine the utility of the segment concept by relating segment characteristics to teacher and pupil behavior.

Framework/Model

Classrooms are viewed as behavior settings which are defined as "standing patterns of behavior-and-milieu with the milieu circumjacent and synomorphic to the behavior" (p. 4). Purely physical (that is, behaviorless), perceptual (based on the meaning of the environment to the individual) or behavioral conceptions of the environment are rejected. Rather, the milieu surrounds or encloses the behavior (circumjacent) and there is a proper "fit" or "match" between the behavior and the milieu (synomorphic). "The present investigation is based upon the idea that complexity and detail [of the classroom] are more or less massive depending upon whether or not the investigator can identify the ecological 'wholes' which, in turn, bind and organize the event details. If analysis of the data separates events into molecular bits and eliminates their ecological anchorage, then the task of classifying and organizing the bits can, indeed, become enormous" (pp. 8–9).

Graphically, the model is:

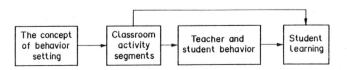

Procedures

1. Observe in two classrooms (third and fourth grades) for 29 hours across 19 days in order to field test methods and concepts. While in the classrooms use a Stenomask (a device that allows for silent dictation to a portable tape recorder) and timed photography (with a snapshot taken every 20 seconds) to make a record of classroom events. In the dictation time was noted every minute or so.
2. Select a sample of six third-grade classrooms. The six teachers were selected from 19 teachers initially observed so that at least two teachers were at the high and low ends on three dimensions: academic capability of pupils based on intelligence tests, novelty of the teacher's presentation, and the managerial efficiency of the teacher.
3   Use three observers in succession to observe in each of the classrooms for two full days. The approach described in step 1 (above) was used during the observations. Classroom materials such as reading assignments and worksheets that helped clarify the classroom activities also were collected.
4. Prepare written transcripts of the dictation.
5. Develop a set of rules to use in determining classroom segments. Use the rules to identify the classroom segments included in the written transcripts. Have several researchers identify the segments on selected transcripts and compare the segments identified.
6. Identify five dimensions on which each segment can be analyzed. These dimensions are: concern, teacher leadership pattern, group quality, pupil activity, and action sequencing.
7. Develop sets of categories to use in coding teacher behavior (from the transcripts) and pupil behavior (from the still photographs). Use multiple coders and compare their codings.
8. Summarize evidence on classroom segments, teacher behavior, and pupil behavior in terms of mean time and percentages.
9. Relate to evidence on classroom segments to evidence on teacher and pupil behavior.
10. Present and discuss results of the study.

Box 10.2   Summary of the Gump (1967) Study.

Following the pilot study, a sample of six third-grade classrooms was selected from a population of 19 classrooms. The classrooms chosen represented extremes in terms of pupil ability, the novelty of the teachers' presentations, and the managerial efficiency of the teacher. Each classroom was observed for two full days, with three observers alternating to complete the observations. Classroom materials such as reading assignments and worksheets were collected by the observers.

Written transcripts of the dictation were prepared and a set of rules was developed to aid in identifying classroom activity segments. To test out the rules, several researchers were asked to identify the segments on selected transcripts. The agreement among the researchers was quite high.

Five dimensions were identified on which each segment could be coded: concern, teacher leadership pattern, group quality, pupil activity, and action sequencing. Each segment was coded in terms of these dimensions. A set of categories was identified for the purpose of coding teacher behavior (from the transcripts) and pupil behavior (from the still photographs). The transcripts and still photographs were coded in terms of these categories.

Evidence pertaining to the five dimensions and the teacher and pupil behavior categories was summarized in terms of mean amounts of time and percentages. Finally, the evidence on the five segment dimensions was related to the evidence pertaining to the pupil and teacher behavior categories.

Several components of the Gump study are particularly important. First, the observers focused their attention on the teacher and the activities in which he or she was directly engaged; the camera was focused on the students. In addition, the observers provided a silent dictation of classroom events; they did not code on observation forms or write field notes. Since writing may distract an observer from the observational task at hand, silent dictation may provide a more accurate and complete description of the classroom. Second, multiple observers were used consecutively in the same classrooms. Because observation is fatiguing, the use of multiple observers is likely to enhance the accuracy of the records made by the observers. Third, and perhaps most importantly, the results of the study lend support to the existence of all six instructional dimensions in naturally occurring classrooms. Gump's study, then, provides an empirical basis for our theoretical perspective on classroom instruction.

Teaching Styles and Pupil Progress (Bennett, 1976)

Bennett begins his book by asserting that "it could be argued that in an ideal educational world new ideas and techniques would be subjected to objective evaluation before being implemented. But this is not an ideal world and practice often seems to be based on myth and assertion rather than objective evidence" (p. 1). As a consequence, the purpose of the study is to "provide evidence on such basic pedagogical questions as 'Do teaching methods (or styles as they are called in this book) have a differential effect on the academic progress of pupils?' and 'Do pupils of differing personality characteristics progress similarly when taught by different approaches?' " (p. xiii). (See Box 10.3.)

Purpose

"To provide evidence on such basic pedagogical questions as 'Do teaching methods (or styles as they are called in this book) have a differential effect on the academic progress of pupils?' and 'Do pupils of differing personality characteristics progress similarly when taught by different approaches?' " (p. xiii).

Framework/Model

A series of hypothesized interrelationships among teacher beliefs, teaching styles, pupil personality, pupil behaviors, and pupil learning outcomes form the framework within which the study was conducted. Teachers' aims and opinions are hypothesized to influence the teaching styles they assume or use. These teaching styles, in turn, are believed to directly influence student behavior. Furthermore, these teaching styles are hypothesized to have differential effects on the achievement of pupils with differing personality characteristics.

Graphically, the model is:

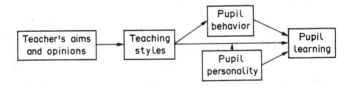

Procedures

PHASE 1

1. Identify the key features or elements that define "progressive" and "traditional" teachers (see Table 10.1). Based on these features develop a questionnaire to measure progressive (informal) and traditional (formal) teaching styles.

2. Administer the questionnaire to large sample of teachers believed to be representative of teachers in northwest England. Use cluster analysis to create typology of twelve teaching styles. Validate typology by observation and content analysis of pupil essays describing the teachers.

3. Collapse seven of the original 12 teaching styles into three categories: informal, mixed, and formal. Eliminate those styles which occurred infrequently.

4. Compare formal, informal, and mixed teachers in terms of their opinions concerning the aims of education, a variety of educational issues, and the strengths and weaknesses of formal and informal teaching methods.

PHASE 2

5. Identify 12 formal, 12 informal, and 13 mixed teachers. Teachers chosen were those whose profiles most closely matched the group profiles of formal, informal, and mixed teachers.

6. Administer reading, mathematics, and English tests to students at the end of the school year prior to the beginning of the study. Based on the test scores, place students into three achievement groups (high, middle, and low).

7. Administer a personality measure to the students in each teacher's classroom at the beginning of the study year. Based on the results of a cluster analysis, divide students into eight personality types.

8. During the year have students write imaginative and descriptive essays. Also during the year conduct observations in each teacher's classroom.

9. Administer the same battery of achievement tests approximately one year after the battery was initially administered.

10. Compare the achievement, behavior, and writing of students who were taught by the three groups of teachers. Also, compare the achievement, behavior, and writing of students with different initial achievement levels and of different personality types who were taught by the three groups of teachers.

11. Present and discuss the results of the study.

Box 10.3 Summary of the Bennett (1976) Study.

The study was conducted in two phases. The first phase began with the identification of the key elements of "progressive" and "traditional" teaching methods (see Table 10.1). A questionnaire was developed that incorporated these key elements and was administered to a large sample of primary school teachers. Based on the teachers' responses to a portion of the items on the questionnaire, twelve teaching styles were identified using

TABLE 10.1

Elements of Progressive and Traditional Teaching Methods

Progressive	Traditional
1 Integrated subject matter	1 Separate subject matter
2 Teacher as guide to educational experiences	2 Teacher as distributor of knowledge
3 Active pupil role	3 Passive pupil role
4 Pupils participate in curriculum planning	4 Pupils have no say in curriculum planning
5 Learning predominantly by discovery techniques	5 Accent on memory, practice and rote
6 External rewards and punishments not necessary, i.e. intrinsic motivation	6 External rewards used, e.g. grades, i.e. extrinsic motivation
7 Not too concerned with conventional academic standards	7 Concerned with academic standards
8 Little testing	8 Regular testing
9 Accent on cooperative group work	9 Accent on competition
10 Teaching not confined to classroom base	10 Teaching confined to classroom base
11 Accent on creative expression	11 Little emphasis on creative expression

Source: Bennett (1976).

cluster analysis. These twelve teaching styles were validated by making observations in the teachers' classrooms and asking pupils to write essays describing their teachers.

Five of the twelve teaching styles were found to occur very infrequently and the other seven styles were collapsed into three categories: formal, informal, and mixed pattern. Teachers were placed in one of these three categories based on their questionnaire responses. Comparisons among these three groups of teachers were made in terms of their opinions concerning the aims of education, various educational issues, and the strengths and weaknesses of formal and informal teaching methods.

The second phase of the study began with the identification of 12 formal, 12 informal and 13 mixed pattern teachers. These 37 teachers were chosen because the profile of their responses to the relevant questionnaire items matched most closely the group profiles of formal, informal and mixed pattern teachers. At the end of the school year prior to the study, students who were to be in these teachers' classes during the forthcoming school year were administered a battery of achievement tests. Three achievement groups were formed (high, medium, and low). At the beginning of the school year during which the second phase of the study was conducted, students were administered a series of personality measures. Based on a cluster analysis of these personality measures, eight personality types were identified.

Around the middle of the school year students were asked to write imaginative and descriptive stories. Near the end of the year, observations took place in each classroom. At the end of the study, the same achievement battery was administered to the students.

Comparisons of the achievement, behavior, and writing of students taught by the three groups of teachers were made. These comparisons were also made for students with different initial achievement levels and of different personality types.

Several of the components of the Bennett study are particularly note-worthy. First, the development of the questionnaire is a model to be followed by those intent on using questionnaires in their classroom research. The movement from the identification of key features that differentiate between the two primary teaching styles to the field testing of the instrument is systematic and thorough. Second, teaching styles were derived from the questionnaires based on responses of teachers in 871 schools. Because of the large sample size, reliable differentiation among the teaching styles was quite likely. Third, observational evidence and content analyses of essays written by students describing their teachers were used to substantiate and support the initial classification of teaching styles based on the questionnaire responses. Multiple sources of evidence enhance the validity of the evidence collected. Fourth, the concept of teaching styles was embedded within an overall quasi-causal model. The relationships of teaching styles with all of the other concepts in the model (e.g., teachers' aims and opinions, pupil behavior, pupil personality, pupil writing, and pupil achievement) was examined.

Experimental Study of Mathematics Instruction (Good and Grouws, 1979)

This study was based on the belief that findings from studies conducted in naturally-occurring classrooms could be translated into experimental programs for teachers that could increase their effectiveness in the class-room. Based on the results of previous studies of teacher effectiveness, several factors associated with increased student achievement were iden-tified. These factors were organized into two clusters: "performance expectations and time utilization" and "interaction between teachers and students." A training manual was prepared that incorporated recom-mendations for mathematics instruction based on the previous research findings. The study was intended to determine whether teachers could be taught to follow the recommendations included in the manual and whether these recommendations, if they were followed by teachers in the classroom, would lead to higher levels of student achievement.

A sample of 40 fourth-grade teachers was selected (see Box 10.4). The researchers met with these teachers to explain the study and to randomly assign them to experimental and control groups.

Purpose

To determine 1) whether teachers could be taught to use a set of behaviors derived from correlational research on teacher effectiveness, and 2) whether these behaviors, if they could be taught to the teachers, would result in higher levels of student achievement.

Framework/Model

The study is based on the assumption that findings from studies conducted in naturally-occurring classrooms can be translated into experimental programs designed for teachers that are intended to improve student learning. Based on the results of a previously conducted study of teacher effectiveness in fourth-grade mathematics, several factors associated with higher levels of student achievement were identified. These factors were placed into two clusters: "performance expectations and time utilization" and "interaction between teachers and students." In combination, these clusters were hypothesized to influence student achievement.

Graphically, the model is:

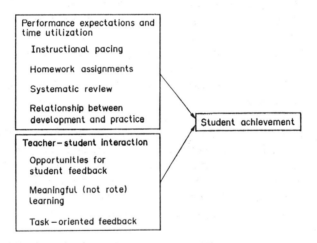

Procedures

1. Based on the results of a prior study (as well as the reviews of other relevant studies), identify those patterns or clusters of variables that differentiate more effective from less effective teachers.

2. Prepare a training manual that incorporates these patterns or clusters of variables.

3. Identify a sample of 40 fourth-grade teachers. Discuss the study with them and then randomly assign the teachers to experimental or control groups. No two teachers in any school are in the experimental *and* the control groups. The control group teachers were informed that they would receive the details of the experimental treatment at the end of the study. The experimental teachers attended a 90-minute meeting concerning the program to be implemented. They were given the manual and asked to read it and plan for the implementation of the program. Two weeks after the study began, the experimental teachers attended another 90-minute meeting during which time they could ask questions about the program.

4. Prior to the study, administer an achievement test, a learning style inventory, and an attitude toward mathematics survey to the students. Also administer to the teachers an instrument measuring their beliefs and preferences concerning mathematics instruction.

5. During the study (which lasted about three months) observe each teacher on six occasions. Collect evidence concerning the extent to which important aspects of the treatment were being implemented. Based on the evidence, estimate the "fidelity of implementation" of the treatment.

6. At the end of the study, re-administer the battery of tests which were administered prior to the study.

7. Compare residual achievement gain scores of the students in the experimental and control groups. Divide both teachers and students into four typologies and compare the impact of the treatment on various types of teachers and students in terms of residual achievement gain scores.

8. Compute correlations between frequency of occurrence of selected teacher behaviors and residual achievement gain scores. Also, compare the relationship between teacher behaviors and residual achievement gain scores for students of various socioeconomic backgrounds.

9. Present and discuss the results of the study.

Box 10.4 Summary of the Good and Grouws (1979) Study.

Those teachers in the control group were told they would receive the details of the experimental treatment at the end of the study. The experimental teachers attended a 90-minute meeting conducted by the researchers during which time they received the manual. They were told to read the manual and plan for the implementation of the instructional program described in it. Two weeks after the study began another meeting was held with the experimental teachers to answer questions and offer clarifications.

Prior to the beginning of the study, students were administered an achievement test, a learning style inventory, and an attitude toward mathematics survey. A questionnaire measuring teachers' beliefs and preferences concerning mathematics instruction was given to the teachers.

During the study, each teacher was observed on six occasions. The primary purpose of the observations was to examine the extent to which the experimental teachers were implementing the program as it was designed. The observations also provided evidence as to the degree to which the control teachers were implementing components of the program on their own.

At the end of the study, the test, inventory, and survey were re-administered to the students. Residual gain scores were estimated for each student and the average residual gain score for each class was computed. Both teachers and students were divided into four typologies; the teachers' typologies were based on their beliefs about mathematics instruction, and the students' typologies were based on the learning style preferences.

Comparisons of the average residual gain scores for students in the experimental and control groups were made. Comparisons of the average residual gain scores for different types of students and different types of teachers in each group were also made. Correlations between the frequency of occurrence of selected teacher behaviors and residual gain scores were computed for the total sample as well as for subsamples that were formed based on the socioeconomic backgrounds of the students.

Several components of the Good and Grouws study are worth noting. First, the treatment given to the experimental teachers is best considered a "minimum" treatment. In light of Cuban's (1984) analysis of the stability of teaching methods, strategies, or styles over the past several decades, one must question the extent to which the ways in which teachers instruct their students can be significantly altered by three contact hours and a 45-page manual. Second, however, Good and Grouws examined the extent to which the experimental teachers actually used the instructional program as it was intended to be used by the researchers. Evidence collected during observation in the classrooms allowed them to estimate the "fidelity of implementation." This observational evidence also provided Good and Grouws with an understanding of the actual instructional differences between the teachers in the two groups. Rather than attributing differences in achievement to a somewhat vague "treatment," achievement differences that do exist can be more precisely attributed to particular aspects or components of the treatment provided that such observational evidence is available. Third, concerns for the possible differential effectiveness of the treatment for different students and different teachers were expressed and considered.

Students were classified according to their learning styles and their socioeconomic status; teachers were classified according to their beliefs about mathematics instruction. In the event that differences between the treatment and control groups were not generally evident, differences between the treatment and control groups for particular types of teachers or students could be examined.

How Schools Work (Barr and Dreeben, 1983)

The study examines the formation of reading groups within first-grade classrooms, the impact of these groups on the pace with which instruction is provided to students, and the effect of the pace of instruction on reading achievement. Barr and Dreeben contend that their research strategy has not been to "devise new measurement and statistical techniques or to test hypotheses in the conventional sense. Rather, it has been directed primarily at recasting the ways in which educational effects have been conceptualized" (p. 4).

The study began with the retrieval of evidence that had been previously collected in fifteen classrooms in six schools in three school districts (see Box 10.5). The evidence had been collected at three time periods during a single year. Measures of student aptitudes, student background, and class size were collected prior to the school year. Measures of basal word knowledge, reading group membership, and pace or content coverage were gathered in mid-year. Finally, measures of basal word knowledge, phonics knowledge, vocabulary and comprehension, and pace or content coverage were collected at the end of the school year. Additional evidence concerning years of teaching experience, difficulty of the reading material, daily class time, and time allocated to instruction in basal reading and phonics was gathered at various times throughout the study.

Purpose

To "develop a formulation about how schools and school systems work, with particular emphasis on classroom instruction" (p. 4). "Our strategy has not been to devise new measurement and statistical techniques or to test hypotheses in the conventional sense. Rather, it has been directed primarily at recasting the ways in which educational effects have been conceptualized" (p. 4).

Framework/Model

Two concepts lie at the heart of this framework: the formation of within-class instructional groups, and the pace at which the students are taught once placed in those groups. The decision to form within-class instructional groups (and, subsequently, the number of groups to form) is the teacher's response to the variation among students in terms of their aptitudes. The mean aptitudes of the group (rather than the aptitude of the individual students) determines the pace at which instruction proceeds and, as a consequence, the amount of content that is covered during any given time period. Pace, or content coverage, is influenced by three factors: the availability of materials, the amount of time available to teach particular topics or content, and the amount of time the teacher supervises the students. Finally, pace, or content coverage, influences student achievement. Graphically,

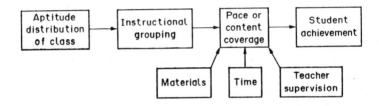

Procedures

1. Retrieve evidence collected previously in 15 classrooms in six schools in three districts. Two schools were located in each district and, with the exception of one school, two or more classrooms were located in each school.

2. Examine evidence collected at three time periods: at the beginning of the school year, about the middle of the school year, and at the end of the school year. Measures of student aptitudes, student background variables, and class size were obtained prior to the school year. Measures of basal word knowledge, reading group membership, and pace or content coverage were collected in mid-year. Measures of basal word knowledge, phonics knowledge, vocabulary and comprehension, and pace or content coverage were gathered at the end of the school year.

3. During the study additional information was collected concerning:
   a. years of teaching experience,
   b. difficulty of the reading material,
   c. daily class time, and
   d. time allocated to reading instruction in basal reading and phonics.

4. Create three data sets based on the available information. The first data set pertained to individual students. The second data set included members of the instructional groups. The third data set contained the 15 classrooms.
5. Examine the relationships of aptitude, content coverage, difficulty of the reading material, and allocated time with student learning (e.g., basal word knowledge, reading vocabulary, and reading comprehension).
6. Examine the relationships of mean class aptitude, the variation in class aptitude, the skewness of the aptitude distribution, the number of low aptitude children, and the size of the class with the formation of instructional groups.
7. Calculate three indexes of group configuration: size inequality index, discreteness index, and group range. Examine the correlations of these indexes with class size, mean aptitude, variation in aptitude, skewness, and number of low aptitude children.
8. Examine the changes in the grouping pattern from fall to spring.
9. Examine relationships of group mean aptitude, difficulty of basal material, years of teaching experience, basal group size, basal instructional time, basal supervision time, and size of class remainder with basal word coverage and phonics coverage.
10. Examine relationship of pacing or content coverage and basal and phonics achievement.
11. Present and discuss results of the study.

Box 10.5   Summary of the Barr and Dreeben (1983) Study.

Three data sets were created. The first set pertained to individual students; the second, to students in the same reading group; and the third, to students in the same classroom. Using the various data sets, several sets of relationships among the variables were investigated, each set of relationships formulated in the context of a causal model. First, the relationship of aptitude, pacing or content coverage, difficulty of reading material, and allocated time with measures of student learning were examined. Second, the relationship of mean class aptitude, variation in class aptitude, skewness of the aptitude distribution, number of low aptitude children, and the size of the class with the formation of instructional groups was considered. Third, the relationship of mean group aptitude, difficulty of basal material, years of teaching experience, basal group size, basal instructional time, basal supervision time, and size of class remainder with basal word coverage and phonics coverage was examined. The relationship of pacing or content coverage and basal and phonics achievement was investigated and the results of all analyses were summarized.

Several of the components of the Barr and Dreeben study are of importance. First, the relationships among three of the six components of instruction are examined empirically. These components are task demands (basal knowledge, phonics knowledge, vocabulary, and comprehension), instructional grouping (the number and composition of reading groups), and time/pacing/coverage (in fact, both time and pacing or content coverage are included). Subject matter is held constant (reading) as is the instructional format (with the teacher working with one group of students while the students in the other groups work on their assignments). The only component not studied or controlled, then, is the specific teacher behaviors or teacher-student interactions in the group setting. Second, data sets at various levels of aggregation are included: individual, reading group, and entire class. These different data sets permit a variety of intriguing questions to be addressed, questions such as whether the pace of instruction is more strongly related to the aptitudes of the individual students or the mean aptitude of the groups in which individual students are members. Third, evidence was collected at multiple points in time. As a consequence, changes in the various components of instruction that may occur over time can be examined. In addition, the collection of evidence over time is important if the evidence is to be analyzed using path analytic techniques. Fourth, and pertaining to path analysis, all of the relationships among the variables were explored within the context of *a priori* causal models. The value of causal models in research on teaching has already been discussed (see Chapter 9). Such models have the same value in research on instruction.

How Teachers Taught (Cuban, 1984)

Cuban was intrigued by the apparent stability of teacher-centered instruction over the past century despite "mighty efforts to move toward student-centered instruction" (p. 5). He offers three explanations for its stability. First, schools are a form of social control and sorting. Teacher-centered instruction produces student behaviors expected by the larger society. Second, the organizational structure of the school and the classroom contribute to the stability of teacher-centered instruction. Third, the culture of teaching "tilts toward stability" (p. 10). That is, those who enter teaching in essence teach the way in which they were taught. Two explanations are offered for any change in methods that may have occurred over time. However, these explanations are offered almost apologetically. (See Box 10.6).

Two historical periods were selected for study. They were selected because they were times during which "reformers tried vigorously to install student-centered teaching practices" (p. 7). Urban and rural school districts were identified that were the most likely to have engaged in student-centered teaching practices during these two time periods.

Purpose

"To determine how stable certain teaching behaviors were decade after decade in the face of mighty efforts to move toward student-centered instruction—not [to determine] the relative value of teacher-centered instruction in achieving student outcomes" (p. 5).

Framework/Model

Three possible reasons for the stability of teacher-centered instruction over time are suggested. First, schools are a form of social control and sorting. Teacher-centered instruction produces student behaviors expected by the larger society. Second, the organizational structure of the school and classroom are responsible for the stability of teacher-centered instruction. Third, the culture of teaching "tilts toward stability" (p. 10). People who become teachers tend to use those practices that they observed in the teachers they had. Two possible reasons are given for a movement from teacher-centered to student-centered instruction. First, ideas about child development, the role of the school, classroom authority, and the place of subject matter in instruction determine teaching practices. As these ideas change, teaching practices change. Second, effective implementation of novel teaching practices increases the likelihood that these practices will replace the more traditional ones.

Graphically, the model is:

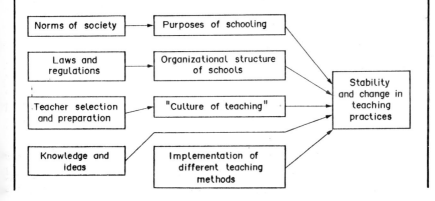

Procedures

1.   Select two historical periods for study: 1920s and 1930s, and 1965–1975. The two periods were selected because they were times during which "reformers tried vigorously to install student-centered teaching practices" (p. 7).
2.   Identify urban and rural school districts during each of these periods that were most likely to embrace, endorse, and use student-centered teaching practices.
3.   Locate primary sources from these school districts that pertain to either of the two historical periods. These sources included:
     a. photographs of teachers and students in classes,
     b. textbooks and tests that were used by teachers and students,
     c. student recollections of their experiences in classrooms,
     d. teacher reports of how they taught,
     e. reports from persons who visited the classrooms (e.g., journalists, parents, and administrators),
     g. student writings in school newspapers and yearbooks,
     h. research studies of teacher behavior in classrooms, and
     i. descriptions of classroom architecture, size of rooms, desk designs and placement.
4.   Create five criteria or dimensions that differentiate "teacher-centered" instruction, "student-centered" instruction, and "mixed patterns" of instruction. The dimensions are: class arrangement, group instruction, classroom talk, class activities, and student movement.
5.   For each dimension, identify a set of observable indicators that are associated with "teacher-centered," "student-centered," and "mixed patterns" of teaching. For example, "movable desks and chairs in rows facing teacher's desk and/or blackboard" is an indicator of "class arrangement" associated with "teacher-centered" instruction.
6.   Using the dimensions and indicators, analyze the primary sources of evidence that were located (see step 3). Each classroom for which a primary source of evidence is available is classified as "teacher-centered," "student-centered," or "mixed patterns" on each of the five dimensions.
7.   Compute the percentages of classrooms classified as "teacher-centered," "student-centered," and "mixed patterns" for each of the five dimensions. Indicate the numbers of classrooms on which the percentages were based.

8. Examine the similarities and differences in these percentages across elementary and secondary schools, urban and rural schools, and the two time periods (1920s and 1930s, and 1965–1975).
9. Present and discuss the results of the study. Use excerpts from primary sources for emphasis and illustration.

Box 10.6 Summary of the Cuban (1984) Study.

Primary sources of evidence from these school districts that were related to either of the two time periods were located and examined. These sources included photographs, textbooks, reports, research studies, and descriptions of classroom architecture and arrangements.

Five criteria or dimensions that differentiated among "teacher-centered" instruction, "student-centered" instruction, and "mixed patterns of instruction" were identified. In addition, sets of observable indicators were established for each criterion or dimension that would enable each classroom for which evidence was available to be classified into one of the three categories of instruction. This classification scheme was then used with all of the primary sources of evidence that were available.

The percentages of classrooms that were placed in each of the three categories of instruction on each of the five criteria or dimensions were computed separately for the two time periods, rural and urban schools, and elementary and secondary schools. Similarities and differences in these percentages across time periods, school location, and school level were examined and discussed.

Several of the components of the Cuban study are noteworthy. First, Cuban establishes explicit relationships among the primary concepts ("teacher-centered," "student-centered," and "mixed patterns"), the criteria or dimensions used to differentiate among the concepts ("class arrangement," "group instruction," "classroom talk," "class activities," and "student movement"), and the indicators related to each criterion or dimension. Thus, the relationship between the evidence and the underlying conceptual framework is quite clear. Second, only primary sources of evidence are used. The use of primary sources enhances the credibility of the evidence. Third, the generalizability of the results is enhanced by comparing the results across different time periods, school locations, and school levels. The use of purposeful sampling permits the limits of the generalizability of results and conclusions to be examined.

Synopses of Other Studies

As was the case for studies of teaching, numerous studies investigating various components of instruction have been conducted over the past several decades. In this section we shall briefly review three of the studies we think are quite important.

Dahllöf (1971)

Dahllöf re-analyzed three separate studies (two from Sweden and one from the United States) in order to test a general paradigm for research on

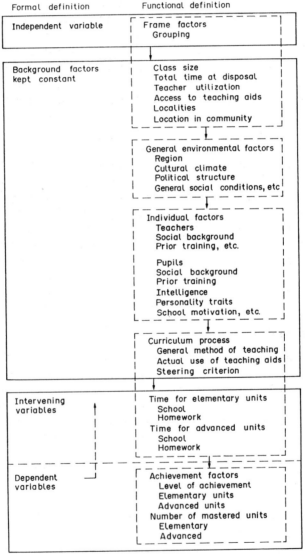

FIG 10.1   A model for research on grouping (from Dahllöf, 1971).

grouping that outlines the relationships among grouping, curriculum, teaching processes, and student achievement. This general paradigm is displayed in Figure 10.1. In summary, grouping practices affect the ability distribution of a class of students which, in turn, determines the ability level of the steering group (that is, that group of students teachers use to pace instruction). The ability level of the steering group influences the pacing of instruction which, ultimately, influences student achievement.

To test his conceptual model, Dahllöf compared the achievement of students who were assigned to ability-grouped classes (either high-ability or low-ability classes) with those who were enrolled in heterogenous classes. He also examined teacher reports on the use of teaching methods and content coverage (e.g., elementary topics, advanced topics). Based on the results from these two analyses, he offers his "theory of steering" to explain the results. He formulated a mathematical model which incorporates his major variables and suggests several hypotheses that could be derived from the model.

Dahllöf's study is important for two reasons. First, like Barr and Dreeben, Dahllöf suggests that instruction must be understood within the context of the distributional properties of classrooms. That is, instructional decisions are made based on groups and subgroups of students, rather than on individual students or the entire class (e.g., the "average" student). Second, Dahllöf introduced the concept of "frame factor," an important concept in understanding the stability of teaching and instruction over time. Briefly, a frame factor is a characteristic of the school environment, which although modifiable, is in place for a long period of time. As such, the environmental characteristic frames the conditions under which instruction and teaching take place.

Fisher et al. (1978)

The *Beginning Teacher Evaluation Study (BTES)* began with a general planning year during 1972–73. The activities of the planning year (Phase I) as well as a subsequent year of field work (Phase II) were conducted by McDonald and Elias (1975/76), representing the Educational Testing Service. The activities of Phase III (which lasted from 1974 through 1978) were completed by a group of researchers at the Far West Laboratory for Educational Research and Development. Phase III was divided into two parts: Phase III–A (from 1974 through 1976) and Phase III–B (from 1976 through 1978). The final report of Phase III–B is summarized below.

The purpose of the study was to evaluate a particular instructional model. According to the model (which was displayed graphically in Chapter 6), student achievement is directly influenced by two factors: student aptitude and student classroom behavior. Furthermore, the most important type of student classroom behavior is that which is task-oriented, content-oriented, and success-oriented. This type of behavior can be defined in a time metric and is referred to as Academic Learning Time (ALT). Specifically, ALT is defined as the amount of time a student spends engaged in a task that is directly related to a defined criterion, and, furthermore, *is achieving success on that task*. According to the model, teaching behaviors and instructional processes will influence student achievement indirectly through their direct influence on ALT.

Twenty-five second-grade classes and 22 fifth-grade classes participated in the study. Student achievement in reading and mathematics, attitudes toward mathematics and reading, and attitudes toward school were assessed at three times during the study. Based on the initial achievement testing, target students falling between the 30th and 60th percentile ranks on both reading and mathematics tests were identified. Within each classroom three target boys and three target girls were selected for observation.

Several different sources of evidence were used: direct observation, teacher logs, interviews, and rating scales. In addition to the quantitative analysis (which involved correlation and regression analysis), a qualitative investigation (involving verbal descriptions of classrooms based on evidence gathered using interviews and field notes) was conducted. The qualitative part of the study focused on eight second-grade classes that differed in the mean residual gain scores.

Phase III–B of the BTES is important for two reasons. First, the study single-handedly introduced the concept of academic learning time into the vocabulary of classroom researchers. Second, as specified in the underlying conceptual model, teaching does not directly influence student achievement. This contention is consistent with our view of instruction that includes teacher-student interactions as but one component of instruction. Two other components of instruction are hidden within academic learning time. "Time/coverage/pacing" is related to the content dimension of ALT. "Task demands" is inherent in both the task dimension and the success dimension.

Stodolsky (1988)

The purpose of this study was to examine the degree to which "what is being taught . . . shapes instructional activity" (p. 1). In addition, "particular attention is paid to the conditions under which different intellectual goals are pursued" (p. 2).

Observations were conducted in 20 elementary mathematics classes and 19 elementary social studies classes. Fifteen of the teachers observed taught both mathematics and social studies. The observations were made by eleven field workers using a semi-structured recording system. The primary emphasis of the recording system was the activities in place in the classroom. The role of the teacher in those activities and the students' involvement in the activities also were noted. In addition to the observations, all teachers were interviewed.

Activity segments were identified and analyzed in terms of a variety of dimensions: instructional format, pacing, cognitive level, student behavior, teacher leadership role, feedback, expected student interaction, task options, student location, and student involvement. Each dimension was divided into several categories which, in essence, defined the dimension. For example, "solve/desk," "question/answer," "blackboard/watch," "checking work," and "listening" were five of the thirteen categories associated with the student behavior dimension. The evidence for each of these dimensions was summarized in terms of the percentages of all segments in which each category was observed to be present. These percentages were computed separately for reading and mathematics.

The Stodolsky study is important for two reasons. First, it is perhaps the most complete study of the components of instruction conducted to date. Evidence on all six components of instruction was gathered during the study. Second, the study uses a semi-structured observation system. Such systems are somewhat rare in classroom research, with most systems lying at either end of the structured-unstructured continuum (as mentioned in Chapter 5).

Comparisons of the Six Primary Studies

The six studies detailed in this chapter tend to be more different than they are similar. Nonetheless, some similarities among them do exist. A comparison of the six studies is shown in Table 10.2.

Purpose of the Study

With the exception of the Cuban study and to a lesser extent the Gump study, the remaining studies are associational. The Johnson and the Good and Grouws studies are experimental, seeking to establish causal relationships between components of instruction and student achievement. The Barr and Dreeben study also seeks to establish causal relationships, but in a non-experimental setting. Path analysis is used to estimate the strength of relationships among the various instructional components as well as to infer causality. The Bennett study examines differences among teachers who use different teaching styles or methods in terms of the achievement of their students. The extent to which these different teaching styles or methods may be more or less effective for different types of students also is examined.

Keys to Improving Student Learning

Quite different keys for improvement are identified by the different researchers. Johnson suggests that teachers must learn to experiment in

TABLE 10.2

A Comparison of Studies of Instruction Along Seven Dimensions

	Studies		
Dimensions	Johnson	Gump	Bennett
Purpose of Study	Associational	Descriptive & Associational	Associational
Key(s) to Improving Student Learning	Having evidence on efficiency of various teaching methods	Understanding behavior settings & classroom activity segments	Increased use of formal or "mixed" teaching styles
Extent of Manipulation	Varying methods used to teach different science experiments	None	None
Sampling	CONV ($n=3$)	PRPS ($n=6$) [Student ability, teacher's presentation, teacher's management]	PRPS ($n=37$) [Formal, informal, and "mixed" styles]
Sources of Evidence	TEST	AUDIO TRANS DOEX	TEST SOBS DOEX
Nature of Evidence	MEANS	FREQ/% MEANS	FREQ/% MEANS MEDIAN GRAPH
Analysis of Evidence	COMPSTAT	CORR	COMPSTAT OTHR (Cluster analysis)

	Studies		
Dimensions	Good and Grouws	Barr and Dreeben	Cuban
Purpose of Study	Associational	Associational	Descriptive
Key(s) to Improving Student Learning	Increasing performance expectations, time utilization, and improved teacher-student interaction	Increasing content coverage or pacing	None

Table 10.2 *(continued)*

Dimensions	Good and Grouws	Barr and Dreeben	Cuban
		Studies	
Extent of Manipulation	Two 90-minute sessions and training manual	None	None
Sampling	CONV (*n*=40)	CONV (*n*=15)	PRPS (*n*=637+) [two time periods, urban vs. rural, elementary vs. secondary]
Sources of Evidence	SOBS TEST	INTR NOTES TEST	DOEX
Nature of Evidence	MEANS	MEANS FREQ/%	FREQ/% EXCRPT
Analysis of Evidence	COMPSTAT CORR OTHR (Cluster analysis)	CORR PATH	COMPARE

Key to abbreviations used in Table 10.2

Sampling
CONV = convenience
PRPS = purposeful

Sources of Evidence
AUDIO = audiotapes
DOEX = documents/exhibits
NOTES = field notes
INTR = interviews
SOBS = structured observation
TEST = tests
TRANS = transcripts

Nature of Evidence
FREQ/% = frequencies, percentages
MEANS = means (and/or standard deviations)
MEDIAN = medians (and/or ranges)
EXCRPT = written excerpts from observations or interviews
GRAPH = graphical displays

Analysis of Evidence
CORR = correlations
COMPARE = comparisons between groups using human inference
COMPSTAT = comparisons between groups using statistical inference (e.g., *t*-test, ANOVA, chi-square, ANCOVA)
PATH = path analysis
OTHR = other

their classrooms and make instructional decisions based on objective evidence rather than on the basis of "conditioned emotional response" (p. 104). Gump suggests an understanding of meaningful classroom units (such as classroom activity segments) is necessary if student learning is to be improved. Such units "bind and organize" the details. Without such units, events are separated into "molecular bits" which make a comprehensive understanding difficult. Bennett suggests that formal (and perhaps mixed formal and informal) teaching methods hold the key to student learning. Good and Grouws suggest that increasing performance expectations and time utilization, and improving teacher-student interactions (by providing increased opportunities for student feedback, meaningful learning, and teacher task-orientated feedback) are the keys to improved learning. Finally, Barr and Dreeben contend that increasing the content coverage or the pace of instruction is likely to enhance student learning.

Extent of Manipulation

As can be expected, manipulation is present in the two experimental studies. Johnson manipulated the methods that were used to teach different science experiments, while Good and Grouws manipulated a series of instructional and teaching variables by meeting with one group of teachers and providing them with a training manual. Furthermore, they examined the success of their manipulation by conducting observations in the teachers' classrooms.

Sampling

Convenience samples were used in both experimental studies. Purposeful samples were included in the majority of the other studies. Gump chose classrooms and teachers that differed along three dimensions: student ability, teacher's presentation, and teacher's management. Bennett identified three groups of teachers who differed in terms of their teaching style as reported by the teachers on a questionnaire. The specific teachers selected were those most like the group profiles on the responses to the various questions. Cuban selected time periods and schools that were most likely to exemplify student-centered instruction. Among the non-experimental studies, only Barr and Dreeben used a convenience sample.

Sources of Evidence

A wide variety of sources of evidence was used in the study. Achievement tests were used in the majority of the studies. Structured observation systems were used in two of the studies (Bennett, Good and Grouws), but in neither case did observation serve as a primary source of evidence.

Bennett used observation to confirm or verify the teaching styles identified using his questionnaire. Good and Grouws used observation to confirm or verify that those teachers who received the training manual and training sessions were behaving in accordance with the recommendations included in the manual and differently from the teachers in the control group. Documents in the form of historical photographs, records, and reports (Cuban), photographs (Gump), and essays written by students (Bennett) were also used as a source of evidence. Questionnaires, used extensively in studies of teachers and teaching, were not used at all in these six studies of instruction.

Nature of Evidence

As in the case of studies of teaching, quantitative evidence predominates. Mean scores and standard deviations were reported in all studies except Cuban. Frequencies and percentages were reported in all of the non-experimental studies. Excerpts from written documents were used only by Cuban, while graphical displays were used only by Bennett.

Analysis of Evidence

Consistent with the nature of the evidence, standard statistical tests are the rule in studies of instruction. Only Cuban did not use inferential statistical techniques. Correlational analysis, analysis of variance, cluster analysis, and path analysis all were used in at least one study.

Recommendations for Research on Instruction

Several of the recommendations made in the context of research on teachers and research on teaching also apply here and are illustrated by the studies reviewed in this chapter. The use of pilot studies to enhance the quality of the research (Gump), the use of multiple sources of evidence to corroborate findings and support interpretations (Bennett), the need to control or estimate the effects of confounding or extraneous variables to increase the validity of interpretations (Johnson), and the use of causal models to plan studies, select appropriate analytic techniques, and move beyond description to explanation (Barr and Dreeben) have all been discussed in one or both of the previous chapters. In addition, however, three more general recommendations concerning the study of instruction can be offered:

1. An increase in studies which include most if not all of the components of instruction is sorely needed. All too frequently, studies of instruction have focused on only one or two components, either neglecting the other components or ignoring them (by holding them constant). Early studies traditionally used this approach. Johnson, for example, simultaneously

varied instructional format and grouping arrangements to create his three treatment conditions. Subject matter and time, pacing, and coverage were held constant. Task demands were equated across treatment groups since the same experiments were given to all students. Classroom behaviors and interactions, however, were allowed to vary. In studies of instruction which include multiple classrooms and teachers, this variation would likely find its way into the error term of the statistical analysis.

If instruction is defined in terms of six primary components, then studies of instruction should routinely include these components (e.g., Stodolsky). In addition, studies that address the relationships among the components would greatly enhance our understanding of classroom instruction (e.g., Barr and Dreeben, Gump).

2. Even in those studies in which the emphasis is on a single component (or perhaps two components), the other components should be considered as the study is planned. These components become extraneous factors that can confound both the interpretation and generalization of the results. As mentioned in Chapter 1, for example, instruction contextualizes teaching. Thus, as studies of teaching are designed, concerns for task demands, instructional format, grouping arrangement, time/pacing/coverage, and, perhaps, subject matter should be considered. As we shall see in the next chapter, the relationship of many of these other components of instruction with student achievement is substantially stronger than that between teacher behavior and classroom interactions and student achievement.

Similarly, researchers who plan studies of time, pacing, and coverage would also do well to consider the other components. Are members of different groups spending the same amount of time with the teacher, or covering the same amount of content at roughly the same pace? Who or what is pacing the instruction? In recitation-type formats teachers pace the instruction, whereas in seatwork-type formats students pace themselves. What are the task demands inherent in the curriculum and instruction and how much time is likely needed for students to achieve those demands? How much time is allocated to the learning of this particular subject matter and do these time allocations communicate to students the value (or lack of value) attached to the subject matter? What is taking place in the classroom during this allocated time? How much structure is provided by the teacher? How many student-initiated queries or responses occur? All of these questions are reasonable for consideration by those planning studies of time, pacing, and coverage.

3. Evidence pertaining to instruction can exist at multiple levels (student, group, and classroom). Furthermore, groups may be formal (as in reading groups) or informal (as in steering groups). Creating data sets and analyzing the evidence at these various levels is likely to yield a more complete understanding of instruction. A variety of sophisticated statistical techniques is available for this purpose (see Chapter 4).

Closing Comments

The six studies reviewed in this chapter represent a variety of conceptualizations of instruction and a variety of research plans and techniques. Studies including multiple components of instruction have been reviewed as have studies including a single, often confounded component. Even when the studies have addressed the same issue (e.g., teaching methods), the approach taken has varied from experimental to naturalistic to historical. More complex and complete studies of instruction are needed before we are likely to understand and improve life in classrooms.

11

Reviewing the Research Reviews

Much of the recent research on teachers, teaching, and instruction has its roots in a meeting that took place on February 26, 1950, in Atlantic City, New Jersey. The primary purpose of this meeting was to discuss criteria that could be used to identify effective teachers and teaching. A Committee on the Criteria of Teacher Effectiveness was appointed shortly after this meeting and subsequently issued two reports (Barr et al., 1952; Barr et al., 1953). In 1957, Professor N. L. Gage was asked to prepare a plan for a handbook of research on teaching. Some six years later, the *Handbook of Research on Teaching* was published (Gage, 1963b). Flanders and Simon (1969) referred to the *Handbook* as the "most important single publication with regard to teaching effectiveness since the third edition of the *Encyclopedia of Educational Research*" (p. 1423). And it was that!

In contrast to the *Encyclopedia* which devoted 41 of its 1564 pages to topics such as "instruction," "methods of teaching," "teacher competencies," "teacher effectiveness," and the "prediction of teacher effectiveness," the *Handbook of Research on Teaching* devoted 813 of its 1172 pages to the study of teachers, teaching, and instruction in general, and the remaining 359 pages to the study of teachers, teaching, and instruction at particular grade levels and in specific subject matters. In many ways, the *Handbook* legitimized teachers, teaching, and instruction as fields of study within education.

If the *Handbook* could be said to have legitimized the study of teachers, teaching, and instruction, the book written by Dunkin and Biddle (1974) about a decade later certainly popularized it. Relying on reports of original research studies, many of them unpublished papers and doctoral dissertations, Dunkin and Biddle produced an impressive set of "boxes" which summarized the research findings on a variety of important topics: classroom climate, management and control, the classroom as a social system, knowledge and intellect, logic and linguistics, and sequential patterns of classroom behavior.

Initially, we intended to replicate Dunkin and Biddle's review strategy. That is, we intended to locate reports of original research studies and, from these studies, produce a set of "boxes" which would update and expand on those produced by Dunkin and Biddle. We abandoned this strategy in short order for two reasons. First, original research studies on teachers, teaching, and instruction proliferated during the decade of the 1970s, making the task of reviewing such studies virtually impossible. This proliferation was readily predictable from Dunkin and Biddle's review. Of their more than 350 references, 119 (or about one-third of them) were from the 1970s, despite the fact that the decade was only about one-third over when the book was written. Subsequently, the decade of the 1970s produced such a large scale studies as the Texas Teacher Effectiveness Project (Brophy and Evertson, 1974; Evertson and Brophy, 1974), the Beginning Teacher Evaluation Study (Fisher et al., 1978), the Instructional Dimensions Study (Cooley and Leinhardt, 1980), and the Observational Research and Classroom Learning Evaluation Studies (ORACLE) (Galton et al., 1980).

Second, during the time that we were planning this book, two major works appeared on the educational scene. The first was the *Handbook of Research on Teaching, Third Edition* (Wittrock, 1986); the other was *The International Encyclopedia of Teaching and Teacher Education* (Dunkin, 1987a). The review chapters or entries pertaining to teachers, teaching, and instruction that appeared in these two volumes were very complete and comprehensive. Our reviews of original studies would likely be a duplication of effort. As a consequence, a decision was made to conduct a review of the reviews, rather than a review of original research studies. This review of reviews was supplemented by our knowledge gained from the original research studies included in the previous three chapters.

We recognize that this decision is not without its drawbacks. Primary sources of evidence are, in essence, replaced by secondary sources with a concomitant loss of precision. In order to counteract the drawbacks to the degree possible, a standard procedure was used to review the reviews and to arrive at generalizations concerning our current state of knowledge about teachers, teaching, and instruction. The reviews included in our review are listed in Table 11.1; the procedure we followed in reviewing them is shown in Table 11.2.

In Table 11.1 the reviews are listed in reverse chronological order. As can be seen in this table, the reviews that we consulted appeared in *The International Encyclopedia of Teaching and Teacher Education,* the three editions of the *Handbook of Research on Teaching,* and the three most recent editions of the *Encyclopedia of Educational Research.*

The procedure we used to conduct our review was relatively straight-forward (see Table 11.2). We began by identifying those chapters of the handbooks or entries of the encyclopedias that dealt primarily with teachers, teaching, or instruction in some general sense. Chapters or entries focusing on particular subject matters or grade levels were excluded at this point in the process. Next, within each chapter and entry that was retained, we identified those portions that most directly addressed the relationships of

TABLE 11.1

Listing of Reviews

Dunkin, M. J. (Ed.) (1987a). *The International Encyclopedia of Teaching and Teacher Education.* Oxford: Pergamon Press.
    Barnes, J. Teaching Experience, pp. 608–612.
    Barr, R. Content Coverage, pp. 364–368.
    Biddle, B. J. Teacher Roles, pp. 625–634.
    Biddle, B. J. and Dunkin, M. J. Effects of Teaching, pp. 119–124.
    Braun, C. Teachers' Expectations, pp. 598–605.
    Calfee, R. C. and Piontkowski, D. C. Grouping for Teaching, pp. 225–232.
    Doenau, S. J. Soliciting, pp. 407–413.
    Doenau, S. J. Structuring, pp. 398–407.
    Doyle, W. Paradigms for Research, pp. 113–119.
    Dunkin, M. J. Lesson Formats, pp. 263–266.
    Gump, P. V. Activities: Structures and Functions, pp. 452–457.
    Levis, D. S. Teachers' Personality, pp. 585–589.
    Medley, D. M. Criteria for Evaluating Teaching, pp. 169–181.
    Posner, G. J. Pacing and Sequencing, pp. 266–272.
    Rosenshine, B. Direct Instruction, pp. 257–262.
    Shavelson, R. J. Interactive decision-making, pp. 491–493.
    Shavelson, R. J. Planning, pp. 483–486.
    Shavelson, R. J. Teachers' Judgments, pp. 486–490.
    Slavin, R. E. Small Group Methods, pp. 237–243.
    Soar, R. S. and Soar, R. M. Classroom Climate, pp. 336–342.
    Withall, J. Teacher-centred and Learner-centred Teaching, pp. 327–336.
    Zahorik, J. A. Reacting, pp. 416–423.

Wittrock, M. C. (Ed.). (1986). *Handbook of Research on Teaching, Third Edition.* New York: Macmillan.
    Biddle, B. J. and Anderson, D. S. Theory, Methods, Knowledge, and Research on Teaching, pp. 230–252.
    Brophy, J. E. and Good, T. L. Teacher Behavior and Student Achievement, pp. 328–375.
    Cazden, C. B. Classroom Discourse, pp. 432–463.
    Clark, C. M. and Peterson, P. L. Teachers' Thought Processes, pp. 255–296.
    Doyle, W. Classroom Organization and Management, pp. 392–431.
    Rosenshine, B. V. and Stevens, R. Teaching Functions, pp. 376–391

Mitzel, H. E. (1982). *Encyclopedia of Educational Research, Fifth Edition.* New York: The Free Press.
    Kleine, P. F. Teaching Styles, pp. 1927–1932.
    Medley, D. M. Teacher Effectiveness, pp. 1894–1903.
    Ryan, K. and Phillips, D. H. Teacher Characteristics, pp. 1869–1876.
    Weil, M. L. and Murphy, J. Instruction Processes, pp. 890–917.

Travers, R. M. W. (Ed.). (1973). *Second Handbook of Research on Teaching.* Chicago: Rand McNally.
    Bidwell, C. E. The Social Psychology of Teaching, pp. 413–449.
    Dreeben, R. The School as a Workplace, pp. 450–473.
    Lortie, D. C. Observations of Teaching as Work, pp. 474–497.
    Nuthall, G. and Snook, I. Contemporary Models of Teaching, pp. 47–76.
    Rosenshine, B. and Furst, N. The Use of Direct Observation to Study Teaching, pp. 122–183.

Ebel, R. L. (1969). *Encyclopedia of Educational Research, Fourth Edition.* New York: Macmillan.
    Anderson, R. H. and Ritsher, C. Pupil Progress, pp. 1050–1062.
    Biddle, B. J. Teacher Roles, pp. 1437–1446.

Flanders, N. A. and Simon, A. Teacher Effectiveness, pp. 1423–1437.
Gage, N. L. Teaching Methods, pp. 1446–1458.
Heathers, G. Grouping, pp. 559–570.

Gage, N. L. (1963b). *Handbook of Research on Teaching.* Chicago: Rand McNally.
Getzels, J. W. and Jackson, P. W. The Teacher's Personality and Characteristics, pp. 506–582.
Wallen, N. E. and Travers, R. M. W. Analysis and Investigation of Teaching Methods, pp. 448–505.
Withall, J. and Lewis, W. W. Social Interaction in the Classroom, pp. 683–714.

Harris, C. W. (1960). *Encyclopedia of Educational Research, Third Edition.* New York: Macmillan.
Mitzel, H. E. Teacher Effectiveness, pp. 1481–1486.
Ryans, D. G. Prediction of Teacher Effectiveness, pp. 1486–1491.
Stiles, L. J. Instruction, pp. 710–715.
Wingo, G. M. Methods of Teaching, pp. 848–861.

TABLE 11.2

Procedure for Reviewing the Reviews

Step Number	Activity
1	Identify those handbook chapters or encyclopedia entries that deal exclusively or primarily with classroom research. Exclude those chapters or entries that deal solely with particular school levels (e.g., early childhood, elementary) or particular subject areas (e.g., reading, science).
2	Skim each chapter or entry and identify those portions that deal directly with activities that take place in classrooms, student learning processes (e.g., behavior, time-on-task), or student learning outcomes (e.g., achievement, attitudes). In the fifth edition of the *Encyclopedia*, for example, the portion of the entry on "Teacher Characteristics" that pertained to simple descriptions of teacher demographics (e.g., age, sex, reasons for choosing teaching as a career, and years of experience) would be excluded. In contrast, the entry on "Teacher Experience" in the *International Encyclopedia* was included since it contained a discussion of the relationship between years of experience and the effectiveness of teachers in classrooms.
3	Read each identified portion of a particular chapter or entry carefully, taking extensive notes and formulating tentative generalizations.
4	Read each successive chapter or entry with an emphasis on checking the validity of previous generalizations and formulating new generalizations. Also, review original research studies included in Chapters 4 through 6 and other reviews of research conducted in recent years (e.g., Dunkin and Biddle, 1974) for verification or expansion of the generalizations.
5	After all generalizations have been formulated, examine the interrelationships among them, combining them into larger generalizations as necessary and appropriate. Quickly re-read relevant chapters and entries looking for counter examples or counter arguments for each major generalization. Eliminate those generalizations for which counter examples or counter arguments were found.

teachers, teaching, or instruction, on the one hand, and students' behavior, involvement, achievement or attitudes, on the other. This somewhat limited focus was consistent with the overall purpose of this volume as described in the Preface.

Next, we carefully read each identified portion of the retained chapters and entries, taking extensive notes and formulating tentative generalizations. As each subsequent chapter, entry, or study summary was read, checks on the validity of these generalizations were made and new generalizations were formulated as necessary and appropriate. In addition, the original studies included in Chapters 8 through 10 and other reviews of which we were aware (e.g., Dunkin and Biddle, 1974, and Medley, 1977) were examined for further verification of the generalizations and for the development of additional generalizations.

At this point in the process, all of the generalizations that had been developed were placed in a single list. The final step was to combine the generalizations into "larger" generalizations where appropriate, and to quickly re-read relevant chapters, entries, and study summaries searching for counter examples or counter arguments to the more global generalizations. If no counter examples or counter arguments were evident, the generalizations were accepted.

Before these generalizations are presented and discussed, a comment on the reviews and the reviewers is in order. One theme that runs through a surprisingly large number of the reviews is the criticism of the studies included in the review by the reviewer on the grounds of inadequate conceptualization, inappropriate research plans (e.g., lack of concern for extraneous variables, the proliferation of instruments), or problems inherent in implementing those plans (e.g., the failure to monitor the implementation of the plans). In fact, the summary sections of these reviews are replete with conclusions about the studies themselves and are somewhat lacking in conclusions of a more substantive nature (such as, what do we currently know about this aspect of teachers, teaching, or instruction?).

Consider, for example, the criticisms focusing solely on the absence of a conceptual framework underlying the studies reviewed. Getzels and Jackson (1963), for example, suggested that research on teachers' personality and characteristics was being conducted in a "theoretical vacuum." Similarly, Flanders and Simon (1969) asserted that much of the research in the area of teacher effectiveness lacked theory and instead "merely seeks to establish a correlation between an outcome and some other situational variable" (p. 1431). Finally, Heathers (1969) contended that research on grouping has been limited by a failure to design the research plan on the basis of an adequate theoretical model. In our terminology, these criticisms pertain to studies of teachers, teaching, and instruction, respectively. Lest the reader think that these criticisms made in the 1960s are no longer applicable, similar concerns have been voiced by Ryan and Phillips (1982) and Weil and Murphy (1982).

Perhaps these reviewers are correct in refraining from substantive conclusions when the studies they are reviewing are replete with problems in conceptualization, planning, and implementation. Nonetheless, without such conclusions we are left with the feeling that researchers spend most of their time criticizing other researchers (Coleman, 1984) or that the results from existing research studies add nothing to our base of knowledge because these studies are hopelessly flawed. We would dismiss this pessimistic and somewhat dismal point of view and cast our lot with Biddle and Dunkin (1987) who assert that:

> It is certainly true, that few universal "facts" have yet appeared in research on teaching effects. This does not mean that the effort is useless. On the contrary, a number of contributions have clearly appeared in this research [including the development of] new concepts for describing teaching and its outcomes, and new propositions about the relationship between these two realms, . . . evidence which is useful for testing theories and telling how teaching works in those contexts studied, . . . practical innovations such as new curricula, methods for teacher training, or techniques for measuring the outcomes of instruction, . . . [and the] stimulation of theory concerning teaching and its effects which has the capacity of affecting future generations of educators (pp. 122–123).

The generalizations that appear in the next several sections of this chapter are offered in this light.

Generalizations About Teachers

Of teachers, teaching, and instruction, generalizations about teachers are the most difficult. One of the reasons for this state of affairs is the change in the study of teachers that has taken place over the past 60 years (see Chapter 8). Concerns for general traits of teachers have given way to the realization that studies of specific cognitive and affective characteristics may be more fruitful (Levis, 1987). Similarly, studies whose purpose was to identify traits that could be used to select teachers have been replaced by those whose intent is to promote the education and growth of teachers (Doyle, 1987). Nonetheless, four generalizations about teachers can be offered with some confidence.

Generalization 1—There is no universal definition of an excellent, good, or effective teacher.

Teachers, students, and supervisors have different views of what constitutes an effective teacher (Getzels and Jackson, 1963). In addition, the school and classroom context do affect the characteristics we would ascribe to an effective teacher (Charters and Waples, 1929). As Ryan and Phillips (1982) argue, for example,

> Teacher characteristics judged successful in a suburban Boston elementary school might be very different from those needed for success in a South Side Chicago high school (p. 1871).

As a consequence, the idea that there is a single, easily measured criterion of teacher effectiveness needs to be replaced with a more complicated, multi-faceted view of effectiveness (Withall and Lewis, 1963).

What would be included in this "complicated, multi-faceted" definition of effectiveness? We are not at all certain. The tasks that teachers have been and continue to be expected to perform are numerous. Teachers are expected to

> "emancipate pupils from their home environment, encourage achievement among pupils, sort out and socialize 'winners' and 'losers' in the achievement game, inculcate societal norms in pupils, teach technical skills, instill interpersonal sensitivity and discipline, and aid pupils in making decisions and training for occupations, . . . maintain order in their classrooms, accept and promote a common curriculum, follow the orders of supervisors, maintain effective communication with parents, and exhibit 'loyalty' to their schools" (Biddle, 1987, p. 632).

Quite likely, some teachers will be more successful on some of these tasks while others may be more successful on others.

Generalization 2—Teachers vary on a wide variety of personal and professional characteristics, at least some of which are related to what transpires in their classrooms.

Teachers differ in their attitudes, interests, values, and motivations (Ryan and Phillips, 1982), their cognitive organization and problem-solving ability (Flanders and Simon, 1969), the expectations they hold for students (Brophy and Good, 1986) and the beliefs they have about them (Clark and Peterson, 1986), and their characteristic ways of planning and making decisions (Clark and Peterson, 1986).

There is little evidence that teachers' attitudes, interests, values, and motivations are related to their performance in the classrooms. On the other hand, there is some evidence that teachers who operate at higher cognitive levels tend to be more flexible in their method of teaching and their handling of classroom discipline problems (Ryan and Phillips, 1982). Similarly, teachers' professional knowledge has been linked to their performance in the classroom (Flanders and Simon, 1969).

The expectations that teachers have for their students are associated with the ways in which they behave toward the students (Good, 1987), as well as the tasks students are assigned by their teachers (Braun, 1987). In general, students for whom teachers hold low expectations are given less time to answer questions, rewarded more frequently for inadequate answers, criticized more often and praised less often, and offered fewer opportunities to interact with the teacher (Good, 1987). These students also are assigned tasks that require little more than rote memorization (Braun, 1987). Similarly, the beliefs teachers have about their students, particularly about the effort students expend on their assigned tasks, is related to the type of feedback teachers provide their students (Clark and Peterson, 1986).

Finally, teacher planning is associated with several of the more important components of instruction. Specifically, teacher planning has been found to be related to content coverage and grouping arrangements (Clark and Peterson, 1986).

Generalization 3—Teacher characteristics do not impact directly on student achievement.

The key phrase in this generalization is "impact directly." The intent of this generalization is *not* to suggest that teacher characteristics have no effect on student achievement. Rather, the intent is to suggest that any effect of teacher characteristics on student achievement must necessarily be *indirect.* Stated somewhat differently, teacher characteristics must be evident to the students if they are to affect them in any way. Thus, teacher characteristics may (or may not) directly affect the way in which teachers act toward their students or treat their students which in turn may (or may not) directly or indirectly affect student achievement.

As this analysis would suggest, attempts to directly link teacher characteristics with student achievement have been futile. There is little if any evidence that differences in personality characteristics (Getzels and Jackson, 1963; Levis, 1987) or general teacher knowledge (Shulman, 1986) are associated with differences in student achievement. More complex models which include contextual or setting variables (Flanders and Simon, 1969) and variables representing likely manifestations of particular teacher characteristics are needed if the relationship between teacher characteristics and student achievement is to be properly studied and understood.

One methodological point must be raised before we move to the next generalization. In many studies, teachers differ little if at all in terms of the characteristics under investigation (e.g., their highest level of education, their knowledge of subject matter, their attitudes toward education). As a consequence, empirical relationships between teacher characteristics and student achievement are impossible to establish using traditional correlational methods. In this regard, there is some evidence that the relationships between certain teacher characteristics and student achievement may be more substantial in experimental or quasi-experimental studies than in naturally occurring settings (Flanders and Simon, 1969). Quite obviously, this finding only applies to teacher characteristics that can be experimentally manipulated.

Generalization 4—Teachers progress through a fairly predictable set of qualitatively distinct stages as they move from novice to expert status.

Estimates of the actual number of stages range from three (Ryan and Phillips, 1982) to five (Berliner, 1988). Since much of this research has been directed toward novices and experts, more is known about these two extreme stages on the developmental continuum.

Novice teachers tend to behave in a relatively inflexible manner, using general, context-free rules to guide their behavior. They have difficulty interpreting events and behaviors, focusing instead on fairly literal descriptions. Perhaps as a consequence, they also have difficulty separating more important events from less important events (Berliner, 1988). Novice teachers are concerned primarily with their own survival in the classroom (Ryan and Phillips, 1982). This personal concern may account in part for the amount of time they spend on classroom management (Anderson et al., 1989).

Expert teachers are characterized by fluid, apparently effortless performance in their classrooms. In Berliner's (1988) terms, they exemplify "knowledge in action." Expert teachers have developed organizing frameworks which help them make sense of classroom events and guide their behavior. They are analytic only when necessary, choosing to rely on routines they have developed over time and predictions concerning likely consequences of their actions (Berliner, 1988). They are concerned primarily with their students' learning and well being, having already achieved a sense of personal competence (Ryan and Phillips, 1982).

Teachers in between these two stages are acquiring experience and developing organizing frameworks. This experience and these frameworks allow them to differentiate important from unimportant events and to make more precise predictions of future events. Their responsibility for their own actions increases and their concerns shift from managing students to instructing students to facilitating and fostering student learning.

The length of these various stages remains a mystery, although there is some evidence that some teachers fixate at certain stages. Such a fixation would explain at least partially the apparent curvilinear relationship between teaching experience and student achievement (Ryans, 1960b; Barnes, 1987). That is, as a group, teachers apparently increase in their effectiveness for the first six or seven years, after which time they tend either to maintain the same level of effectiveness or actually experience a decline.

Generalizations about Teaching

In contrast to the relatively few generalizations that can be made about teachers, numerous generalizations can be drawn about teaching. The problem in reviewing the reviews on teaching, then, quickly became how to limit the generalizations to avoid a long "laundry list." The problem was solved, at least to our satisfaction, by combining specific generalizations into more global ones. In the process, four fairly global generalizations were derived.

Generalization 1—Teachers assume a very central, directive, and active role in their classrooms.

Teachers spend the majority of their time talking *to* students, talking *with* students, and supervising students while they engage in academic work at their seats, desks, or tables. A shorthand notation for all of this talking/ listening and supervising/working is "recitation-seatwork' (Dunkin and Biddle, 1974). Teachers also maintain control of their classrooms—they make the majority of the decisions and arrange most of the activities. While different researchers have used different terminology to describe this role—"ringmaster" (Smith and Geoffrey, 1968; Biddle, 1969), "teacher-centered" (Cuban, 1984), or "direct instruction" (Rosenshine, 1987)—few question its pervasiveness (Biddle, 1987) or stability over time (Cuban, 1984).

It is not surprising, then, that classroom researchers have either questioned the appropriateness of this role (Flanders, 1960; Bennett, 1976), pondered over possible reasons for its stability over time (Dreeben, 1973; Cuban, 1984), or simply accepted it as a "given", choosing instead to examine the ways in which teachers could be more effective in this role (Brophy and Good, 1986). Given this widely-accepted role of the teacher it also is not surprising that calls for "child-centered" instruction (Cuban, 1984), "adaptive instruction" (Wang, 1984), or "informal methods" (Bennett, 1976) are either rejected, met with skepticism, or, if accepted, typically short-lived.

The vast majority of the research on teaching has accepted the central, directive, and active role of the teacher. Consider, for example, the major subheadings used by Brophy and Good (1986) to summarize their review of research on teacher behaviors and student achievement: giving information, questioning the students, reacting to student responses, and handling seatwork and homework assignments. The first three subheadings are associated with "recitation", while the fourth is "seatwork" (either completed in school or at home).

Even those who disagree that teachers should assume such a role have used their knowledge that teachers *do* assume such a role in planning and conducting their studies. For example, while the results of studies conducted in the socio-linguistic tradition have focused on the students' role in the classroom, these investigations have typically been made in classrooms in which teachers have assumed a fairly traditional role (Morine-Dershimer, 1985). As a result, their findings concerning teacher behaviors are quite similar to those of other researchers.

One final point should be made relative to this generalization. Research conducted in classrooms in which teachers have assumed non-traditional roles has produced quite impressive results. For example, cooperative learning, an approach to classroom teaching and learning that encourages student-student interaction and requires teachers to assume a less direct and more supportive and facilitative role (Johnson and Johnson, 1989), has been associated with higher student achievement and more positive attitudes (Slavin, 1987). Additional research on the effectiveness of alternative teacher roles appears to be important and worthwhile.

Generalization 2—Differences in individual teaching behaviors are not reliably associated with differences in student achievement.

This generalization has been known for some time (Morsh and Wilder, 1954). What we have learned over the past 30 or 40 years are some reasons for this generalization. At this time, at least three reasons can be given. First, different teachers tend to behave in much the same way when teaching in their classrooms. Dreeben (1973) suggests that organizational properties of schools and classrooms constrain teachers to behave as they do, primarily as activity managers and recitation leaders. If, for whatever reason, it is impossible to reliably differentiate among teachers based on their classroom behaviors, differences in these behaviors cannot be found to be linked with differences in mean student achievement (Anderson et al., 1989).

Second, and related to the first reason, differences in teaching behaviors are more likely to reflect the subject matters or grade levels that they teach, the occasions on which they are observed (e.g., early in year vs. late in year, Monday vs. Friday), or the aim or purpose of the lesson or class session being observed than stable, consistent differences in teaching behavior among the teachers themselves. As a consequence, it seems unlikely that the teacher behaviors associated with achievement in one setting are necessarily associated with achievement in other settings or at another point in time. Soar and Soar (1987) have provided several examples in which a teaching behavior which was positively correlated with student achievement in one study was negatively correlated with student achievement in another.

A third reason for the lack of a relationship between teaching behaviors and student achievement is that most research on teaching presumes a stable classroom setting in which the effects of teaching on achievement are evident almost immediately. As Biddle and Dunkin (1987) suggest, however, the "real world is far from stable, and teaching may have effects that cumulate or are delayed" (p. 123). [Also, see our postscript to Chapter 2.]

Generalization 3—If teaching behaviors are to be reliably associated with student achievement, then patterns, groupings, or clusters of these behaviors must be identified. Furthermore, experimental or quasi-experimental studies may be necessary to produce the variation in these behavioral clusters that is needed to properly examine the relationship between teacher behavior and student achievement.

As early as 1945, Jayne (1945) demonstrated that while discrete teaching behaviors were largely unrelated to student achievement, clusters of these behaviors were found to have substantial correlations with student achievement. More recently, Weil and Murphy (1982) suggested that

> Many of the isolated behaviors identified as part of the direct instruction repertoire of effective teachers can be more powerfully characterized . . . by describing them in terms of a teaching strategy (p. 912).

While the importance of clusters of strategies has long been recognized, the problem of how clusters should be formed or strategies developed remains to be solved.

Clusters of behaviors can be formed using solely empirical means, solely conceptual arguments, or some combination of conceptual and empirical. Empirically, one can manipulate the data until the strongest relationship between teacher behavior and student achievement has been established.

Unfortunately, without an underlying conceptual framework the interpretation of the cluster of behaviors is problematic. Conceptually, one can arrange behaviors into a cluster independently of whether empirical evidence supports (or at least does not refute) this *a priori* clustering. Consistent with the point of view expressed throughout this book, the combination of conceptual and empirical is likely to provide the greatest payoff.

Two clusters of behaviors that hold some promise in future classroom research have been derived largely from this combined conceptual-empirical approach. The first cluster has been labeled "structuring behavior" (Bellack et al., 1966) or "structure" (Doenau, 1987). The second cluster has been termed "feedback and correctives" (Bloom, 1976) or "corrective feedback" (Zahorik, 1987).

Defined by example, structure includes a wide variety of teaching behaviors: reviewing, outlining, previewing or providing overviews, stating aims or objectives, using verbal markers to highlight important points, and summarizing (Doenau, 1987). All of these behaviors are intended to help students identify important ideas or concepts and form the necessary relationships among these ideas or concepts. Several findings related to structure are particularly noteworthy. First, structuring is most important for students who apparently need it the most (e.g., less able students, more anxious students). Second, although teacher behaviors associated with structuring have been identified, student perceptions of structure may be more valid and hence more important in classroom research than the more objective records made by classroom observers (Doenau, 1987; Anderson et al., 1989).

In addition to "structuring behaviors," the structure of the lessons provided to students by teachers is worthy of continual examination. Good, Grouws, and Ebmeier (1983), for example, have suggested a lesson structure for mathematics that has produced rather impressive empirical results.

The second cluster of behaviors is termed "feedback." Feedback is simply informing students of the correctness, adequacy, or appropriateness of their answers or work. Corrective feedback implies that students whose answers or work are incorrect, inadequate, or inappropriate are subsequently helped to correct their errors and overcome their misunderstandings. As in the case of structure, several teacher behaviors have been associated with feedback and corrective feedback (e.g., praises, gives answers, acknowledges answers, discusses *how* the answers could be derived). In combination, the results of classroom studies in which feedback was included in the conceptual framework support the conclusion that feedback is "consistently related to increases in student achievement in basic skills at the elementary school level" (Zahorik, 1987, p. 421).

Generalization 4—Considering teaching from a functional, rather than behavioral, point of view is more likely to result in a greater understanding of teaching in general and effective teaching in particular.

One means by which teaching behavior can be combined into clusters is to consider the intended or actual consequences of the behaviors. Behaviors that are intended to serve or do serve the same function can be grouped in a single cluster. Examining behaviors from a functional perspective simply asks the researcher to identify the reason a particular behavior is being exhibited and/or the impact that behavior has on student behavior or learning. Considering Brophy and Good's (1986) major subheadings as summarized in Generalization 1, one would begin to ask *why* the information is being presented, *why* the questions are being asked, *why* teachers react in the way they do, and *why* the work is being assigned.

Fortunately, several functional categories of teacher behaviors already exist. Both "structure" and "corrective feedback" are examples of such categories. Rosenshine and Stevens (1987) have identified several additional functional categories, as have Weil and Murphy (1982).

Many behaviors exhibited by teachers serve multiple functions. While students are engaged in seatwork, for example, a teacher's supervisory behaviors serve at least two functions. First, they keep students engaged in learning or on-task. Second, they allow teachers to identify students' learning problems as early as possible so that they can be corrected before they accumulate and interfere with future learning. Similarly, the questions that teachers ask serve several functions. They can be the starting point for a lecture or discussion (as in the case of rhetorical questions), they can be used to gain the attention of a wayward student, or they can be used to check students' understanding of a point being made. Frequency counts of the numbers of questions asked hide these functional distinctions. Brophy (1981) has performed a similar analysis of the functions of teacher praise.

In many respects the formation of functional categories requires that researchers begin to examine teaching behavior from the students' point of view. Rather than asking what behaviors teachers are exhibiting and how frequently they are exhibiting those behaviors, the fundamental questions become what the teachers are trying to accomplish with those behaviors and what the actual consequences of those behaviors are on students (e.g., Morine-Dershimer, 1985).

Generalizations about Instruction

Our generalizations concerning instruction are organized around five of the six major components of instruction (see Table 1.1). Generalizations pertaining to the sixth component, classroom behaviors and interactions, have been addressed in the previous section. For each of the remaining components—subject matter, task demands, instructional format, grouping arrangement, and time/pacing/coverage—a single generalization has been drawn.

Generalization 1—The subject matter being taught impacts on some, if not all, of the other components of instruction.

Since most classroom research has been conducted within a single subject matter, this generalization is not supported by many of the reviews. However, the results of several of the original research studies included in Chapter 10, most of which have been conducted at the elementary school level, lend support to this generalization.

For example, differences in the task demands on fifth grade students in social studies and mathematics were documented by Stodolsky (1988). The vast majority of tasks assigned to students in mathematics (about 80 percent) required students to understand concepts and apply skills. In contrast, fewer than one-fourth of the tasks assigned to students in social studies demanded students to exhibit this same level of understanding and application. Instead, the majority of tasks assigned to students in social studies required them either to recall facts (a somewhat lower level task) or to engage in research skills (a somewhat higher level task).

Subject matter impacts on the grouping arrangements in the elementary school classroom. For example, within-classroom grouping is far more common in reading than in mathematics (Barr and Dreeben, 1983). Subject matter also impacts on the way in which time is allocated and used in the elementary school. Galton et al. (1980) found that primary school students spent two-thirds or more of their time in mathematics or language arts. Other subject areas such as science, social studies, art, and music received considerably less emphasis. One important element of these studies is that most elementary school teachers teach different subject matters. Thus, differences in teachers cannot account for the differences in task demands or grouping arrangements.

Additional research in this area may lead to additional support for this generalization. Such research would require recognition of the fact that subject matter influences the demands placed on students, the format of instruction, the grouping configuration used in the classroom, the time allocated to the study of the subject matter and the pace with which the subject matter is covered, and the way in which teachers and students behave and interact (Stodolsky, 1988). Perhaps, the impact of subject matter on these other components of instruction is so obvious to many researchers that its study may be deemed unimportant or trivial (see Chapter 1). Nonetheless, subject matter remains one of the primary dimensions of instruction.

Generalization 2—While the academic demands on students tend to be fairly minimal, the greater the emphasis on those demands and the students' need to meet those demands, the greater their achievement in the basic skills.

At least two sets of findings suggest that the academic demands placed on students while they are in the classroom are quite minimal. First, much time in classrooms is spent reviewing previously taught knowledge or practicing previously taught skills (Anderson et al., 1989; Burns, 1984). Second, the cognitive level at which students are expected or required to operate is fairly low. Few classrooms questions require students to go beyond the recall of previously encountered information (Galton et al., 1980). Most objectives stress knowledge, comprehension, and application; rarely are students expected to analyze, synthesize, or evaluate the information they are given (Stodolsky, 1988). In many ways, these findings represent the "bad news."

The "good news" is that greater academic focus or task-orientation in the classroom is related to higher levels of student achievement in basic skills (Weil and Murphy, 1982). The frequency with which students are asked memory or recall questions is positively related to their achievement (Medley, 1977). Furthermore, the more that students are held accountable for the completion and quality of their work, the higher their levels of achievement (Weil and Murphy, 1982).

Generalization 3—While lecture, recitation, and seatwork predominate in classrooms, there is little if any evidence that changes in format would result in higher levels of student achievement.

The prevalence of lecture, recitation, and seatwork in classrooms has been well-documented (Dunkin, 1987b). Doyle (1986) has suggested that the prevalence of these formats is related to classroom management. That is, the use of familiar activities such as recitation and seatwork, and the routinization of classroom procedures are reasonable strategies for maintaining order.

While some may bemoan teachers' reliance on these common, routinized instructional formats, there is very little evidence to support the effectiveness of other available formats (e.g., discussion, the use of audiovisual aids). In fact, no single instructional format has been found to be superior in enhancing student achievement (Wallen and Travers, 1963; Gage, 1969). Furthermore, no single instructional format producing superior students achievement is likely to be found because different formats are based on different principles of learning (Wallen and Travers, 1963) and are directed toward different learning objectives (Weil and Murphy, 1982).

Generalization 4—While most teaching and learning takes place in whole-class settings, there is increasing evidence that grouping within the classroom is beneficial for student learning.

Whole class instruction occurs far more frequently than either small group instruction or individual student tutoring (Dunkin, 1987b). Once again, the reliance on whole class instruction may be due to the need for teachers to manage their classrooms and maintain order. Teachers tend to form groups within classrooms when they become aware of the diversity that exists among the students in their classroom (Barr and Dreeben, 1983) and when instructional materials appropriate for different ability or achievement levels are available (Calfee and Piontkowski, 1987).

There is evidence to support the superiority of whole-class instruction over within-class grouping (Medley, 1977). There also is evidence supporting the superiority of within-class grouping over whole-class instruction (Calfee and Piontkowski, 1987). This disagreement suggests that simply grouping or not grouping is not the real issue. Rather, the superiority of within-class grouping, when it is in fact superior, can be attributed to a number of factors. For example, homogeneous within-class grouping tends to be superior when students receive definite assignments that can be completed with little if any intervention by the teacher, and where student progress on the assignments is monitored by the teacher, aide, or other source (Calfee and Piontkowski, 1987). Cooperative grouping, that is, heterogeneous grouping in which students are expected or required to work together, tends to be superior in a great variety of circumstances. Students working together on tasks or projects (Weil and Murphy, 1982; Slavin, 1987) or students helping other students (Rosenshine, 1987) tend to produce quite impressive results in terms of student achievement and attitude.

Generalization 5—Instructional time, content coverage, and pacing are associated with higher levels of student achievement.

This generalization is supported by several of the reviews (Barr, 1987; Kleine, 1982; Rosenshine, 1987; Weil and Murphy, 1982) as well as several of the original studies included in Chapter 10 (Nuthall and Church, 1973; Anderson et al., 1989). From a purely descriptive point of view, however, there is evidence that the majority of time in classrooms, approximately 85 percent, is instructional time (that is, time that students are being taught and expected to learn some academic content) (Burns, 1984), that the pacing of instruction is relatively slow (Barr, 1987) with a great deal of review occurring in most classrooms (Burns, 1984), and that the content actually covered in class, or at least that portion of the content that is related to end-of-term or end-of-year achievement tests, differs widely across class-rooms (Anderson et al., 1989).

Discussion

In this chapter we have offered 13 generalizations concerning teachers, teaching, and instruction. In formulating these generalizations we were unable to find any evidence to refute them. Thus, they stand as fairly conservative generalizations.

In many ways, these generalizations represent the culmination of more than 50 years of classroom research. Our hope is that these generalizations serve two major purposes. First, we hope that they promote a dialogue among researchers and practitioners concerning what is known and what remains to be known. Consistent with our value orientation, these generalizations represent what we believe to be true about teachers, teaching, and instruction. Certainly not all readers will agree as to the validity of these generalizations; however, we would encourage these readers to offer additional generalizations supported by existing evidence.

Second, these generalizations are still in the form of a "laundry list." We encourage researchers and practitioners to begin to integrate the knowledge included in these generalizations first into coherent conceptual frameworks and ultimately into theories that are capable of guiding research efforts into the future. Theoretically-based conceptual frameworks are needed if we are to move beyond a knowledge of "what works" to a deeper understanding of "why it works." Without such understanding, the likelihood that research in classrooms will accomplish its primary purpose, that of improving student learning, is small indeed.

References

Adams, R. S. (1972). Observational studies of teacher role. *International Review of Education, 18,* 440–459.

Allport, G. W. (1961). *Pattern and growth in personality.* New York: Holt, Rinehart, and Winston.

Amidon, E. and Hunter, E. (1967). *Improving teaching: The analysis of classroom verbal interaction.* New York: Holt, Rinehart, and Winston.

Anderson, L. W. (1984). Concerns for appropriate instrumentation in research on classroom teaching. *Evaluation in Education: An International Review Series, 8,* 133–152.

Anderson, L. W. (1986). Understanding teacher behavior in the classroom: A must for sound evaluation. *NASSP Bulletin, 70* (490), 42–50.

Anderson, L. W. (n.d.) *Handbook on evaluating annual and continuing contract teachers.* Columbia, SC: Office of Research, South Carolina Department of Education.

Anderson, L. W. (1987). Opportunity to learn. In M. J. Dunkin (Ed.), *The international encyclopedia of teaching and teacher education* (pp. 368–371). Oxford: Pergamon.

Anderson, L. W., Ryan, D. W. and Shapiro, B. J. (1989). *The IEA Classroom Environment Study.* Oxford: Pergamon.

Anderson, N. H. (1963). Comparison of different populations: Resistance to extinction and transfer. *Psychological Review, 70,* 162–179.

Ashton, P. T. and Webb, R. B. (1986). *Making a difference: Teachers' sense of efficacy and student achievement.* New York: Longman.

Barker, R. (1968). *Ecological psychology: Concepts and methods for studying the environment of human behavior.* Stanford, California: Stanford University Press.

Barnes, J. (1987). Teaching experience. In M. Dunkin (Ed.), *International encyclopedia of teaching and teacher education* (pp. 608–612). Oxford: Pergamon.

Barr, A. S. (1929). *Characteristic differences of good and poor teachers.* Bloomington, Illinois: Public School Publishing Company.

Barr, A. S. (1952). Teaching competencies. In W. S. Monroe (Ed.), *Encyclopedia of educational research* (2nd ed.) (pp. 1446–1454). New York: Macmillan.

Barr, A. S., Bechdolt, B. V., Coxe, W. W., Gage, N. L., Orleans, J. S., Remmers, H. H. and Ryans, D. G. (1952). Report of the committee on the criteria of teacher effectiveness. *Review of Educational Research, 22,* 238–263.

Barr, A. S., Bechdolt, B. V., Gage, N. L., Orleans, J. S., Pace, C. R. Remmers, H. H. and Ryans, D. G. (1953). Second report of the committee on criteria of teacher effectiveness. *Journal of Educational Research, 46,* 641–658.

Barr, R. (1973/74). Instructional pace differences and their effect on reading acquisition. *Reading Research Quarterly, 9,* 526–554.

Barr, R. (1975). How children are taught to read: Grouping and pacing. *School Review, 83,* 479–498.

Barr, R. (1987). Content coverage. In M. J. Dunkin (Ed.), *International encyclopedia of teaching and teacher education* (pp. 364–368). Oxford: Pergamon.

Barr, R. and Dreeben, R. (1977). Instruction in classrooms. *Review of Research in Education, 5,* 89–162.

Barr, R. and Dreeben, R. (1983). *How schools work.* Chicago: University of Chicago Press.

Bellack, A., Kliebard, H., Hyman, R. and Smith, F. (1966). *The language of the classroom.* New York: Columbia University Press.

Bennett, S. N. (1976). *Teaching styles and pupil progress.* Cambridge, Massachusetts: Harvard University Press.

Bennett, S. N. (1978). Recent research on teaching: A dream, a belief, and a model. *British Journal of Educational Psychology, 48,* 127–147.

Bennett, N., DesForges, C., Cockburn, A. and Wilkinson, B. (1984). *The quality of pupil learning experiences.* Hillsdale, New Jersey: Erlbaum.

Berliner, D. C. (1983). Developing conceptions of classroom environments: Some light on the T in classroom studies of ATI. *Educational Psychologist,* **13,** 1–13.

Berliner, D. C. (1988). *The development of expertise in pedagogy.* Washington, DC.: AACTE Publications.

Berliner, D. C. and Tikunoff, W. J. (1976). The California Beginning Teacher Evaluation Study: Overview of the ethnographic study. *Journal of Teacher Education,* **27,** 24–30.

Berliner, D., Filby, N., Marliave, R., Moore, J. and Tikunoff, W. (1976). *Experimental teaching units and the identification of a special sample of classrooms for conducting research on teaching* (Technical Report 76–12–1). San Francisco: Far West Laboratory for Educational Research and Development. (ERIC ED 147 278).

Biddle, B. J. (1969). Teacher roles. In R. L. Ebel (Ed.), *Encyclopedia of educational research* (4th ed.) (pp. 1437–1446). New York: Macmillan.

Biddle, B. J. (1987). Teacher roles. In M. J. Dunkin (Ed.), *International encyclopedia of teaching and teacher education* (pp. 625–634). Oxford: Pergamon.

Biddle, B. J. and Anderson, D. S. (1986). Theory, methods, knowledge, and research on teaching. In M. C. Wittrock (Ed.), *Handbook of research on teaching* (3rd ed.) (pp. 230–252). New York: Macmillan.

Biddle, B. J. and Dunkin, M. J. (1987). Effects of teaching. In M. J. Dunkin (Ed.), *International encyclopedia of teaching and teacher education* (pp. 119–124). Oxford: Pergamon.

Bloom, B. S. (1972). Innocence in education. *School Review,* **80,** 332–352.

Bloom, B. S. (1976). *Human characteristics and school learning.* New York: McGraw-Hill.

Bloom, B. S. (1981). New directions in educational research and educational practice. In B. S. Bloom (Ed.), *All our children learning* (pp. 1–12). New York: McGraw-Hill.

Blumer, H. (1969). *Symbolic interactionism: Perspective and method.* Englewood Cliffs, N.J.: Prentice-Hall.

Bogdan, R. C. and Biklen, S. K. (1982). *Qualitative research for education: An introduction to theory and methods.* Boston: Allyn and Bacon.

Bolster, A. (1983). Toward a more effective model of research on teaching. *Harvard Educational Review,* **53,** 294–308.

Braun, C. (1987). Teachers' expectations. In M. Dunkin (Ed.), *International encyclopedia of teaching and teacher education* (pp. 598–605). Oxford: Pergamon.

Bridgman, P. W. (1927). *The logic of modern physics.* New York: Macmillan.

Brophy, J. (1981). Teacher praise: A functional analysis. *Review of Educational Research,* **51,** (1), 5–32.

Brophy, J. and Evertson, C. (1974). *The Texas Teacher Effectiveness Project: Presentation of non-linear relationships and summary discussion* (Research Report No. 74–6). Austin: University of Texas R & D Center for Teacher Education (ERIC ED 099 345).

Brophy, J. and Good, T. L. (1986). Teacher behavior. In M. C. Wittrock (Ed.), *Handbook of research on teaching* (3rd ed.) (pp. 328–375). New York: Macmillan.

Brunswik, E. (1955). Representative design and probabilistic theory in a functional psychology. *Psychological Review,* **62,** 193–217.

Brunswik, E. (1956). *Perception and the representative design of psychological experiments.* Berkeley: University of California Press.

Bruyn, S. T. (1966). *The human perspective in sociology: The methodology of participant observation.* Englewood Cliffs. N.J.: Prentice-Hall.

Bryk, A. S. and Weisberg, H. I. (1977). Use of the nonequivalent control group design when subjects are growing. *Psychological Bulletin,* **84,** 950–962.

Bryk, A. S. and Raudenbush, S. W. (1987). Application of hierarchical linear models to assessing change. *Psychological Bulletin,* **101,** 147–158.

Burns, R. B. (1984). How time is used in elementary schools: The activity structure of classrooms. In L. W. Anderson (Ed.), *Time and school learning: Theory, research, and practice* (pp. 91–127). Beckenham, Kent: Croom Helm.

Burns, R. B. and Anderson, L. W. (1987). The activity structure of lesson segments. *Curriculum Inquiry,* **17** (1), 31–53.

Burstein, L. (1980). The analysis of multilevel data in educational research and evaluation. *Review of Research in Education,* **8,** 158–233.

Burstein, L. (1987). Units of analysis. In M. Dunkin (Ed.), *The international encyclopedia of teaching and teacher education* (pp. 155–162). Oxford: Pergamon.

Bussis, A. M., Chittenden, E. A. and Amarel, M. (1976). *Beyond surface curriculum.* Boulder, Colorado: Westview Press.

Calderhead, J. (1981). A psychological approach to research on teachers' classroom decision making. *British Educational Research Journal,* **7,** 51–57.

Cahen, L. S., Filby, N., McCutcheon, G. and Kyle, D. (1983). *Class size and instruction.* New York: Longman.

Calfee, R. C. and Piontkowki, D. C. (1987). Grouping for teaching. In M. J. Dunkin (Ed.), *International encyclopedia of teaching and teacher education* (pp. 225–232). Oxford: Pergamon.

Campbell, D. T. (1975). "Degrees of freedom" and the case study. *Comparative Political Studies,* **8,** 178–193.

Campbell, D. T. and Stanley, J. C. (1963). Experimental and quasi-experimental designs for research on teaching. In N. L. Gage (Ed.), *Handbook of research on teaching* (pp. 171–246). Chicago: Rand McNally.

Carroll, J. B. (1964). Words, meanings, and concepts. *Harvard Educational Review,* **34,** 178–202.

Centra, J. A. and Potter, D. A. (1980). School and teacher effects: An interrelational model. *Review of Educational Research,* **50,** 273–291.

Charters, W. W. and Waples, D. (1929). *The commonwealth teacher-training study.* Chicago: University of Chicago Press.

Clark, C. M., Gage, N. L., Marx, R. W., Peterson, P. L., Stayrook, N. G. and Winne, P. H. (1979). A factorial experiment on teacher structuring, soliciting, and reacting. *Journal of Educational Psychology,* **71,** 534–552.

Clark, C. M. and Peterson, P. L. (1986). Teachers' thought processes. In M. C. Wittrock (Ed.), *Handbook of research on teaching* (3rd ed.) (pp. 255–296). New York: Macmillan.

Clark, G. K. (1967). *The critical historian.* London: Heineman Educational Books, Ltd.

Coleman, J. S. (1984). How might policy research in education be better carried out. In R. Glaser (Ed.), *Improving education: Perspectives on educational research* (pp. 4–13). Pittsburgh: National Academy of Education.

Cook, T. D. and Campbell, D. T. (1979). *Quasi-experimentation: Design and analysis issues for field settings.* Chicago: Rand McNally.

Cook, T. D. and Reichardt, C. S. (Eds.). (1979). *Qualitative and quantitative methods in evaluation research.* Beverly Hills: Sage.

Cook-Gumperz, J., Simons, H. D. and Gumperz, J. J. (1981). *Final Report on School/Home Ethnography Project* (National Institute of Education Grant No. G–78–0082). Washington, D.C.: U.S. Department of Education (ERIC ED 233 915).

Cooley, W. and Leinhardt, G. (1980). The Instructional Dimensions Study. *Educational Evaluation and Policy Analysis,* **2,** 7–25.

Cooley, W. W. and Lohnes, P. R. (1976). *Evaluation research in education: Theory, principles, and practice.* New York: Irvington.

Corey, S. M. and Monroe, W. S. (1941). Methods of teaching. In W. S. Monroe (Ed.), *Encyclopedia of educational research* (pp. 725–731). New York: Macmillan.

Crocker, R., Brokenshire, G., Boak, T., Fagan, M. and James, E. (1978). *Teaching Strategies Project: Manual for classroom observers.* St. Johns, Newfoundland: Institute for Educational Research and Development, Memorial University of Newfoundland.

Cronbach, L. J. (1957). The two disciplines of scientific psychology. *American Psychologist,* **12,** 671–684.

Cronbach, L. J. (1975). Beyond the two disciplines of scientific psychology. *American Psychologist,* **30,** 116–127.

Cronbach, L. J. and Snow, R. E. (1977). *Aptitudes and instructional methods: Handbook for the study of interactions.* New York: Irvington/Naiburg.

Cronbach, L. J. and Suppes, P. (Eds.). (1969). *Disciplined inquiry for education.* Toronto, Ontario: Collier-MacMillan.

Cronbach, L. J. with J. E. Dikers and N. Webb (1976). *Research on classrooms and schools: Formulation of questions, design, and analysis* (Occasional Paper). Stanford, CA: Stanford Evaluation Consortium.

Cuban, L. (1984). *How teachers taught: Constancy and change in American classrooms 1890–1980.* New York: Longman.

Cusick, P. A. (1973). *Inside high school: The student's perspective.* New York: Holt, Rinehart, and Winston.

Dahllöf, U. S, (1971). *Ability grouping, content validity, and curriculum process analysis.* New York: Teachers College Press.

Denzin, N. K. (1970). *The research act: A theoretical introduction to sociological methods.* New York: McGraw-Hill.

Doenau, S. J. (1987). Structuring. In M. J. Dunkin (Ed.), *International encyclopedia of teaching and teacher education* (pp. 398–406). Oxford: Pergamon.

Doyle, W. (1977). Learning the classroom environment: An ecological analysis. *Journal of Teacher Education,* **28** (6), 51–55.

Doyle, W. (1978). Paradigms for research on teacher effectiveness. In L. S. Shulman (Ed.), *Review of Research in Education,* **5,** 163–198.

Doyle, W. (1986). Classroom organization and management. In M. C. Wittrock (Ed.), *Handbook of research on teaching* (3rd ed.) (pp. 392–431). New York: Macmillan.

Doyle, W. (1987). Paradigms for research. In M. J. Dunkin (Ed.), *International encyclopedia of teaching and teacher education* (pp. 113–119). Oxford: Pergamon.

Dreeben, R. (1973). The school as a workplace. In R. M. W. Travers (Ed.), *Second handbook of research on teaching* (pp. 450–473). Chicago: Rand McNally.

Dunkin, M. J. (Ed.). (1987a). *The international encyclopedia of teaching and teacher education.* Oxford: Pergamon.

Dunkin, M. J. (1987b). Lesson formats. In M. J. Dunkin (Ed.), *International encyclopedia of teaching and teacher education* (pp. 263–266). Oxford: Pergamon.

Dunkin, M. J. and Biddle, B. J. (1974). *The study of teaching.* New York: Holt, Rinehart, and Winston.

Dyer, H. C. (1976). *The interview as a measuring device in education.* Princeton, N.J.: ERIC Clearinghouse on Tests, Measurements, and Evaluation.

Ebel, R. L. (Ed.). (1969). *Encyclopedia of educational research* (4th ed.). New York: Macmillan.

Emerson, R. M. (1983). *Contemporary field research: A collection of readings.* Boston: Little, Brown.

Erickson, F. (1982). Classroom discourse as improvisation: Relationships between academic task structure and social participation structure in lessons. In L. C. Wilkinson (Ed.), *Communicating in the classroom* (pp. 153–181). New York: Academic.

Erickson, F. (1986). Qualitative methods in research on teaching. In M. C. Wittrock (Ed.), *Handbook of research on teaching* (3rd ed.) (pp. 119–161). New York: Macmillan.

Evertson, C. M. (1986). Personal communication.

Evertson, C. and Brophy, J. (1974). *Texas Teacher Effectiveness Project: Questionnaire and interview data* (Research Report No. 74–5). Austin: University of Texas R & D Center for Teacher Education (ERIC ED 099 346).

Evertson, C. M. and Green, J. L. (1986). Observation as inquiry and method. In M. C. Wittrock (Ed.), *Third handbook of research on teaching* (pp. 162–213). New York: Macmillan.

Firestone, W. A. (1987). Meaning in method: The rhetoric of quantitative and qualitative research. *Educational Researcher,* **16** (7), 16–21.

Fisher, C. W. and Berliner, D. C. (Eds.). (1985) *Perspectives on instructional time.* New York: Longman.

Fisher, C. W., Filby, N. N., Marliave, R. S., Cahen, L. S., Dishaw, M. M., Moore, J. E. and Berliner, D. C. (1978). *Teaching Behaviors, Academic Learning Time, and Student Achievement: Final Report of Phase III-B, Beginning Teacher Evaluation Study* (Technical Report V-1). San Francisco: Far West Laboratory for Educational Research and Development. (ERIC ED 183 525).

Fisher, C. W., Berliner, D. C., Filby, N. N., Marliave, R., Cahen, L. S. and Dishaw, M. M. (1980). Teacher behaviors, academic learning time, and student achievement: An overview. In C. Denham and A. Lieberman (Eds.), *Time to learn* (pp. 7–32). Washington, DC.: National Institute of Education.

Fiske, D. W. (1978). *Strategies for personality research: The observation versus interpretation of data.* San Francisco: Jossey-Bass.

Flanders, N. A. (1960). *Teacher influence, pupil attitudes, and achievement.* (Cooperative Research Project No. 397). Minneapolis: University of Minnesota.

Flanders, N. (1965). *Teacher influence, pupil attitudes, and achievement.* Washington, DC.: U.S. Department of Health, Education, and Welfare.

Flanders, N. A. and Amidon, E. J. (1981). *A case study of an educational innovation: The history of Flanders Interaction Analysis System.* Oakland, California: Ned A. Flanders.

Flanders, N. A. and Simon, A. (1969). Teacher effectiveness. In R. L. Ebel (Ed.), *Encyclopedia of educational research* (4th ed.) (pp. 1423–1437). New York: Macmillan.

Franck, I. (1986). Psychology as a science: Resolving the idiographic-nomothetic controversy. In J. Valsiner (Ed.), *The individual subject and scientific psychology* (pp. 17–36). New York: Plenum.

Gage, N. L. (1963a). Paradigms for research on teaching. In N. L. Gage (Ed.), *Handbook of research on teaching* (pp. 94–141). Chicago: Rand McNally.

Gage, N. L. (Ed.). (1963b). *Handbook of research on teaching.* Chicago: Rand McNally.

Gage, N. L. (1969). Teaching methods. In R. L. Ebel (Ed.), *Encyclopedia of educational research* (4th ed.) (pp. 1446–1458). New York: Macmillan.

Gage, N. L. (1978). *The scientific basis for the art of teaching.* New York: Teachers College Press.

Gage, N. L. (1985). *Hard gains in the soft sciences: The case of pedagogy.* New York: Phi Delta Kappa.

Gage, N. L. and Needels, M. C. (1989). Process-product research on teaching. A review of criticisms. *Elementary School Journal, 89,* 253–300.

Galton, M. (1987). Structured observation. In M. J. Dunkin (Ed.), *International encyclopedia of teaching and teacher education* (pp. 142–147). Oxford: Pergamon.

Galton, M., Simon, B. and Croll, P. (1980). *Inside the primary classroom.* London: Routledge and Kegan Paul.

Geertz, C. (1973). *The interpretation of culture.* New York: Random House.

Getzels, J. W. and Jackson, P. W. (1963). The teacher's personality and characteristics. In N. L. Gage (Ed.), *Handbook of research on teaching* (pp. 506–582). Chicago: Rand McNally.

Ghory, W. J. (1984). Breakthroughs and breakdowns: A case study of the implementation of the Stallings Effective Teaching Practices Training Programme. In L. W. Anderson (Ed.), *Time and school learning: Theory, research, and practice* (pp. 228–252). London: Croom-Helm.

Giesen, P. and Sirotnik, K. A. (1979). *The methodology of classroom observation in a study of schooling* (Technical Report No. 5). Los Angeles: Graduate School of Education, University of California at Los Angeles.

Glaser, B. G. and Strauss, A. (1967). *The discovery of grounded theory: Strategies for qualitative research.* Chicago: Aldine.

Glass, G. V. and Stanley, J. C. (1970). *Statistical methods in education and psychology.* Englewood Cliffs: Prentice-Hall.

Goetz, J. P. and LeCompte, M. D. (1984). *Ethnography and qualitative design in educational research.* Orlando: Academic.

Good, C. V. (1959). *Dictionary of education* (2nd ed.). New York: McGraw-Hill.

Good, C. V. (1973). *Dictionary of education* (3rd ed.). New York: McGraw-Hill.

Good, T. L. (1987). Teacher expectations. In D. C. Berliner and B. V. Rosenshine (Eds.), *Talks to teachers* (pp. 159–200). New York: Random House.

Good, T. L. and Grouws, D. A. (1979). *Experimental study of mathematics instruction in elementary schools, Final report.* (National Institute of Education Grant No. NIE-G-79-0103). Columbia: University of Missouri Center for the Study of Social Behavior.

Good, T. L., Grouws, D. A., and Ebmeier, H. (1983). *Active mathematics teaching.* New York: Longman.

Goodlad, J. I. (1984). *A place called school.* New York: McGraw-Hill.

Goodlad, J. I., Klein, M. F. and Associates (1970). *Behind the classroom door.* Worthington, OH: Charles A. Jones.

Gordon, I. J., Fattu, N., Hughes, M. M., Lund, G., Smith, E. B. and Travers, R. M. W. (1968). *Theories of instruction.* Washington, DC.: Association for Supervision and Curriculum Development.

Green, J. L. (1983). Research on teaching as a linguistic process: A state of the art. *Review of Research in Education, 10,* 151–252.

Greenberg, S. (1970). *Selected studies of classroom teaching: A comparative analysis* . Scranton, PA: International Textbook Company.

Guba, E. (1978). *Toward a methodology of naturalistic inquiry in educational evaluation.* Los Angeles: Center for the Study of Evaluation.

Guba, E. G. and Lincoln, Y. S. (1987). Naturalistic inquiry. In M. J. Dunkin (Ed.), *International encyclopedia of teaching and teacher education* (pp. 147–151). Oxford: Pergamon.

Gump, P. V. (1967). *The classroom behavior setting: Its nature and relation to student behavior* (Final Report, Project No. 2453). Lawrence, Kansas: Midwest Psychological Field Station, University of Kansas.

Gump, P. V. (1968). Persons, settings, and larger contexts. In B. Indik and F. Berrien (Eds.), *People, groups, and organizations* (pp. 233–249). New York: Teachers College Press.

Gump, P. V. (1969). Intra-setting analysis: The third grade classroom as a special but instructive case. In E. P. Willems and H. L. Raush (Eds.), *Naturalistic viewpoints in psychological research* (pp. 200–220). New York: Holt, Rinehart, and Winston.

Gump, P. V. (1971). What's happening in the elementary classroom? In I. Westbury and A. Bellack (Eds.), *Research into classroom processes: Recent developments and next steps* (pp. 155–165). New York: Teachers College Press.

Gutting, G. (Ed.). (1980). *Paradigms and revolutions: Appraisals and applications of Thomas Kuhn's philosophy of science.* Notre Dame: University of Notre Dame Press.

Hage, J. (1972). *Techniques and problems of theory construction in sociology.* New York: Wiley.

Hamilton, D. and Delamont, S. (1974). Classroom research: A cautionary tale. *Research in Education,* **11,** 1–15.

Harris, C. W. (Ed.). (1960). *Encyclopedia of educational research* (3rd ed.). New York: Macmillan.

Hawkins, R. P. (1982). Developing a behavioral code. In D. P. Hartman (Ed.), *Using observers to study behavior* (pp. 21–35). San Francisco: Jossey-Bass.

Hayduk, L. A. (1987). *Structural equation modeling with LISREL: Essentials and advances.* Baltimore: The Johns Hopkins University Press.

Heathers, G. (1969). Grouping. In R. L. Ebel (Ed.), *Encyclopedia of educational research* (4th ed.) (pp. 559–570). London: Collier-Macmillan.

House, E. R. (1980). *Evaluating with validity.* Beverly Hills: Sage.

Howe, K. R. (1985). Two dogmas of educational research. *Educational Researcher,* **14** (8), 10–18.

Hughes, D. C. (1973). An experimental investigation of the effects of pupil responding and teacher reacting on pupil achievement. *American Educational Research Journal,* **10,** 21–37.

Hughes, M. and Associates (1959). *Assessment of the quality of teaching in elementary schools.* Salt Lake City: University of Utah.

Hull, C. L. (1937). Mind, mechanism, and adaptive behavior. *Psychological Review,* **44,** 1–32.

Jackson, P. W. (1968). *Life in classrooms.* New York: Holt, Rinehart, and Winston.

Jackson, P. W. (1986). *The practice of teaching.* New York: Teachers College Press.

Jacob, E. (1987). Qualitative research traditions: A review. *Review of Educational Research,* **57,** 1–50.

Jayne, C. D. (1945). A study of the relationship between teaching procedures and educational outcomes. *Journal of Experimental Education,* **14,** 101–134.

Johnson, P. O. (1928). A comparison of the lecture-demonstration, group laboratory experimentation, and individual laboratory experimentation methods of teaching high school biology. *Journal of Educational Research,* **18,** 103–111.

Johnson, D. W. and Johnson, R. T. (1989). Cooperative learning. In L. W. Anderson (Ed.), *The effective teacher: Study guide and book of readings* (pp. 175–184). New York: Random House.

Jöreskog, K. and Sorbom, D. (1986). *LISREL VI: Analysis of linear structural relationships by maximum likelihood, instrumental variables, and least squares methods.* Uppsala, Sweden: University of Uppsala.

Kaplan, A. (1964). *The conduct of inquiry: Methology for behavioral science.* San Feransicso: Chandler.

Kelly, G. A. (1955). *A theory of personality: The psychology of personal constructs.* New York: W. W. Norton.

Kerlinger, F. N. (1973). *Foundations of behavioral research* (2nd ed.). New York: Holt, Rinehart, and Winston.

Klauer, K. J. (1985). Framework for a theory of teaching. *Teaching and Teacher Education*, **1**, 5–17.

Kleine, P. F. (1982). Teaching styles. In H. E. Mitzel (Ed.), *Encyclopedia of educational research* (5th ed.) (pp. 1927–1932). New York: The Free Press.

Krathwohl, D. R. (1985). *Social and behavioral science research*. San Francisco: Jossey-Bass.

Kratz, H. E. (1896). Characteristics of the best teachers as recognized by children. *Pedagogical Seminary*, **3**, 413–418.

Kuhn, T. S. (1962). *The structure of scientific revolutions*. Chicago: University of Chicago Press.

Kuhn, T. S. (1970). *The structure of scientific revolutions* (2nd ed.). Chicago: University of Chicago Press.

Kulik, J. A. and Kulik, C. C. (1988). Effects of ability grouping on student achievement. *Equity and Excellence*, **22**, 22–30.

Lakatos, I. (1978). *The methodology of scientific research programmes*. Cambridge: Cambridge University Press.

Leacock, E. (1969). *Teaching and learning in city schools: A comparative study*. New York: Basic.

Lehner, P. N. (1979). *Handbook of ethological methods*. New York: Garland STPM Press.

Leinhardt, G. and Greeno, J. (1986). The cognitive skill of teaching. *Journal of Educational Psychology*, **78**, 75–95.

Levis, D. S. (1987). Teachers' personality. In M. J. Dunkin (Ed.), *International encyclopedia of teaching and teacher education* (pp. 585–589). Oxford: Pergamon.

Light, R. J. (1973). Issues in the analysis of qualitative data. In R. M. W. Travers (Ed.), *Second handbook of research on teaching* (pp. 318–381). Chicago: Rand McNally.

Lincoln, Y. S. (1980, April). *Documentary analysis and the use of records*. Paper presented at the annual meeting of the American Educational Research Association, Boston.

Lincoln, Y. S. and Guba, E. G. (1985). *Naturalistic inquiry*. Beverly Hills: Sage.

Magoon, A. J. (1977). Constructivist approaches in educational research. *Review of Educational Research*, **47**, 651–693.

Malinowski, B. (1950). *Argonauts of the western Pacific*. New York: E. P. Dutton.

Mandeville, G. K. (1984). Re-analyzing teaching research data: Problems and promises. *Evaluation in Education: An International Review Series*, **8**, 153–166.

Manning, P. K. (1983). Analytic induction. In R. B. Smith and P. K. Manning (Eds.), *Qualitative methods: Volume II of Handbook of social science methods* (pp. 273–301). Cambridge: Ballinger.

Marsh, H. W. (1987). Student evaluations of teaching. In M. J. Dunkin (Ed.), *International encyclopedia of teaching and teacher education* (pp. 181–187). Oxford: Pergamon.

Mathison, S. (1988). Why triangulate? *Educational Researcher*, **17** (2), 13–17.

McCutcheon, G. (1981). On the interpretation of classroom observations. *Educational Researcher*, **10** (5), 5–10.

McDonald, F. J. and Elias, P. J. (1975/76). *The Effects of Teaching Performances on Pupil Learning* (Beginning Teacher Evaluation Study: Phase II. Final Report: Volume I). Princeton, New Jersey: Educational Testing Service.

Medley, D. M. (1972). Early history of research on teacher behavior. *International Review of Education*, **18**, 430–439.

Medley, D. M. (1977). *Teacher competence and teacher effectiveness: A review of the process-product research*. Washington, DC.: American Association of Colleges for Teacher Education.

Medley, D. M. (1982). Systematic observation. In H. E. Mitzel (Ed.), *Encyclopedia of educational research* (5th ed.) (pp. 1841–1851). New York: The Free Press.

Medley, D. M. (1987). Criteria for evaluating teaching. In M. Dunkin (Ed.), *The international encyclopedia of teaching and teacher education* (pp. 169–181). Oxford: Pergamon.

Medley, D. M. and Mitzel, H. E. (1963). Measuring classroom behavior in systematic observation. In N. L. Gage (Ed.), *Handbook of research on teaching* (pp. 247–328). Chicago: Rand-McNally.

Meehl, P. E. (1986). What social scientists don't understand. In D. W. Fiske and R. A. Shweder (Eds.), *Metatheory in social science* (pp. 315–338). Chicago: The University of Chicago Press.

Mehan, H. (1979). *Learning lessons: Social organization in the classroom.* Cambridge, MA: Harvard University Press.

Merton, R. (1982). The normative structure of science. In A. Rosenblatt and T. F. Gieryn (Eds.), *Social research and the practicing professions* (pp. 3–16). Cambridge: Abt Books.

Messick, S. (1984). The psychology of educational measurement. *Journal of Educational Measurement,* **21,** 215–237.

Miles, M. B. and Huberman, A. M. (1984). *Qualitative data analysis: A sourcebook of new methods.* Beverly Hills: Sage.

Mitzel, H. E. (Ed.) (1982). *Encyclopedia of educational research* (5th ed.). New York: Macmillan.

Morine-Dershimer, G. (1985). *Talking, listening, and learning in elementary school classrooms.* New York: Longman.

Morsh, J. E. and Wilder, E. W. (1954). *Identifying the effective instructor: A review of the quantitative studies, 1900–1952* (Research Bulletin No. AFPTRIC-TR-54-44). San Antonio, Texas: USAF Personnel Training Center, Lackland Air Force Base.

Mouly, G. J. (1963). *The science of education research.* New York: American Book Company.

Neisser, U. (1967). *Cognitive psychology.* New York: Appleton-Century-Crofts.

Nuthall, G. A. (1968). Studies of teaching II. Types of research on teaching. *New Zealand Journal of Educational Studies* **3,** 125–147.

Nuthall, G. and Church, J. (1973). Experimental studies of teaching behaviour. In G. Chanan (Ed.), *Towards a science of teaching* (pp. 9–25). Windsor, Berks: NFER Publishing Company.

Nuthall, G. A. and Lawrence, P. J. (1965). *Thinking in the classroom: The development of a method of analysis.* Wellington: New Zealand Council for Educational Research.

Nuthall, G. and Snook, I. (1973). Contemporary models of teaching. In R. M. W. Travers (Ed.), *Second handbook of research on teaching,* (pp. 47–76). Chicago: Rand McNally.

Oosthoek, H. and Van Den Eeden, P. (Eds.). (1983). *Education from the multi-level perspective: Models, methodology, and empirical findings.* New York: Gordon and Breach Science Publishers.

Overman, B. (1979). *A study of schooling: Methodology* (Technical Report No. 2). Los Angeles: Graduate School of Education, University of California at Los Angeles.

Patton, M. Q. (1980). *Qualitative evaluation methods.* Beverly Hills: Sage.

Pedhazur, E. (1982). *Multiple regression in behavioral research* (2nd ed.). New York: Holt, Rinehart, and Winston.

Pelto, P. (1970). *Anthropological research: The structure of inquiry.* New York: Harper and Row.

Pelto, P. J. and Pelto, G. H. (1978). *Anthropological research: The structure of inquiry* (2nd ed.). Cambridge: Cambridge University Press.

Pike, K. (1954). *Language in relation to a unified theory of the structure of human behavior* (Part I: Preliminary Edition). Ann Arbor, MI: Braun-Brumfield.

Polkinghorne, D. (1983). *Methodology for the human sciences: Systems of inquiry.* Albany, N.Y.: State University of New York Press.

Popper, K. (1959). *The logic of scientific discovery.* New York: Basic.

Rabinowitz, W. and Travers, R. M. W. (1953). Problems of defining and assessing teacher effectiveness. *Educational Theory,* **3,** 212–219.

Remmers, H. H. (1963). Rating methods in research on teaching. In N. L. Gage (Ed.), *Handbook of research on teaching* (pp. 329–378). Chicago: Rand McNally.

Robertson, E. (1987). Teaching and related activities. In M. J. Dunkin (Ed.), *International encyclopedia of teaching and teacher education* (pp. 15–18). Oxford: Pergamon.

Robinson, W. S. (1951). The logical structure of analytic induction. *American Sociological Review,* **16,** 812–818.

Roehler, L. R., Duffy, G. G., Herrmann, B. A., Conley, M. and Johnson, J. (1988). Knowledge structures as evidence of the 'Personal': Bridging the gap from thought to practice. *Journal of Curriculum Studies,* **20** (2), 150–165.

Rogosa, D., Brand, D. and Zimowski, M. (1982). A growth curve approach to the measurement of change. *Psychological Bulletin,* **90,** 726–748.

Rosenshine, B. V. (1987). Direct instruction. In M. J. Dunkin (Ed.), *International encyclopedia of teaching and teacher education* (pp. 257–262). Oxford: Pergamon.

Rosenshine, B. V. and Furst, N. (1973). The use of direct observation to study teaching. In R. M. W. Travers (Ed.), *Second handbook of research on teaching* (pp. 122–183). Chicago: Rand McNally.

Rosenshine, B. V. and Stevens, R. (1986). Teaching functions. In M. C. Wittrock (Ed.). *Third handbook of research on teaching* (pp. 376–391). New York: Macmillan.

Rumelhart, D. E. and Norman, D. A. (1978). Accretion, tuning, and restructuring: Three modes of learning. In J. W. Cotton and R. L. Klatzky (Eds.), *Semantic factors in cognition* (pp. 37–53). New York: Wiley.

Ryan, K. and Phillips, D. H. (1982). Teacher characteristics. In H. E. Mitzel (Ed.), *Encyclopedia of educational research* (5th ed.) (pp. 1869–1876). New York: The Free Press.

Ryans, D. G. (1960a). *Characteristics of teachers*. Washington, D.C.: American Council on Education.

Ryans, D. G. (1960b). Prediction of teacher effectiveness. In C. W. Harris (Ed.), *Encyclopedia of educational research* (3rd ed.) (pp. 1486–1491). New York: Macmillan.

Rychlak, J. (1968). *A philosophy of science for personality theory*. New York: Houghlin Mifflin.

Rychlak, J. (1977). *The psychology of rigorous humanism*. New York: Wiley.

Scarr, S. (1985). Constructing psychology: Making facts and fables for our times. *American Psychologist*, **40**, 499–512.

Schafer, J. (1981). Situational properties of competence: A case study of one child's behavior in two educational settings. In Cook-Gumperz, J., Simons, H. D. and Gumperz, J. J., *Final Report on School/Home Ethnography Project* (National Institute of Education Grant No. G-78-0082). Washington, D.C.: U.S. Department of Education. (ERIC ED 233 915).

Schneider, W. and Treiber, B. (1984). Classroom differences in the determination of achievement changes. *American Educational Research Journal*, **21**, 195–211.

Scott, W. A. (1955). Reliability of content analysis: The case of nominal coding. *Public Opinion Quarterly*, **19**, 321–325.

Shavelson, R. J. (1987). Interactive decision-making. In M. J. Dunkin (Ed.), *International encyclopedia of teaching and teacher education* (pp. 491–493). Oxford: Pergamon.

Shulman, L. S. (1981). Disciplines of inquiry in education: An overview. *Educational Researcher*, **10**, 5–12, 23.

Shulman, L. S. (1986). Paradigms and research programs in the study of teaching: A contemporary perspective. In M. C. Wittrock (Ed.), *Handbook of research on teaching* (3rd ed.) (pp. 3–36). New York: Macmillan.

Shulman, L. S. (1988). *Knowledge growth in teaching: A final report to the Spencer Foundation*. Stanford, California: Stanford University School of Education.

Simon, A. and Boyer, E. G. (Eds.). (1967). *Mirrors for behavior: An anthology of classroom observation instruments*. Philadelphia: Research for Better Schools.

Simon, A. and Boyer, E. G. (Eds.). (1970). *Mirrors for behavior: An anthology of classroom observation instruments continued*. Philadelphia: Research for Better Schools.

Simon, H. A. and Newell, A. (1956). Models: Their uses and limitations. In L. D. White (Ed.), *The state of the social sciences* (pp. 66–83). Chicago: The University of Chicago Press.

Skinner, B. F. (1950). Are theories of learning necessary? *Psychological Review*, **57**, 193–216.

Slavin, R. E. (1987). Small group methods. In M. J. Dunkin (Ed.), *International encyclopedia of teaching and teacher education* (pp. 237–243). Oxford: Pergamon.

Smith, B. O. (1987). Definitions of teaching. In M. J. Dunkin (Ed.), *International encyclopedia of teaching and teacher education* (pp. 11–15). Oxford: Pergamon.

Smith, B. O. and Meux, M. O. (1962). *A study of the logic of teaching*. Urbana, Illinois: Bureau of Educational Research, University of Illinois (mimeographed).

Smith, L. (1979). An evolving logic of participant observation, educational ethnography, and other case studies. *Review of Research in Education*, **6**, 316–377.

Smith, L. M. and Geoffrey, W. (1968). *The complexities of an urban classroom: An analysis toward a general theory of teaching*. New York: Holt, Rinehart, and Winston.

Snow, R. E. (1968). Brunswikian approaches to research on teaching. *American Educational Research Journal*, **5**, 475–489.

Snow, R. E. (1973). Theory construction for research on teaching. In R. M. W. Travers (Ed.), *Second handbook of research on teaching* (pp. 77–112). Chicago: Rand McNally.

Snow, R. (1974). Representative and quasi-representative designs for research on teaching. *Review of Educational Research*, **44**, 265–291.

Snow, R. E., Federico, P.-A. and Montague, W. E. (Eds.). (1980). *Aptitude, learning, and instruction (Volumes 1 and 2)*. Hillsdale, N.J.: Erlbaum.
Soar, R. S., Medley, D. M. and Coker, H. (1983). Teacher evaluation: A critique of currently used methods. *Phi Delta Kappa*, **83**, 239–246.
Soar, R. S. and Soar, R. M. (1987). Classroom climate. In M. J. Dunkin (Ed.), *International encyclopedia of teaching and teacher education* (pp. 336–342). Oxford: Pergamon.
Soltis, J. F. (1984). On the nature of educational research. *Educational Researcher*, **13** (10), 5–10.
Spindler, G. (1982). *Doing the ethnography of schooling: Educational anthropology in action*. New York: Holt, Rinehart, and Winston.
Spradley, J. (1979). *The ethnographic interview*. New York: Holt, Rinehart, and Winston.
Stallings, J. (1977). *Learning to look: A handbook on classroom observation and teaching methods*. Belmont, California: Wadsworth.
Stein, J. S. (1984). *The Random House college dictionary, revised edition*. New York: Random House.
Steinberg, R., Haymore, J. and Marks, R. (1985). *Teachers' knowledge and structuring content in mathematics*. Paper presented at the annual meeting of the American Educational Research Association, Chicago.
Stiles, L. J. (1960). Instruction. In C. W. Harris (Ed.), *Encyclopedia of educational research* (3rd ed.) (pp. 710–715). New York: Macmillan.
Stodolsky, S. S. (1983). *Classroom Activity Structures in the Fifth Grade*. (Final Report, NIE Contract No. 400-77-0094). Washington, DC.: U.S. Department of Education (ERIC ED 242 412).
Stodolsky, S. S. (1984). Teacher evaluation: The limits of looking. *Educational Researcher*, **13** (9), 11–18.
Stodolsky, S. S. (1988). *The subject matters*. Chicago: University of Chicago Press.
Strike, K. A. (1972). Explaining and understanding: The impact of science on our concept of man. In L. G. Thomas (Ed.), *Philosophical redirection of educational research* (pp. 26–46). Chicago: The University of Chicago Press.
Suppe, F. (Ed.) (1974). *The structure of scientific theories*. Urbana, Il: University of Illinois Press.
Taft, R. (1987). Ethnographic methods. In M. J. Dunkin (Ed.), *International encyclopedia of teaching and teacher education* (pp. 151–155). Oxford: Pergamon.
Taylor, S. J. and Bogdan, R. (1984). *Introduction to qualitative research methods: The search for meanings*. New York: Wiley.
Tikunoff, W. J., Berliner, D. C. and Rist, R. C. (1975). *Special Study A: An Ethnographic Study of Forty Classrooms of the Beginning Teacher Evaluation Study Known Sample* (Technical Report 75-10-5). San Francisco: Far West Laboratory for Educational Research and Development (ERIC ED 150 110).
Travers, R. M. W. (Ed.) (1973). *Second handbook of research on teaching*. Chicago: Rand McNally.
Treiber, B. (1981). Classroom environments and processes in a multilevel framework. *Studies in Educational Evaluation*, **7**, 75–84.
Tyler, R. W. (1973). Assessing educational achievement in the affective domain. *Measurement in Education*, **4** (3), 1–8.
Walberg, H. J. (1984). Improving the productivity of America's schools. *Educational Leadership*, **41** (8), 19–27.
Walker, R. and Adelman, C. (1975). Interaction analysis in informal classrooms: A critical comment on the Flanders' system. *British Journal of Educational Psychology*, **45**, 73–76.
Wallen, N. E. and Travers, R. M. W. (1963). Analysis and investigation of teaching methods. In N. L. Gage (Ed.), *Handbook of research on teaching* (pp. 448–505). Chicago: Rand McNally.
Wang, M. C. (1984). Time-use and the provision of adaptive instruction. In L. W. Anderson (Ed.), *Time and school learning: Theory, research, and practice* (pp. 167–203). Beckenham, Kent: Croom Helm.
Watson, J. B. (1913). Psychology as the behaviorist views it. *Psychological Review*, **20**, 158–177.
Webb, E. J., Campbell, D. T., Schwartz, R. D. and Sechrest, L. (1966). *Unobstrusive measures: Nonreactive research in the social sciences*. Chicago: Rand McNally.
Webb, E. J., Campbell, D. T., Schwartz, R. D., Sechrest, L. and Grove, J. B. (1981). *Nonreactive measures in the social sciences* (2nd ed.). Boston: Houghton Mifflin.

Weil, M. L. and Murphy, J. (1982). Instruction processes. In H. E. Mitzel (Ed.), *Encyclopedia of educational research* (5th ed.) (pp. 890–917). New York: The Free Press.

Wilkinson, L. C. (Ed.). (1982). *Communicating in the classroom.* New York: Academic.

Willems, E. (1969). Planning a rationale for naturalistic research. In E. Willems and H. Raush (Eds.), *Naturalistic viewpoints in psychological research* (pp. 44–71). New York: Holt, Rinehart, and Winston.

Willems, E. P. and Raush, H. L. (1969). Introduction. In E. P. Willems and H. L. Raush (Eds.), *Naturalistic viewpoints in psychological research* (pp. 1–10). New York: Holt, Rinehart, and Winston.

Wilson, S. (1977). The use of ethnographic techniques in educational research. *Review of Educational Research,* **47,** 245–265.

Wilson, S., Shulman, L. and Richert, A. (1987). 150 different ways of knowing: Representations of knowledge in teaching. In J. Calderhead (Ed.), *Exploring teachers' thinking* (pp. 104–124). London: Cassell Educational Limited.

Wineburg, S. S. (1986). *Interview 2, Designing a teaching sequence.* Unpublished manuscript, Stanford University Teacher Assessment Project.

Wineburg, S. S. (1987). *Interview 2, Scope and organization of teaching sequence.* Unpublished manuscript, Stanford University Teacher Assessment Project.

Wineburg, S. S. and Wilson, S. (1986). *Suggestions for conducting interviews.* Unpublished manuscript, Stanford University Teacher Assessment Project.

Withall, J. and Lewis, W. W. (1963). Social interaction in the classroom. In N. L. Gage (Ed.), *Handbook of research on teaching* (pp. 683–714). Chicago: Rand McNally.

Wittrock, M. C. (Ed.). (1986). *Handbook of research on teaching* (3rd ed.). New York: Macmillan.

Wold, H. (1982). Soft modeling: The basic design and some extensions. In K. G. Jöreskog and H. Wold (Eds.), *Systems under indirect observation, Part II.* Amsterdam: North-Holland.

Worthen, B. R. (1968). Discovery and expository task presentation in elementary mathematics. *Journal of Educational Psychology* (Monograph Supplement, Pt. 2), **59,** 1–13.

Wright, H. F. (1967). *Recording and analyzing child behavior.* New York: Harper and Row.

Wright, C. J. and Nuthall, G. A. (1970). Relationships between teacher behaviors and pupil achievement in three experimental elementary science lessons. *American Educational Research Journal, 7,* 477–491.

Zahorik, J. A. (1987). Reacting. In M. J. Dunkin (Ed.), *International encyclopedia of teaching and teacher education* (pp. 416–423). Oxford: Pergamon.

Znaniecki, F. (1934). *The method of sociology.* New York: Farrar and Rinehart.

Name Index

Name Index

Name Index

Subject Index

Interpretive inquiry 59, 67–70, 72–80, 96–98, 105
 contrasted with confirmatory inquiry 67, 72–80, 96–98, 105
Interviews 117–118
 contrasted with questionnaires 117–118
 see also Questioning

Knowing 48–49
 contrasted with knowledge 48
 sources of 48–49
Knowledge 48–50
 contrasted with knowing 48
 defined 49
 scientific 49–50
 sources of 48–49
Knowledge claims 49–50, 108–111, 113

Linking power *see* Internal validity

Meaning of evidence 103–104, 163–186
 conceptual frameworks and 164
 connotative 163
 denotative 163
 intended vs. actual 163
 recommendations for enhancing 181–186
Models 30–35, 37–41
 illustrations of 31–35, 37–39
 purposes of 31–35, 37–39
 relation with theories 30

Naturalistic design 78–80
Nomothetic explanation 76
Non-equivalent groups *see* Analysis of numerical evidence

Objectivity 187–190
 and observer agreement 187–190
 as detachment 188–190
 defined 187
Observation 103, 135–141, 143, 145–147
 recommendations concerning 145–147
 strengths 140–141
 weaknesses 143
Observation techniques and methods 136, 139–140
 classroom chronicles 136, 139–140
 ethnography 139–140
 field notes 136
 naturalistic records 139–140
 rating scales 136, 139–140
 specimen records 136, 140
 structured observation systems 136, 139–140
 see also Specific techniques and methods

Open-ended responses 120, 122
 strengths 120
 weaknesses 122
Opportunity to learn (OTL) *see* Instruction, components of

Pacing *see* Instruction, components of
Paradigms 17–21, 40
 defined 17, 21
 in classroom research 19–21
Purposeful sampling 19–102
Purposes of classroom research 86–88
 associational 87
 descriptive 87

Qualitative data *see* Analysis of verbal evidence
Quality of evidence 104, 186–199
 objectivity 186–190
 validity of association 195–199
 validity of description 191–195
Questioning 103, 115–121, 123–134
 examples and illustrations 126–134
 prompts 116
 recommendations 123–126
 standardization 117
 stimulus and response 116
 strengths 118–119
 weaknesses 120–121
Questionnaires 117–118
 contrasted with interviews 117–118
 see also Questioning

Research and human values 14–15, 113
Research design *see* Research plan
Research methodology 45–58, 81
 contrasted with research techniques 46
 examples 51–58
 philosophy and 58
 quantitative vs. qualitative 46–47
Research plan 94–98, 100–102
Research programs 17, 22
Reviews of classroom research 338–339
Roles of classroom observers 137–138
 detached recorder 137–138
 involved interpreter 137–138

Sampling of evidence 98–102
 purposeful 99
 random 101
 theoretical 102
Scientific community, defined 18–19
Semi-standardized questionnaires and interviews 119–122
 strengths 119
 weaknesses 122

Ada